Giving Preservation a History

Giving Preservation a History
Histories of Historic Preservation
in the United States

Edited by
Max Page
and
Randall Mason

ROUTLEDGE
NEW YORK AND LONDON

Published in 2004 by
Routledge
711 Third Avenue
New York, NY 10017
www.routledge-ny.com

Published in Great Britain by
Routledge
2 Park Square, Milton Park
Abingdon, Oxon OX14 4RN
www.routledge.co.uk

10 9 8 7 6 5 4 3 2

Library of Congress Cataloging-in-Publication data

Giving preservation a history / edited by Max Page and Randall Mason.
    p. cm.
  ISBN 0-415-93442-7 (HB : alk. paper)—ISBN 0-415-93443-5 (PB : alk. paper)
    1. Architecture—Conservation and restoration.   2. Art—Conservation
and restoration.   3. Cultural property—Protection.   I. Page, Max.
II. Mason, Randall.
  NA105.G48 2003
  363.6'9—dc21

                                      2003010962

ACKNOWLEDGMENTS

The authors would like to thank the Graham Foundation for Advanced Studies in the Fine Arts and the Center for Architectural Design and Research at the University of Maryland, both of which generously supported the publication of this book. We would also like to thank the staff at Routledge—especially our editor David McBride and his assistant Angela Chnapko—and Richard Rothschild at Print Matters, for their enthusiasm and professionalism. Finally, we would like to thank our contributors, who have collectively advanced the understanding and practice of historic preservation.

CONTENTS

I
Introduction

RETHINKING THE ROOTS OF THE HISTORIC PRESERVATION MOVEMENT

Max Page
Randall Mason

HISTORIC PRESERVATION has been one of the broadest and longest-lasting land-use reform efforts in this country. It is therefore ironic that we have so little understanding of its history. Scholars have written prolifically on the history of museums, national monuments, and historical artifacts, but very little on the effort to preserve historic buildings and places. Advocacy and scholarship have both suffered from this lack of perspective. The potential of historic preservation as a social movement is immense; it has the capacity to help forestall the destructive and unregulated development that threatens to destroy the places Americans love. But before it can achieve its vision, the preservation movement must lose its blinders and open itself to the new possibilities that only an understanding of history can provide. The essays in this book are intended to contribute to that process.

We begin with three recent preservation controversies: one from New York City, one from Chicago, and one from the desert of California.

The Lower East Side of Manhattan is hot these days. Tenement apartments that immigrants labored desperately to escape are now selling for a million dollars. In 2001, the Lower East Side neighborhood was honored by the National Park Service, which placed the district on the National Register of Historic Places. But not the whole neighborhood—just a carefully carved section of it, the bizarre shape of which looked less like a coherent neighborhood than a gerrymandered voting district, similar to the snaking Twelfth Congressional District of North Carolina, which the Supreme Court approved on the very same day that the Lower East Side district received its designation. It hardly resembled the area that either current residents or those who lived there a century ago would consider the Lower East Side. This map-making fiction said little about history, and much more about cultural politics and the practice of historic preservation today.

Some argued that the National Register listing of the Lower East Side was a victory over architectural elitism. The district was listed because of its cultural importance rather than its significant buildings; its primary historic significance is as home to countless immigrants who arrived after 1880 and continue to arrive every day. But in order to have a district accepted onto the revered list, advocates had to jump through the anachronistic hoops of the National Register, focusing on the quality of the architecture and reassuring officials that there were enough "contributing" buildings (buildings close to their "original" appearance) to make the district feel historic. And they had to choose a specific "period of significance." For some obvious reasons, they focused on the great era of immigration, from 1820 to 1940, especially 1880 to 1924, during which millions of Jews flowed from Eastern Europe into New York and the Lower East Side. The nomination cites "cultural affiliations" to include primarily "German immigrants and Eastern European Jewish immigrants," even though the Lower East Side has been home to the Dutch, African Americans, Irish, Chinese, Vietnamese, Cambodian, and on and on.

Preservation advocates had to draw lines on the map to include buildings that helped build their case, and excluded many others of equal cultural significance. The map lassoed in the old Forward Building on East Broadway, the Educational Alliance Building, the Henry Street Settlement, as well as the Lower East Side Tenement Museum building (previously designated a National Historic Landmark). On the west side of the district, a little bump is designed to incorporate the 1886 Eldridge Street Synagogue, which is actually a block beyond the district's Allen Street border. But they couldn't incorporate buildings to the east, including St. Mary's Church (an anchor of the once strong Irish community here), nor Beit Hamedrash Hagadol, on Norfolk Street (once a black Baptist church and now an Orthodox Jewish synagogue), because both are surrounded by modern buildings and can't "contribute," in preservation parlance, to the feel of an historic district. The result was not a logical outline of a historic neighborhood but a segregated excerpt. It was really a Jewish Lower East Side historic district—and an incomplete one at that—offered as a stand-in for the history of the whole neighborhood. It was ironic that just as the 2000 census was revealing that the United States, and New York City, were more diverse than ever, the National Register was approving a landmark district based only on the history of one group, in the neighborhood best defined as a crucible of multiple cultures.

The image from Chicago was painful: aging blues singer Jimmie Lee Robinson walked to the middle of the famous Maxwell Street in the fall of 2000 to sing "Maxwell Street Blues," as demolition crews tore down a block of buildings that once framed one of the most vibrant places of cultural creativity in America. In the 1940s and 1950s, as waves of African Americans migrated from the South, Maxwell Street and its bustling market became the birthplace of the urban electric blues, a place where Muddy Waters, Robert Nighthawk, Little Walter, Hound Dog Taylor, and dozens of other musicians found ready audiences and turned an African American musical form into a foundation of modern popular music.

But by the 1970s, Maxwell Street had already begun its long slide, and by the 1980s it was a shell of its former self. The University of Illinois in Chicago—Maxwell Street's neighbor to the north and west—became the force for renewal in the Near West Side neighborhood. Some considered UIC a vibrant institution that would transform the decrepit strips of stores into an academic village, while others saw it as a colonial power, violently displacing a venerable immigrant neighborhood and outdoor market. By the time of Jimmie Lee Robinson's last stand, despite a vocal fight by blues musicians and neighborhood activists, the end was inevitable.

Community advocates were appalled by this act of urban renewal that hearkened back to the days of Robert Moses. Preservationists rightly asked: Why did we let Chicago's Maxwell Street die an unnatural death? In a time when we are once again embracing the vibrancy of our great cities, celebrating the contributions of diverse groups to American culture, preserving and valuing our physical past as never before, how could America allow the bustling urban area, the birthplace of the blues, to be demolished?

Manzanar, in California's interior desert, was the site of an internment camp—some have termed it a concentration camp—for Japanese-Americans during World War II. It was declared a National Historic Landmark in 1985, and in 1992 the National Park Service acquired it and began to plan for its preservation and for the presentation of the site's history to the public. As a preservation project, Manzanar embodies some of the most important challenges faced recently by the preservation field. How can we grapple with shameful but defining aspects of our nation's history—in this case, official discrimination against a minority group? How can we accommodate the desires of different stakeholders, some of whom wish the site to be carefully preserved, some of whom wish to forget the experience of internment, some of whom may even see the camp as fully justified? How can we craft a preservation strategy for a site where little material integrity of buildings and landscape has survived? How much should we materially reconstruct a place in order to get it to tell a memorable story? This preservation dilemma continues to unfold.[1]

The stories of these three places tell us a lot about preservation at the beginning of the new millennium, and they pose some of the central questions of the field: Whose history is important? What are legitimate boundaries of a "historic" district? Should physical integrity of a building or landscape be the primary test of whether it might be protected? How can we focus more attention on the interpretation of historic buildings and sites? What is the relationship between economic development and historic preservation?

In suggesting an approach to answering these questions, we offer a very simple observation, rarely noted in preservation practice: Contemporary preservation battles, and the preservation field itself, have a history. Our goal in this volume is to convince our readers of that simple fact. We do not pretend to provide a new history of historic preservation—although that story certainly needs to be written. Rather, we hope through these essays to sketch the approaches of a new generation of scholarship on the history of historic preservation. In the process, we want to suggest how preservation today might look different if we took into account an accurate history of the movement.

This book is no antiquarian project, nor one of interest purely to scholars. For historic preservation touches more Americans than any other public history endeavor. In their landmark study of American attitudes toward the past, Roy Rosenzweig and David Thelen found that more than half of respondents had chosen to visit a historic building or site in the previous year.[2] Approximately a million houses lie within National Register of Historic Places historic districts, or are eligible for such status. In a country long seen as uninterested in the past, these are remarkable statistics, showing the power of historic places—and historic preservation—in connecting Americans with their past.

If you ask preservationists about the history of preservation, they might start with one of two stories—both of which are important parts of the larger history of preservation, but have taken on the kind of mythic dimensions that make us stop asking critical historical questions. One is the heroic effort of Ann Pamela Cunningham and her collaborators to save Mount Vernon beginning in 1853. It is an appealing starting point: It was the "first" grassroots preservation effort, it demonstrated the contributions of women to public life, and, not least, it was successful. The other story you are likely to hear is the more recent failure to save New York's Pennsylvania Station in 1963. This story demonstrates, to many preservationists, the evils against which mid-twentieth-century preservationists organized—corporations, greed, urban renewal. Though it failed, the effort to save Penn Station inspired the modern preservation movement, armed with toothy local preservation laws, a savvy public-relations apparatus, and experienced professionals.

Such stories are so familiar, they seem to tell all we need to know about preservation: It is a battle of good and evil, where sometimes preservation prevails, and more often development wins out. Preservation, in these stories, works through the Sisyphean efforts of well-intentioned, public-minded individuals. Those of us in the preservation field hold dear these cherished myths. This book seeks to complicate those myths.

Opening up the field of historic preservation to critical historical inquiry, however, is difficult. More than virtually any other historical undertaking, preservation scholarship has been dominated by a single work. The traditional history, as told first and most effectively by Charles Hosmer, focused largely on individuals and institutions, largely in the Northeast, and the great "saves" they achieved. In addition to the stories of Mount Vernon and Penn Station, the efforts of John D. Rockefeller at Williamsburg, Henry Ford at Greenfield Village, William Sumner Appleton in Boston at the Society for the Preservation of New England Antiquities, George Sheldon and the Pocumtuck Valley Memorial Association, and Helen and Henry Flynt in Deerfield are well documented. Most histories portray these individuals as members of a brave upper class eager to stem the tide of destruction endemic to a rapidly growing, industrializing, and urbanizing nation.

The narrative of Herculean individual efforts continues, in midcentury, with an increasing emphasis on the role of governments—local, state, and federal—in historic preservation. Key laws and other institutional achievements advanced the progress of preservation: the 1906 Antiquities Act, Charleston's historic districting law from 1931, the Historic Sites Act of 1935, the work of the Historic American Buildings Survey in the 1930s, the 1949 creation of the National Trust for Historic Preservation, and then, finally, the 1966 National Preservation Act. This institutional history, focusing on the deployment of state power as the ultimate test of successful preservation, skips lightly over vast social and cultural shifts that shaped historic preservation.

This traditional history has been sustained by the limited amount of serious historical research on the preservation movement. Indeed, the field and practice of preservation remain dominated by Charles Hosmer's three-volume work. That work, written by the foremost historian of the preservation field, was broad in its scope but held a narrow view of preservation's undertaking. Preservation historians are now influenced by the new social history, by the proliferation of public history practice and scholarship, and by the strong assertion of subaltern histories in the last generation.

One particular shortcoming has been an overwhelmingly linear narrative of preservation's history, a sense that today's ideas are the logical and positive culmination of the developments of earlier years. In fact, as we discuss below, preservation has waxed and waned, with ideas coming back and falling out of favor, with as many disappointments and dead ends as victories and achievements. The innovations have come from the local level as much as nationally.

By suggesting that wealthy individuals or the national government have driven the evolution of the preservation field, this traditional history misleads us and fails to inspire. It leaves unaddressed what was happening on the ground, in cities and localities across the country, as citizens, officials, activists, and professionals practiced preservation with reference to specific buildings and sites, and concerns about the quality of their local environments—their senses of place. Is there a national story of the preservation field? Certainly. Is it the most important story? We think not—and the chapters herein present some evidence of what is gained by looking at preservation unfolding as a local practice.

The persistence of this dominant narrative suggests a surprising lack of curiosity among preservationists about their own field. A self-organized group of intelligent professionals and civic-minded advocates, motivated by the notion that the "spirit and direction of the Nation are founded upon and reflected in its historic heritage," as the National Historic Preservation Act of 1966 declared, could be expected to feel the need to examine, understand, criticize, and rethink their own work.[3] Charles Hosmer opened the first volume of his three-volume study of the history of American preservation with this observation. "It seems logical," he wrote in *Presence of the Past*, "that historians should study the evolution of the American preservation movement." But alas, while "certain aspects of the early history of preservationism have been recorded . . . the larger, more comprehensive story has been left largely untouched."[4] His massive chronicle began to create a national historical memory for the preservation field, and it has been accepted as part of the preservation catechism, but it did not stimulate a great deal more work.

Fortunately, the field of historic preservation is changing, and for the better. The current generation of practicing preservationists are creating a watershed for the field. The techniques, theories, and public policies inherited by today's practitioners hark to the time when the inherent historical values of old buildings, and the material integrity of those artifacts, were seen as sufficient foundations for the field. Now, in the wake of epistemological and political revolutions since the 1960s—from civil rights and women's rights to postmodernism—the political values of preservation, and its value in shaping personal, social-group, and national identity, are paramount. Economic interests, once banished as the enemy, play an ever-greater role in preservation—sometimes for better and sometimes for worse. Preservation now operates in a different world from that in which its roots were planted, and slowly the field is managing to reimagine and retool itself to thrive in changed circumstances.

The rethinking of the preservation field must be informed by serious reflection on the field's history. This book seeks to fill the void of historical curiosity about preservation, and fuel self-critical reflection within the field (and from outside as well) as preservation passes through its watershed. Hosmer created a fine and substantial chronicle. But critical research needs to be done to make the history of preservation usable for preservationists working today. Where Hosmer stressed the commonalities among preservation efforts in different locales, the essays in this volume speak more to the differentiations, cleavages, conflicts, and tensions evident in the practice and effect of historic preservation in places across the country and over time. Written by scholars trained largely outside the field of preservation, they are case studies, but each seeks to connect to other themes and trajectories of social history, as well as to "the larger, more comprehensive story" of American preservation.[5]

PRINCIPLES FOR A NEW HISTORY OF HISTORIC PRESERVATION IN THE UNITED STATES

The contributions in this volume are unified by several themes that have emerged in recent scholarly writings on the social construction of the past, as well as the history of architecture and urbanism. The burgeoning literature on the social construction of the past has helped to reinvigorate urban and social history by showing the centrality of battles over the past in contemporary social and political debates. Out of the work of many scholars come a series of principles and themes for a new history of historic preservation in the United States.

First, this volume demonstrates that the history of historic preservation extends across the whole span of the nineteenth and twentieth centuries. Preservation is not simply a phenomenon of the 1960s and after. Many of the institutions and ideals that animate preservation of the physical past were born and debated in the late nineteenth and early twentieth centuries. We also need to understand the roots of American preservation in European culture, what makes the American project of preservation different, even "exceptional," to use a phrase that makes historians shudder.

Rudy Koshar's essay sets the stage for understanding American preservation by outlining the social crises that stimulated a preservation movement in Germany in the middle of the nineteenth century. David Lowenthal's essay charts the contemporary Western fascination—for some an obsession—with heritage. His work sketches the definitions and dilemmas of history and heritage, and sheds both historical and contemporary light on the cultural politics of preservation. Americans inherited the essential tension between the attitude of John Ruskin and William Morris (who sought to protect historic sites exactly as they were—the anti-scrape ideology, as it is sometimes known) and that of Viollet (who imagined a much more active re-creation and re-building of historic buildings and sites). Several of the essays in the volume—including those by Randall Mason, James Lindgren, and Chris Wilson—show how these debates played out on the American scene.

Second, we want to suggest how the American preservation movement diverged from its European predecessors. On the one hand, preservation in the United States has always been driven by patriotism—not just national patriotism but also a more local "civic patriotism" that has been closely allied with boosterism. On the other hand, preservation was, from early on, involved in debates about the character and pace of urban development. This history shows that preservation has not been simply an oppositional movement in the United States—not only a campaign to parcel off a few buildings from the depredations of the market—but rather a movement often pursued in concert with urban development.

Third, historic preservation cannot be seen in isolation. It is one part of a larger "history industry" that includes museums, monuments and memorials, collecting, historical fiction, and other historical undertakings. This industry first blossomed at the turn of the twentieth century. This volume is in part designed to place historic preservation alongside, and even at the heart of, these broad efforts of American society to come to terms with the politics of memory in the modern world. Indeed, this collection would have been impossible without two decades or more of writing on memory and public history, on the means and effects of individuals and societies remembering in public. It seemed most appropriate that this volume begin with an essay by David Lowenthal, who has pioneered the study of history, memory, and heritage in the modern world.

Fourth, the scholars in this volume see historic preservation as a social reform movement, in tandem with—and at times in conflict with—other social movements of the past century. Preservation arose as part of a broad effort among Progressive reformers to transform the nature of urban space—its aesthetic character, its social uses, what it signified to society, how it was used, and who controlled it—as a means of transforming society. The new history outlined in *Giving Preservation a History* focuses more on the preservation as a *process*, than as a set of *results* (that is, a set of preserved historic sites and artifacts), or personalities, or specific places. The authors ask questions about who was involved in struggles over preservation, their motivations, and how and why they made decisions about preservation.

Sixth, scholars are recognizing that historic preservation was far more than a pet issue of the waning blue-blood elite. Across the country, preservation was often pushed hardest by the most active and powerful city-builders, and was placed at the center of public debates about the character of urban development. Preservation has to be understood not as a particular stylistic take on architecture, not simply as a version of museum curatorship, but rather as a reform movement related to the many other constructive reforms of capitalist society. Michael Holleran's chapter, for instance—as well as Mason's—argues that *urban planner* and even *real estate developer* were often just other names for *preservationist*, especially in the early twentieth century.

Links between preservation and economic development are one of the enduring issues in contemporary preservation practice and policy, and the history of these relations is more complicated and longstanding than commonly thought. The two ends of this debate—that preservation is anathema to the market, or that preservation pays and should be promoted as an economic investment—are both too simplistic. There are many aspects to the preservation-economics relationship: preservation as means to increase property values; the marketing and collecting of antiques; and the promotion of tourism. The economic history of preservation did not start with Rockefeller's land purchases at Williamsburg or the federal tax credits of the last generation. Chapters by Briann Greenfield and Chris Wilson in particular explore this terrain.

Seventh, the story of historic preservation commonly told has mimicked traditional stories of American history: That everything can and must be traced back to New England or Virginia. While these places were certainly important in providing energy and ideas for the emerging preservation movement (discussed in the chapters by James Lindgren and Michael Holleran), regional differences, influences, and variations are crucial to understanding the movement in the twentieth century. In order to challenge the "declension" model of preservation historiography—that original ideas all flow from New England and the Mid-Atlantic—we have intentionally sought stories from a range of regions in the United States. The historical consciousness of the preservation field, where it exists, may be rooted in the Northeast and the South (Boston, Williamsburg, Charleston, New Orleans), but its development over the late nineteenth and early twentieth centuries is truly a national phenomenon, so we have included scholarship on the Midwest and West. By the middle of the twentieth century, preservation had become a truly national phenomenon.

While the evolution of preservation tools and thinking took different paths in different places, it is difficult to argue that it was "invented" in one place or region and diffused to others. While such a diffusion model may be true of the technical preservation tools and policies developed in the 1960s and afterward—when the federal government pushed to regularize preservation rules under the 1966 National Historic Preservation Act—it seems not to be true of the earlier period when preservation was in its formative stages. In each chapter, the practical demands of metropolitan urban development and the political challenge of forging good "American" citizens out of the dramatically pluralistic populace combined to give rise to differing preservation institutions, projects, and traditions. The creation of "instant civic identity" in Denver (described by Judy Morley) led to very different notions of preservation from Santa Fe (as examined by Chris Wilson), where the weight of a Spanish past—part real and part invented—galvanized preservation. In the Chicago that Daniel Bluestone describes, divided so sharply between black and white, preservation became a tool for community empowerment.

A further reason for telling regionalized or localized histories of historic preservation is that in the American setting, preservation has largely been and even now remains a local political phenomenon. Local politics and the decentralization of land-use debates and decision-making is one of the bedrock insights about the American landscape, and it figures prominently in the evolution of historic preservation. Far too often, the preservation field as a whole makes too much of the federal government's role (or lack of it) in historic preservation (especially in narrating the history of preservation before the 1960s). The truer index of preservation's importance is the local scene. Federal developments are easier to document and analyze, of course. But the lack of federal presence in the first half of the twentieth century does not mean that preservation was absent or less important in regional and local geographic contexts.

The scholars in this volume are united by a belief that attitudes toward historic preservation are valuable windows into much broader issues of social and cultural change in society, beyond the specific battles to preserve individual buildings and places. Each chapter demonstrates this in the context of its particular time and place. Most of the scholars in this volume are both historians and preservation activists, involved in the contemporary debates and battles around preservation. Therefore, the historical essays are written in the present, about the past, but with an eye toward the future of historic preservation in the United States. We intend this volume to help ask the simple and important question: How might preservation look different in the future if practitioners examined critically their movement's history?

THE FUTURE OF PRESERVATION—VIEWS FROM HISTORY

This collection was intended as a set of "views from history" that can and should shape the contemporary practice of historic preservation in the United States. We specifically chose the word *views* because we do not intend our observations as concrete, unchangeable "lessons." Rather, taking a long view of the history of historic preservation, the scholars writing in this collection offer new perspectives, to be generated by the readers as well as the writers, and new ways to conceive of the practice of preservation.

We hope that preservationists find the history of the field useful. A sense of history serves as inspiration. It also enables a realistic evaluation of accomplishment and failure within the preservation movement. Ideally, this can lead to more openness and self-critique of the practices of preservationists, and pave the way for evaluating the impacts of the movement on society. Too many preservationists have held as an article of faith that virtually any act of preservation is a benefit to society. The views from history in this volume question that faith, and examine the results achieved.

History and progress

One of the particular insights of these chapters is that the history of preservation has not been a simple progression. For example, recent interest in preservation of cultural landscapes harkens back to the nineteenth-century interest in preserving houses and their gardens, or battlefields, or urban parks. The most recent developments in the field aren't necessarily the best developments. The success and relevance of preservation has waxed and waned; innovation and success are, as ever, highly dependent on local politics.

There is a widespread sense that the early twentieth century was an ineffectual, muddled period in the history of the preservation movement—featuring neither the triumphs of Mount Vernon nor the twentieth-century innovations such as historic districts. On the contrary, many of the arguments and institutions that would sustain the preservation movement throughout the century were founded and elaborated at this time—including the notions of a national trust and comprehensive federal legislation.

Many preservationists seem to view the distant era before 1966 and the National Historic Preservation Act as a hazy world of ineffective or purely patriotic endeavors. In fact, new histories of historic preservation recognize how important these early efforts were in establishing the ethos of historic preservation, in establishing key organizations, and in linking preservation, planning, and social reform in addressing larger cultural concerns.

Connecting historic preservation to other history and reform movements

Preservationists should see their work as intimately linked up with other history institutions such as museums and monuments, and not an isolated undertaking. If the goal of preservationists is to preserve elements of the past and make their beauty and meaning available to the public, then preservationists will have to more thoughtfully and aggressively engage with other history industries. Implicitly, this also means that preservationists will have to think far more rigorously about interpretation as part of their job. Focusing exclusively on saving the historic resource, preservationists have failed to talk about the essential need for interpretation of historic places.

Looking back over more than a century of preservation history, we can see that some advocates of preserving the physical past pushed the boundaries of how the past would be merged with the present. Some envisioned a didactic Americanization. Others linked Progressive housing and economic reform with protecting the past, attempting to broaden the fabric of the past that would be preserved, and even developing a critique of the private real-estate market that lay behind the speedy disappearance of historic structures.

If preservationists could recognize the social reform roots of their movement, they would be more apt to see their project not as simply saving individual structures, but as shaping healthier urban and rural environments. While some practitioners—often those who are most literate in the history of the movement—have made bridges to the environmental movement, the smart-growth movement and others, too many remain mired in older, narrow views of preservation practice. Preservation could become an anchor of approaches to regulating the urban environment against sprawl and other destructive developments. In this regard, there are hopeful signs, especially the National Trust's commitment to downtowns, fighting sprawl, and working closely with its allies in the environmental movement.

Undesirable pasts

The academic field of American history has been fundamentally transformed over the past generation. Historians now routinely seek out the variety of perspectives on a particular time or place, and we value many formerly invisible and disturbing aspects of our history. But where is historic preservation in the task of recovering a fuller sense of our past? While there are many promising examples of historic preservation efforts designed to broaden and diversify the physical landmarks of the past, these efforts need much greater attention and investment of the movement's resources. At the same time, preservationists need to confront undesirable aspects of the movement's own history—in perpetuating limited notions of American identity, in keeping the history of immigrants and African Americans off the National Register for so many years, in using history to perpetuate white racial supremacy. To this day, you can go long and far throughout the South, into cities and plantations, and learn very little about slavery, segregation, or racial violence. Preservationists have played their part in the cover-up; they can now be part of the ongoing reevaluation of American history.

Public and private benefits of urban preservation

The argument of several of the contributors to this volume—that the most passionate preservationists have often been the shrewdest private developers in cities—should serve as a warning to preservationists.

The preservation field has lived a dual life when it comes to the market. On the one hand, opposition to developers (whether moralistic or political) has been a mainstay of preservation theory and action. Developers seek private gain; preservationists are interested in the public good. On the other hand, preservationists have often entered into a marriage with developers, bending over backward not to be against development. In the process of garnering a bit of the market's power, they often promote the very policies and forces that destroy the historic fabric of a place. The twinning of these two aspects of preservation—as public history and collective memory, and as development strategy—and the unresolved relationship between them, is an ongoing theme in preservation. This relationship has often defined the politics of preservation, and must be one of the primary lines of inquiry among scholars and advocates attempting to understand the history of preservation.

NOTES

1. Updates on developments at Manzanar, as well as access to background studies, are available at www.nps.gov/manz
2. Rosenzweig, Roy, and David Thelen. *The Presence of the Past: Popular Uses of History in American Life* (New York: Columbia University Press, 1998).
3. National Historic Preservation Act of 1966 (16 U.S.C. 470), Section 1(b)(1).
4. Charles B. Hosmer, Jr. *Presence of the Past* (New York: Putnam, 1965), p. 21.
5. Some other, recent scholarship has begun expanding the historical understanding and critique of historic preservation, especially with regard to women's history and the heritage of ethnic and other minority groups. See Gail Dubrow and Jennifer Goodman, eds. *Restoring Women's History Through Historic Preservation* (Baltimore: Johns Hopkins University Press, 2003); Moira Kenney in Leonie Sandercock, ed. *Making the Invisible Visible: a Multicultural Planning History* (Berkeley: University of California Press, 1998); Dolores Hayden, *The Power of Place* (Yale University Press, 1995); essays by Gail Lee Dubrow and Luis Apontes-Pars in Robert Melnick and Arnold Alanen, eds. *Preserving Cultural Landscapes in America* (Baltimore: Johns Hopkins Press, 2000).

II

Origin Stories: Finding the Roots of Historic Preservation in the United States

1

THE HERITAGE CRUSADE AND ITS CONTRADICTIONS[1]

David Lowenthal

HERITAGE IS EVERYWHERE—in the news, in the movies, in the market-place—in everything from galaxies to genes. It is the chief focus of patriotism and a prime lure of tourism. One can barely move without bumping into a heritage site. Every legacy is cherished. From ethnic roots to history theme parks, Hollywood to the Holocaust, millions are busy lauding (or lamenting) some past.

Why this rash of backward-looking concern? What makes heritage so popular in a world beset by poverty and hunger, enmity and strife? We seek its comfort partly to allay these griefs. In recoiling from tragic loss or fending off a fearsome future, people the world over revert to ancestral legacies. As hopes of progress fade, heritage consoles us with tradition. Against what's dreadful and dreaded today, heritage is *good*—indeed, it perhaps first appears in Psalm 16's "goodly heritage."

Yet much that we inherit is far from "goodly," some of it downright diabolical. Heritage brings manifold benefits: it links us with ancestors and offspring, bonds neighbors and patriots, certifies identity, roots us in time-honored ways. But heritage is also oppressive, defeatist, decadent. Miring us in the obsolete, the cult of heritage immures life within museums and monuments. Breeding xenophobic hate, it becomes a byword for bellicose discord. Perverting the "true" past for greedy or chauvinist ends, heritage undermines historical truth with twisted myth. Exalting rooted faith over critical reason, it stymies social action and sanctions passive acceptance of preordained fate.

Its benefits hyped and its perils exaggerated, heritage by its very nature excites partisan extremes. Heritage passions play a major role in national and ethnic conflict, in racism and resurgent genetic determinism, in museum and commemorative policy, in global theft, illicit trade, and rising demands for repatriating art and antiquities. Decisions about what to conserve and what to jettison, about parenthood and adoption, about killing or converting or cosseting those of rival faiths all invoke heritage to explain how we feel and to validate how we act.

Heritage is as old as humanity. Prehistoric peoples bequeathed goods and goals; legacies benign and malign suffuse Homeric tales, the Old Testament, and Confucian precepts. But only in our time has heritage become a mass crusade whose shrines and icons daily multiply and whose praise suffuses public discourse. Concern with roots and recollection saturates the West and encroaches more and more on the rest of the world. Nostalgia for things old and outworn supplants dreams of progress. A century or even fifty years ago, the untrammeled future was all the rage; today we laud legacies bequeathed by has-beens. Once patrimony implied provincial backwardness or musty antiquarianism; now it denotes nurturance and stewardship.

Devotion to heritage is a spiritual calling "like nursing or being in Holy Orders," as James Lees-Milne termed his own career of rescuing historic English country houses. A National Trust successor's verbal slip, "When I joined the Church—I mean, the Trust," reinforces the parallel. Heritage everywhere betokens piety. Australians are held to "spend more of their spiritual energy" in quests for enshrined symbols of identity than in any other pursuit; "worship of the past [is] one of the great secular religions."[2]

The creed of heritage fills needs for ritual devotion where formal faith has dwindled. Like religious causes, heritage fosters exhilarating fealties. The quest for and defense of patrimonial legacies is likened to the Crusades—bitter, protracted, and ruthless. And like religion, heritage relies on revealed faith rather than rational proof. We elect and exalt our legacy not by objectively weighing its claims to truth, but in passionately feeling that it *must* be right. Its mainstay is not mental effort but moral zeal.

Heritage is mandatory. It comes to us willy-nilly, and cannot be shed however shaming it may be. To share a legacy is to belong to a family, a community, a race, a nation. What each inherits is in some measure unique, but common commitments bind us to our group. Inheritors are fellow countrymen—not just patriots but *compatriots*. Mutual identity demands mutual allegiance. Those deprived of a legacy are rootless and bereaved; those who spurn one are unnatural ingrates. Nations bereft of birthrights today lament their loss much as Esau did in the book of Genesis, and intone UNESCO's Convention on the Repatriation of Cultural Property as Holy Scripture.

The traits that align heritage with religion help explain its potent pull, but they also pose serious risks. A dogma of roots and origins that must be accepted on faith denies the role of reason and forecloses compromise. Credence in a mythic past crafted for some present cause flies in the face of the past's actual complexity and precludes impartial historical knowledge. Touting our own heritage as uniquely splendid sanctions narrow ignorance and breeds belligerent bigotry.

Heritage's potential for both good and evil is huge. On the one hand, it offers a rationale for self-respecting stewardship of all we hold dear; on the other, it signals eclipse of reason and regression to embattled tribalism. Benign and baneful consequences are intertwined; heritage vice is inseparable from heritage virtue. Yet heritage is customarily either admired or reviled in toto. Devotees ignore or slight its threats; detractors simply damn its ills and deny its virtues.

I begin by tracing how and why heritage has come to matter so much.

HERITAGE RAMPANT

Heritage is not our sole link with the past. History, tradition, memory, myth, and memoir variously join us with previous times, with forebears, and with our own earlier selves. These diverse routes to the past are neither fixed nor firmly bounded; they overlap and shift their focus. Much that was once termed *history* or *tradition* is now *heritage.* But the lure of heritage now outpaces other modes of retrieval. Neither history nor tradition ever commanded the ubiquitous reach of heritage today. Heritage may be heir to the "continuous nourishing tradition" that the historian Carl Schorske, by no means alone, fears history has abdicated.[3]

Never before have so many been so engaged with so many different pasts. Spanning the centuries from prehistory to last night, heritage commingles Mesozoic monsters with Marilyn Monroe, Egyptian pyramids with Elvis Presley. Memorials and monuments multiply, cities and sites are restored, historic exploits reenacted, flea-market bygones reborn as antiques. Retrofashion rages; camcorders perpetuate yesterday's trivia. Historic sites multiply from thousands to millions; 95 percent of existing museums postdate the Second World War. Nothing seems too recent or trifling to commemorate; in Budapest, for example, museums of everyday life enshrine the telephone and the tram, pastries and pharmaceuticals, advertising and animal husbandry.

Fifty years back, book titles and indexes suggest, heritage dwelt mainly on heredity, probate law, and taxation; it now stresses antiquities, roots, identity, belonging. Prior possession once mainly legitimated title to land or lucre; today it sanctions claims to sites and relics. On both sides of the Atlantic, modern preoccupation with heritage dates from about 1980, France's official "Year of Patrimony," when Larousse redefined it from construing the civil code to celebrating the national estate.[4]

Each people esteems its newly inflated heritage concerns as unique, reflecting some trait of character or circumstance, some spirit of veneration or revenge peculiarly its own. But the pull of the past differs less than most suppose. Vaunting our own legacy, we are unaware how similar our neighbors' often is. Here is a 1994 travel brochure list of Canadian heritage goodies:

> Chestnut canoes . . . golden wheat fields of the prairies . . . Blackfoot medicine wheels . . . Haida totem poles . . . fishing villages on Fogo Island . . . donning skates on a crisp winter's morning . . . Northern Lights . . . Anne of Green Gables . . . soapstone carvings . . . loons . . . igloos . . . toboggans . . . maple syrup.

These items are quintessentially Canadian, to be sure. But their invocation of nature, ethnicity, and childhood typify most heritages. Maxims in Manchester and Minneapolis, Madagascar and the Marquesas sound alike. "If wealth is lost, nothing is lost," say Sikhs; "if *heritage* is lost, *you* are lost." To a Cameroon diplomat, heritage is "beyond price, beyond value; it unifies the tribe [and] is the spirit of the nation, what holds us together." Inuit and Indians term "everything part of our heritage." Everywhere, heritage is avowed a nutriment as vital as food and drink.[5]

Most heritage is amassed by particular groups, but global media diffusion make it ever more common coin. The same concerns with precedence and antiquity, continuity and coherence, heroism and sacrifice surface again and again. Heritage care and conveyance conjoin the stewardship of relics unique to Australia or Amazonia, New Mexico or New Guinea. Display and tourism imprint diverse legacies with like facades. Legacies of nature, prehistory, art, and architecture are hyped in terms ever more alike. Exotic dragonflies and endangered dialects are not yet shown alongside Old Master paintings in Sotheby's catalogues, but their collectors and protectors talk the same legacy lingo.

Today's heritage impulse is Western in origin, language, and leadership. The first historic monuments meeting in 1931 engaged Europeans alone; Tunisia, Mexico, and Peru joined in 1964; by 1979, eighty nations from all continents crafted the World Heritage Convention.[6] With conservation techniques devised in Rome and London and California, Swedish and German firms dominate heritage work in Asia and Africa. Zimbabwe's national patrimony—a "living" Shona village; the replica Old Bulawayo Heritage Centre—are typical products of Euro-American enterprise.

CAUSES OF MODERN HERITAGE CONCERN

Why does heritage loom so large today? Answers differ from place to place. Heritage in Britain is said to reflect nostalgia for imperial self-esteem, in America to requite angst for lost community, in France to redress wartime disgrace, in Australia to supplant the curse of European recency with indigenous antiquity.[7] But no explanation specific to one people can account for a cause so contagious. What is involved is a cluster of trends whose premises, promises, and problems are truly global.

These trends engender isolation and dislocation of self from family, family from neighborhood, neighborhood from nation—even oneself from one's former selves. Such changes involve manifold aspects of life: increasing longevity, family dissolution, loss of familiar locales, genocide and wholesale migration, accelerated obsolescence along with a rising fear of technology. They erode future expectations, spur nostalgia, and instill among millions the conviction that they need and are owed a heritage.

Runaway innovation stokes demands for heritage. Market forces swiftly outdate most things now made or built; migration uproots millions from native locales; new modes of transport and machinery transform urban and rural landscapes at shocking speed. Beleaguered by loss and change, we keep our bearings only by clinging to remnants of stability. Hence preservers' aversion to let anything go, manias for period styles, pagan cults at megalithic sites. We long for islands of security in seas of change. "In a throwaway society where everything is ephemeral," London's College of Arms explains the vogue for ancestor hunts, people "begin to look for something more lasting."[8]

Legacies at risk are cherished for their very fragility. The heritage of rural life is exalted because everywhere at risk, if not already lost. So rapid is French scenic and social decay that tourists were urged in 1993 to "see France while it is still there." Landscape is Britain's archetypal legacy; two centuries of city celebrants made country life a metaphor for the national soul, yearning to "win back a share in the common heritage filched from them with Enclosure and the Industrial Revolution." The historian Herbert Butterfield lauded Englishmen's "inescapable heritage" of Whig history as "part of the landscape of

English life, like our country lanes or our November mists or historic inns."[9] At the height of the "mad cow" epidemic in the late 1990s, leaders of a dozen English amenity groups joined to warn that the wholesale slaughter of livestock threatened, above all else, to doom the pastoral landscape—the nation's spiritual heartland.

Genocide and iconoclasm intensify needs for abiding legacies. Europe's doomed Jews resolved to leave ineffaceable witnesses to the Holocaust. Along with human butchery we mourn the carnage of irreplaceable art. To save Giotto's frescoes, Harold Nicolson would have sacrificed himself, and sooner than lose St. Mark's, Venice, would have given up his sons.[10] A pace of loss "peculiar to our times," declared UNESCO in 1972, menaced mankind's cultural and natural heritage and mandated its protection. The deliberate demolition of Mostar's bridge and Sarajevo's library underscore the gravity of continuing loss.

Yet horror at upheaval is not new. Each generation since the French Revolution has felt buffeted by turbulent times. After Napoleon, many felt stranded between the past, when life had been much the same from eon to eon, and a present that sundered each year from the last. They were the first to mourn the recent as beyond recall and to limn a childhood unimaginable to their own children. Marx's 1848 *Communist Manifesto* noted the "constant revolution of productions, the uninterrupted disturbance of all social relations, ideas becoming obsolete before they can ossify." Our great-great-grandparents were more severed from their past than we, who as heirs to two centuries of change are habituated to expect—and until recently to welcome—innovation.[11]

Ruing lost familiar vistas much as we do, our precursors were no less estranged by novelty.[12] But they were less ceaselessly reminded of their loss. Nor did a socially accepted nostalgia sanction their yearnings; on the contrary, they were enjoined to praise the new. They suffered change often as violent as ours; but we *perceive* ourselves to be its unexampled victims. Modern media magnify the past's remoteness. Even recent visual images (street scenes, home decor, hairstyles, and clothing) at once strike us as anachronistic. Old photos posed in studios seem inconceivably remote. Our great-grandparents look more like foreigners than forebears. Growing longevity cuts us off even from our own pasts. Bereft of familiar scenes and companions, our memories become unrecognizable to others. "If you age a lot, there is finally almost nobody left who shared your vast experience" of a bygone world. You look around for "*anyone* of the older generation . . . to satisfy your curiosity about some detail of the landscape of the past. There is no longer any older generation. You have become it, while your mind was mostly on other matters," notes William Maxwell.[13]

To those conscious of being poised between two worlds of thought and action, heritage seems of crucial import. "My Breton-speaking contemporaries will perhaps be the very last people to have spoken Breton on their mothers' laps," says the folklorist Hélias. Hence his stewardship duty transcends that of his predecessors and successors. "The former were not much concerned with the fate of their idiom"; the latter will condemn us for failing to protect their heritage.[14] We feel uniquely accountable. Previous generations likewise looked back to a congenial world just gone, but their laments were formulaic; ours harden into heritage dogma.

Massive migration sharpens nostalgia. This century's diaspora have suffered incomparable displacement. Fleeing violence, hatred, and hunger, tens of millions take refuge in alien lands. Mass exodus has many precedents, to be sure—the Middle Passage, the Irish Famine. But refugee exodus, up twentyfold in thirty years, is now a global commonplace. More than half of all Palestinians, Liberians, Afghans, Rwandans, and Bosnians mourn lost homelands. So do billions of rural folk forced into cities. "Displaced persons are displaced not just in space but in time; they have been cut off from their own pasts," writes Penelope Lively, severed from her own Egyptian childhood by removal to England. "If you cannot revisit your own origins—reach out and touch them from time to time—you are for ever in some crucial sense untethered."[15]

From such traumas ensue quests for roots. "The more people are on the move," observes a columnist, "the more they will grasp at tangible memorials of their collective past."[16] Urban newcomers domesticate alien milieus with rural furnishings and old farm tools; mementos of bygone lifestyles console those torn from native scenes. Diaspora are notably heritage-hungry. Five out of six ancestry searches in Italy are made by Italian-Americans. Dublin is deluged with inquiries from Sons of Erin abroad, some seeking a long-lost legacy, others an heir on whom to bestow one.

A heritage past need not have been known firsthand. "I come from Rotuma," says a Fijian who has never been in Rotuma; home is where his ancestors came from. Until recently, fourth-generation New Zealanders spoke of Britain as "home" with no intention of ever living there. Descendants of Confederate planters who fled to Brazil still cleave to old Dixieland ways, exalting a heritage of slavery so as to "pass cherished values on to future generations."[17]

Heritage is also nurtured by technophobic gloom. The horrors of fascism, the failure of communism, above all the threat of nuclear and biological catastrophe corrode former faith in progress. Many doubt their leaders' vision or ability to sustain a livable globe; dismayed by today's world, they hark back to a simpler past whose virtues they inflate and whose vices they ignore.

The dismayed are newly legion: heritage looms larger because more people now have a share in it. In times past, only a small aristocratic minority sought forebears, amassed antiquities, enjoyed Old Masters, or toured museums and historic sites. Such pursuits now lure the multitude. Millions now hunt their roots, protect beloved scenes, cherish mementos, and generally dote on times past.

Heritage growth thus reflects traumas of loss and change and fears of a menacing future. How many preservationists does it take to change a light bulb? Four—one to insert the bulb, one to document the event, and two to lament the passing of the old bulb. Heritage is not promoted only by felt decline; it sometimes celebrates success. But devotion to legacies is far more apt to mourn loss than to laud gain.

FACETS OF GROWTH

Until modern times most peoples trusted tradition, lived in accordance with what was constant and consistent, and customarily communed with ancestors. Handing down modes of life and thought to descendants was more a matter of ingrained habit than of deliberate effort; the inheritance of land and livestock, lineage and repute was socially codified and largely closed to personal decision. Few clung to artifacts that had outlasted practical or spiritual use. By contrast, heritage now reflects not just habit but conscious choice. Ways of valuing the past that arose in Renaissance and Enlightenment Europe and were bolstered by nationalism and populism are now adopted everywhere.

Earlier folk largely fused past with present. Stability and cyclical recurrence muted marks of change and averted the breaches that now sunder old from new, obsolete from usable, the dead from the living. Spirits of the departed remained intimately involved with everyday life, bonding what could be seen and touched with what was veiled or imagined. For most peoples, the past was not a foreign country but their own.[18]

While in our world the new replaces the old, in theirs the new was but another aspect of the eternal. Hence few desired to preserve what was old. The only vestiges of the past that medieval Europeans systematically conserved were princely talismans and spiritual icons—the vestments and bodily traces of saints and sovereigns. Ancient edifices were allowed to decay or were demolished with little sense of loss. The razing and rebuilding of St. Peter's in Rome in the 1500s was wholly consonant with stewardship as then seen. The old stones meant nothing in themselves; only the remembered site signified the Church's indestructible permanence.[19]

Over ensuing centuries, material relics played an increasing role, as emblems first of power and piety, then of popular purpose. Ever more secular, more social, and more substantial, heritage today augments in manifold ways. Three aspects of growth merit special note: from the elite and grand to the vernacular and everyday; from the remote to the recent; and from the material to the intangible.

Vernacular Bents

Like its new mass clientele, the past doted on is more and more populist. Formerly about splendid monuments, unique treasures, and great heroes, heritage now also touts the typical and evokes the vernacular. The homes and haunts of Everyman and Everywoman have spread from Scandinavian open-air museums into historical theme parks the world over. Colonial Williamsburg privileges dirt, ruin, and decay (unmown grass, peeling paint, and horse manure) in an everyday scene more authentic, and hence more virtuous, than the genteel fictions of previous restorers. Unhappy Williamsburg craftsmen are now required to turn out shoddy replicas true to supposed eighteenth-century prototypes.[20]

Run by the well born and the well off, heritage remains more an elite than a folk domain. But if palaces are more lavishly stewarded than haunts of the humble, the latter are better loved. Historic-house visitors flock to kitchens and servant and slave quarters; folk museums stress the humdrum over the exquisite, the ordinary more than the unusual, the popular along with the patrician. In reenacting the past, peasants and pop stars gain center stage. The bedroom carpet and plastic houseplant from Elvis Presley's Graceland are his fans' *Mona Lisa* and Elgin Marbles. Old baseball cards, beer cans, Coke bottles, and barbed wire thrill more collectors than do Queen Anne chairs or mahogany highboys. Genre scenes, decoy ducks, and mangle boards that once cluttered lofts and attics get reclaimed as art. Pop memorabilia however trivial or tawdry becomes treasure trove.

The more who engage with heritage, the less esoteric and exacting it grows. If the weak and the meek have not inherited the earth, they increasingly become keepers of its castoffs. Vestiges of folkways formerly scorned as backward are now prized as quaint.[21] Sanctuaries once exclusively elite now cater to hoi polloi. Exhibitions at London's Victoria & Albert Museum hype New Age grunge and "street cred." The generals and grandees who glower down from the walls of Britain's National

Portrait Gallery are now outfaced by grinning athletes, pop stars, and media celebrities.

Some decry such plebeian trends. "Can a perfectly ordinary house in a perfectly ordinary town really be a part of our national heritage?" So carped a critic in 1993, when England's National Trust was bequeathed a Victorian semidetached house in Worksop, Nottinghamshire, that had been left in a sixty-year time warp. Rather than "a worm's-eye view" of the past, the Trust should "illustrate the *finest* examples of architecture and furnishings."[22] Yet *Our Grimy Heritage* (1971) and SAVE Britain's Heritage's *Satanic Mills* (1984) had already won accolades from heritage fanciers.

The populist trend is worldwide. France in the 1980s legitimated a wide range of working-class legacies: "a simple oven or a village lavatory elicits the patrimonial ardor once given an artistic masterpiece."[23] American heritage began to be folksy a century ago, with George Washington repackaged from austere aristocrat into common man, Abraham Lincoln refashioned into a rustic rail-splitter, and log cabins de rigueur as presidential birthplaces; today the vernacular is all the rage. Australians zealously promote their folk past. Museums dwell on migration and newcomers, the poor and the imprisoned, the notorious Ned Kelly gang. This reflects a general view that they *have* no elite past worth notice—no monuments to wealthy taste, no heroic episodes, no formative documents like Magna Carta. Anything pompous gets mercilessly mocked.[24]

Genealogy typifies the populist trend. Millions of *Roots*-related quests spawned fifty thousand American family-tree experts. Since 1970 French ancestor hunting has become a veritable national sport. "Not long ago genealogy was a hobby for aristocrats, maiden aunts, and eccentrics," noted a 1988 survey, and "most Europeans would have stared blankly if asked to give their great-grandmother's name." With humble origins newly chic, all forebears are now ancestral worthies.[25] "When I was a boy at Harrow School in the 1920s," the architectural historian Sir John Summerson told me sixty years later, "I did all I could to prevent *any*one finding out my grandfather was a common labourer. Today I'd make sure *every*one knew." The writer Jonathan Raban relates his father's switch from genteel to rougher roots. In the 1950s he mounted an "antique truffle hunt [for] an unbroken arc of pure ancestry, a trail of blood [from] helmeted centurions [and] Anglo-Saxons in mead halls" down through army officers and minor gentry. But in the 1980s Raban *père* was digging up "our criminal past," ancestors "engaged in smuggling, privateering and the slave trade," showing that "rapine, plunder, fiddling the books and dealing under the counter ran in our blood."[26]

Convict forebears who once disgraced Australian descendants now lend them radical chic. Some limits remain: "murder, rape—no, we wouldn't brag about that," says a genealogist. "We would brag about highway robbery, though." More typically, roots' seekers hope to find "simple, honest, law-abiding" ancestors, in Carol Shields's words, whose "robustly rounded" lives will compensate for their own complex fears and doubts.[27]

Instant Tradition

Once confined to a distant past—pre-1750 buildings, centuries-old antiques, Old Master paintings—heritage now engulfs yesterday. Houses become "historic" in mere decades, school history takes on events within living memory, a "Heritage" car is one made before 1970. The commemorative pace quickens from centennials to fiftieth and twenty-fifth anniversaries. Heritage today hails even the living. Indiana fans of Dan Quayle boast the first museum honoring an extant vice president, featuring Bible-school snapshots and his Little League baseball uniform. "A lot of people wait fifty years, after the person is gone, but we had all his stuff lying right here, so why not do it while he's still living?" A New Jersey museum of Bruce Springsteen memorabilia opened *and* closed while the rock star yet lives.

Stress on recent heritage mirrors its mass clienteles—the British working-class cult of steam trains, for example. Notably for those with little schooling, things within living memory have a relevance absent from remoter times. And recent souvenirs rapidly gain scarcity value. Fountain pens are already rare, antique TVs and extinct Web sites the latest collectibles.[28]

Novelties at first decried in the end gain legacy status, and the end is nigh ever sooner. From hated eyesores, Victorian railway viaducts mutated into beloved scenery defended more zealously than ancient abbeys. The passage from horror to heritage once took a century; now it happens in two decades. Once proscribed by Australian towns as shabby reminders of a hated past, Victorian verandas by the 1970s became valued heritage, and in the 1980s were often added to buildings that had never had verandas.[29] The golden arches of McDonald's eateries are concurrently a detested novelty in London's Hampstead and a cherished legacy in California.

Like populism, the vogue for recency shows that heritage is open to improvement. A mean or meager legacy can always be augmented, a brief time span lengthened. Today's new clients supplant or supplement preexisting legacies with icons of their own. "Other great Americans will be born whose birthdays will force their way in to the calendar," cautioned a 1911 essay against a fixed ancestral canon. "Our boundaries of national gratitude are not finally set."[30] They never will be. Rosters of historic persons and places continue to annex what becomes newly salient and to shed what loses pertinence.

The pace of replacement does exact costs. As heritage expands closer to the present, it becomes more ephemeral. Fads for things barely past, like most icons of popular culture, hasten the attrition of historical memory and diminish shared canonical legacies. The accrual of ever more recent relics also makes heritage harder to demarcate from the ongoing present. Yesterday's traces merge with those of today; conserved legacies coalesce with current locales. Proximity to the present makes heritage ever more relevant to, but ever less distinct from, our own world. At length all that distinguishes heritage is its history of previous use.

Living Folkways

Along with the recent and the vernacular, heritage today stresses intangible folkways—kinship, language, poetry, music. Such concerns are not novel: Homeric lineages bolstered feudal perquisites; folk legacies sustained European nation-states. Indeed, two centuries ago the philosopher Johann Gottfried von Herder considered language and folklore the crux of collective heritage. Yet tangible monuments and memorials dominated the discourse of national patrimony well into the twentieth century. Safeguarding architectural antiquities became an overriding concern, as myriad legislative acts attest. Even now, heritage restitution campaigns concentrate more on buildings and bones than on quatrains or cookery.

But legacy concerns increasingly focus on ideas and images. This shift reflects the values of cultures that do not share the Western bias toward material objects. Koreans cherish masked plays, musical genres, and skills like knot making, brass smelting, and pot glazing. "Living Cultural Treasures" betoken Japanese admiration for ancient forms and skills, whereas ancient buildings (save for sacred shrines) are shunned as *furukusai*—so old they stink. Western conservation has small allure for peoples who build little meant to last. The transcendent value accorded original stone and brickwork in UNESCO's Venice Charter of 1966 "leave[s] other cultures and traditions ill at ease, [for] *they* place more emphasis on spiritual values, on authenticity of thought, than on material symbols." Indeed, as the purpose of preserving traditional skills is to ensure the continuity of creative practice, the retention of material artifacts may be actively discouraged. "When the product is preserved and venerated, the impulse to repeat the process is compromised," writes Chinua Achebe of Nigerian art. "The Igbo choose to eliminate the product and retain the process so that every occasion and every generation will receive its own impulse and kinesis of creation."[31]

Cultural heritage stresses words over things above all in China, where esteem for tradition goes hand in hand with recurrent demolition of material remains. Revering ancestral memory and calligraphy, the Chinese hold the past's purely physical traces in small regard; indeed, old works must perish so that new ones can take their place. Memory of art, not its physical persistence, suffuses awareness and spurs new artistic creation.[32] "We in the West tend to equate the antique presence with authentically ancient physical objects," observes a Sinologist. "China has no ruins comparable to the Roman Forum, or even to Angkor Wat"—not for want of skills "but because of a different attitude about how to achieve an enduring monument." Ancient cities became sites of heritage through "a past of words, not of stones."[33] The Chinese heritage is not imperishable monuments but imperishable words.

Sentiments linked with sites can override tangible concerns even in the West. In North Carolina, a folklorist found many old homesteads empty and neglected but periodically used for family reunions; what mattered was "not the walls, the roof, and the foundation [but] the memory of the experiences within. [They] preserve stories about old houses better than they preserve the structures themselves."[34] The marginalized poor are most apt to discount material legacies. Preserving old houses is more of a bane than a boon to working-class or ethnic neighborhoods at risk of being gentrified. Heritage to them is more likely to mean folkways (faiths, foods, forms of music and dance) than fabric, live performance more than finished artifact.[35]

Intangible folkways now attract mainstream support. Winners of National Endowment for the Arts heritage fellowships in 1995 included a blues guitarist, a cowboy balladeer, a basket weaver, a step dancer, a luthier, a quiltmaker, and a blacksmith. A publican, a thatcher, a cheesemonger, and an umbrella-handle maker figure among Britain's *Country Life* "living national treasures." In 2002, UNESCO launched an international charter to register and protect a list of the "Masterpieces of the Oral and Intangible Heritage of Humanity," ranging from polyphonic singing in Georgia to puppet theater in Sicily.

VULNERABLE AND DISPUTED LEGACIES

We value our heritage most when it seems at risk; threats of loss engender stewardly fervor. Civil war roused seventeenth-century antiquaries to save England's imperiled ecclesiastical monuments. Only

when English antiquaries wrote of "saving" ruined Norman abbeys by
dismantling and shipping them across the Channel did the French rescue them from further neglect; only when a London museum bought
the 's Hertogenbosch seventeenth-century rood-loft did the Dutch
rally to defend their national legacy; only when Americans were about
to export Tattershall Castle brick by brick did Britain in 1913 legislate
to protect its built legacy. "Heritage never means more to us than
when we see it inherited by someone else."[36]

The conservation of England's architectural heritage owes much to
a 1930s student binge at historic Rousham, Oxfordshire. Helplessly
watching his drunken host take potshots at garden statuary and slash
family portraits with a hunting crop roused in young James Lees-
Milne "some deep atavistic compassion for ancient architecture so
vulnerable and transient, and some paternal instinct to protect and
safeguard all tangible works of art." Thus inspired, Lees-Milne became
the guiding genius of the National Trust's country-house crusade; during and after the Second World War scores of the greatest estates in
England were brought into public ownership and thus saved from
ruin.[37]

Conservation in England is commonly couched in terms of some
national legacy in peril, be it Wren churches, fox-hunting, ducal collections of Greek and Italian art, or the aristocracy itself. "We are now
down to 25 breeding dukes," warned the Duke of Buccleigh in 1992.
"At this rate we shall soon need our own rare breed society." Extinction
seems always imminent for legacies of nature. In World Wildlife Fund
appeals every bird is on the brink, every mammal all but doomed. So
scarce was the bald eagle, America's national bird, that corporations
launched a costly (and successful) drive to restock eaglets. To save
shrinking rain forests, conservers cry havoc over trees felled, species
lost, ecosystems ravaged. As developers despoil and robbers ransack,
the world's cultural legacy shrinks like the rain forest. So does its cere-
bral patrimony; nine-tenths of the globe's six thousand existing languages are expected soon to vanish.

Such fears are not chimerical. Many dwindling legacies are destined
to die out. But alarmism is endemic in the heritage mind-set. "Hurry.
The bulldozers are coming. Historic buildings are falling," warned
America's National Trust in 1970; thirty years on the same entreaty re-
echoes. British patrimonial alarm is perpetual—yet their legacy is
probably the world's best protected. Aghast at the drain of treasures
abroad, they forget that the flux was ever thus. "Precious things are
going out of our distracted country," agonized a Henry James grandee
a century ago, "at a quicker rate" than they ever came in.[38]

Heritage depletion is better understood as part of an ongoing dynamic process than as irreplaceable loss. To expunge the obsolete and restore it as heritage are, like disease and its treatment, conjoint and even symbiotic. The Nazis gutted Old Warsaw to obliterate an icon of Polish identity; postwar Poles speedily rebuilt it to imply unbroken cultural continuity. The world's greatest technocrats married genius for annihilation with instincts to preserve: the inventor of dynamite, long the globe's most explosive substance, is now best recalled for the Nobel Peace Prize; Henry Ford and John D. Rockefeller, whose juggernauts of progress doomed older modes of life, became exemplary collectors and custodians, at Ford's Old Dearborn and Rockefeller's Colonial Williamsburg, of the heritage their engines and oil outmoded.

Heritage felt offensive to new orthodoxies is jettisoned in turn. Afghanistan's Buddhas blasted by the Taliban, dismantled Soviet heroic statues are just the latest victims of chronic acts of iconoclasm. "Bolsheviks topple czar monuments, Stalin erases old Bolsheviks, Khrushchev tears down Stalin, Brezhnev tears down Khrushchev . . . No difference," says a Russian critic. "This is classic old Moscow technique: either worship or destroy."[39]

Heritage also succumbs because ravished by admirers—loved to death. Devotees wear down old floors, abrade ancient stones, erode prehistoric trackways. The more we learn of the ill effects of light, the less can old fabrics and watercolors be displayed. Since breath is lethal to the cave paintings, legacies like Lascaux are closed to public view; to see Leonardo's *Last Supper,* visitors must first be decontaminated. Ecotourism swamps the fragile sites it was designed to safeguard. To protect Galápagos tortoises and birds, an annual ceiling of twelve thousand visitors was set three decades ago; this "ultimate environmental experience" now disastrously lures five times that many.

The best intentions prove lethal; the more heritage is appreciated, the sooner it decays or turns to dross. The very act of designating a building as worth conserving often has the opposite effect; the owner's fear that it may come under legal protection triggers hasty demolition to avert the burden of care.

Stonehenge, Britain's heritage archetype and a renowned World Heritage Site, typifies global heritage dilemmas. It has long served and suffered for myriad purposes. Some locals took stones for fencing and building, others rented tools to tourists to chip off bits of sarsen—one antiquary grumbled at being "Obliged with a Hammer to labour hard three Quarters of an Hour."[40] National property since the First World War, Stonehenge is now safe from religious zealots, farmers, and souvenir hunters. But it endures endless custodial folly. Access is through a dank concrete tunnel; barbed wire intermittently festoons the stones; car parks, lavatories, a cramped gift shop, a dingy café's Sarsen Sandwiches degrade the ambience. "We've managed to separate the stones from their setting," bragged English Heritage; "we've surrounded a great monument to the genius of the early British with the worst excesses of the 20th century."[41] Cult status and commercial pressure aggravate these woes. To make Stonehenge seemly for paying tourists, its custodians in the mid-1980s banned New Age cultists, hippies, ley-line mystics, and "Druids." English Heritage pledged a purified Stonehenge as honeypot and sanctuary. Still a self-styled "national disgrace," Stonehenge today "is a monument above all to the modern British vandal."[42]

Stonehenge's woes reflect confusion over heritage goals and means common to many famous sites. Popularity equally degrades Mont-Saint-Michel. Bandits drawn by the antiquities market machine-gun their way into Angkor Wat, ill-protected even though floodlit and wired like a concentration camp; tourists must evade land mines planted to halt plunder, sometimes by the very soldiers deputized to guard the place. Art-historical hyping of Cycladic figurines led to the looting of thousands of Dodecanese graves and a flood of Cycladic fakes.

A million and a half ritual and cultural objects are being returned from American museums to Indian tribes under the 1991 Native American Graves and Repatriation Act. Most are reburied, some exposed to the elements, many destroyed for purposes of purification. Similar fates befell bones and grave goods repatriated to Australian Aborigines after 1984. Some argue that this deprives indigenes' own better-educated (in other words, Westernized) descendants of an invaluable legacy. One archaeologist surmises that "Aboriginal people may come to acknowledge the good fortune that European collectors preserved fragments of their cultural heritage."[43]

Or they may continue to deplore that preservation. Aborigines who have lived with loss remark that "white people don't know what to remember and what to forget, what to let go of and what to preserve." American whites try to keep it all. At one meeting with tribal leaders, a curator recalls anthropologists opposing the reburial of grave goods lest knowledge be lost.

> Finally one Native American activist said, "Why do you white people need to know all this stuff? Why can't you just let it go?" Listening, I had such a visceral reaction of horror, I knew he had hit on something very sacred to *my* culture. The thought of deliberately letting knowledge perish was as

sacrilegious to me as the thought of keeping one's ancestors on a museum shelf was sacrilegious to the Indians.[44]

Such disputes are myriad.

The past is more accessible, more controversial, and more vulnerable than ever before. Heritage appetites outpace heritage growth. Awareness of its fragility endears what we inherit; ever more popular, heritage becomes ever more perishable. And squabbling over heritage spoils its integrity for all claimants. The long-disputed Stone of Scone was stolen from Westminster by 1950s Scottish Nationalists, who copied it before returning it; in 1996 it was again sundered from the accompanying Coronation chair and officially "repatriated" to Scotland, but no one knows if this is the "real" Stone or a copy.[45] Rivalry often causes treasures to be withdrawn from view entirely. Forbidden to take out of Britain a Lucian Freud painting she had bought at auction in London, an American locked it away in a bank vault. "If Britain's export laws could stop her hanging it in her collection, she would stop Britain's public galleries hanging it in theirs."[46]

Quarrels over possession and stewardship aggravate these risks. The passions for possession that enrich victors traumatize victims. The tangible classical heritage has been so long admired—and collected—abroad that little of it survives intact in Greece.[47] Given the avarice of private collectors and the chauvinism of nation-states, no policing can stem the evil impact of illicit excavation and smuggling. Antiquities stripped from site, sundered from context, are lost not only to their lands of origin but also to the global community.[48]

HERITAGE DEPRIVATION, HERITAGE POSSESSION

Yet in many monument-rich lands, the sacred national patrimony means little except to ruling elites or as an adjunct to tourism. Most people are too poor not to market any antiquities they can unearth. "To be rich, dig up an ancient tomb," runs a Chinese peasant saying; "to make a fortune, open a coffin." Indeed, illicit exports of antiquities from Mexico and Guatemala may feed more mouths than any other resource. Against such acts, legal codes are impotent and moral entreaty otiose. Why should the indigent not hawk their heritage to feed their families?

Do they even view it as *their* heritage? Peruvian villagers about to loot a newfound pre-Incan grave site were persuaded not to "steal from the ancestors" or "sack their father's sacred tomb." But such veneration is rare. When told that plundering Mayan sites was destroying their own legacy, Yucatán peasants were unrepentant. "The ancient people made it; it is not a part of what we are."[49] Even those who cherish "the ancient people" may sell them off. Tomb robbers in Sicily and Tuscany feel fully justified in smuggling antiquities to Swiss dealers. "They consider that these tombs contain the bodies of their ancestors and they are therefore entitled to the contents," explains a Sicilian. Tuscan tomb robbers avow endorsement from Etruscan forebears who tell them when and where to dig, and which tombs to leave inviolate. *Tombaroli* skills are handed down within particular families, with proceeds shared among the whole community.[50]

A heritage in alien hands is felt not worth husbanding. "The issue is ownership and control," says an American civil-rights crusader campaigning to conserve and interpret that movement's sites. "If we don't tell the story or control the telling, then it is no longer about us." Egyptians whose antiquities have mostly ended up in Europe, and Jamaicans whose beaches are fenced off for exclusive use by tourists, cannot suppose these legacies of culture and nature are truly their own. Similar dispossession is legion. Westernized Javanese cut off from indigenous roots by Dutch imperial rule felt exiled in their own land; "living in a hotel owned by others, we seek neither to improve nor equip it as we do not feel that it is ours." A chronicler lays Sicilian despondency to awareness "that none of the[ir] riches—the Greek temples, the Byzantine mosaics, Catalan-Gothic churches—are really" theirs. A dozen faceless, limbless statues of the goddess Cybele, hacked to pieces by a peasant angered by tourists trampling his onions, attest "the danger presented by a people that feels that its past doesn't belong to it."[51]

Legacies are especially crippling where a conquered people are coerced into the conviction they *had* no proper patrimony. Children in French colonial Africa were taught to revere "our ancestors, the Gauls." Throughout the Caribbean, British colonizers built schools and libraries where "you distorted or erased my history and glorified your own," charges Jamaica Kincaid; West Indians were left with "no motherland, no fatherland, no gods, . . . no tongue." Earlier legacies offer no solace. "No periods of time over which my [African] ancestors held sway, no documentation of complex civilizations, is any comfort to me." To redeem ancient legacies as national heritage is harder still. Third World efforts to forge emblems of tradition are mocked as imitative and obsolete, not "authentic" heritage but an opéra bouffe simulacrum of flags and folk costumes.[52] Heritage is truly transmitted, suggests V. S. Naipaul, only in "dead countries, or secured and bypassed ones—where men can cherish the past and think of passing on furniture and china to their heirs"—places like Sweden and Canada. "Everywhere else the past can only cause pain."[53]

Merely to gain a heritage is fruitless, warns a British custodian; inheritors must be actively cognizant they are "heirs to the past, heirs to the collections which they own, free to decide for themselves what they are going to do with the past, what it means for them now and what it may mean for them in the future."[54] Choices are constrained, to be sure; most heritage comes prepackaged by our precursors. But for the past to enrich our present, we must make its legacy our very own.

The supreme merit of heritage identity was underscored by an Israeli archaeologist addressing army recruits at Masada:

> When Napoleon stood among his troops next to the pyramids of Egypt, he declared: "Four thousand years of history look down upon you." . . . What would he not have given to be able to say: "Four thousand years of *your own* history look down upon you."

Our own heritage indeed matters most to us. But we have a stake in what others care for, too. "History did not need to be mine in order to engage me," writes a Haitian. "It just needed to relate to someone, anyone. It could not just be The Past. It had to be someone's past."[55] Heirs of commingled legacies, we gain more from attachment to many pasts than from exclusive devotion to our "own"—assuming we could decide which past was truly just ours.

Not only is no past exclusively ours, no past people are enough like ourselves to justify essentialist claims to a particular history. Rather than exclusively tribal secrets, our cosmopolite ancestors have things to say to all their cosmopolite descendants, never just to a few self-chosen ones. Globally cherished legacies demand shared possession and control. All heritage is in any case ours for only a brief spell, before we in turn pass it on to no less myriad heirs.

HAZARDS OF HERITAGE GLUT

Our newly augmented heritage answers a congeries of needs, but the magnitude and momentum of its growth give rise to their own perils. Heritage of every kind accumulates to counter the transience of everything newly made. We cordon off more and more relics of the past against the rapid demise of the disposable. A legacy of protected sites and objects piles up as the felt opposite of obsolescence. Salvaging ever more from erosion and discard, we strive to rectify the imbalance between the ephemeral and the enduring.[56] Fending off irreversible change, we preserve, restore, or replicate. Any extinction is considered a crime.

Heritage accumulates by its very nature: stockpiling is its raison d'être. We amass out of habit, and then contend that keeping stuff is good for us and for posterity. Parsimony sanctions the storage bags labeled PIECES OF STRING TOO SHORT TO USE, the jars of excrement their begetter could not bear to part with, the auto-icon of Jeremy Bentham left in perpetuity to University College London. Sir Vauncey Harpur-Crewe stuffed shells and shards and rocks and swords on to every shelf of every room in Calke Abbey, now a National Trust shrine to his anal-retentive obsession.[57] Such hoards can be lethally toxic. Like Mark Twain's *Connecticut Yankee,* mortally marooned among the rotting corpses of his electrocuted enemy knights,[58] many heritage custodians would sooner perish amid putrescence than cull their collections.

Crusades to save endangered heritage seldom heed limited custodial resources. Archaeologists bemoan sites plundered or lost to developers, yet more gets excavated than can be appraised, conserved, or displayed.[59] Archival accretion has multiplied holdings a thousandfold within decades. Each American president's papers are said to outnumber those of all his predecessors combined. Every enterprise becomes memorable; not only banks but also bakeries and beauty shops file dossiers:

> No epoch has deliberately produced so many archives as ours, due alike to technical advances in reproduction and conservation and to our superstitious respect for these traces. As traditional memory fades, we feel obliged religiously to accumulate the testimonies, documents, images, and visible signs of what was, as if this ever-proliferating dossier should be called on as evidence in some tribunal of history. Hence the inhibition against destroying, the retention of everything. . . . In classical times, only great families, the church, and the state kept records; today memories are recorded and memoirs written not only by minor actors in history but by their spouses and doctors.

Once reproached for saving too much, archivists are now adjured to keep everything. The glut causes chaos; reduced publication and maintenance funds make their expanded stocks ever less accessible. New acquisitions go unreported, their very existence unknown to the public lest some seek to use them.[60] Heirs to a growing legacy of unsorted verbiage, chroniclers, like Tristram Shandy, are losing ground all the time.

Heritage overload is not a new problem, to be sure. "The world is accumulating too many materials for knowledge," observed Hawthorne after a day at the British Museum in 1855, "and as each generation leaves its fragments & potsherds behind it, such will finally be the desperate conclusion of the learned."[61] Only in our time, though, has the glut become suffocatingly unmanageable. Yet heritage is such a sacred cow that none can halt its growth. For example, Italy is so stuffed with treasure that only a fraction of it is cataloged, let alone cared for, least of all open to the public.[62] Everyone knows this, yet no steward dares publicly affirm it. To asperse so sacred a realm goes against the grain. As a heritage activist, I myself almost instinctively applaud the renewal of local pride in ancestral roots, the protection of relics threatened by erosion or plunder, and the rescue of cherished legacies from purblind greed.

Indiscriminate retention bares other heritage faults. The sheer magnitude of tangible mementos and documentary traces inhibits creative action. Worship of a bloated heritage invites passive reliance on received authority, stifles rational inquiry, replaces unpleasant reality with feel-good history, and saps creative innovation. And all too often it ignores the needs of local inhabitants whose involvement is essential. That heritage is viable only in a living community is a tenet widely accepted but seldom acted on. To sustain a legacy of stones, those who dwell among them also need stewardship. "*We* are the heritage," declaimed a mayor of Dijon of plans to conserve that indigent city; the French government should "extend patrimonial solicitude to us." Traditional Georgia Sea Islands' crafts have been revived, but rampant tourism beleaguers the people themselves: "We, the black native population of these islands, have become the new endangered species."[63]

The past is a scarce resource, remarked an anthropologist about historical memory in India.[64] With regard to relics, scarcity seems ipso facto evident. Yet it is not true; scarcity is only a cultural construct, its definition varying with circumstance. The West today attaches high value to what is unique, hence rare and induplicable, such as the Dead Sea Scrolls or a Shakespeare first folio. We have forsworn, if not forgotten, earlier modes of enlarging sacred heritage. In medieval Christendom, miraculous intervention made scarce relics, such as fragments of the True Cross, infinitely replicable. Mere proximity to a relic could sanctify other relics. The productivity of late nineteenth century relic factories enabled the Vatican to buy back many more sacred treasures than it had lost after 1870, when Italy expropriated religious properties.[65] Moreover, as shown above, not every realm of memory requires tangible or even visible mementos. Memorials become compelling by means of absences as well as presences. Ghostly monuments to the Holocaust in several German cities—shafts lowered gradually below ground, leaving nothing beyond the memory of their disappearance but a plaque on the surface, are more poignant than solid mausoleums.[66]

Finally, heritage is not a static finished product pickled in amber but an ever-changing palimpsest. New creations and recognitions more than make up for what is lost through erosion, demolition, and changing tastes. Care for what we inherit requires active embrace of what we add to it. To conserve the past is never enough; good caretaking involves continual creation. Heritage is ever revitalized. Our legacy is not purely original, for it includes our forebears' alterations and additions along with their first creations. We treasure that heritage in our own protective *and* transformative fashion, handing it down reshaped in the faith that our heirs will also become creative as well as retentive stewards.

We benefit our successors less by encumbering them with a bundle of canonical artifacts and structures than by handing down memories. The future may be better served by inheriting from us not specific material relics but knowledge of traditional creative skills, institutions in good working order, and habits of resilience in coping with the uncertain vicissitudes of existence.

NOTES

1. This essay distills and extends the argument in chapters 1 and 10 of my book *The Heritage Crusade and the Spoils of History* (New York: Cambridge University Press, 1998).
2. James Lees-Milne, *People and Places: Country House Donors and the National Trust* (London: Murray, 1992), 5; author's interview with Martin Drury, 1977; Les A. Murray, *Persistence in Folly: Selected Prose Writings* (London: Angus & Robertson/Sirius, 1984), 114, 26.
3. Carl Schorske, *Fin-de-Siècle Vienna* (New York: Cambridge University Press, 1981), xvii.
4. Alain Bourdin, *La patrimoine réinventé* (Paris: Presses universitaires de France, 1984), 18; Pierre Nora, "L'ère de la commémoration," in his *Lieux de mémoire* (Paris: Gallimard, 1984–92), III.3, 995.
5. Heritage attestations in *Museum* 33 (1981), 117–23, and in John Henry Merryman, "The Nation and the Object," *International Journal of Cultural Property* 3 (1994), 68–9; UNESCO, *Conventions and Recommendations . . . Concerning the Protection of Cultural Heritage* (Paris: UNESCO, 1985).
6. Françoise Choay, *L'Allégorie du patrimoine* (Paris: Seuil, 1992), 10–12.
7. Kevin T. Walsh, *The Representation of the Past: Museums and Heritage in the Post-Modern World* (London: Routledge, 1992), 52; James Marston Fitch, *Historic Preservation: Curatorial Management of the Built World* (New York: McGraw-Hill, 1982); Alfred Grosser, *Le crime et la mémoire* (Paris: Flammarion, 1989); Murray, *Persistence in Folly*, 109–29; Graeme Davison, "Heritage: From Patrimony to Pastiche" in his *The Use and Abuse of Australian History* (Sydney: Allen and Unwin, 2000), 110–30.
8. Peter Spurrier quoted in "Europe's Genealogy Craze," *Newsweek*, 7 March 1988, 58–9; see also Michael Kammen, *Mystic Chords of Memory* (New York: Vintage Books, 1991), 642.
9. C. H. Warren (1943) quoted in Malcolm Chase, "This Is No Claptrap, This Is Our Heritage," in Christopher Shaw and Malcolm Chase, eds. *The Imagined Past* (Manchester: Manchester University Press, 1989), 131; Herbert Butterfield, *The Englishman and His History* (Cambridge: University Press, 1944), 2; Reg Gammon, "Our Country, All Earthly Things Above, As Always," *The Field* 282 (May 1990), 82–3.
10. Harold Nicolson (1944) quoted in John Henry Merryman, "Two Ways of Thinking about Cultural Property," *American Journal of International Law* 80 (1986), 840.

11. François Furet, "L'Ancien Régime et la Révolution," in Nora, *Lieux de mémoire*, III.1, 107–39; Roy Pascal, *Design and Truth in Autobiography* (London: Routledge & Kegan Paul, 1960), 57; Richard Terdiman, "The Mnemonics of Musset's *Confession*," *Representations* 26 (spring 1989), 26–48.

12. It is a common belief that technical invention has soared without precedent in recent decades. But is it true? Have television, computers, nuclear power, and space flights altered life more in our time than did the auto, telephone, electric light, airplane, radio, and cinema between 1900 and 1950? Or the railroads, gas lights, steamships, telegraph, factory-made clothing, and household goods that transformed the Western world between 1800 and 1860? No one from the 1750s could have imagined the new world of 1800; in contrast, no one from the 1950s would find most present-day scenes unfamiliar. While the 1890s seemed like the Dark Ages in 1945, sixty years on 1945 seems like only yesterday, laptops and mobile phones aside.

13. William Maxwell, "The Man in the Moon," in his *Billie Dyer and Other Stories* (New York: Gale, 1993), 57.

14. Pierre-Jakez Hélias, *The Horse of Pride: Life in a Breton Village* (New Haven, CT: Yale University Press, 1978), 343.

15. William B. Wood, "Forced Migration: Local Conflicts and International Dilemmas," *Annals of the Association of American Geographers* 84 (1994), 607–34; Penelope Lively, *Oleander, Jacaranda: A Childhood Perceived* (London: Viking, 1994), 175.

16. Simon Jenkins, "Dead and Dismembered on the Nile," *The Times* (London), 9 January 1993, 12.

17. Ron Crocombe, "The Continuing Creation of Identities in the Pacific Islands," in David Hooson, ed., *Geography and National Identity* (Oxford: Blackwell, 1994), 317; Brazilian quoted in Michael Kepp, "Rebels Who Stay True to Dixie," *Observer on Sunday* (London), 2 August 1992, 11.

18. I explore what made the past foreign in *The Past Is a Foreign Country* (Cambridge: Cambridge University Press, 1985), and in "The Past Is a Foreign Country," in Tim Ingold, ed., *Key Debates in Anthropology* (London: Routledge, 1996), 206–12, 229–45.

19. Roberto Weiss, *The Renaissance Discovery of Classical Antiquity* (Oxford: Blackwell, 1959), 65–70, 98–104; Marc Guillaume, *La politique du patrimoine* (Paris: Galilée, 1980), 99–100.

20. Eric Gable and Richard Handler, "Deep Dirt: Messing Up the Past at Colonial Williamsburg," *Social Analysis* 34 (1993), 3–16.

21. Kammen, *Mystic Chords of Memory*, 681–2.

22. Catherine Milner, "The Last Straws," *Times Magazine* (London), 3 April 1993, 38.

23. Nora, "L'ère de la commémoration," 1000–5.

24. David Lowenthal, "Uses of the Past in Australia," in Brian Hocking, ed., *Australia Towards 2000* (Basingstoke, England: Macmillan, 1990), 46–54; Alistair Thomson, *Anzac Memories: Living with the Legend* (Melbourne: Oxford University Press, 1994).

25. Robert M. Taylor Jr. and Ralph J. Crandall, "Historians and Genealogists," in their (eds.) *Generations and Change* (Macon, GA: Percer University Press, 1986), 14–15; survey in "Europe's Genealogy Craze," *Newsweek*, 7 March 1988, 58–9; André Burguière, "La généalogie," in Nora, *Lieux de mémoire*, III.3, 20.

26. Jonathan Raban, *Coasting* (London: Picador, 1987), 152, 172.

27. Graeme Davison, "The Broken Lineage of Australian Family History," in Donna Merwick, ed., *Dangerous Liaisons: Essays on Honour of Greg Dening* (Parkville: University of Melbourne History Dept., 1994), 335; Norma Tuck of the Society of Australian Genealogists, quoted in Seth Mydans, "Those Convict Fathers? Not so Bad," *New York Times*, 3 February 1988, 4; Carol Shields, *The Stone Diaries* (London: Fourth Estate, 1993), 166.

28. Paul Andrews, "The Virtual Dead Live On in Museum of Web Failures," *International Herald Tribune*, 25 May 2001; Shannon Henry, "Dot-com Era's Froth to Be Kept for Posterity," *International Herald Tribune*, 29 June 2002.

29. Tom Griffiths, *Hunters and Collectors: The Antiquarian Imagination in Australia* (Melbourne: Cambridge University Press, 1996), 240–2.

30. James Lane Allen (1911) quoted in Kammen, *Mystic Chords of Memory*, 256–7.

31. Olgierd Czerner, "Communal Cultural Heritage in a Unified Europe," *ICOMOS News* 1:1 (March 1991), 25. Chinua Achebe, "The Igbo World and Its Art," in his *Hopes and Impediments: Selected Essays, 1965–1987* (London: Heinemann, 1988), 43.

32. Wang Gungwu, "Loving the Ancient in China," in Isabel McBryde, ed., *Who Owns the Past?* (Melbourne: Oxford University Press, 1985), 175–95; Pierre Ryckmans, "The Chinese Attitude towards the Past" [1986], in Simon Leys (pseudonym for Ryckmans), *The Angel and the Octopus: Collected Essays 1983–1998* (Sydney: Duffy & Snelgrove, 1999), 3–24.

33. F. W. Mote, "A Millennium of Chinese Urban History: Form, Time, and Space Concepts in Soochow," *Rice University Studies* 59:4 (1973), 49–53.

34. Michael Ann Williams, "The Realm of the Tangible," in Burt Feintuch, ed., *The Conservation of Culture* (Lexington: University Press of Kentucky, 1988), 199–200.

35. Antoinette J. Lee, "Discovering Old Cultures in the New World," in Robert E. Stipe and A. J. Lee, *The American Mosaic: Preserving a Nation's Heritage* (Washington: US/ICOMOS, 1987), 179–205; idem, "Cultural Diversity in Historic Preservation," *Historic Preservation Forum* 6:4 (1992), 28–41.

36. Details in my *Past Is a Foreign Country,* 394.

37. James Lees-Milne, *Another Self* (London: Faber, 1970), 93–5; idem, *People and Places,* 1; Simon Jenkins, *The Selling of Mary Davies and Other Writings* (London: J. Murray, 1993), 99–103.

38. Henry James, *The Outcry* [1911] (New York: H. Fertig, 1982), 43–5.

39. Vitaly Komar quoted in Lawrence Wechsler, "Slight Modifications," *New Yorker,* 12 July 1993, 59–65.

40. Robert Townson (1799) quoted in Christopher Chippindale, *Stonehenge Complete* (rev. ed., London: Thames & Hudson, 1994), 91.

41. English Heritage chairman Jocelyn Stevens quoted in Alexander Frater, "The Lasting Lure of the Stones," *Observer on Sunday,* 20 June 1993, 49–50.

42. Christopher Chippindale et al., *Who Owns Stonehenge?* (London: Batsford, 1990); English Heritage, *Conservation Bull.* November 1994; Christopher Chippindale, "Putting the 'H' in Stonehenge," *History Today* 43 (April 1993), 6–7; Barbara Bender, "Stonehenge—Contested Landscape," in her (ed.) *Landscape: Politics and Perspectives* (Providence, RI: Berg, 1993), 245–79; Simon Jenkins, "Let Stonehenge Rise, or Suffer the Curse of Og," *The Times* (London), 8 February 2002.

43. D. J. Mulvaney, "A Question of Values: Museums and Cultural Property," in McBryde, *Who Owns the Past?,* 87–8; idem, "Past Regained, Future Lost: The Kow Swamp Pleistocene Burials," *Antiquity* 65 (1991), 12–21.

44. Australian Aborigine quoted in Griffiths, *Hunters and Collectors,* 226; Carolyn Gilman to the author, 29 June 1995, recalling a 1989 symposium.

45. Paul Binski, "Even More English than Scottish," *Spectator,* 13 July 1996, 11–16.

46. Quoted in Dalya Alberge, "Buyer Frustrates Art Export Laws," *The Times* (London), 5 March 1996.

47. Roger Just, "Cultural Certainties and Private Doubts," in Wendy James, ed., *The Pursuit of Certainty: Religious and Cultural Formulations* (London: Routledge, 1995), 285–308 at 290.

48. Colin Renfrew, *Loot, Legitimacy and Ownership* (London: Duckworth, 2000).

49. Archaeologist Walter Alva quoted in Sidney D. Kirkpatrick, *Lords of Sipán* (New York: Morrow, 1992), 139–42; Mary Dempsey, "Protectors of Peru's Shining Past," *New Scientist,* 20 August 1994, 23–5; "Stones of Their Ancestors," *Newsweek,* 11 September 1989, 57.

50. Giuliana Luna (1976) quoted in John Henry Merryman, "A Licit International Trade in Cultural Objects," *International Journal of Cultural Property* 4 (1995), 36; Diura Thoden van Velzen, "The World of Tuscan Tomb Robbers: Living with the Local Community and the Ancestors," *International Journal of Cultural Property* 5 (1996), 111–26.

51. Ki Hadjar Dewantara [Suwardi Surjaningrat] (1929) quoted in Denys Lombard, "Indonesia: Pulling Together the Strands of Time," *UNESCO Courier,* April 1990, 26–8; Fernanda Eberstadt, "The Palace and the City," *New Yorker,* 23 December 1991, 41–84.

52. Jamaica Kincaid, *A Small Place* (New York: Virago, 1988), 31, 36–7; Orvar Löfgren, "Materializing the Nation in Sweden and America," *Ethnos* 58 (1993), 164–5.

53. V. S. Naipaul, *A Bend in the River* (London: Deutsch, 1979), 152–3.

54. Neil MacGregor, "Scholarship and the Public," *Journal of the Royal Society of Arts* 139 (1991), 191–4.

55. Yigael Yadin (1963) quoted in Amos Elon, *The Israelis: Founders and Sons* (New York: Weidenfeld & Nicolson, 1971), 288 (my emphasis); Michel-Rolph Trouillot, *Silencing the Past: Power and the Production of History* (Boston: Beacon Press, 1995), 142.

56. André Chastel, "La notion du patrimoine," in Nora, *Lieux de mémoire,* II.2, 446; Guillaume, *Politique du patrimoine,* 149; Bernard Smith, "Art Objects and Historical Usage," in McBryde, *Who Owns the Past?,* 83–4.

57. Martin Drury, "The Restoration of Calke Abbey," *Journal of the Royal Society of Arts* 136 (1988), 497.

58. Mark Twain, *A Connecticut Yankee in King Arthur's Court* (New York: Harper & Brothers, 1889), 404–5.

59. Thomas F. King, "Beneath the American Mosaic: The Place of Archaeology," in Stipe and Lee, *American Mosaic,* 260.

60. Nora, "Entre mémoire et histoire," in his *Lieux de mémoire,* I:xxv–xxviii (my translation; see Marc Roudebush's in *Representations* 26 [spring 1989], 7–24); Lisa B. Weber, ed., *Documenting America: Assessing the Conditions of Historical Records in the States* (Albany, NY, 1983), notably essays by Richard J. Cox (19–36) and William L. Joyce (37–46).

61. Nathaniel Hawthorne, 29 September 1855, *The English Notebooks,* ed. Randall Stewart (New York: Modern Language Association of America, 1941), 242.

62. Christopher Gordon, *National Cultural Policy in Italy: A Report for the Council of Europe* (Strasbourg: Council of Europe, 1995).

63. R. Poujade (1980) quoted in Guillaume, *Politique du patrimoine,* 167–70; Emory Campbell (1984) quoted in Dale Rosengarten, "'Sweetgrass is Gold': Natural Resources, Conservation Policy, and African-American Basketry," in Mary Hufford, ed., *Conserving Culture: A New Discourse on Heritage* (Urbana: University of Illinois Press for the American Folklife Center, 1994), 152–63 at 153.

64. Arjun Appadurai, "The Past as a Scarce Resource," *Man* 16 (1981), 201–19.

65. Patrick J. Geary, *Furta Sacra: Thefts of Relics in the Central Middle Ages* (Princeton, NJ: Princeton University Press, 1978); idem, *Living with the Dead in the Middle Ages* (Ithaca, NY: Cornell University Press, 1994), 200–5; Lowenthal, *Past Is a Foreign Country,* 290–1, 408.

66. James E. Young, *The Texture of Memory: Holocaust Memorials and Meaning* (New Haven, CT: Yale University Press, 1993), 27–48.

2

ON CULTS AND CULTISTS

German Historic Preservation in the Twentieth Century

Rudy J. Koshar

ALOIS RIEGL PUBLISHED "The Modern Cult of Monuments: Its Form and Origins" in 1903.[1] In this seminal essay, the Viennese art historian analyzed a desire for monuments that had swept through the world of educated Europeans at the turn of the century. Riegl also laid the basis for the modern concept of monuments, stressing that a broad appreciation of incessant change rather than aesthetic or historical values gave monuments their special appeal to the modern viewer. For Riegl, and for most literate Europeans, monuments included not only those statues, busts, plaques, coins, and other movable or immovable objects designed to commemorate a historical personality or event. They also increasingly encompassed buildings, squares, cityscapes, eventually whole towns and nature—indeed any part of the physical environment that drew attention to the presence of the past. The German term for monument, *Denkmal,* reinforced this richness (or maddening open-endedness) because it was used so ubiquitously, extending from historic sites and buildings to musical compositions and even great works of literature. Three-quarters of a century after Riegl wrote, the Hessian historic preservationist Reinhard Bentmann published an essay with the suggestive title "The Battle Over Memory."[2] He, too, used the term *cult of monuments* (*Denkmalkultus*), linking it to a wave of nostalgia in the Federal Republic of Germany in the mid-1970s. In the last decade of the twentieth century, the notion of a Denkmalkultus not only persisted but actually gained new life. Preservationists used the term with reference to postmodernism and other late-millennial concepts.[3] Given this continuity of terminology in a century that was anything but continuous, is it not worth asking what was behind the term and what its specific meaning was for its users?

Addressing such questions is as much a matter of focusing on the people who adhered to the cult of monuments as it is of considering the forms and internal meanings of the artifacts themselves. This is the point of departure for the following essay. Monuments by definition create an orientation to the past, whether this takes the form of history or memory, whether the goal is glorification of a great ruler or mourning the mass slaughter of innocents. Group orientations to the past, as Iwona Irwin-Zarecka tells us, are dependent not only on the internal meaning of the "texts" that transmit history and memory, but also on "intermediaries" such as professors, museum directors, teachers, pastors, public officials, architects, artists, poets, media specialists, journalists, and of course preservationists.[4] Intermediaries may have different goals and intentions than either rulers or the general public. It is thus a matter of analyzing the "preservationists," in the broadest sense of the term, as key historical actors in the complex formation of a late modern cult of monuments.

It is also worth emphasizing that a cult is by definition a system of worship. Riegl did not equate moderns' desire for monuments with Christianity, but he saw parallels between how Greek philosophers paved the way for the Christian religion and how historians disseminated knowledge about the past to encourage the public's embrace of historic artifacts and buildings.[5] Historic preservation, like Christianity, had ethical and altruistic elements that potentially placed it beyond the pull of egoism, whether national or individual, argued Riegl. The care and superintendence of monuments, or *Denkmalpflege*, would lead to a broad acceptance of all aspects of human creation and, because the rise and fall of historic buildings recalled the cyclical rhythm of life itself, to the adoration of Nature and its Creator. Preservationists thereby became the guardians of the church, the apostles and missionaries of a faith who ministered to the needs of the flock. Old buildings became the relics, vestments, and symbols of a commemorative liturgy grounded in historiographical practice.

The focus will be on Germany, although it will not be claimed that this country had (or has) more monuments. Other nations may lay claim to this distinction, as will be shown. Sheer numbers do not in any case convey the degree to which a country can be considered to have a strong and developed cult of monuments, especially for the second half of the twentieth century, when wholesale reconstruction of buildings increased the number of "historic" artifacts even after major disasters such as war wiped them out, or when the United States manufactured historical fantasy worlds in places such as Disneyland, in which, it should be noted, Cinderella's Castle was adapted from the deranged Bavarian monarch Ludwig II's Neuschwanstein. It was not only Riegl, surveying the culture of fin-de-siècle Vienna, who thought that the cult of monuments was especially well developed in German-speaking Europe. The Edinburgh art historian G. Baldwin Brown argued in 1905 that Germany was about to become the leading country in Europe in the race to protect historical architecture. He argued this could be attributed above all to the productive manner with which German preservationists responded to the challenges of modernity, however that was to be defined. Germany's protectors of historic edifices were not "extremists," wrote Brown, but "practical men who are familiar with the exigencies of modern life."[6] The German cult of monuments had an international profile. Preservationists such as the art historian Georg Dehio and the art historian–conservator Paul Clemen, whose career spanned the era from imperial Germany (1871–1918) to the immediate post–World War II period, were well known throughout the Euro-American world to both academic specialists and (in Dehio's case, for reasons to be made clear below) to cultured tourists. Twentieth-century Germany led the world not only in historic preservation but also in the destruction of monuments, as the rebuilt cities of Warsaw, Coventry, Rotterdam, and Stalingrad attest. German historic places and their curators deserve attention, then, not because of the presence of relatively many monuments, but because the German cult of monuments had a deep and abiding impact within and outside German-speaking Europe.

HISTORICAL BUILDINGS AND NATIONAL BEING

A variety of individual and collective motivations inspired those who acted as the advocates and curators of historic buildings. Even so, one can detect a certain continuity in the argument that preservationists gave about the rationale for their work over the decades. In Germany, relatively late national unification, rapid and extensive social and economic change, the strong persistence of regional ties, and the growth of democracy within a political culture still shaped by monarchical and aristocratic values created much uncertainty about the new nation's relation to both past and future. A great public surge of interest in historic places at the beginning of the twentieth century stemmed in part from the need to resolve the tensions of German historical consciousness and its relationship to national identity.[7] This was the argument given in the first edition of *Die Denkmalpflege*, published in 1899 as the first German-language journal to deal specifically with historic preservation and related activities such as archaeology and urban planning. One of the coeditors was Oskar Hoßfeld (1848–1915), an architect, university lecturer, and Prussian building official who would be influential in Heimatschutz, a movement to promote local and regional cultures. Hoßfeld and his coeditor Otto Sarrazin wrote that, despite the importance of the "historical sciences" for all nations, in Germany "broad strata of the population are oddly indifferent or blind toward the most valuable kinds of study aids of historical research, toward the documents of stone that have come down to us, the architectural monuments and everything that goes with them." So serious was the indifference, the editors averred, that it created doubts about the "level of cultural attainment that our time so willingly claims for itself."[8] Traffic planning that stressed the geometries of circulation rather than stability; public health policy that saw old buildings as seedbeds of disease and epidemics; destructive restorations and the cognate practice of "disencumbering" historic buildings from their surroundings; and an unthinking desire for the new—all promoted indifference toward artifacts of the past.[9] The editors were criticizing what may be called a national historicide, a violent disengagement of the nation from its origins. Historic preservationists would set themselves against such cultural suicide, and striving for national continuity in the face of public insensitivity would determine the logic of their practice for the century to come.

Unlike the growing throng of turn-of-the-century cultural pessimists, whom historians have often identified as natural allies of the preservation movement,[10] Hoßfeld and his allies were optimistic about the future. Indeed, Hoßfeld predicted that the ailing national community would recover due to both enlightened state initiatives and growing public awareness: "Slowly it has dawned on people that shortsighted actions must be stopped, that for monuments there is also validity to Bismarck's golden words that it is of greatest harm to a nation when it allows the living consciousness of its connection to its heritage and history to fade."[11] This reference to the Iron Chancellor was unintentionally ironic, to be sure, since he had been a Prussian monarchist who was unwilling to promote nationalist symbols of loyalty to the Reich. But it was equally unsurprising that the journal editors should have evoked Bismarck, since they themselves were working in a thoroughly Prussian institution. Even so, the editors were convinced that preservation's newfound influence stemmed not only from functional responses to historicide but also from a new sense of the nation. Previous generations of preservationists were also motivated by national aims: "But these initiatives stemmed too greatly from general and unfocused Romantic dispositions that lacked the solid ground of a powerful national consciousness," they wrote.[12] A new nation, or rather a new and more profound orientation to the nation, meant recognition and embrace of national symbols, wherever one found them. This reorientation demanded the rediscovery of a national genealogy and an awareness of the nation's deep and enduring roots in the past. This point of view was of course hardly unprecedented or unique to the German preservationist movement; many European advocates of cultural heritage from the nineteenth century fully endorsed the liberal French Catholic Montalembert's idea that "long memories make great peoples." Yet the relative newness of the German national state as well as the convergence of multiple streams of change—political, social, cultural, and economic—gave efforts to create strong national loyalties a greater degree of urgency than elsewhere.

The issue of national continuity was registered most substantively in an important address given in Strasbourg by Georg Dehio on 27 January 1905.[13] Celebrating the kaiser's birthday at the university of this Alsatian city on Germany's western frontier, Dehio's speech was delivered before an audience consisting of Wilhelm II himself, faculty, and students. It was the first such academic presentation to deal exclusively with the subject, indicating the new status of historic preservation. Beside exploring the historical roots of monument protection and outlining the state of the discipline at the beginning of the new century, Dehio maintained that the nurturing of historic buildings was motivated above all by a political goal: "We conserve a monument not because we consider it beautiful, but because it is a piece of our national life. To protect monuments is not to pursue pleasure, but to practice piety. Aesthetic and even art-historical judgments change, but here an unchanging criterion is found."[14]

Dehio's nationalist emphasis stemmed in part from the context in which he spoke. Strasbourg was seized by Germany in the Franco-Prussian war in 1870–71, and tensions between the German state and local inhabitants persisted right up until the end of World War I, when Alsace-Lorraine returned to French control. Historic preservation's cultural remit took on stronger political features in this contentious climate. But the speech also contributed to an international conversation in which the Strasbourg art history professor and Riegl were among the main interlocutors.[15] Their concerns spoke not only to preservation's political-cultural functions but also to its techniques and procedures; indeed, Dehio's address illustrated that matters of power and method were closely intertwined. Dehio and Riegl disagreed vehemently on many things, to be sure, but it is important to point out the broad areas of common ground as well.

Let us begin with questions of preservationist method before returning to political implications. Both Dehio and Riegl aggressively attacked restorationists, arguing that they did more to destroy monuments than to protect them. In the last quarter of the nineteenth century, preservationists were still strongly influenced by historicism, which was above all based on thinking one's way into earlier historical epochs. Historicism demanded that when valued buildings were preserved, their guardians "restored" them to the condition deemed appropriate for a particular monument, regardless of the actual condition of the artifact or the quality of modifications performed on it. Radical interventions in the building substance ensued, often to the point of rebuilding a fragment or remain from a bygone era on the basis of the sparsest historical evidence. Restoration derived from the assumption that a select group, or canon, of monuments and buildings possessed universal historical value. Ultimately, as the famous French architect and preservationist Eugène Viollet-le-Duc once pronounced, it mattered little if the building in question had ever existed in the form restoration gave it. More important was the idea that a monument captured a certain historical type or genre, whether Baroque, Renaissance, Gothic, or Romanesque. This technique had come in for heavy criticism already in the 1870s and 1880s, and by 1900 the idea of "conserve, don't restore" had gained a considerable following, especially among preservationists influenced by Dehio and Riegl but also by the Bonn conservator Paul Clemen. Dehio was one of the most vociferous critics of the restorationists—"the doctors are more dangerous than the illness itself," he said in 1905[16]—and he led successful public opposition to proposed plans to rebuild the Heidelberg Castle ruins, one of the most controversial issues in German preservation before World War I.

Riegl was more theoretically incisive than Dehio on the issue of restoration. He questioned absolute standards of beauty, arguing that historical additions on monuments were documents of the specific "artistic intention" of past ages. Opposed to any technique that would do away with such accretions from the past, or such products of a bygone artistic intention, Riegl favored a radical conservation policy by which buildings were maintained but eventually allowed to deteriorate and to amortize their full age value (*Alterswert*) "naturally."[17] He maintained that the proper objects of art-historical study extended from great works of art and architecture to ornament, crafts, and the applied arts. In regard to monuments, the artistic and historical evaluation of artifacts from the past had given way to an appreciation of the monument as a complex marker of age and development. Emphasizing the Alterswert of monuments potentially opened the way toward a very broad definition of historic objects. Riegl recognized that this tendency devalued the creators and original characteristics of monuments, but he also thought that regarding monuments by their age value was the sine qua non of modernity, in which incessant change destabilized or relativized all standards. Riegl thought that the tendency was "socialistic" because it created equality among monuments and made a broad array of monuments accessible to a public without specialized knowledge of art or history.[18] One could argue that Riegl's thought pointed toward the popularization, or even democratization, of the cult of monuments and a potentially unlimited widening of the number of historic artifacts to be considered. But even if Riegl's conservationist theories carried the day, in practical terms many preservationists, builders, and state officials continued to restore historic buildings and sites. It could be argued indeed that restorationism became stronger, not weaker, especially in response to the depredations of the world wars, as we will see.

Both Dehio and Riegl used the term *socialism* to describe historic preservation, although in contrast to Riegl's more philosophical view of the term, Dehio had in mind a pragmatic abrogation of private property rights and judicious limits on liberal economic systems. But on this issue, differences ran much deeper. Dehio thought Riegl's emphasis on age value was hedonistic, seeing it as a concept associated with an era of individualized pleasure and decadence, or more seriously as the product of a fin-de-siècle fascination with death and decay. For Dehio, only national piety was a reliable motivation for monument preservation, and only safeguarding the symbols of "national being" could prevent the overly individualized and ultimately decadent appropriation of monuments that Riegl's theory allegedly implied.[19]

Riegl responded to Dehio's challenge in a 1905 review by arguing that nationalist motivations for protecting historical places were not pious at all but rather egoistic.[20] He argued that the cult of monuments led ultimately to a form of identity beyond national selfishness, toward international understanding and altruism. Riegl's ideas did not logically presuppose an end to national identity, to be sure. International brotherhood began with the premise of self-conscious national communities interacting on a basis of equality and openness. In one sense, Dehio's position was close to that of Riegl's insofar as national patriotism, in its eighteenth- and nineteenth-century variation, was also based on a notion of equal nations interacting freely in international exchange and communication. But Dehio's vision was set on national priorities and the continuation of national existence, whereas Riegl's theory, when taken to its logical extreme, was rooted in a sense of immutable change and human mortality, implying both the end of national entities and the imminent crumbling of monuments on which those entities relied for their symbolic currency. It shall be noted in the conclusion that these differences did not in any case preclude either the synthesis of Dehio's and Riegl's ideas or the retention of national identity as an important motivation of historic preservation when using Riegl's notion of age value. But in the context of the time, the two found themselves at odds, and their differences roiled the waters of preservationist debate for years to come.

THE BELIEVERS

Just as early Christianity depended on zealots and small groups of the faithful gathered around them, so the early formation of a cult of monuments depended greatly on the aptitude and action of single individuals, whose energy could compensate, if only sporadically, for lack of trained personnel, insufficient public support, and limited financial resources—all characteristics of the early preservationist movement. Who were these faithful?

The question is more difficult to answer than one might assume because the activity of conserving historic buildings did not exist as a coherent discipline even though its late modern origins lie firmly in the historical sciences of the nineteenth century.[21] No highly institutionalized and widely recognized profession had developed to organize and regulate the preservation of historical places. No highly visible research institutes or university curricula emerged to give preservation a coherent intellectual and scientific identity. No truly centralized, national interest groups mobilized to present the case for historic artifacts. Throughout the first half of the twentieth century, many groups supported the cause of historic preservation—from the main professional organization of German historians to architects' associations, from women's groups and church societies to "homeland clubs" (*Heimatvereine*), and from "beautification leagues" to local cultural and history groups such as Düsseldorfer Jonges. But by the standards of an age of mass, centralized organization, such groups were relatively small and, because they were so often focused on regional or local history, highly dispersed.[22] It was precisely for reasons of this incoherence that Dehio gave his 1905 address in an attempt to give meaningful form to a fragmented range of initiatives.

The institutional backbone of the emergent preservationist lobby was state-sponsored monument conservation.[23] But here, too, there was as much competition as there was coherence. Just as the various German states had contributed to the development of the highly respected German university system, so the persistence of federal states in the late modern era also contributed to the advance of historic preservation. Since early in the nineteenth century, Prussia and Bavaria, the former Protestant and shaped by the Hohenzollern monarchical tradition, the latter Catholic and deeply concerned about defending the Wittelsbach dynasty's status in the new national state, vied with one another for cultural hegemony. They sponsored several highly visible and popular conservation projects, including, in Prussia above all, the completion of the medieval Cologne Cathedral and the restoration of the badly deteriorated Marienburg fortress in East Prussia, a citadel of German power in the Slavic East. During the imperial period, quasi-state, provincial associations were formed in the Prussian provinces to decentralize administration and mobilize popular sympathies for the Prussian government. Such hybrid, self-governing bodies had jurisdiction over historic preservation and many other cultural activities. Smaller states such as Hesse, which passed an influential preservation law in 1902 that was studied throughout Europe as a landmark of cultural policy, also distinguished themselves as innovators in historic preservation as they tried to maintain their legitimacy vis-à-vis their larger German cousins. The viability of the federal state tradition ensured that tremendous variation in funding, personnel, and institutional dynamics would mark the preservation movement right through the century.[24]

It was in the nineteenth century that Prussia, Bavaria, Hesse, and other states began appointing conservators who were responsible for administering state-controlled historic sites. Ferdinand von Quast, a student of the great architect Karl Friedrich Schinkel, was the first Prussian conservator of monuments in 1843. In the Second Empire, as Prussia devolved more cultural authority onto its provinces, it appointed fourteen provincial conservators and created mechanisms for a more ambitious program of monument protection at lower levels of authority. At first the provincial conservators received no salary, although some of their expenses were covered with provincial and state moneys. Bavaria had eight conservators in this period, more than any other non-Prussian federal state. Each conservator also had an additional small supporting staff, as did municipal conservators, the first of which was appointed for the Rhenish city Cologne in 1913.[25]

The influence of the conservators in the German preservation movement would far outweigh their rather meager numerical importance as well as their salary. The first conservator of the Prussian Rhineland, Paul Clemen, organized more than two hundred volunteers as "correspondents" who considerably extended his range of knowledge and influence in the province. He also kept up active relations with church authorities and with the many Heimat, architects', and cultural associations that were involved in the protection of historic edifices. Clemen was a cofounder of the Rhenish Association for Historic and Cultural Preservation (Rheinischer Verein für Denkmalpflege und Heimatschutz, or RVDH), an elite organization established in 1906.[26] Newspapers regularly reported on the activities of conservators, who would find a public forum for their views in the Preservation Congress (Tag für Denkmalpflege), first held in 1900.

For most of the century, conservators were bourgeois, university educated, and male. Out of forty-four individuals who served as provincial or district conservators in Prussia from 1890 to the end of the Weimar Republic (1933), only two came from aristocratic families. Although conservators have sometimes came from the educated laity, most often they were trained as art historians, government building officials, architects, or artists. As professionals, the conservator and the preservationist have had rather inchoate roles dependent on the specific educational background, initiative, and personality of the individual. Regional political, administrative, and cultural conditions often determined who would be chosen as conservator. In the Prussian Rhine province up to World War II, for example, the rich palette of architectural monuments from the medieval age called for a conservator such as Clemen, who had an art-historical background, whereas in Wiesbaden museum officials assumed this role and, in the Prussian district of Kassel in Hesse, autodidacts with broad regional knowledge took the lead.[27]

The most important German conservator of the twentieth century—and one of the most important single contributors to the broader evolution of the German cult of monuments—was the aforementioned Clemen, whose career spanned the years from 1890 to 1947. Hailed as the "actual creator of Rhenish preservation,"[28] the Bonn art historian was close to the Hohenzollern monarchy, serving often as tour guide and art-historical adviser to Crown Prince Wilhelm and the Kaiser Wilhelm II himself. Beside holding the position of

Fig. 2.1 Marienburg. (Bildarchiv Foto Marburg.)

Rhenish conservator from 1893 to 1911, he was the founder of the Bonn university's Art Historical Institute, organizer of the German cultural protection program in World War I, and chair of the Preservation Congress from 1923 to 1932. While serving in the Rhineland, he was responsible for more than one-quarter of all historic buildings in the Prussian monarchy, and thus had more monuments from the medieval period under his supervision than any conservator in Europe at the time. His book *German Art and Historic Preservation: A Confession,* published in 1933 with essays and lectures from the preceding two decades, was a central text of German monument preservation in the first half of the century.[29] It had detailed discussions of issues related to conservation policy as well as philosophical digressions on the nature, symbolism, and meaning of monuments. The book was also an embarrassment to many preservationists in the second half of the century because of its obvious debt to the mystical elitism of Stefan Georg and his circle, its language of myth and nationalism, and its brief praise for Adolf Hitler. While he stressed the importance of historic preservation for the national heritage, Clemen was also very cosmopolitan. An exchange professor at Harvard University in 1907, Clemen admired and wrote expertly on French medieval architecture, traveled widely throughout Europe and the Middle East, and read John Ruskin, H. G. Wells, Oscar Wilde, and Le Corbusier. Before his death, he would help to reestablish official preservation in the Rhineland in the first two years after World War II.

No national professional organization of conservators existed, although the above-mentioned Tag für Denkmalpflege, which grew out of the professional association of German historians, operated as a quasi-official interest group for preservationists, if not for conservators specifically. The congress's pre–World War I conferences attracted as many as seven hundred participants (1913) and often aroused much public attention, as when the Dresden conference of 1900 touched off debate over proper preservation techniques (conservation or restoration?), or when the Cologne conference of 1930 stimulated criticism from the German press and others over maintenance of the facade of the Cologne Cathedral, marred by gradual deterioration as well as urban pollution.[30] In general, however, the conservators retained a rather eclectic profile that fit the amorphous nature of historic preservation as a cultural practice.

The hybrid nature of the conservator gave rise to the argument that monument preservation somehow stood "between" the disciplines. It was said that the conservator required a unique combination of political experience, administrative acuity, artistic talent, practical knowledge of building technique and artisanal practice, and the ability to educate not only craftsmen and construction foremen but also the uninitiated public. It was appropriate in this context to speak of "pastoral preservation," as one commentator did with reference to Robert Hiecke, a Prussian state conservator.[31] The conservator ministered to his flock as if he were a Protestant pastor, who advised the errant believer, counseled the troubled married couple, and visited the sick and incapacitated. The preservationist approached his subject in an undogmatic way. He understood that "practical preservation," the application of preservation theory in daily life, remained "the art of the single case and the science of the borderline, tolerating no principle that failed to imply its refutation or at least an exception."[32] This attachment to a rather vague and eclectic set of professional criteria and insistence on flexibility and case-by-case procedures had implications for how preservationists participated in the key cultural and political developments of the day.

Beyond the rather small circle of conservators and their staffs, the major personalities who had an impact on preservation right through the century belonged mainly to the pre–World War I generation. They included Dehio (1850–1932), trained by the historians Leopold von Ranke and Heinrich von Sybel. Dehio taught art history in Königsberg, Strasbourg, and Tübingen. Among the German public, Dehio was best known not for his 1905 address but as the compiler of five-volume survey of German monuments funded by the royal government and completed in 1912. This compilation was (and still is) widely used as a guide to German historic buildings by preservationists and tourists alike. There was also the Dresden art historian Cornelius Gurlitt (1850–1938), whose collected writings on art history and culture amounted to more than ninety volumes, and who was an active participant in the preservation movement until the interwar period. One must also mention Paul Schultze-Naumburg (1860–1949), an architect, cofounder of the Heimatschutz movement, and leading cultural critic of his day. Although he never wrote specifically about preservationist technique, he championed the cause of historic buildings and constantly criticized the shoddy construction of contemporary architecture in comparison with historical models. His publications became obligatory reading for building authorities and other state officials in the first third of the century.[33] Schultze-Naumburg was also an anti-Semite, and his increasingly radical political views led him to support the National Socialist party after World War I.[34]

These individuals, along with Clemen, Riegl, and Max Dvořák, Riegl's successor at the University of Vienna, started their careers before World War I, and their initiatives and ideas remained influential for the rest of the century. There were other individuals who had long careers or who distinguished themselves with records of public accomplishment, as did Robert Hiecke (1876–1952), who became Prussian state conservator in 1918 and who endeavored unsuccessfully until after World War II to have national preservation legislation passed. Yet it was the prewar group whose theoretical and organizational efforts continued to shape preservation. At the end of the twentieth century, German protectors of monuments still turned to Clemen, Riegl, Dehio, and Gurlitt (though not Schultze-Naumburg) for inspiration, and their writings constituted the canon of preservationist tradition.[35]

Women remained on the periphery of such developments. There were female conservators only after World War II, as in Cologne, where two women, Hanna Adenauer and Hiltrud Kier, were appointed in 1953 (though unofficially Adenauer had been acting as municipal conservator since 1948) and 1978, respectively. But this is not to argue that female underrepresentation was (or is) a peculiarity of German historic preservation. In many cognate disciplines, such as architecture, urban planning, and academic art history, women either faced obstacles or chose not to seek access. Women were not absent from the world of historic preservation, to be sure. Popular illustrated magazines such as *Die Gartenlaube*, a favorite of middle-class women and their families, showed a great deal of concern for monuments of history and nature.[36] As tourists, women viewed historical buildings and referred to tourist guidebooks, of which the Baedeker, with concise accounts of cultural-historical monuments and indexes devoted to literary and artistic personalities, were particularly good at addressing women, albeit as cultural ancillaries to male heads of households.[37] Often acting to collect funds for the restoration of a local landmark and publicize the plight of an old building at risk of demolition, women's societies also contributed to public debates over preservation. But they did so largely as marginal participants, adherents and spectators rather than active movers and doers.

At a somewhat more abstract level, women occupied a subordinate symbolic position as well. European historical architecture was full of elaborate female forms, including sylphs, muses, goddesses, dryads, caryatids, nymphs, and angels. National-political iconographies had been full of such images, as France had its Marianne, Germany its Germania, and Serbia its Maiden of Kosovo. Such figures were part of a broader allegorical tradition in classical and Christian civilization in which symbolic representations of females expressed widely held values. But the strength and pervasiveness of this allegorical tradition often depended on women's being excluded from the possibility of practicing the values in question. From another angle, tourists and preservationists who valued scenic villages or historic urban centers reinforced dominant interpretations of "picturesque" settings, to which both male and female viewers often ascribed "feminine" characteristics such as beauty and naturalness—but also lack of organization and incompleteness. Those who preserved or reorganized such settings assumed a masculine position as they cared for and "completed" a feminized landscape.[38]

What patterns of preservation proceeded from these social and gender premises? We can address the question in part by focusing on inventorization, one of the great tasks of modern historic preservation.[39] Just as scientific worldview had demanded classification and itemization of nature, the better to subdue and manipulate it, so preservation demanded sweeping assessments and definition of the available "historical substance." Clemen began his association with preservation not as a conservator but as the medieval art specialist in charge of inventorying Rhenish monuments, a project that produced fifty-six volumes while Clemen directed it. The inventories reflected official memory's sense of historical architecture because they were cooperative efforts undertaken by conservators and local citizens, and they were usually subsidized with government grants. The size of the inventories reflected the degree to which the number of monuments increased in the first three decades of the century. The 1894 inventory for Düsseldorf city and county concentrated on the Middle Ages, avoided almost all architecture built after the early nineteenth century, which meant almost all Neoclassicist buildings, and was only 172 pages long. By contrast, the interwar inventories of Cologne and Münster would have almost six hundred pages each for "profane" monuments alone.[40]

Until well into the twentieth century, most German preservationists favored the monuments of medieval history, above all churches and other religious buildings. In 1929, it was estimated that within Prussia the state owned more than 90 percent of the buildings that preservationists regarded as historically important, and that three-quarters of those consisted of religious edifices.[41] Only slowly were preservationists willing to expand the canon to include residential structures or even the artifacts of economic and social history, or so-called technical monuments, but even then they were cautious about including historical buildings dating from anytime after the early nineteenth century. Still, throughout the last decades before World War I and into the interwar period, the line that divided the early nineteenth century from later periods slowly eroded. The preservation of historical windmills, factories, artisanal shops, and peasant dwellings had supporters before

World War I, but only in the interwar period did such artifacts have significant public attention, in part because of the growing populist nationalism of the times, and only in the 1970s did they become a truly important dimension of historic preservation.[42]

The foregoing indicates that historic preservation was very much a product of that German-bourgeois, cultural individualism that originated in the eighteenth century but reached its fullest development in the nineteenth. Although historic preservation developed most consequentially in Germany as a state-organized practice, it relied ultimately on individuals who considered their cultural self-formation as a constitutive factor of modern being. Cultural self-formation relied in turn on reverence for the historical, for the "classics," and for everything inherited from the past that was deemed enlightening and uplifting. The great works of church architecture enjoyed a special place in this worldview, while residences or artifacts of social history occupied a secondary place, unless they could be recast as objects of nostalgia, or of a sentimentalized understanding of the history of the *Volk*. For the most part, buildings that reminded the observer of the messy facts of everyday life, of social oppression or injustice, to say nothing of the ugliness and egotism that allegedly shaped modern economic existence, were disfavored. Historic preservation, right alongside a love for history, an appreciation of the "monuments" of classical music, great works of art, and the literature of Goethe, Schiller, and their successors, thereby became one of many variations on the same theme: the elaboration and self-examination of the "cultured bourgeoisie" (*Bildungsbürgertum*).[43] When the German Bürgertum looked at beautifully restored old buildings, it saw its reflection in the mirror of history.

Even so, preservation's statist, bourgeois, and masculine (to say nothing of regionalist) interests were subsumed within the broader national motivation of the historic preservation movement for much of the twentieth century. Not that the national meaning of preservation remained static. When Dehio made his pronouncement on the political mission of cultural preservation, his sense of the nation was already out of step with that which was taking hold in significant parts of German society. Like the majority of the Bildungsbürgertum from which he came, Dehio had a conservative notion of nationality based on cultural criteria such as language, shared history, and custom. *His* nation was necessarily selective, the product of a small leadership with the heritage, education, and economic wherewithal to shape destiny. But the mass nationalism of the era used harsher images and developed more radical political visions. Race and ethnicity, not cultural criteria; political power, not taste and grace determined radical na-

Fig. 2.2 Rothenburg: Historic cityscape as tourist attraction. (Author's collection.)

tionalism's orientation. The mobilization of the entire Volk, not the concentrated engagement of the most conscientious representatives of the educated classes, was the prerequisite of the new mass national-ism.[44] While Dehio's "national being" pointed back to the nineteenth century, that of the mass nationalists pointed to the twentieth, to World War I, the "Volk community," and Hitler. This is not to argue for a deep underlying determinism or inevitability; still, the connec-tions cannot be overlooked, just as the differences between Dehio's na-tion and that of a more dynamic radical nationalism should not be underestimated.

PRESERVATION AND MASS NATIONALISM

It was the events of the two world wars that brought historic preserva-tion into the stream of troubled waters agitated by the new national-ism. In World War I, German conservationists were put in the unenviable position of defending the German military's destruction of great monuments in France, Belgium, and elsewhere. They did so more or less enthusiastically. Clemen and others conducted battlefield preservation efforts first in France and Belgium and then anywhere the German military operated. Military defeat and the founding of a dem-ocratic republic in 1919 were profound shocks. Although preserva-tionists such as Clemen were closely identified with Wilhelmine culture, they nonetheless found that the Weimar Republic offered more specific legal guarantees for the protection of historical property than the empire had. Article 150 of the Weimar Constitution stated: "The monuments of art, history, nature, and the landscape enjoy the protection and guardianship of the state."[45] Despite having a poten-tially more secure legal basis on which to conduct their work, preser-vationists could not avoid the politicization of cultural issues that occurred in the Weimar Republic. Leading advocates of architectural preservation such as Konrad Nonn, editor of the Prussian finance minister's architectural journal, participated fully in the nationalistic assault on the "cultural-Bolshevist" Bauhaus and on modernist archi-tecture. Paul Schultze-Naumburg's racism became ever more pro-nounced, as did that of significant sections of the homeland preservation movement, which also opposed the new functionalist styles. Initially indifferent to such controversies, the Nazis would ex-ploit this grassroots cultural criticism, identifying with those who felt threatened by the cosmopolitan and allegedly "Jewish" characteristics of modernist "new building."[46]

But preservationists were not uniformly opposed to modernist architecture; nor were they fully imbued with the growing racism and hypernationalism of the era. The 1928 Preservation Congress was notable for its attempt to find a common ground between the views of modernists such as the Frankfurt planner Ernst May and Heimatschutz conservatives.[47] Conservators and their allies often shunned the harsh light of late-Weimar cultural debates. Yet they were not immune to the nationalism of the age, and important conservators such as Franz Graf Wolff Metternich of the Prussian Rhine province employed the language of the Volk community (*Volksgemeinschaft*) in their public pronouncements.[48] In his *German Art and Historic Preservation: A Confession,* Clemen quoted with approval Adolf Hitler's invocation to "the great tradition of our people."[49] Imbued with the idea that national piety was at the heart of their practice, preservationists saw the right-wing nationalism of late Weimar and the dynamism of National Socialism as potential sources for a more forceful defense of German history and culture.

Preservationists' willingness to look to radical nationalism for support provided the basis for their cooperation with Nazism in the first years of the dictatorship. Nazism coordinated the institutions of historic preservation and related cultural activities in the Reich Federation for Culture and Homeland (Reichsbund Volkstum und Heimat). The first Nazi-era Preservation Congress, held in Kassel in 1933 and titled "Historic Preservation and Homeland Protection in the Reconstruction of the Nation," occurred under the auspices of the Reich Federation.[50] Nazi party agencies and publications trumpeted the benefits of historic preservation, and individual Nazi leaders such as Heinrich Himmler supported the saving of architectural monuments, though often for idiosyncratic and even bizarre personal reasons. As for Hitler, he had written adoringly of German historical architecture in his political autobiography, *Mein Kampf,* but it was clear he was most interested in the great urban monuments; a thousand-year Reich would demand not the humble patina of medieval town architecture but colossal cityscapes and overpowering monuments that symbolized the brute power of the new regime. Planning projects such as urban renewal, a hot topic of the Nazi era, appeared to combine a wish for modernity with respect for historical values. Some of the urban renewal projects started under the National Socialist regime resembled postwar developments insofar as they created highly modern urban ensembles in which historic buildings were sanitized and prettified to accommodate shoppers, drivers, and tourists. Other schemes, especially chief architect Albert Speer's plan to remake Berlin as the world capital of the Nazi racial empire, showed disregard for everything but Hitler's megalomania.[51]

For the most part, preservationists responded enthusiastically, especially when such projects provided more financial support and increased status for them. Yet they were uneasy about the centralization of cultural authority. They insisted that practical preservation should be the result of cautious and step-by-step procedures rather than ideological zeal, and they remained committed to the pious embrace of historical values. Such positions could be compatible with Nazism's cultural politics, but they could also contradict a regime whose main goal was ideological mobilization and racial war. Nazism wanted racialization of the nation, while preservationists continued to aim for that spiritualization of nationality that only history and a well-developed cult of monuments could provide. The deep and abiding differences between the regime's cultural policy and the goals of historic preservation could be seen in the last, horrific years of World War II. As the bombs fell on German cities, the Nazi propaganda chief Joseph Goebbels celebrated the end of the bourgeois era, saying that the historic cityscapes of the nation could now be swept aside to make room for the Nazi revolution.[52] Preservationists once railed against a historicide born of indifference or unthinking passion for the modern; but *this* historicide was far more total, and far more vengeful, than anything they encountered in the past. Regrettably, they had done much to legitimize it.

RECONSTRUCTIONS

National motivations for preservation did not disappear after the tremendous destruction of World War II. Indeed, in the first decade after the war, historic preservationists, like their counterparts in the Heimatschutz movement, tried to disengage themselves from Nazi cultural policy and to represent themselves as advocates of the "real" German nation. Their argument was that Nazism misused architectural and homeland preservation in particular and German national feeling in general for the purposes of a radical policy of destruction wholly out of line with the best traditions of Goethe, Humboldt, and other cultural luminaries of the German past. The support many preservationists showed for Nazism early in the Third Reich was forgotten. In its place was a memory of the destruction of German cities and their monuments, and a characterization of historical conservation programs as part of a broad resistance against Nazi barbarism and the evisceration of German culture. Like the ethnic German groups expelled from Eastern Europe or German POWs, the preservationists were to be seen as victims, the historic buildings as innocent bystanders.[53]

In practical terms, preservationists were overcome by events. The level of destruction in World War II was too great to allow the old maxim of "conserve, don't restore" to be upheld in any strict sense. The need to clear away rubble, find temporary housing for the homeless, and rebuild bombed-out cities and factories took precedence over the careful nurturance of historic buildings.[54] Urban planners and architects gained in stature and importance over preservationists in the context of such tasks. Political considerations proved to be overpowering as well. Not only the Allied occupiers but also many German political leaders wanted to destroy the traces of the Nazi regime, but even salvageable artifacts from earlier historical periods were destroyed if they were deemed to be politically unsavory. Against the protests of preservationists on both sides of the German–German border, the East German regime leveled the damaged Berlin Castle in a truly spectacular act of destruction ending in 1951.[55] The most obvious symbols of Nazi barbarism, the concentration camps, were plowed under by the Allies (Bergen-Belsen), retooled by communists as internment camps for the enemies of Stalinism (Buchenwald, Sachsenhausen), used for housing refugees from the East (Dachau), or simply ignored. Only later would preservationists turn their attention seriously to these documents of National Socialist crime, and then often only after public pressure and official action had turned them into either memorial sites for various victim groups or, in the East, elaborate memorial stages designed to commemorate "anti-fascist" resistance by communists.[56]

Yet preservationists were successful in preserving a sense of institutional as well as national continuity in the face of such changes. In contrast to the centralizing intentions of the Nazi era, state-organized preservation remained very much a matter of the federal states in the democratic Federal Republic of Germany, for example. As before World War I, such diversity also resulted in enormous disparities in funding and practice.[57] At first glance, it appeared that conservators had become both more properly organized and more professional. After World War II, state conservators in the Federal Republic created an organization more specifically designed to represent their interests, professional requirements, and opinions. But appearances were deceiving even when the generation that had come to maturity after World War I made way for a new cadre. Hartwig Beseler, state conservator of Schleswig-Holstein, bemoaned the continued lack of coherence and professionalization of conservators: "State preservationists [still] operate on an ad hoc basis," he wrote in 1975. "One or the other may have had a course at the university or technical college on the subject of historical preservation, but in no way can one speak of systematic preparation."[58] What was once praised as a necessary attribute of the "science of the borderline," namely eclecticism and resistance to overly specialized training, was now derided as lack of professionalization. The critique reflected the new aspirations of some preservationists just as it highlighted the continuation of older, more "generalist," and (for some) amateurish practices.

There was a degree of continuity in the types of historic artifacts favored by official preservationism as well. More in the West than in the East, historic churches were lovingly restored, as the Allied authorities (above all the United States and Great Britain) incorrectly regarded the churches as having been politically uncompromised in the Nazi regime. Germans saw the churches as important symbols of Christianity and of Occidental culture. But the Christian churches were also important symbols of German national identity, especially when they reminded Protestants of the close interface between their faith and national tradition. Where the churches were also constitutive of local identities, as in Catholic Cologne, there were added incentives to rebuild them as quickly and completely as possible. Preservationists supported such restorations and contributed where they could. But both the Protestant and Catholic churches could also rely on international support, which enabled them to implement plans over which municipal or state-appointed preservationists had only indirect control. It was for this reason that the techniques of preservation relied more on restorationist than on conservationist tradition, as with the Romanesque churches of Cologne, or with many churches in Munich's historical city center.[59] Rarely did West Germany allow ruined churches to stand alone as reminders of German victimization (or sin?) amid the modernized hustle of rebuilt urban centers. The most famous such instance was Berlin's Kaiser Wilhelm Memorial Church, built as a neo-Romanesque conceit of the Hohenzollern dynasty before World War I, badly damaged by Allied bombers in World War II, and allowed to stand as an evocative fragment next to a modern chapel in what became the commercial heart of West Berlin, where shoppers, punk rockers, and tourists would later mingle in the shadows of this gigantic ruin.[60] As for the East German communist regime, the German Democratic Republic, many demolished churches were left where they stood, either because financial means and building materials were in short supply, or because the Socialist Unity party deemed it politically incorrect to salvage the traces of Christianity on communist soil. East German preservationists made a virtue of necessity, as government conservators discussed "ruins in the city" as a planning paradigm for future policy initiatives.[61]

Whether the subject is historic churches or ruins, it is clear that the reconstruction of German cities was a compromise between the old and the new, between architectural and local tradition on the one side and a desire to begin anew by using the language of international functionalism on the other.[62] By the mid-1950s, this compromise, which preservationists and their allies in the public had done much to bring about, was more or less abandoned as many cities succumbed to the attractions of modernization, commercialization, and the imagery of the "car-oriented city." Whereas the old had been a symbol of a German cultural continuity, it now came to stand for the reactionary and the antiquated. Modernist architects did the preservation lobby no favors when, implicitly and often explicitly, they associated saving historic buildings with "fascist" and authoritarian traditions.[63] Their intentions were democratic and reformist, but their language put them uncomfortably close to communist rhetoric, in which historic preservation was derided as a product of "imperialist barbarism." German national identity, whether expressed in the political language of the Christian Democratic finance minister Ludwig Erhard's "social market economy," or of a modernized socialist nation on the other side of the German–German border, was now decisively linked with the future. That future spoke a language not of piety or history but of speed, consumption, functionality, and spectacle.

POWER TO THE PEOPLE

From the point of view of the end of the twentieth century, one can see that the rupture with previous traditions of preservation was short-lived. But it was intense, and highly moralistic. The postwar generation's willingness to be silent about the war and Nazism was questioned in the 1960s by a new generation of university graduates who sometimes violently wielded history as a weapon against their parents. Their brand of history was not of the Dehioan variety, affirmative and bourgeois; instead, they deployed what Nietzsche had called a "critical" species of history, in which the past was held up to the harsh light of the present, and always found wanting.[64] But by the early 1970s in the Federal Republic, the idea of a future utopia of unlimited economic growth had run its course, just as initiatives for radical political

Fig. 2.3–4 The Berlin Castle ruin leveled, 1951. (Bildarchiv Preußischer Kulturbesitz.)

reform and social-liberal experimentation, first under Social Democratic chancellor Willi Brandt and then under Helmut Schmidt, became exhausted. One of the most notable results of the cultural and political confusion of the age was that those formerly indifferent or opposed to historic preservation gradually became enamored with monuments and the past. Influenced by the views of Italian communist administrations in cities such as Bologna, the West German left came to believe that preservation was "revolution." Workers' housing and once decried "founders' era" (*Gründerzeit*) architecture, the often garish product of the new German nation's economic boom of 1870–73, now became more popular. Cultural criticism shifted, as the advocates of modernization and economic growth were portrayed as indifferent to historical nuance and tradition. What had started as an idealistic and critical mobilization of the past by university students and antiwar activists had either degenerated into political terrorism (the Red Army Faction), or reappeared as nostalgia for old things, including historic buildings.[65]

West Germany's leading daily, the *Frankfurter Allgemeine Zeitung,* recognized what was brewing when it wrote of preservation as a "people's movement."[66] The grassroots effort was impressive indeed, as citizens' initiatives, socialist and trade union cultural groups, history workshops, and a variety of other often ad hoc entities mobilized. Their efforts were diverse: An initiative might be formed to save a newly historic windmill or pub threatened by urban renewal, or a "history workshop" would be formed to interrogate the local built environment for traces of the Holocaust. The university-educated, the young, and women increasingly found their place at the head of such groups, often identifying with the memories held by victims of Nazi repression. So strong was public interest that by the mid-1970s, one began to hear conservators from the Federal Republic argue that there was too much popular concern for monuments, a situation entirely different from that which had existed just ten years previously. This criticism only became stronger as official preservation increasingly felt itself to be overburdened by a public thirsty for instant history.[67] Conservators went from rags to riches, trading historiographical austerity for commemorative largesse, and often regretting that for which they had so fervently prayed.

Under very different political conditions—and without the broad social movement evolving in the democratic West—the East German state belatedly also came to see the value of the German past, whether in the form of a "jubilee preservation" that capitalized on the cultural legitimacy of important historical figures such as the Prussian

monarch Frederick the Great and Martin Luther, or in the less propa-
gandistic form of expanding the day-to-day operations of state-run
preservation agencies.[68] Indeed, anti-fascism, the official ideology of
the East German regime, relied on history for its legitimacy, since neither territory nor cultural tradition defined the new entity. Preservation would participate in a socialist cultural politics in which the
healthy, socialist traditions of the German past were nurtured and
elaborated for future generations, while authoritarian, fascist, and imperialist impulses were to be obliterated.

Neither in the West nor in the East was the past a "foreign country"
any longer.[69] Indeed, Germans showed they did not merely want to visit
the past; they wanted to inhabit it. This desire was reflected in a mass re-
definition of the physical environment as historically significant. Consider for a moment how radically assessments of the number of
historical places increased in this period. Estimates for the former Federal Republic ran as high as eight hundred thousand monuments and
historic buildings in 1976, and as high as fifty thousand in the 1980s for
the German Democratic Republic. The high count for West Germany
may be accounted for in part by the fact that urban "ensembles" were included in the total, but the number is extraordinary nonetheless given
that at the end of the 1960s, experts in the Federal Republic claimed no
more than two hundred thousand monuments.[70] Of course, regional
variation again calls for interpretive caution. At the end of the century,
Bavaria was said to be particularly monument-rich, having approximately one hundred thousand historic sites. But even the much smaller
state of Rheinland-Pfalz was estimated to have seventy-five thousand
(up from thirty-five thousand in a 1970s estimate).[71]

Other countries had more monuments, to be sure. With a population 13 percent smaller than that of the former Federal Republic, Italy
counted 4.5 million historical places in the 1970s. Among Eastern Bloc
countries, Czechoslovakia was estimated to have approximately eight
times more historic buildings per capita than the former East Germany had.[72] Yet the German "monument-boom," as pundits were fond
of writing, was both sudden and impressive, especially when considering that West Germany was the economically most advanced state in
Cold War Europe.

What happened to people's sense of national continuity, one of the
central goals of the preservation movement, in the light of such developments? Both among preservationists as well as in the politically conscious public, it was common to argue that by 1970 at the latest, West
Germans had abandoned the ground of national identity as it had
been understood for most of the previous century. For intellectuals

Fig. 2.5 Kaiser Wilhelm Memorial Church, Berlin. (Bildarchiv Foto Marburg.)

such as Günter Grass, this was not only understandable but morally imperative because *Auschwitz*, which was then becoming the key word of West German political culture, made "normal" nationhood impossible for the two Germanys. For Grass, only a loose confederation of German states was imaginable.[73] The argument that Germans neither had, nor deserved to have, a normal national identity resonated at other levels of cultural politics. Preservationists noted that at international conferences, West German participants exhibited the least amount of national pride or consciousness.[74] The practice of historic preservation had come to stand not for national but for a new kind of social memory. Whether one saved a broad urban ensemble (or "city-monument") or a nineteenth-century factory, a Bavarian cultural landscape or an important historic cathedral, the nation was said to have abandoned its once lofty position as the object and motivation of cultural policy. In its place stood a multiplicity of groups with a multiplicity of orientations to the past. National identity no longer gave coherence or meaning to this panoply of memories. A pluralistic concept of the monument—and not the focused national symbolism of Dehioan practice—now appeared best suited for the new situation.[75]

Although things were quite different in East Germany, here, too, it was assumed that a deep rupture in national continuity had occurred. From its beginning, the communist regime argued it had disengaged itself from its imperialist and fascist past, helping not only to establish the first socialist nation on German soil, but also to ensconce workers and peasants as the heirs of German cultural tradition. As the East German republic consolidated its cultural authority, the historical German nation of 1871 seemed to have become an artifact of a past that was, if not fully "overcome," then at least incapable of being revived.[76]

The argument of a deep break in historical continuity was convincing to many Germans on both sides of the border in the 1970s and 1980s. For supporters of the idea, still inspired by the political and cultural lessons of the 1960s, the German past was an object of critical scrutiny, and the protector of historic sites would be called on to nurture a broad array of monuments meaningful to an increasingly diverse culture. Old monuments would be redefined, often to point out the nationalist and authoritarian sins of one's forefathers, while newly historic edifices would be restored to highlight the struggles and fates of political and religious dissidents, workers, women, homosexuals, and Holocaust victims. Emphasizing those who had been left out of the historical record presupposed a new continuity—that of the "other Germany," with its democratic, multicultural, more sexually progressive, and "alternative" values.

Fig. 2.6 Digging for traces of Nazi atrocities at former Gestapo headquarters, West Berlin, 1985. (Aktives Museum für Faschismus und Widerstand Berlin, photo by Juergen Henschel.)

For critics of this new dispensation, the only solution was to rediscover the threads of national continuity through large-scale cultural projects, such as the organization of a German National History Museum, promoted most forcefully by the West German Christian Democratic chancellor Helmut Kohl in the 1980s.[77] Even the most disturbing traces of German history would be mobilized in this historiographical politics. Holocaust monuments, from former synagogues to more "tourist-friendly" concentration camp sites, from the Wannsee Villa (site of an infamous meeting associated with the planning of Nazi extermination policies) to a controversial scheme to build a single definitive monument in Berlin commemorating all European Jewish victims of genocide, could now be used to tell an undifferentiated story of *all* Germans' victimization under the hegemony of Nazism and war. Preservationists would be called on to save historic artifacts in such a way that they revealed either the accomplishments or tribulations of an entire nation, not a battery of individuated groupings with incompatible religious, historical, political, and sexual identities. The emphasis on rediscovery of the nation only drew more attention to the sensation of discontinuity even as it resurrected the well-established practice of calling on preservationists to address the blind spots and shortcomings of German political identity. A national "heritage" was again at stake, though the issue was very much in doubt as to whose national heritage would dominate public opinion, and whether that heritage deserved to be called "national" in the first place.

Reunification tipped the balance of the debate in favor of the advocates of restored national continuity, although disagreement remained. On the one hand, a triumphant Federal Republic treated the forty years of East German rule as a bad dream of German history. The dreaming patient from the East, the humiliated "Ossi," would be helped to overcome his guilt feelings after proper therapy, after the appropriate work of mourning, and of course with the aid of substantial injections of financial medication. The physical traces of the East German state, its monuments and public buildings, its Wall and its "antifascist tradition cabinets," its street names and Holocaust memorials, its monumental avenues and housing projects, would be either obliterated or preserved in such a way as to remind everyone of the superiority of West German culture and politics. German history now consisted of two major "parentheses," both now to be overcome, both the products of political dictatorships whose values were antipathetic to Western democracies, among which the Federal Republic quite understandably counted itself as a leading member. On the other hand, although they admitted to complete defeat of the German Democratic Republic and the impossibility of a "third way" in German history, many Germans, especially those who had lived in the East, asked that the public not forget what had been left behind after forty years of socialist nationhood. Their motto was aptly stated in writer Daniella Dahn's controversial *Westwards and Never Forget: On Discontent in Unity*.[78] A minority position in the new, Europeanized Federal Republic, the Brechtian invocation "never to forget" the positive, or potentially positive, elements of the East German past revived the need for continuity, for looking back, just as directly as the victors' stress on German nationhood did. Such desires also permeated everyday life, as people on both sides of the border evidenced a growing nostalgia for the material culture of the former East Germany, from the Trabant automobile to kitchen appliances, furniture, and other items.[79]

It was thus not surprising to see that preservationists again regarded their role as one in which "historical continuity" was a central ethical motivation. The Bavarian preservationist Michael Petzet stated the matter clearly in 1994:

This concept of historical continuity, which plays an absolutely central role in the cult of monuments at the end of the twentieth century, and which must be maintained—and which of course is found not only in our historical buildings—also provides moral legitimacy for the practice of historic preservation. Humankind is an "historical essence," and its necessary orientation to history and memory must not be torn away. One therefore preserves monuments, and to protect them from destruction is not only a matter of self-interest but of morality.[80]

With its emphasis on the human being as a historical phenomenon and its invocation of the moral calling of monument protection, this statement would have found approval among the founding fathers of modern preservation, most notably Dehio and Riegl. Dehio and Riegl differed on the matter of nationality, but as indicated above, even Riegl's conception of an international brotherhood of historical feeling, even his idea of a "socialist" preservation accessible to a broad range of people outside the educated classes, was not without a basis in national thinking. Given the political and cultural atmosphere of Europe after the fall of communism, it is difficult in any case to understand how an emphasis on historical continuity and a postmodern cult of monuments would *not* somehow lead back to the nation. It is possible that a pluralistic concept of the monument, based at least in part on the age value of historic sites, helped to transform German conceptions of the nation, fostering more "civic" or "political" loyalties in addition to cultural categories, and bringing about a more "lateral" national community shaped by a plurality of groups rather than the vertical authority of the state and elites. In this sense, it united Dehio and Riegl in a new synthesis, a more populist, perhaps democratic, practice of historic preservation that drew on the best intentions of both individuals' thought. Through that synthesis, what had been a cult became the established state religion.

NOTES

1. Alois Riegl, "Der Moderne Denkmalskultus. Sein Wesen und seine Entstehung," in *Gesammelte Aufsätze* (Augsburg and Vienna: Filser, 1928), 144–93.
2. Reinhard Bentmann, "Der Kampf um die Erinnerung. Ideologische und methodische Konzepte des modernen Denkmalkultus," in Ina-Maria Greverus, ed., *Denkmalräume-Lebensräume* (Gießen: Schmitz, 1976), 213–46.
3. Michael Petzet, "Der neue Denkmalkultus am Ende des 20. Jahrhunderts," *Die Denkmalpflege* 52:1 (1994), 22–32.
4. Iwona Irwin-Zarecka, *Frames of Remembrance: The Dynamics of Collective Memory* (New Brunswick, NJ, and London: Transaction Publishers, 1994).
5. Margaret Olin, *Forms of Representation in Alois Riegl's Theory of Art* (University Park: The Pennsylvania State University Press, 1992), 177–8.

6. G. Baldwin Brown, *The Care of Ancient Monuments* (Cambridge: Cambridge University Press, 1905), 27.

7. Rudy Koshar, *Germany's Transient Pasts: Preservation and National Memory in the Twentieth Century* (Chapel Hill and London: University of North Carolina Press, 1998), 18–29; idem, *From Monuments to Traces: Artifacts of German Memory, 1870–1990* (Berkeley and Los Angeles: University of California Press, 2000), 52–8.

8. Otto Sarrazin and Oskar Hoßfeld, "Zur Einführung," *Die Denkmalpflege* 1:1 (4 January 1899), 1–2 at 1.

9. For examples, see Brian Ladd, *Urban Planning and Civic Order in Germany, 1860–1914* (Cambridge, MA: Harvard University Press, 1990).

10. See for example Klaus Bergmann, *Agrarromantik und Großstadtfeindschaft* (Meisenheim: Anton Hain Verlag, 1970).

11. Sarrazin and Hoßfeld, "Zur Einführung," 1.

12. Ibid.

13. Georg Dehio, "Denkmalschutz und Denkmalpflege im neunzehnten Jahrhundert," in Marion Wohlleben, ed., *Konservieren nicht restaurieren. Streitschriften zur Denkmalpflege um 1900* (Braunschweig and Wiesbaden: Vieweg & Sohn, 1988), 88–103.

14. Ibid., 92.

15. For the following discussion, see Wohlleben, "Vorwort," in *Konservieren nicht restaurieren,* esp. 11–14.

16. Dehio, "Denkmalschutz und Denkmalpflege," 101.

17. Olin, *Forms of Representation,* 175–8; see also Kurt Forster, "Monument/Memory and the Mortality of Architecture," *Oppositions* 25 (fall 1982), 2–19.

18. Olin, *Forms of Representation,* 117–8, 175–7; see also Henri Zerner, "Alois Riegl: Age, Value, and Historicism," *Daedalus* 105: 1 (winter 1976), 177–88.

19. Wohlleben, "Vorwort."

20. Olin, *Forms of Representation,* 177.

21. Stephen L. Kern, *The Culture of Time and Space 1880–1918* (Cambridge, MA: Harvard University Press, 1983), 36–64.

22. Celia Applegate, *A Nation of Provincials: The German Idea of Heimat* (Berkeley and Los Angeles: University of California Press, 1990); Alon Confino, *The Nation as a Local Metaphor: Württemberg, Imperial Germany, and National Memory, 1871–1918* (Chapel Hill and London: University of North Carolina Press, 1997).

23. The most comprehensive institutional study of German historic preservation is Winfried Speitkamp, *Verwaltung der Geschichte. Denkmalpflege und Staat in Deutschland, 1871–1933* (Göttingen: Vandenhoeck & Ruprecht, 1996); see also Michael Siegel, *Denkmalpflege als öffentliche Aufgabe: Eine ökonomische, institutionelle, und historische Untersuchung* (Göttingen: Vandenhoeck & Ruprecht, 1985).

24. Koshar, *Germany's Transient Past,* 29–44.

25. Ibid., 37–40.

26. Landschaftsverband Rheinland, ed., *"Der Rhein ist mein Schicksal geworden": Paul Clemen, 1866–1947. Erster Provinzialkonservator der Rheinprovinz* (Cologne: Rheinland-Verlag, 1991); see also Rheinischer Verein für Denkmalpflege und Landschaftsschutz, ed., *Erhalten und gestalten. 75 Jahre Rheinischer Verein für Denkmalpflege und Landschaftsschutz* (Neuß: Gesellschaft für Buchdruckerei, 1981).

27. Speitkamp, *Die Verwaltung der Geschichte,* 263–85.

28. Johannes Horion, *Die rheinische Provinzialverwaltung, ihre Entwicklung und ihr heutiger Stand* (Düsseldorf: Schwann, 1925), 11.

29. Paul Clemen, *Die Deutsche Kunst und die Denkmalpflege. Ein Bekenntnis* (Berlin: Deutscher Kunstverlag, 1933).

30. Tag für Denkmalpflege, ed., *Tag für Denkmalpflege und Heimatschutz. Köln, 1930. Tagungsbericht* (Berlin: Deutscher Kunstverlag, 1931).

31. Dagobert Frey, "Der Denkmalpfleger: Robert Hiecke zum sechzigsten Geburtstage," *Deutsche Kunst und Denkmalpflege* 38:10 (1936), 297.

32. Rudolf Pfister, review of Hans Hörmann, *Methodik der Denkmalpflege* (München 1938), *Deutsche Kunst und Denkmalpflege* 40:2/3 (1938), 109.

33. Speitkamp, *Die Verwaltung der Geschichte*, 30–1.

34. Barbara Miller Lane, *Architecture and Politics in Germany 1918–1945* (Cambridge, MA: Harvard University Press, 1968), 157–60.

35. See the examples in Norbert Huse, ed., *Denkmalpflege. Deutsche Texte aus drei Jahrhunderten* (Munich: Beck, 1984).

36. Kirsten Belgum, *Popularizing the Nation: Audience, Representation, and the Production of Identity in* Die Gartenlaube, *1853–1900* (Lincoln and London: University of Nebraska Press, 1998).

37. Rudy Koshar, *German Travel Cultures* (Oxford and New York: Berg, 2000), 39–41.

38. Marina Warner, *Monuments and Maidens: The Allegory of Female Form* (New York: Atheneum, 1985), xvii–xx, 18–37; Koshar, *From Monuments to Traces*, 70–2; idem, *Germany's Transient Pasts*, 52–4.

39. Speitkamp, *Die Verwaltung der Geschichte*, 201–13.

40. Koshar, *Germany's Transient Pasts*, 35–6.

41. Ibid., 113–4.

42. Koshar, *From Monuments to Traces*, 57–8; Ulrich Linse, "Die Entdeckung der technischen Denkmäler. Über die Anfänge der Industriearchäologie in Deutschland," *Technikgeschichte* 53:3 (1986), 201–22.

43. Thomas Nipperdey, *Deutsche Geschichte, 1866–1918*, vol. 1: *Arbeitswelt und Bürgergeist*, 3rd ed. (Munich: Beck, 1993), 382–9.

44. David Blackbourn, *The Long Nineteenth Century: A History of Germany, 1780–1918* (Oxford and New York: Oxford University Press, 1997), 425–40.

45. Cited in Koshar, *Germany's Transient Pasts*, 109.

46. Lane, *Architecture and Politics in Germany*, 69–86.

47. Tag für Denkmalpflege und Heimatschutz, ed., *Tag für Denkmalpflege und Heimatschutz. Würzburg und Nürnberg, 1928: Tagungsbericht* (Berlin: Guido Hackebeil, 1929), 99–117.

48. Winfried Speitkamp, "Denkmalpflege und Heimatschutz in Deutschland zwischen Kulturkritik und Nationalsozialismus," *Archiv für Kulturgeschichte* 70 (1988), 164.

49. See the preface to Clemen, *Die Deutsche Kunst und die Denkmalpflege.*

50. Burkhard Meier, "Der Denkmalpflegetag in Kassel," *Die Denkmalpflege* 35:6 (1933), 193–209.

51. Koshar, *Germany's Transient Pasts*, 152–66.

52. Hans-Dieter Schäfer, *Das gespaltene Bewußtsein: Deutsche Kultur und Lebenswirklichkeit, 1933–1945* (Munich: Carl Hanser, 1982), 132.

53. Koshar, *Germany's Transient Pasts*, 209–27.

54. Jeffry M. Diefendorf, *In the Wake of War: The Reconstruction of German Cities After World War II* (New York: Oxford University Press, 1993).

55. Gerd Zuchold, "Der Abriß der Ruinen des Stadtschlosses und der Bauakademie in Ost-Berlin," *Deutschland-Archiv* 18:2 (1985), 178–207.

56. For examples: James E. Young, *The Texture of Memory: Holocaust Memorials and Meaning* (New Haven, CT, and London: Yale University Press, 1993).

57. Koshar, *Germany's Transient Pasts*, 29–44, 298.

58. Hartwig Beseler, "Berufsbild und Berufsausbildung der Denkmalpfleger," in *Denkmalräume-Lebensräume*, 279–86 at 284.

59. See examples in Gavriel Rosenfeld, *Munich and Memory: Architecture, Monuments, and the Legacy of the Third Reich* (Berkeley and Los Angeles: University of California Press, 2000).

60. Brian Ladd, *The Ghosts of Berlin: Confronting German History in the Urban Landscape* (Chicago and London: University of Chicago Press, 1997), 177, 181.
61. Koshar, *Germany's Transient Pasts,* 255.
62. Diefendorf, *In the Wake of War,* esp. chap. 4.
63. Ibid., 73.
64. Friedrich Nietzsche, "On the Uses and Disadvantages of History for Life," in R. J. Hollingdale, ed., *Untimely Meditations* (Cambridge: Cambridge University Press, 1983), 75–7.
65. Koshar, *From Monuments to Traces,* 228–43.
66. "Denkmalschutz als Volksbewegung," *Frankfurter Allgemeine Zeitung,* 21 January 1975.
67. Koshar, *Germany's Transient Pasts,* chap. 7.
68. Ibid., 303–4.
69. David Lowenthal, *The Past Is a Foreign Country* (Cambridge: Cambridge University Press, 1985).
70. Beseler, "Berufsbild und Berufsausbildung," 281.
71. Klaus von Beyme, *Der Wiederaufbau. Architektur und Städtebaupolitik in beiden deutschen Staaten* (Munich: Piper, 1987), 239, table 9.1.
72. Koshar, *Germany's Transient Pasts,* 300, 305.
73. Günter Grass, *Two States—One Nation?* (San Diego and New York: Harcourt Brace Jovanovich, 1990).
74. Georg Mörsch, "Wer bestimmt das öffentliche Interesse an der Erhaltung von Baudenkmalen? Mechanismen und Problematik der Auswahl," *Deutsche Kunst und Denkmalpflege* 38 (1980), 126–9.
75. Willibald Sauerländer, "Erweiterung des Denkmalbegriffs?" *Deutsche Kunst und Denkmalpflege* 33 (1975), 117–30.
76. Koshar, *Germany's Transient Pasts,* 222–3.
77. Peter Reichel, *Politik mit der Erinnerung: Gedächtnisorte im Streit um die nationalsozialistische Vergangenheit* (Munich: Carl Hanser, 1995).
78. Daniela Dahn, *Westwärts und nicht vergessen. Vom Unbehagen in der Einheit* (Reinbek bei Hamburg: Rowohlt, 1997).
79. Paul Betts, "The Twilight of the Idols: East German Memory and Material Culture," *Journal of Modern History* 72:3 (September 2000), 731–65.
80. Petzet, "Der neue Denkmalkultus," 31.

III
The Many Movements for Preservation in the United States

3

ROOTS IN BOSTON, BRANCHES IN PLANNING AND PARKS[1]

Michael Holleran

BOSTONIANS, LIKE OTHER URBAN Americans in the mid–nineteenth century, embraced a culture of change in the built environment. Change was progress, change was good; change was in any case inevitable. This culture was not friendly to the survival of old buildings. Antiquarians appreciated them but took no actions to save them. The embryonic preservation efforts before the Civil War were outside of cities.

During the last third of the nineteenth century, Boston residents grew uncomfortable with environmental change and began to defend features of the city that they valued, not only buildings but also landscapes. Boston was in the forefront of American reactions against environmental change. Preservation became an urban movement in the 1870s with the success at saving Boston's Old South Meetinghouse. Architects became preservationists in the 1890s with the campaign to save the Bulfinch State House. Efforts to maintain the state house's Beacon Hill setting at the turn of the century laid foundations for land-use regulation in the United States, and the same locale saw some of the country's first neighborhood restoration. Starting in 1910, William Sumner Appleton's Society for the Preservation of New England Antiquities set patterns of professional preservation practice for much of the twentieth century.

Bostonians first learned the difficulties of preservation in the city in an unsuccessful effort to save John Hancock's house, which stood next

Fig. 3.1 Hancock House, photographed by Edward Lamson Henry, c. 1863. (Courtesy of the Society for the Preservation of New England Antiquities.)

door to the Beacon Hill statehouse whose site he donated. In 1859, just after Mount Vernon was purchased by preservationists, the Hancock family offered the house for sale to the commonwealth of Massachusetts. The governor recommended and the legislature approved buying it, but then they dithered over whether it should become an official governors' residence. In 1863, the family sold the land for redevelopment and offered to donate the structure to the city. The city council began making arrangements to move it, with individuals pledging much of the cost, but the effort faltered when the council learned its estimate was low.[2] As a last resort, preservationists, in a large handbill, appealed to the new owners themselves to save the house "by an act of simple self-denial."[3] The house came down.

The Hancock house effort had all the ingredients of successful preservation, except the success. Both state and city governments recognized that preservation could be a legitimate aim of public policy and a legitimate object of public expenditure. Private individuals, too, assumed financial responsibility for preservation, bringing the Mount Vernon precedent to the city. Bostonians had gone beyond regretting the loss of urban landmarks to try saving one. The Hancock house would become the movement's martyr, a nineteenth-century version of New York's Pennsylvania Station.

THE OLD SOUTH MEETINGHOUSE

In the years after the Hancock house fell in 1863, Bostonians lost more prominent old buildings, especially as churches migrated to the new Back Bay. The greatest American preservation effort of the nineteenth century began when the Old South congregation decided that it, too, would move.

The Old South Meetinghouse dated from 1729, a brick barn of a building with a unique Revolutionary role as the site of gatherings too large for Faneuil Hall, such as the one that launched the Boston Tea Party.[4] Efforts to preserve the meetinghouse went through three phases: First, a faction within the congregation sought to block any move. Then opponents both within and outside the church challenged its right to move. Finally, preservationists campaigned to save the building independently of the congregation.

By the years after the Civil War, the Old South proprietors complained of the changing neighborhood, "hardly a suitable place for females to walk in the evening,"[5] and in 1869 they bought land at Copley Square in the Back Bay. The well-to-do "standing committee" who managed the church's business mostly lived in that neighborhood. The church's charter prohibited selling or leasing the meetinghouse,[6] but the standing committee informally entertained offers. In April 1872, the society voted, over many objectors, to ask the next legislature for authority to sell it.[7]

That November, the Great Fire destroyed downtown Boston, stopping at the Old South through some combination of divine intervention and the heroic efforts of firefighters. Troops quartered at the meetinghouse while guarding the burned district, and the standing

BOSTON.—SCENE AT THE GREAT FIRE—EFFORTS TO SAVE THE OLD SOUTH CHURCH.—SEE PAGE 513.

Fig. 3.2 The Great Fire: heroic efforts to save the Old South Meetinghouse. (Courtesy Boston Public Library, Print Department.)

committee offered it as a temporary post office during rebuilding. They petitioned the legislature not for that use, however, but also for removal of all restrictions on its disposal.[8]

The campaign now entered its public phase. Nineteen of the church's proprietors—only twenty-one had voted for the post office lease—asked the legislature to deny the request, as did other opponents from all around New England, who saw the proprietors as "trustees of an edifice of first-class historical interest."[9] The standing committee rejected this view of its responsibility. Deacon Charles Stoddard saw "no sense in having such a sentimental veneration for bricks and mortar, for even if the British did do something or other in the church, that was nothing to do with the work of Christ."[10] Both sides agreed that the structure's appeal was not architectural. "They say the Old South is Ugly!" said preservationist Wendell Phillips. "I should be ashamed to know whether it is ugly or handsome. Does a man love his mother because she is handsome?"[11] The congregation offered the meetinghouse to the Massachusetts Historical Society for its appraised value, but no one attempted to raise the hundreds of thousands of dollars that this would cost.[12]

The legislature approved not a complete release but only a two-year lease for the post office. The congregation moved services to a chapel in Copley Square,[13] and over the objections of its preservationist members built a $450,000 church there, dedicated in December 1875.[14] Meanwhile the standing committee sought permission to dispose of the old building, first from the legislature, and then from the Supreme Judicial Court,[15] which in 1876 noted that the law made no allowance for "patriotic and historical" considerations, and granted the release.[16] On Thursday, 8 June—less than four weeks before the national centennial—the Old South was auctioned for $1,350 as salvage. On Saturday, the buyer began dismantling the steeple.[17]

The following day, the third and most extraordinary phase of the preservation effort began as department store owner George W. Simmons secured a week's delay in demolition. He hung from the steeple a banner reading:

THE ELEVENTH HOUR!

MEN AND WOMEN OF MASSACHUSETTS!

Does Boston desire the humiliation which is to-day a part of her history since she had allowed this memorial to be sold under the hammer?

SHALL THE OLD SOUTH BE SAVED?

We have bought the right to hold this building uninjured for seven days, and will be conditionally responsible for raising the last $100,000 to complete its purchase.[18]

Bostonians packed the building for a meeting at which Wendell Phillips invoked the centennial: "The saving of this landmark is the best monument you can erect to the men of the Revolution. . . . Shall we tear in pieces the roof that actually trembled to the words which made us a nation?"[19]

A committee chaired by the governor raised funds for the building's preservation. They obtained a month's extension from the demolition contractor, and on the last day the church's officers named their price for the land: $420,000, cash, to be paid in two months. They expressed skepticism that preservationists would raise it, and required that the committee agree in writing that "you will not ask us for any further extension."[20] "The society," editorialized *The Commonwealth*, "does not mean that two edifices bearing the name of 'Old South' shall stand at the same time in the city of Boston—one to be a continual reminder of the unpatriotic course of the controllers of the other!"[21]

The women of Boston did most of the work toward saving the Old South.[22] Women canvassed as fund-raisers. While the preservation committee wrangled over the land, twenty women bought the structure itself from the salvage contractor and engaged architects to prepare plans for moving it. As its new site they proposed a vacant lot at Copley Square, opposite the new Old South Church.[23] The Old South was ultimately rescued by one woman. The building's purchase, and the moving plans, were organized by Mary Hemenway, recent widow of the richest man in New England. Shortly before the deadline, she anonymously offered one hundred thousand dollars to the preservation effort. Together with a $225,000 mortgage, the preservation committee was able to take title on 11 October 1876.[24] Preservationists worked for years to pay down the mortgage,[25] with the legislature grudgingly providing the last ten thousand dollars.[26]

Boston's greatest contribution to American preservation was saving the Old South Church. The significance of the Old South campaign was that, despite overwhelming odds, it worked. It was the first time Americans challenged the culture of change head-on and won. The building occupied some of the most valuable real estate in America; its owners were hostile to its continued existence; demolition had actually begun before the preservation effort got under way. If the Old South could be saved, anything could.

Bostonians noted this lesson, and began working to save everything that they liked. They liked a lot: not just historic buildings, but also Boston's Common, its old burial grounds, and disappearing rural landscapes. They mounted an effort to save H. H. Richardson's new Brattle Square church—then just nine years old—after the congregation disbanded.[27]

Most directly, the Old South's preservation altered a long debate about the future of the nearby Old State House, Massachusetts's capitol from 1712 to 1798. It had been threatened off and on throughout the nineteenth century, meanwhile packed with commercial tenants in what one modern preservationist calls "adaptive abuse."[28] But once the Old South was out of danger, the *Evening Transcript* noted that the Old State House "does not require redemption from other hands, but is already the property of the people, and therefore can easily be preserved."[29]

Common Council president William H. Whitmore had worked on the Old South effort and helped found the Bostonian Society, which took up the cause of the Old State House when its leases expired in 1881.[30] Whitmore secured an appropriation to restore the exterior and assembly halls[31] to their "appearance when used by the Legislature."[32] This was the brand of restoration that John Ruskin opposed as "a lie," and Bostonians made similar objections. "So far as the interior is concerned we cannot make it a relic," said one Common Council member. "We can only make an imitation. It will be a spurious relic."[33] Whitmore directed this restoration, and the Bostonian Society was made the building's custodian.

Both the Old South and the Old State House were saved for historical associations rather than architectural qualities; they were monuments rather than landmarks, not valued yet for their contribution to the visible cityscape. Another contemporary preservation cause—the protection of the city's old public landscapes—had everything to do with the city's appearance.

Park advocates responded to disappearing green spaces within and around cities. Boston produced many of the ideas behind the American parks movement, but no parks until annexation of neighboring towns in the 1870s. Boston's park system was born in the years of the Old South campaign, largely through the efforts of Uriel H. Crocker, one of the preservationist leaders within the congregation.[34] Franklin Park and Jamaica Pond, the biggest pieces, were chosen to preserve existing landscapes where parks commissioners worried that "the scenery will probably be hopelessly destroyed within a few years."[35]

The oldest part of the system was Boston Common, originally a seventeenth-century pasture that predated the very idea of a park. Many of the Old South's defenders, fresh from victory there and led by William H. Whitmore, turned their attention to the Common in 1877, when the Charitable Mechanic Association proposed housing its triennial industrial exhibition in a temporary six-hundred-foot-long crystal palace there. "We simply want to have the use, for a short period," explained the association's representative, "of a small portion of a large tract of unused land."[36] The proposal was not out of line with traditional uses of the space, but it did not fit the new idea of parkland. The Common Council rejected the mechanics' proposal on the motion of

Fig. 3.3 Old State House, 1876. Signs cover much of the building's exterior. A mansard roof has been added to increase rentable space. A portico added in 1830 projects into traffic. (Courtesy of the Society for the Preservation of New England Antiquities.)

Fig. 3.4 Jamaica Pond, from *Ballou's Drawing Room Companion,* 1855. (Courtesy of the Society for the Preservation of New England Antiquities.)

Uriel H. Crocker,[37] and no further serious attempts were made to place substantial buildings there. A more utilitarian threat was the need for access to downtown. Traffic in the 1870s brought proposals for streets on the Common, all defeated.[38] By the early 1890s, the problems led some suburban residents to propose an elevated railroad across the Common. Protests rained from as far away as Virginia, with women once again taking an active preservationist role.[39] The extraordinary solution was the first subway in the nation, under the edge of the Common, "a safeguard to the Common," according to its author, "as it would prevent a demand for a larger portion of it."[40] The transit commissioners were friends of the Common who worked to protect trees[41] and to relocate graves respectfully, and engaged Olmsted, Olmsted & Eliot for a landscape restoration.[42]

Another set of historic landscapes, the Granary and King's Chapel burial grounds, also received a preservationist bounce from the Old South campaign. In the late 1870s, the board of health proposed ending interments in the center of the city and calculated that a fine rural cemetery could be financed by selling the burial grounds.[43] Tomb owners asserted their rights in the graveyards, out of a "desire to maintain these grounds as monuments."[44] History could not address the public health arguments against burial grounds, but the parks movement could: King's Chapel, wrote Dr. Oliver Wendell Holmes Sr., was "an open breathing-space in a crowded part of the city."[45] The city council kept the burial grounds.

Outside the city center, landscape preservation was practiced at ever-greater scales. Massachusetts activists helped establish the Adirondack Forest in New York and national parks in the West, and as suburbs grew, they brought the parks movement back to the region around Boston. In 1890, Charles Eliot, who would soon join the Olmsted firm as a partner,[46] gathered "persons interested in the preservation of scenery and historical sites in Massachusetts," invoked the Old South and other preservation successes, and suggested that more people would undertake such efforts if a statewide organization could act as a guardian for the resources they saved.[47] The 1891 legislature chartered the Trustees of Public Reservations, a private, tax-exempt custodian for "beautiful and historic places." British preservationists cited this group as a model for their National Trust for Places of Historic Interest or Natural Beauty, founded in 1893 (it was in turn the model for the American National Trust for Historic Preservation).

These groups shows the kinship between parks and preservation: Both scenic and historical resources were threatened and needed to be saved. The first preservationist interest in the Common and burial grounds, as at the Old South, was nominally historic, but eventually it became clear that people valued these places less as symbols than as visible pieces of the urban environment.

THE BULFINCH FRONT

For buildings as for landscapes, people began defining significance by visual rather than historical importance. The fulcrum for this shift was the statehouse on Beacon Hill, designed by Charles Bulfinch and completed in 1798. The Bulfinch State House—how many capitols are known by their architect's name?—inspired the first major preservation campaign in the country that was more about architectural than other kinds of history.

By the 1880s, the statehouse, though well loved, was clearly inadequate. The Hancock house site next door suggested that demolition was not the answer, and the legislature in 1886 began planning a massive addition.[48] Three construction commissioners, appointed to build it, were not sympathetic to the Bulfinch building. In 1893 they revived the question

> whether the whole State House should not be made new. . . . It is some hundred years old. Its outer walls and wooden finish will not be in keeping with what, while called an extension, will really be five-sixths of the whole building. The dome is of wood, subject to the impairment of age,

Fig. 3.5 Bulfinch State House. (Courtesy of the Society for the Preservation of New England Antiquities.)

and should be of iron. It is hardly possible that many years will pass before, in any event, this old and most conspicuous part, facing Beacon Street and the Common, will be made new and of equal quality with the rest.[49]

This remarkable passage reveals a paradoxical conflict between preservation and permanence. The commissioners sought a permanence of materials not "subject to the impairment of age." They could not find this perfection in an old building.

Architects led the fight to save the Bulfinch State House, a first for the profession in this country. The Boston Society of Architects promoted preservation in two ways: First, it answered doubts about the building's condition and the practicality of preserving it. Both sides agreed that parts of the building—in particular the dome—had deteriorated. The BSA proposed solutions using the new technology of steel construction, thus framing preservation as another form of progress.[50] Second, the architects explained the building's place in the history of American architecture. As the Colonial Revival was becoming popular, old buildings gained new utility as a canon for emulation.

92 • Michael Holleran

Ironically, this visual focus worked against the Bulfinch building, leading to the strangest episode of the story, an officially endorsed plan to replace the statehouse with a replica—eventually a larger-than-life replica. The commissioners "recognized of course that no change would ever be permitted in the now historic and always admirable" design, but their admiration did not encompass the fabric in which the design was realized.[51] "Will a proper appreciation of Mr. Bulfinch require that the building should be carried forward in pine wood . . . until it shall burn down?" asked commissioner William Endicott Jr. "Is it not a truer loyalty to put the idea of Mr. Bulfinch into enduring materials and pass it down the centuries?"[52] Endicott would "preserve the structure in new material." At a hearing, one skeptic challenged him: "I fail to see how you can preserve the building by substituting a new structure." Endicott answered, "We desire to preserve the idea."[53] Did Charles Bulfinch produce an "idea" or a particular artifact? As the annex took shape, the awkwardness of the new ensemble became clear: "a building five hundred feet long with a dome at one end"; an enormous tail for a "little dog."[54] The construction commissioners decided to get a bigger dog. "Bulfinch originally intended a wider front," claimed one, "and there is some reason to believe that he contemplated with it a higher dome."[55]

Although the legislature's State House Committee approved this plan, five of its eleven members dissented, saying "the way to preserve the State House is to preserve it." Only this promise had allowed the project to go ahead. "The annex was built to preserve the State House and to harmonize with it. We are told, now, that the State House must be destroyed and rebuilt so that it may harmonize with the annex." The minority instead proposed "so thorough a repairing and fireproofing of the present structure that the question of its preservation will be permanently solved. . . . The State House can thus be put into a condition almost unexampled among historic buildings for safety and solidity and we desire to repeat that this is the only kind of preservation that is worthy of the name."[56] Finally, they disagreed that building a new front would improve the appearance of the complex as a whole, and argued that even on these grounds preservation was preferable, since "it will serve to emphasize the fact that the State House and annex are in reality two buildings, the former having been specially preserved for the people, and the union of the two will not be subject to the strict criticism to which one modern building would be exposed."[57] This early discussion of the proper relationship between new and old building fabric showed the sophistication of public discourse resulting from Boston's two decades of successful preservation efforts.

After the commissioners won early rounds, architects in 1896 made the "Bulfinch Front" a nationwide cause, and preservationists—particularly the Daughters of the American Revolution—made it a statewide political fight.[58] The legislature took the restoration out of the commissioners' hands to be supervised instead by three architects who were active in the preservation campaign. Work was finished in time for the building's 1898 centennial, "fresh from the hand of the rehabilitator," said one of its champions, "old yet new."[59]

A block away at the Park Street corner of the Common, another preservation controversy four years later was also about architecture. "The interest in Park Street Church," wrote one of its defenders, "is not due to great antiquity or wealth of historic associations, like the Old South Church. . . . The chief interest lies in the fact that the church is an impressive architectural monument, situated at a strategic point in the landscape of the city."[60] The strategic point was the new Park Street station at the corner of the Common, where thirty thousand people a day emerged to daylight at the 1808 steeple. Late in 1902, developers offered $1,250,000 for the Park Street Church site. The offer, said pastor John L.Withrow, was "the Lord's doing,"[61] and the congregation—with an old bylaw excluding women from voting—gave an option on the property.[62]

Nearby residents organized a Committee for the Preservation of Park Street Church, and quickly announced pledges totaling one hundred thousand dollars, then two hundred thousand, then three.[63] They invoked other preservation victories: The church was "the beginning of the noble approach to the State House," which would be "ruined," said architect John L. Faxon, by a tall structure there. The Granary burial ground next door could become "merely a well or backyard for office buildings." Like the Trustees of Reservations, they linked preservation and parks: "a monument on this corner constitutes a part of the beauty of the Common."[64] "There is as much reason for the preservation of a unique building like Park Street Church," said the committee's chair, "as there is for preserving notable natural features in the State,"[65] and offered the committee's pledges toward park acquisition.[66] The interior could be gutted for state offices.[67]

As the economy began to tighten, the developers let their option lapse.[68] Preservationists offered their funds as an endowment if the church would remain.[69] Instead, the congregation sought another buyer.[70] By spring 1904, they had a proposal from the *Boston Herald*.[71] Preservationists began a new kind of lobbying campaign, aimed at the church members themselves. They questioned the *Herald*'s financial

Fig. 3.6 Park Street Church, with Park Street subway entrance in the foreground, photographed by Henry Peabody, 1906. (Courtesy of the Society for the Preservation of New England Antiquities.)

proposal. They tapped the congregation's pride: The *Herald* claimed that the popular press was an appropriate successor to the evangelical pulpit. "Shall the church assent to this humiliation?" asked preservationists.[72] The deacons eventually withdrew the proposal without putting it to a vote.[73] Preservationists' role in saving Park Street Church is not easy to gauge, because unlike their counterparts at the Old South, they achieved their aims out of the public eye, through the congregation itself.

A similar private drama played out during the same years among the proprietors of the Boston Athenaeum, housed in an 1849 Renaissance palace around the corner from Park Street. In 1901, as tall new office buildings cut off their light, the Athenaeum's trustees prepared to build a new, bigger palace in the Back Bay.[74] But library members, who included activists from every preservation campaign since the Old South, began to have second thoughts, and a group of them started a new preservation campaign for a structure that had just turned fifty. The Athenaeum benefited from the same development slump that saved Park Street Church; selling the old building would not pay for a new one. The proprietors began renovations in 1904, and seven years later built a fireproof replica of the interior within the old walls.[75]

At the Bulfinch State House, Park Street Church, and the Athenaeum, the chronological threshold for preservationist attention—previously limited to the heroic period of the Revolution—advanced until at the Athenaeum it encompassed preservationists' own lifetimes. Architects at Park Street and the Athenaeum continued in the roles of preservation experts and advocates that they first took at the statehouse. All three campaigns were not about historic events but about architecture and urban views—not monuments but landmarks.

Efforts to maintain these views—centered on the statehouse dome, "the hub of the solar system" in the words of Oliver Wendell Holmes Sr.[76]—brought preservationists into urban planning. If tall buildings "dwarfed" the statehouse, wrote the *Transcript* in 1886, "the historical landmark would have lost its chief claim for preservation."[77] William H. Whitmore soon suggested preserving views by limiting building heights around the dome.[78] No American city yet regulated building heights (Boston initiated the practice four years later as a citywide fire safety measure).[79] Once the Bulfinch State House restoration was completed in 1899, preservationists renewed the call for height limits, proposing that no structure within a thousand feet of the dome rise higher than its base.[80] The bill was amended to offer compensation, but even this did not satisfy opponents. "Powers of eminent domain can be extended only to public uses," said a former state attorney general. "To prevent interference with a view of the State House is not a public use."[81]

The legislature limited heights in a small area immediately adjacent to the statehouse.[82] Massachusetts Chief Justice Oliver Wendell Holmes Jr. in 1901 upheld the restrictions, "passed," he wrote, "to save the dignity and beauty of the city at its culminating point."[83] His decision encouraged the idea that such measures could be enacted without compensation under the police power,[84] the key to modern land-use regulations, since eminent-domain controls are cumbersome and expensive, even where, as on Beacon Hill, property owners favored them. In 1904, Massachusetts passed the first police-power height districts in the country,[85] lowering allowable heights on all of Beacon Hill west of the statehouse.[86] The U.S. Supreme Court upheld these districts in 1909,[87] an important precedent for New York City's comprehensive zoning.[88]

This was a high-water mark of preservation as a movement to manage change in the large-scale urban environment. Bostonians had saved a remarkable ensemble of important public buildings—the Bulfinch State House, Park Street Church, the Athenaeum—and the historic green spaces that formed their setting, then shaped new development to fit the old, in ways that laid the groundwork for all of American land-use regulation in the twentieth century.

THE SOCIETY FOR THE PRESERVATION OF NEW ENGLAND ANTIQUITIES

After the turn of the century, preservation in Massachusetts matured from a string of spontaneous efforts to an institutionalized movement. In the process, both its aims and its methods were transformed.

Nineteenth-century Boston did not really have any organization dedicated to preservation in general. The Bostonian Society was meant as such an organization, but its appetite was sated by the single project of looking after the Old State House.[89] The Trustees of Reservations, while nominally interested in historic structures, in practice declined to accept any for years because they had no means of maintaining them.[90] The national Daughters of the American Revolution, organized in 1890, included preservation in its mission; Massachusetts chapters quickly found an outlet in the Bulfinch State House campaign.[91]

America's first standing regional preservation institution grew indirectly out of another ad hoc effort, restoration of Paul Revere's house in Boston, the oldest remaining structure in the city, dating from sometime between 1676 and 1681. Antiquarians endured, as one put it, "the vile odors of garlic and onions" in the immigrant North End to gaze at the greatly altered structure.[92] Revere descendants and others formed the Paul Revere Memorial Association to purchase it and, in 1907, began a restoration unlike any other Boston had seen.[93] The Old South Church and the two statehouses were major public buildings, their treatment a matter of widespread amateur debate. The Revere house, on the other hand, was outside the daily ambit of its preservers, and had undergone radical and unrecorded changes. Its restorers aimed to return it "to its original condition," so its treatment became a matter for expert investigation, not architecture but archaeology.[94] The memorial association's greatest contribution to preservation was in awakening its secretary, William Sumner Appleton Jr., to his life's work. The Revere House turned his attention from patriotism to architecture,[95] and in 1910 he chartered the Society for the Preservation of New England Antiquities (SPNEA).[96] (Appleton himself admitted he had coined an unfortunate mouthful, and his successors are not offended if it is pronounced *spih-NEE-uh.*)

Fig. 3.7 William Sumner Appleton Jr., c. 1917. (Society for the Preservation of New England Antiquities.)

In the society's first *Bulletin*, Appleton issued a preservation mani-festo of unprecedented ambition. The cover featured a photograph of the John Hancock house: BUILT 1737 BY THOMAS HANCOCK. DESTROYED 1863. "Our New England antiquities are fast disappearing," began the text, "because no society has made their preservation its exclusive ob-ject." What Appleton had in mind was "a large and strong society, which shall cover the whole field"—all six New England states—"and act instantly wherever needed to lead in the preservation of notewor-thy buildings and historic sites."[97] Appleton nowhere mentioned the Old South or either statehouse; the only Boston buildings he discussed were of domestic scale. The society's program embraced only such modest structures, aiming to acquire them "through gift, purchase, or otherwise, and then to restore them, and finally to let them to tenants under wise restrictions."[98]

By the end of the society's second year, it owned two houses[99] and had already refined the techniques of private intervention that it would follow for decades. Appleton husbanded resources, using inno-vative means of acquiring properties: seeking gifts and bequests, buy-ing houses subject to life occupancy, and financing restorations in return for reversion of property on their owners' deaths. In 1912, he originated the now familiar "revolving fund."[100] He relied on local groups, keeping SPNEA as a purchaser of last resort. He honed adap-tive use as a preservation tool, rather than making every acquisition a house museum. Appleton's purpose was to stretch SPNEA's funds, but the idea that restored buildings could continue in the lives of their communities was a powerful one.

Appleton recognized that ongoing preservation required financial endurance. The 1773 West Roxbury Meetinghouse in Boston, "saved" by an ad hoc committee, was destroyed in 1913 after SPNEA refused to accept it with a mortgage. Appleton was even prepared to decline properties offered unmortgaged but unendowed: "some houses might be jeopardized by this policy, but the security of the Society as a whole would be much increased."[101] The security of the society was central to Appleton's vision of preservation. He was deeply skeptical of any scheme other than ownership by some institutional guardian, prefer-ably SPNEA.

William Sumner Appleton saved a lot of buildings—when he died in 1947, SPNEA owned fifty-one—and in the process reshaped both the practice and the theory of preservation. The growing field was ripe for organizing ideas, and Appleton's had particular force because of his unique position as head of the country's largest and most rigorous preservation organization. Appleton made systematic an activity that had been ad hoc, and his system steered the movement in new directions.

Turning away from heavy restorations such as the Revere House, he argued that buildings should display the visible record of change over time. He promoted "the Society's thoroughly conservative rule that what is left today can be changed tomorrow, whereas what is removed today can perhaps never be put back." He aimed to conserve not only materials but the "documentary value" of buildings, by making his interventions evident and therefore reversible.[102] "I am . . . the most conservative restorer of the entire lot," wrote Appleton, "and a building is in the safest hands when I have charge of it."[103] Appleton insisted on a rigorous regimen of investigation and recording in the restoration process, laying the basis of a cumulative body of professional knowledge. This approach increased reliance on experts and nurtured restoration architecture as a distinct field.

Like earlier efforts, SPNEA necessarily responded to immediate threats, but from the beginning Appleton meant to do so within systematic priorities. He saw houses as antiques that could be classified and graded, and he was not shy about concluding that many were "not of sufficient importance to interest our Society."[104] As professional preservationists gained the expertise to evaluate individual structures, they lost the amateur's ability to appreciate them subjectively together, "tout ensemble," as New Orleans preservationists later put it.[105] Appleton saw buildings not as parts of the environment, but as objects complete in themselves. He was willing to give up on most of the city.

He was not alone; as Brahmins lost power in Boston to an Irish-dominated political machine, many disengaged from civic life in the city and adopted nativist attitudes, turning their minds to bygone days and to the countryside. They no longer looked to government as an agent of preservation. James Michael Curley, mayor off and on from 1914 until 1949, proposed selling the Public Garden,[106] and his building commissioner threatened to tear down the colonial Shirley-Eustis mansion for code violations.[107] Aristocratic Bostonians would not put environmental stability in the hands of government while the government was in hands like Curley's. Appleton made halfhearted attempts at enlisting state and federal aid for preservation, but at heart he thought government involvement "dangerous."[108]

While some preservationists turned away from the city, others took up the cause of their urban neighborhoods, first on Boston's Beacon Hill. By the 1880s, the area was perceived as declining. Height restrictions in 1899 came as residents began working to reverse that decline, and helped relieve pressures for replacement of existing old houses with large apartment and office buildings. Beacon Hill had maintained a core of aristocratic residents, among them real estate broker William Coombs Codman, who shortly after the turn of the century began restoring and reselling old houses there. Architect Frank A. Bourne moved from the Back Bay and began providing up-to-date interiors within quaint exteriors.[109] They, like Appleton, were practicing preservation by purchase, not through philanthropy but through the housing market.

Beacon Hill residents saw that their preservation efforts required reinforcement through government powers, removing the barriers between preservation and planning. In 1922, the neighborhood organized the Beacon Hill Association,[110] and it immediately lobbied for zoning in Boston. "A direct benefit of zoning," according to the planning board, "perhaps of more value in Boston than in any other city in the United States, will be the protection and preservation of old historical buildings and sites," such as the "famous Beacon Hill district."[111] Once Boston's zoning took effect in 1924, significant new development required zone changes, and the Beacon Hill Association set up a Zoning Defence Committee to fight them.[112]

Appleton did not make common cause with neighborhood preservationists—he did not seem to understand them as part of the same movement—and his purist preservation steered away from any large-scale interest in townscape or landscape. Meanwhile, the parks and planning movements were themselves headed away from their preservationist origins: Planners turned their backs on anything that smacked of aesthetics; parks proponents emphasized active recreation over landscape preservation.

But Appleton despite himself laid the groundwork for a broad movement. Turning from patriotic traditions to the ordinary life of earlier generations—even if conceived as an affirmation of Anglo-Saxon precedence—eventually worked against nativism. It defined an inclusive subject matter that would encourage later preservationists to take an interest in the very groups their predecessors sought to exclude. Appleton's consistency and comprehensiveness, even if intended as strategies of private action, were essential in providing the appearance of objectivity that would make historic districts permissible under the police power. The motivation for such districts was not objective; they grew out of the same sort of amateur appreciation that had saved so much of the center of Boston. Boston relinquished its leadership to southern cities, though it did become the first northern city to enact historic district zoning, for Beacon Hill in 1955.[113] As preservationists in the second half of the twentieth century made alliances with planners and environmentalists, revitalizing historic districts and saving rural landscapes, it was less an innovation than a belated family reunion.

NOTES

1. This chapter is based on my *Boston's "Changeful Times": Origins of American Preservation and Planning* (Baltimore: Johns Hopkins University Press, 1998).

2. *Massachusetts Acts & Resolves,* 1859, Acts chap. 175; Boston City Council, *Preservation of the Hancock House*; Charles B. Hosmer Jr., *Presence of the Past: A History of the Preservation Movement in the United States Before Williamsburg,* 3 vols. (New York: G. P. Putnam's Sons, 1965), 39.

3. O. H. Burnham, publisher, "Bostonians! Save the Old John Hancock Mansion" (6 June 1863), SPNEA library, Boston.

4. *Boston Globe,* 4 December 1872: 4; G. G. Wolkins, *Freedom and the Old South Meeting-house,* Old South leaflets, no. 202 (Boston, 1945), 17. See Frederic C. Detwiller, "Thomas Dawes's Church in Brattle Square," *Old-Time New England* 69 (1979), fig. 7, 8–9.

5. April 30, 1866 report by Charles Stoddard, Loring Lothrop, Avery Plumer, and the church's two pastors, quoted in Hamilton Andrews Hill, *History of the Old South Church (Third Church) Boston: 1669–1884* (Boston: Houghton Mifflin, 1890), 524. They were speaking of the congregation's Spring Lane chapel, on another side of the same block; the congregation voted to give up the chapel and rent one on Beacon Hill instead.

6. 19 October 1869 meeting, "Extracts from the Records of the Old South Church," 2, in Massachusetts Supreme Judicial Court, *Old South Society v. Crocker; Attorney General v. Old South Society* (Boston, 1874–96), various papers bound as 1 vol., Boston Public Library (BPL). Jacob Dresser, quoted in *Boston Globe,* 27 November 1872, 4; Old South Society, *Report of Committee to Consider Building on Boylston Street,* 24 June 1870, 2. Hill, *History,* 507–8. See "Brief for the Attorney General," 11, in Supreme Judicial Court, *Old South Society v. Crocker,* BPL.

7. Hill, *History,* 527–9.

8. [Charles Francis Adams], "The Fate of an Historic Edifice," *The Nation* 15 (28 November 1872), 346; Hill, *History,* 528; Dana, *Argument,* 3.

9. [Adams], "Fate of an Historic Edifice," 347.

10. Stoddard in *Boston Globe,* 23 November 1872, 4.

11. Massachusetts General Court, Committee on Federal Relations, *Hearing . . . March 4, 1878,* 31.

12. "Extracts from the Records," 6, in Supreme Judicial Court, *Old South Society v. Crocker,* BPL; Hill, *History,* 530–1.

13. Hill, *History,* 531; *Massachusetts Acts & Resolves,* 1872, Special session, Acts chap. 368.

14. *Old South v. Crocker,* 119 Mass. 1; Hill, *History,* 547.

15. *Old South v. Crocker,* 119 Mass. 1 (1875), at 7; *Massachusetts Acts & Resolves,* 1874, Acts chap. 120.

16. *Old South Society v. Crocker.* This decision was not published in the *Massachusetts Reports,* but appears in *Transactions of the Colonial Society of Massachusetts* 3 (1896), 264–7 at 267.

17. *Boston Globe,* 9 June 1876, 2; 10 June 1876, 4.

18. Everett W. Burdett, *History of the Old South Meetinghouse in Boston* (Boston: B. B. Russell, 1877), 89.

19. *Old South Meeting House,* Old South leaflets no. 183, 7.

20. Quoted in *Boston Globe,* 14 July 1876, 4.

21. Quoted in *Boston Globe,* 8 July 1876, 4.

22. Already at the first mass meeting on 14 June, journalist Curtis Guild spoke "highly commending the part women took in such movements," according to Burdett (*History,* 97), in apparent reference to the preservation of Mount Vernon.

23. *Boston Globe,* 20 July 1876, 5. If they bought the Copley Square lot, "rumor states that an injunction restraining the erection of the ancient edifice will be applied for by the Old South Society." *Boston Globe,* 19 July 1876, 2. This, said the chairman of the standing committee, was "a lie"; *Boston Globe,* 27 July 1876, 5.

24. *Dictionary of American Biography,* 518–9; *Boston Globe,* 19 June 1876, 2; 13 July 1876, 4; 14 October 1876, 2. Did Simmons's "last $100,000" offer indicate an arrangement with Hemenway from the beginning?

25. *Boston Globe,* 21 June 1878, 4; Old South Association, *The Old South Association in Boston. List of Officers, members, Committees* (Boston, 1912), 17–24.

26. *Massachusetts Acts & Resolves,* 1878, Resolves chap. 26.

27. *Boston Evening Transcript,* 11 October 1881, 4; 16 June 1881, 4; advertisement cited in letter to the editor, *Boston Evening Transcript,* 11 October 1881, 5; [George B. Chase], "Brattle St. Church Tower" MS subscription book, T. Chase papers, Massachusetts Historical Society. The New Brattle Square building is now the First Baptist Church.

28. Sara B. Chase, "A Brief Survey of the Architectural History of the Old State House, Boston, Massachusetts," *Old-Time New England* 58 (1978), 31–49 at 43; Elizabeth Reed Amadon, *Old State House. Historical Report* (Boston, 1970).

29. *Boston Evening Transcript,* 1 June 1881, 4.

30. *Boston Evening Transcript,* 14 January 1880, 1; 11 February 1880, 1. At its inception it was called the Boston Antiquarian Club.

31. *Boston Evening Transcript,* 10 June 1881, 2.

32. *Boston Evening Transcript,* 24 June 1881, 2, 3.

33. *Boston Evening Transcript,* 27 May 1881, 2.

34. In city council debate, 1 April 1875, quoted in Boston City Council, *Public Parks in the City of Boston. A Compilation of Papers, Reports, and Arguments, Relating to the Subject* (City doc. 125, 1880), 34; Cynthia Zaitzevsky, Frederick Law *Olmsted and the Boston Park System* (Cambridge, MA: Harvard University Press, 1982), 37–43.

35. *Second Report of the Board of Commissioners of the Department of Parks for the City of Boston* (City doc. 42, 1876), 31, 29; Alexander von Hoffman, *Local Attachments: The Making of an American Urban Neighborhood, 1850 to 1920* (Baltimore: Johns Hopkins University Press, 1994), 87–8.

36. Boston City Council, *Hearing on the Charitable Mechanics Building,* 65.

37. *Boston Globe,* 9 March 9 1877, 4; *Massachusetts Acts & Resolves,* 1877, Acts chap. 223.

38. *Boston Globe,* 10 April 1872, 8; 23 May 1874, 4; 17 November 1874, 2.

39. Charles W. Cheape, *Moving the Masses: Urban Public Transit in New York, Boston, and Philadelphia, 1880–1912* (Cambridge, MA: Harvard University Press, 1980), 120, 124, 134–6; Nathan Matthews to Horace G. Allen, 14 March 1893, Nathan Matthews papers 4, 237, Littauer Library, Harvard; *Massachusetts Acts and Resolves,* 1893, Acts chap. 481.

40. *Boston Evening Transcript,* 18 December 1893, 8.

41. Boston Transit Commission, *First Annual Report* (Boston, 1895), 17, 30.

42. Boston Transit Commission, *First Annual Report,* 19; *Boston Evening Transcript,* 11 August 1896, 4.

43. *Fifth Annual Report of the Board of Health* (City doc. 67, 1877), 19.

44. *Report on Intramural Interments* (1879), 55 ("as monuments"), 56, 60; *Boston Evening Transcript,* 5 September 1879, 1, 4; *Proceedings of the Common Council* (9 October 1879), 586.

45. *Report on Intramural Interments* (1879), 56.
46. Charles W. Eliot, ed., *Charles Eliot, Landscape Architect* (Boston: Houghton Mifflin, 1902), 204.
47. Trustees of Public Reservations, *First Annual Report . . . 1891* (Boston, 1892), 5, 7–8.
48. *Massachusetts Acts and Resolves,* 1886, Resolves chap. 87; *House Journal,* 1886, 739. See also the account of the act's passage by Dr. William A. Rust, then member of the House, in Massachusetts General Court, Committee on the State House, *Hearings Mar. 16, 17, 18, 1896, concerning the Bulfinch Front,* typescript, Massachusetts State Library Special Collections, 1:2–4.
49. Massachusetts State House Construction Commissioners, *Fourth Annual Report, 1892* (House doc. 6, 1893), 8.
50. Clement K. Fay, in Massachusetts General Court, *Hearings concerning the Bulfinch Front,* 3:17. The committee consisted of Fay, H. Langford Warren, William R. Ware (1:14–5).
51. State House Construction Commissioners, *Fourth Annual Report, 1892,* 8.
52. Letter, *Boston Evening Transcript,* 2 February 1894, 5.
53. *Boston Evening Transcript,* 26 February 1894, 1.
54. Fay, in Massachusetts General Court, *Hearings concerning the Bulfinch Front,* 1:9; *American Architect and Building News,* 10 March 1894, 109.
55. Letter, *Boston Evening Transcript,* 2 February 1894, 5. See Arthur T. Lyman letter, *Boston Evening Transcript,* 22 April 1896, 6: "Even if we had Bulfinch's original plans, it would be absurd to reproduce them when the building that we have is the building that he erected."
56. Massachusetts General Court, Committee on the State House, *Views of a Minority . . . on the Preservation of the State House* (Senate doc. 189, 1894), 2–3.
57. Massachusetts General Court, *Views of a Minority,* 4. The committee was adopting a position earlier taken by the Boston Society of Architects. See William G. Preston letter, *Boston Evening Transcript,* 7 February 1894, 8.
58. *Boston Morning Journal,* 27 March 1896, 10; *American Architect and Building News,* 25 April 1896, 33; *Boston Evening Transcript,* 13 May 1896, 7; Massachusetts State Archives, legislative documents, 1896 Acts, chap. 531; *Boston Morning Journal,* 16 April 1896, 1; Massachusetts General Court, *Centennial of the Bulfinch State House. Exercises before the Massachusetts Legislature, January 11, 1898* (Boston, 1898), 30; *American Architect and Building News,* 18 April 1896, 32; 27 April 1896, 33; 5 May 1896, 45–7; Roe in Massachusetts General Court, *Centennial,* 19–20; see also James M. Lindgren, *Preserving the Old Dominion: Historic Preservation and Virginia Traditionalism* (Charlottesville: University Press of Virginia, 1993), 206.
59. Massachusetts General Court, *Centennial,* 25 ("old yet new"); 28 (architects); 1896 Senate bill 253 (as amended Senate bill 259).
60. Prescott F. Hall, "Circular of the Preservation Committee," 7 February 1903, in Committee for the Preservation of Park Street Church, *The Preservation of Park Street Church, Boston* (Boston: Committee for the Preservation of Park Street Church, 1903), 35.
61. *Springfield Republican,* 17 December 1902, quoted in Committee for the Preservation of Park Street Church, *Preservation,* 52.
62. *Boston Herald,* 8 December 1902, 12; 14 December 1902, 7; 18 December 1902, 8; H. Crosby Englizian, *Brimstone Corner: Park Street Church, Boston* (Chicago: Moody Press, 1968), 204; Committee for the Preservation of Park Street Church, *Preservation,* 22–3.
63. Committee for the Preservation of Park Street Church, *Preservation,* 31; Prescott F. Hall letter, *Boston Evening Transcript,* 31 December 1902, at 51. Pledges: *Boston Evening Transcript,* 15 January 1903; *Boston Globe,* 2 April 1903, quoted in Committee for the Preservation of Park Street Church, *Preservation,* 32, 64; Englizian, *Brimstone Corner,* 205.

64. "Ruined": *Boston Evening Transcript,* 27 February 1903, 1; Committee for the Preservation of Park Street Church, *Preservation,* 60 ("noble approach": "M.N.O." letter to the editor, *Boston Evening Transcript,* 31 January 1903); 50 ("a well": *Boston Evening Transcript,* 31 December 1902); 5–6 ("monumental building).

65. *Boston Evening Transcript,* 27 February 1903, 1.

66. Hosmer, *Presence of the Past,* 146; 1903 House bill 712; *Boston Evening Transcript,* 27 February 1903, 1.

67. Edwin D. Mead and Prescott Hall testimony at legislative hearing, *Boston Evening Transcript,* 27 February 1903, 1.

68. Hosmer, *Presence of the Past,* 111; *Boston Herald,* 7 March, 2 April, 1903; *Springfield Republican,* 10 February 1903, quoted in Committee for the Preservation of Park Street Church, *Preservation,* 32. On 9 March, three days after the Parker House meeting, the legislature received a negative report on the Park Street church bill from the Committee on the State House, which had held the hearing. *House Journal,* 1903, 542.

69. *Boston Evening Transcript,* 27 February 1903, 1; Firey, *Land Use in Central Boston,* quoting *Boston Sunday Journal,* 15 March 1903.

70. *Boston Herald,* 2 April 1903; also *Boston Globe,* 1 July 1903, *Boston Morning Journal,* 1 July 1903, both quoted in Committee for the Preservation of Park Street Church, *Preservation,* 71–4; see also *Preservation,* 22–3.

71. *Boston Herald,* 15 June 1904; Englizian, *Brimstone Corner,* 205–6.

72. Quoted in Englizian, *Brimstone Corner,* 207.

73. Englizian, *Brimstone Corner,* 207.

74. Ronald Story, *Harvard & the Boston Upper Class: The Forging of an Aristocracy, 1800–1870* (Middletown, CT: Wesleyan University Press, 1980), 13–19; *Boston Globe,* 14 January 1873; Trustees' circular letter to proprietors, 1 December 1903, in William Sumner Appleton scrapbook [10], SPNEA.

75. *Boston Evening Transcript,* 23 May 1901; *Boston Herald,* 17 February 1912; *Boston Sunday Post,* 3 December 1911; petition in Appleton scrapbook [10]; Jane S. Knowles, *Change and Continuity: A Pictorial History of the Boston Athenaeum* (Boston: Athenaeum, 1985).

76. Oliver Wendell Holmes Sr., *The Autocrat of the Breakfast Table* [1858] (Boston: Houghton Mifflin, 1886), 125.

77. *Boston Evening Transcript,* 27 November 1886 [n.p.: clipping in Massachusetts State Library Special Collections].

78. *American Architect and Building News,* 26 March 1887, 145.

79. See Michael Holleran, "Boston's 'Sacred Sky Line': From Prohibiting to Sculpting Skyscrapers, 1891–1928," *Journal of Urban History* 22 (1996), 552–85.

80. *American Architect and Building News,* 11 February 1899, 41; Massachusetts State Archives, legislative documents, 1899 Acts, chap. 457; 1899 House bill 681, §1.

81. *Boston Morning Journal,* 4 April 1899, 5; *Boston Evening Globe,* 17 March 1899, 4.

82. *Massachusetts Acts and Resolves,* 1899, Acts chap. 457; 1901, Acts ch. 525; 1902, Acts 543.

83. *Parker v. Commonwealth,* 178 Massachusetts 199 (1901), at 203–4.

84. *Parker v. Commonwealth,* 178 Massachusetts 199, at 204–5.

85. *Massachusetts Acts & Resolves,* 1904, Acts chap. 333, §1; Commission on Height of Buildings in the City of Boston, *Final Report* (City doc. 133, 1905), 18; 1904 House bill 507, submitted by petition of G. H. Richards and others; *Boston City Council Minutes,* 1904, 113 (24 March).

86. Commission on Height of Buildings (Boston), *Final Report.* See also *Boston Evening Transcript,* editorial, 6 December 1904, 12.

87. Justice Rufus W. Peckham's decision also opened a door through which would eventually come historic district zoning: "That in addition to these sufficient facts, con-

siderations of an aesthetic nature also entered into the reasons for their passage, would not invalidate them." *Welch v. Swasey*, 214 U.S. 91, at 106–8.

88. New York City's zoning commissioners took the unusual step of holding a public hearing in Boston, and on the steamboat that brought them back home they discussed what they had heard about that city's experience with height districts. As commission vice chairman Lawson Purdy recalled, they concluded that this was indeed "the answer" for New York; Lawson Purdy, quoted in S. J. Makielski Jr., *The Politics of Zoning: The New York Experience* (New York: Columbia University Press, 1966), 20; Seymour Toll, *Zoned American* (New York: Grossman, 1969), 167.

89. *Proceedings of the Bostonian Society* (1903), [74]. John Ritchie, a neighbor of the Bulfinch State House who would later join the preservation committee to save it, said at the 1887 hearings that he was "astounded that the Bostonian Society . . . did not appear to enter their plea. . . ." *Boston Evening Transcript*, 24 March 1887, 1.

90. Trustees *Ninth Annual Report . . . 1899* (Boston, 1900), 19–20.

91. Lewis Barrington, *Historic Restorations of the Daughters of the American Revolution* (New York: R. R. Smith, 1941), preface; Hosmer, *Presence of the Past*, 131–2.

92. Samuel Adams Drake, *Our Colonial Homes* (1893), quoted in James M. Lindgren, *Preserving Historic New England* (New York: Oxford University Press, 1995), 37.

93. The effort was spearheaded by a Revere descendant, real estate developer John Phillips Reynolds Jr., who bought the house in 1902 as he was trying to tear down Park Street Church. Printed circular letter (1905); "Paul Revere's House Saved," unidentified clipping (1907), both in North Square/Paul Revere scrapbook, SPNEA.

94. "original condition": WSA letter, *Boston Post*, 16 June 1905, in North Square/Paul Revere scrapbook, SPNEA; Joseph Everett Chandler, "Notes on the Paul Revere House," *Handbook of the Paul Revere Memorial Association* (Boston: Paul Revere Memorial Association, 1950), 17–25; Chandler letter to Walter Gilman Page, 2 March 1907, in North Square/Paul Revere scrapbook, SPNEA; William Sumner Appleton, "Destruction and Preservation of Old Buildings in New England," *Art & Archaeology* 8 (1919), 144.

95. William Sumner Appleton Jr.'s background is best described in Lindgren, *Preserving Historic New England;* and Katherine H. Rich, "Beacon," *Old-Time New England* 66 (1976), 42–60. Other information below comes from Hosmer, *Presence of the Past*, 237–9; and "William Sumner Appleton, 1874–1947," *Old-Time New England* 38 (1948), 71–2.

96. See Lindgren, *Preserving Historic New England*, 60–7.

97. *SPNEA Bulletin* 1 (1910), 4, 5.

98. *SPNEA Bulletin* 1 (1910), 6.

99. *SPNEA Bulletin* 3 (1912), 14. The second property was the 1808 Fowler house in Danversport, bought subject to life occupancy by its owners.

100. *SPNEA Bulletin* 1 (1910), 6 ("wise restrictions"); 3 (1913), 11; Lindgren, "Gospel of Preservation," 293.

101. *SPNEA Bulletin* 4 (1913), 28 ("security of the Society"); 3 (1912), 2:19; 6 (1915), 1:13; *American Architect and Building News*, 10 December 1913, 234. See Lindgren, *Preserving Historic New England*, 127.

102. *Old-Time New England* 11 (1920), 167–8 ("thoroughly conservative"); *SPNEA Bulletin* 9 (1918), 34 ("documentary value"); Lindgren, *Preserving Historic New England*, 134–44. Appleton preached the Ruskinian "anti-scrape" gospel of England's Society for the Protection of Ancient Buildings, and called "the spirit of the work of the two societies . . . almost identical." *SPNEA Bulletin* 5 (1914), 19.

103. Letter to Murray Corse, 16 May 1919, quoted in Hosmer, *Presence of the Past*, 285.

104. *SPNEA Bulletin* 5 (1914), 7.

105. Morrison, *Historic Preservation Law*, 47.

106. Jack Beatty, *The Rascal King: The Life and Times of James Michael Curley, 1874–1958* (Reading, MA: Addison-Wesley, 1992), 167–8.

107. *Massachusetts Special Acts & Resolves,* 1915, Acts chap. 306; Lindgren, "Gospel of Preservation," 273. O'Hearn was not being arbitrary; on the contrary, he systematically enforced Boston's building and fire codes for the first time, causing the demolition of 654 substandard structures in his first fifteen months in office; *Boston Evening Transcript,* 12 May 1915, III.3.

108. Ronald F. Lee, *The Antiquities Act of 1906* (Washington:Office of History and Historic Architecture, 1970); Appleton to Charles D. Walcott, 2 December 1912, microfiche correspondence archive, "Preservation legislation," SPNEA, Massachusetts Constitution, amendments art. 51; in *Massachusetts General Acts,* 1919, Act 63.

109. Firey, *Land Use in Central Boston* (Cambridge, MA: Harvard University Press, 1947), 120.

110. Deland, "Regeneration of Beacon Hill," 95; *Boston Evening Transcript,* 6 December 1922, quoted in Firey, *Land Use in Central Boston,* 111; *Old-Time New England* 11 (1920), 171.

111. Boston City Planning Board, *Zoning for Boston,* 34 ("direct benefit"), 29; Kenneth T. Jackson, *Crabgrass Frontier: The Suburbanization of the United States* (New York: Oxford University Press, 1985), 242; Marc A. Weiss, *Rise of the Community Builders* (New York: Columbia University Press, 1987), 11–2.

112. Firey, *Land Use in Central Boston,* 129–32; *Boston Herald,* 2 October 1926; Beacon Hill Association, Zoning Defence Committee, *The Menace to Beacon Hill* (Boston, 1927); *Boston Herald,* 22 June, 29 June 1929; *Boston Evening Transcript,* 8 March 1933; *Boston Herald,* 7 April 1933.

113. Morrison, *Historic Preservation Law,* 12–4. The historic district campaign on Beacon Hill was led by John Codman (Jacobs, "Architectural Preservation in the United States," 328), son and business successor of William Coombs Codman (1 October 1932 clipping in W. C. Codman papers, SPNEA).

4

"A SPIRIT THAT FIRES THE IMAGINATION"

Historic Preservation and Cultural Regeneration in Virginia and New England, 1850–1950

James M. Lindgren

WHILE THE NATION CELEBRATED Jamestown's tercentenary in 1907, Bruton Parish Church was being reconsecrated in nearby Williamsburg after a two-year restoration, one whose donors included Andrew Carnegie, Theodore Roosevelt, and King Edward VII. In his remarks, the Reverend William A. R. Goodwin told the assembled dignitaries of the illustrious history of the former colonial capital. To mark the occasion, Goodwin assembled a commemorative volume, in which he repeated his belief that "the spirit of the days of long ago haunts and hallows the ancient city and the homes of its honored dead; a spirit that stirs the memory and fires the imagination" of the living. At a time of social and economic flux, however, he declared that Williamsburg's inheritance held "priceless value," asking his audience "to guard these ancient landmarks and resist the spirit of ruthless innovation which threatens to rob the city of its unique distinction and its charms." He stressed, "No cost should be spared to preserve them."[1]

An influential member of the Association for the Preservation of Virginia Antiquities (1889), the nation's first statewide preservation organization, Goodwin was surely an important figure in preservation history. In his chronicle of the movement, the historian Charles B. Hosmer Jr. emphasized his courting of John D. Rockefeller Jr. as he convinced the magnate in 1926 to bankroll the most costly, trendsetting enterprise in the annals of historic preservation, the reconstruction of

Williamsburg. As such, according to Hosmer, he helped the movement make the transition from the APVA's supposed amateurism to Colonial Williamsburg's professionalism. Like many, Hosmer was awed by the project's architectural expertise, archaeological research, and business wizardry, all of which he used to define *professionalism*.[2] Yet a preservationist like Goodwin should be primarily understood as a skilled warrior in the cultural battles of his day, for the story of historic preservation is essentially concerned less with methodology, whether amateur or professional, than with a contest over the shaping of present and future. Cultural politics defines the meaning of historic preservation. After all, as Shakespeare said, "What is past is prologue"—but the question is, Whose past?[3]

Goodwin's work falls into a well-established tradition, one that achieved national attention half a century earlier when the fate of George Washington's plantation was unclear. The modern preservation movement began in 1853 with the formation of the Mount Vernon Ladies Association of the Union, the first national preservation society in the United States. The MVLA's efforts are best understood in the context of the political, economic, and social conflicts of the day, which is to say the making of the era's cultural politics. Apparently, after a syndicate had proposed turning the deteriorated estate into a hotel with a racetrack and saloon to lure the nouveaux riches, Ann Pamela Cunningham rallied to prevent its corruption by founding the MVLA. "Pilgrims to the shrine of pure patriotism," she wrote in the *Charleston Mercury*, would find Mount Vernon "forgotten, [and] surrounded by blackening smoke and degrading machinery!—where money, only money enters the thought; and gold, only gold, moves the heart or nerves the arm." Like many southerners reared in an agrarian, aristocratic tradition, she pictured the North as a land of Mammon, where cities, factories, and debauchery prevailed.[4]

In Cunningham's day, most women of property and social standing were influenced by the tradition of republican motherhood. While ladies safeguarded the home's moral authority, and their public activity was thus limited to that sphere, men were busy in the increasingly aggressive, but to many corrupting, world of business and politics. Influenced by domesticity and acting as a counterweight to the impersonal market economy, women developed the philosophy of personalism. Whether on an individual or social level, they sought intimate bonds where personal attachments were prized and fostered. Thinking that those sentiments were linked to material and natural things, women commonly focused their interests on the homes, furnishings, manners, and landscapes associated with the revered founders of the nation, leaders of their community, or patriarchs and matriarchs of their family. An artifact could represent such values as individual character, love of family, or public duty. Personalism was not limited to women, however. Even into the twentieth century, many gentlemen subscribed, but cynics dismissed their alleged romanticism as impractical and unscientific.[5]

Further shaping Cunningham's crusade in the 1850s was the vicious debate between the North and the South. Repudiating those who clamored to either limit or end slavery, she claimed that the agitators had forgotten the Founding Fathers and put the national union in jeopardy. She heralded Washington as a model for the ages. But as the unmarried daughter of a South Carolina planter, she left the public speaking to such gentlemen as Edward Everett, a former Massachusetts statesman, diplomat, and Harvard president. Having just retired from the Senate, he raised money for the MVLA by presenting an oration on the character of Washington some 130 times to packed lecture halls. He deplored his era's sectionalism, as well as Boston's politics and immigrants—as did Cunningham, who condemned the "degeneracy . . . who crowd our metropolis." They both revealed their disillusionment, if not disgust, with politics, and imagined a happier, holier time. Of course, much of their thinking was the invention of mythmakers and ideologues, but the MVLA would reify it through Mount Vernon, which it purchased in 1858.[6]

After the Civil War, Cunningham repeated her criticism through a number of tried-and-true guises, most obviously by deifying the Founders and sentimentalizing early American history. While tradition-minded ladies thus expressed their message through innuendo and analogy, their gentlemen openly used landmarks and heritage to combat perceived foes, whether populists, working-class radicals, or immigrants who challenged America's historical order. Cunningham's influence rippled through women's society and inspired others to form such groups as the Valley Forge Association (1878), the Ladies' Hermitage Association (1889), and the APVA. As was the case, gender segregation restricted women from the more powerful, male-only, historical and patriotic societies. Most preservation work would be regarded as women's task, but men influenced its ideological content.

That was surely the case in 1889 when tradition-minded Virginians, including many of the state's most prominent families, organized the APVA. In its formative years, it acquired a range of colonial buildings, including Jamestown's seventeenth-century ruins, Williamsburg's arsenal, and an Eastern Shore debtors' prison. Like the MVLA, its ambitious work can best be understood within the context of the era's cultural politics. The Confederacy's defeat in the Civil War and the advent of Reconstruction spun Virginia topsy-turvy. "The calamity was overwhelming," said Williamsburg preservationist Lyon G. Tyler, son of the U.S. president. "As a result, the past was severed from the present, the people who survived went about in a stunned condition. After a little, they came to their consciousness, only to face a struggle for self-preservation against reconstruction and negro domination, foisted upon them by their merciless conquerors." After the traditions of social hierarchy, black subservience, and political orthodoxy were toppled, the Readjuster party won control in the late 1870s and 1880s. Backed by newer entrepreneurs, workers, and freedmen, the coalition rode "into power on ignorance and viciousness," claimed Joseph Bryan, Richmond's leading traditionalist. When the populist movement followed, the conservatives' nightmare worsened. As a result, the preservation movement formed, led by many families whose social standing, prized lineage, or property was in doubt, and it strove to preserve the Old Dominion and encourage progress.[7]

The APVA launched its drive at a Richmond public meeting in 1890. Setting the tone, Thomas Nelson Page, a popular writer who mixed history and fiction, recounted the sweet flavor of the antebellum civilization, while Bryan, seconding his remarks, regretted that the proud past had become a "shadowy tradition." One whose family lost two plantations (and more than one hundred slaves) with the war, he focused on the family home. Reminding his audience that "the birthplace of a parent is approached with a sense of reverence and awe," he said: "The long-vacated home of some great man is regarded as partaking of his spirit, and is often—but not too often—carefully preserved, that the virtue of its illustrious master may be the more forcibly perpetuated and impressed on the visitor." Writing an editorial in his *Richmond Times*, he urged his readers to lend their "most ardent support" to the APVA.[8]

Headed by his spouse, Belle—who was not only a descendant of Colonel William Byrd of Westover but also "a special pet" of General Robert E. Lee—the APVA partly acted as a women's society. In 1890, for example, it honored Mary Ball Washington, the president's mother, by acquiring her Fredericksburg home, which Chicagoans had just tried to remove to the Columbian Exposition. As the house became a shrine, the APVA remade her image; it rejected the "disparaging" picture of her as stern and hot-tempered and recast her as "a woman of strong will . . . but kind." The APVA suggested that Mary had taught her son, unlike many shameless modern men, "the principles of truth and honor from which he never swerved, and she was accustomed to say, 'George has been a good boy, and he will certainly do his duty.'"[9]

As republican motherhood had ordained, the APVA preserved many family graveyards and church buildings, leading it to acquire the ruins of Jamestown's church in 1893. As the first permanent English colony in the New World, Jamestown was, according to Virginians, the nation's birthplace, thus implying that the Old Dominion's social order took priority. The APVA fancifully prized the island as the home of Virginia's "Adam and Eve." Appreciating its natural landscape, but distressed by modernity's flux, the association's historian Mary Newton Stanard predicted that the APVA would "preserve the atmosphere of quaintness and calm to which belong so much of beauty and enchantment in contrast to the newness and restlessness of to-day."[10] The APVA's romanticization of Jamestown did not deter it, however, from either inventing a church nave to blend with the existing early-seventeenth-century tower or transforming the island into a bustling shrine for pilgrims. The APVA even invented an Old Dominion tradition, casting 13 May, the day of John Smith's landing, as Virginia Day.

The APVA's own birthplace, Williamsburg, was thoroughly depressed in the 1880s. The association's organizer, Cynthia Coleman, a descendant of the town's famous Tucker family, was so sensitive about the town's plight that she resented northern tourists who came in the wake of the Yorktown Centennial. Upon hearing that an editor from *Harper's Magazine* was coming, she snapped, "I do not like these fat, sleek Yankees to come and spy upon our poverty." Her husband noted ironically that the largest employer, a state hospital, set the town's tone, and "Williamsburg, in the minds of many, has come to mean a lunatic asylum." Tourists more easily heard the shrieks of the patients than imagined the stirring oratory of Patrick Henry. The first step in recovering the town's past would be the preservation of its Powder Horn. Joseph Bryan spurred the cause in a *Richmond Times* editorial by equating the magazine with Fort Sumter: "It was to the colonies in 1775 what Lincoln's proclamation proved to be to the Southern States of America in 1861." Built in 1715 "to suppress negro insurrection," but preserved in the Jim Crow era, it connected the past and present, and, perhaps, the future.[11]

As was the case, the APVA aided the emerging civil religion by enshrining "meccas" where Americans could pay homage to the founders. Virginians, of course, added their own twist to the American tale of patriotism. States' rights, white supremacy, and limited democracy were principal ingredients in the APVA's historical rendition.

Fig. 4.1 Church Tower, Jamestown, Virginia, 1890. Its church had been constructed perhaps in 1639, but the extant tower, which was probably constructed later in the century, came to symbolize the Anglo-Saxon founding of Virginia for traditionalists who were pressed by repeated waves of change after the Civil War. For the tercentennial in 1907, a nave was speculatively reconstructed to display various plaques. (Courtesy of the Association for the Preservation of Virginia Antiquities.)

Moreover, its caliber of preservation in the late nineteenth and early twentieth centuries was that of a revitalization movement, one through which traditionalists reconstituted a waning culture and reestablished their identity through history. That revitalization, however, entailed a discriminating adoption and adaptation of their traditions. "We cherish our *past* for the sake of our *future*," said a Jamestown preservationist, "so that while preserving the one we are building the other for ages yet to come." As a result, preservation often meant dedicating plaques and highlighting object lessons more than preserving actual buildings. At Jamestown, for example, the APVA's landscape became what F.F.V. iconoclast James Branch Cabell called "a mere mob of monuments and memorial tablets." Yet the erection of commemorative markers was typical in the nation, especially by patriotic societies.[12] In the end, then, the regeneration of traditionalism succeeded. As seen in the state constitution of 1902, political conservatives retook the reigns of government, further enabling preservationists to restore a society in which elites professed their respect for tradition and held sway over the multitude.

One who joined the APVA in 1907, but diverged significantly from its path, was William Sumner Appleton Jr., a Boston antiquary with Brahmin roots and an inheritance that enabled him to live independently. He began his preservation career in 1905, drawn to a narrow street in a neighborhood that was "the most crowded one hundred acres of land on earth." Once the bastion of colonial elite, Boston's North End was now home to diverse immigrants. Amid it all stood a decrepit wooden tenement, built about 1685 but later enlarged as the home of Paul Revere. Samuel Adams Drake, a prolific antiquarian writer, voiced his contempt. "Pure air is indeed a luxury" there, he scoffed.

> Pah! the atmosphere is actually thick with the vile odors of garlic and onions—of maccaroni and lazzoroni. The dirty tenements swarm with greasy voluble Italians. . . . One can scarce hear the sound of his own English mother-tongue from one end of the square to the other; and finally (can we believe the evidence of our own eyes?), here is good Father Taylor's old brick Bethel turned into a Catholic chapel! . . . Shade of Cotton Mather! has it come to this, that a mass-house should stand within the very pale of the thrice consecrated old Puritan sanctuary?[13]

The successful campaign to preserve Revere's home coalesced important factions of the budding preservation movement. While architects and antiquarians valued Boston's last example of seventeenth-century construction, patriotic groups such as Appleton's Sons of the Revolution rallied to create a shrine. It would become, he said, "a

Fig. 4.2 "Jamestown Day!" *Richmond Times-Dispatch* (1927) cartoon by Fred O. Seibel. Despite his rough-and-tumble career before 1607, John Smith came to represent the strong leader that many Virginians desired, particularly in the late nineteenth and early twentieth centuries. (Courtesy of the Association for the Preservation of Virginia Antiquities.)

Fig. 4.3 The Paul Revere House, Boston. At the time of this photograph (c. 1900–06), the building housed a bank, storefront, and tenement for Italian immigrants. During the Revolution, the third floor housed Revere's large family. (Photograph by Henry Peabody. Courtesy of the Society for the Preservation of New England Antiquities.)

constant incentive to patriotic citizenship and the study of our national institutions."[14] Those Yankees who wanted newcomers to Americanize stressed that Revere had been a civic-minded artisan whose immigrant family lived humbly and adopted Anglo-American habits. In the restoration, however, not only was Revere's image selectively repackaged, but his house was also spectacularly reinvented as a

Fig. 4.4 The Paul Revere House, Boston. Restored by Joseph E. Chandler to its assumed appearances of the late seventeenth century, the house represents a postmedieval type, one that accorded well with traditionalists who were fascinated not only by the supposedly pure and rugged pioneers, but also the medieval spirit and culture. With a museum promoting Americanization, the building contrasted considerably with its North End neighborhood, thus implying a modern cultural decline and drift. (Photograph by Halliday Historic Photograph Co. Courtesy of the Society for the Preservation of New England Antiquities.)

postmedieval construct—something perhaps that Revere himself would not have recognized. The chief workhorse in the campaign, Appleton re-created the coalition in 1910 when he founded the Society for the Preservation of New England Antiquities.

New England's unsettling changes in population, economy, and society defined the era's cultural politics and set the context for SPNEA's campaign. By 1910, 70 percent of Boston's population was either the foreign-born or their children. Equally significant, industrialization was altering traditional patterns of individualism, class deference, and social order. The subsequent turn by the working classes to political machines, unions, and strikes was little understood by the tradition-minded groups that organized and supported the preservation movement. Massachusetts politics had dramatically changed as well. The Irish had come to power in Boston through the political skills of John "Honey Fitz" Fitzgerald and James Michael Curley, though Yankees still did control the state government and economy. Curley, for one, bitterly recalled his mother scrubbing the floors in the "castles" owned by "the feudal barons who exploited Irish labor." He derided their posh Boston neighborhood as "the most aristocratic rectangle in America." Yankee preservationists expressed nothing but dismay, as did SPNEA president Charles Knowles Bolton, who claimed that only "a democracy run mad" could have elected such "surely ridiculous rulers."[15] Yet preservationists could not ignore the fact that Yankees held only a vague consensus about cultural preservation and little agreement about the importance of historic buildings.

Since the days of the MVLA, preservationists were sailing in the currents of the Colonial Revival, a movement that encouraged both the conservation and emulation of historic forms. Accommodating progress, its advocates harked back to older cultural models—art, architecture, and decorative materials—to kindle respect for traditions, some of which were being remade for modernity. Like Goodwin, they believed this spirit would "stir the memory and fire the imagination." Appleton followed suit. Son of a noted antiquary, he had studied art and architecture at Harvard under Charles Eliot Norton and Denman Ross, both of whom would lead Boston's Arts and Crafts movement. Perceiving a decline in both aesthetics and ethics, Norton, America's foremost cultural critic, stressed the importance of protecting ancestral lines and historical continuity in society. Believing that buildings linked past, present, and future, he wrote:

> To maintain in full vigor the sense of the dependence of the individual life upon the past, more is needed than a mere intellectual recognition of the fact. Such is the frailty of our nature that our principles require to be supported by sentiment, and our sentiments draw nourishment from material things, from visible memorials, from familiar objects to which affection may cling.[16]

The demolition of family homes, Norton thought, created a disoriented people. Yet their identity could be rediscovered, Appleton learned, through the preservation of ancient buildings and materials.

Appleton opened SPNEA's roster to the public, but its leadership overwhelmingly derived from the ranks of the Social Register and particularly the professions. An advocate of private initiative, he soon regarded the APVA as amateurish, but also warned that if government took charge of preservation, it would become "the foot ball of politics," which in Boston meant Irish politics.[17] Appleton led SPNEA until his death in 1947, while it acquired almost fifty buildings, ones that not only illustrated the art of building and the social standards of their eras, but also symbolized the ancestral lines, inherited values, and, when contrasted with modern construction, cultural drift of New England.

Reflecting his cultural politics, Appleton was most impressed by the medieval flavor, rugged simplicity, and Anglo-Saxon character of seventeenth-century buildings. Knowing that they were being fast destroyed or remodeled, he gave them his highest priority. His consulting architect J. Frederick Kelly, for example, suggested that framed buildings, which were constructed without "affectation or sham," revealed not only the practicality of the settlers but also "the unmistakably pure and virile" roots from which later Yankees developed. Appleton and Kelly claimed, meanwhile, that modern buildings were thoroughly inferior with their artificial decoration and shoddy construction. If buildings symbolized an era, modernity appeared "pathetically, not to say ludicrously frail."[18]

SPNEA's buildings were said to characterize such old-time values as a respect for law, civic pride, and honest work. For example, the "Scotch"-Boardman House, a postmedieval dwelling in Saugus, Massachusetts, represented the proper immigrant, said Appleton. Implicitly questioning the worthiness of modern immigrants, he noted that the Scots, as indentured servants, had been "a worthy and cleanly lot" and "carefully selected" as workers. Typifying the proper Americanization, they had adopted the new culture and showed their patriotism in the Revolution. Interestingly, however, Appleton had taken an undocumented (and inaccurate) legend that the house was built for those Scots, publicized it in an (unsuccessful) appeal to Carnegie, and thus invented a piece of history.[19]

Yet the acquisition of such simple dwellings disappointed some SPNEA supporters, including historian Samuel Eliot Morison, who was more interested in Georgian artistry and his own forebears. Contributing generously, he proposed the purchase of the first Harrison Gray Otis House in Boston as the society's headquarters. With Curley sitting in the mayor's office, the newspapers interviewed Morison, who helped remake Otis's image and repeated his approving comment that Otis had "hated democracy . . . and believed that the country should be governed by men of education and wealth." SPNEA acted, however, only after the handsome Bulfinch-designed house was "threatened" by a "Jewish corporation" that wanted to use it "as a home for aged women." Such genteel anti-Semitism was common, and Appleton voiced it in his fund-raising appeal.[20] Anti-Semitism played a conspicuous role, moreover, in the 1923 acquisition of Monticello, the Charlottesville home of Thomas Jefferson, by a memorial foundation. In the prior decade, the popular press labeled its owner, Congressman

Fig. 4.5 William Summer Appleton Jr. (1874–1947) at Manchester, Massachusetts, c. 1920. Of all the individuals in the history of American historic preservation, none perhaps has matched Appleton's legacy. More than half a century after his death, his brand of preservation is, by and large, the American standard. (Courtesy of the Society for the Preservation of New England Antiquities.)

Fig. 4.6 The Harrison Gary Otis House, Boston, c. 1916. The first of three houses that Boston's Federalist leader built, this structure was designed by Charles Bulfinch and built in 1796. Its neighbor, West End Church, designed by Asher Benjamin in 1806, later became a library for diligent immigrants. The two were left standing, but some fifty acres of the old West End were demolished 1958–60 in what was perversely called urban renewal. (Photograph by Frank Cousins Art Co. Courtesy of the Society for the Preservation of New England Antiquities.)

Jefferson M. Levy, an "alien" and a "foreigner" because of his religion, and alleged (incorrectly) that he neglected the mansion.[21]

All the while, Appleton set a professional methodology for preservation. As a result, preservationist William Murtagh later credited SPNEA with "almost single-handedly" reorienting the field from a preoccupation with romanticized history to one stressing architectural aesthetics, scientific method, and historical scholarship. According to Murtagh, Appleton's organization developed "the philosophical dictates which still guide the conscientious professional today." That said, Appleton's methodology departed significantly from that of either William Morris or Eugène Emmanuel Viollet-le-Duc in Europe.[22] Through a trial-and-error approach, Appleton established the primary trend in America—an acceptance of restoration guided by scientific method. Focusing on the nitty-gritties of archaeology and construc-

Fig. 4.7 The Harrison Gary Otis House, Boston, 1925. When Cambridge Street was widened by order of Mayor James Michael Curley, who disdained old Yankee culture, the house was moved forty feet to its rear in 1924. In the house's restoration, SPNEA chose to illustrate the aesthetics of Bulfinch, which represented proper, refined tastes. (Courtesy of the Society for the Preservation of New England Antiquities.)

tion, Appleton also helped masculinize the field for years to come. Although women maintained a strong foothold in smaller societies with a local or feminine agenda, major preservation organizations increasingly advocated a "professional" approach developed by not only SPNEA but also the National Park Service (1916) and Williamsburg Restoration, Inc. (1926, aka Colonial Williamsburg Foundation).[23]

The formation of Colonial Williamsburg was a milestone in the preservation movement. Quickly outpacing SPNEA and displacing the APVA, it stressed architectural aesthetics, scientific method, and corporate organization. The Rockefeller family, whose largesse there reached almost one hundred million dollars, created an aura that even Henry Ford could not match at Greenfield Village. As its Boston-based architects implemented cutoff dates for the town's remaking, Colonial Williamsburg would demolish or move more than 700 buildings from the district, reconstruct some 350, and restore 88, many of the latter being small outbuildings. Within such a dramatic (but invented) back-drop, traditionalists told the story, as Rockefeller put it, of the "patriotism, high purpose, and unselfish devotion of our forefathers to the common good." Yet that story was selectively told, ignoring class and racial problems and creating more of a mythology than a history. Even its motto, "That the future may learn from the past," leaves one wondering, Whose past? Still, what Cabell called "that bric-a-brac but instructive subsidiary of the Standard Oil Company of New Jersey" drew 31,000 visitors in 1934, more than 90,000 by 1936, and almost 1.3 million paid admissions in 1976. Though Frank Lloyd Wright and Lewis Mumford lamented the power of the colonial cult, preservationists praised the undertaking. Appleton did dissent from its emphasis on reconstruction, however—but did so privately, because he hoped also to win Rockefeller's favor.[24]

Williamsburg's reconstruction, euphemistically called a restoration, accelerated the development of both period rooms and living history museums, both of which jeopardized in situ preservation. One of Appleton's colleagues, George Francis Dow, actually introduced both at

Fig. 4.8 The Powder Horn, Williamsburg, Virginia. Built about 1715, the magazine had evolved from an ancestral storehouse whose weapons were used to suppress slave insurrections, resist British masters, or buttress Confederate rebels, to a changing symbol. Whereas in the late nineteenth century, the Powder Horn was used to rally anti-Yankee traditionalists, it is now a more generic symbol of the Revolution. The hospital (at right) was built after the cutoff date of the Rockefeller-funded "restoration," and it was demolished by Colonial Williamsburg. (Courtesy of the Colonial Williamsburg Foundation.)

the Essex Institute in Salem, first in 1907 with "authentic" period interiors and then in 1912 with the John Ward House's furnished rooms, costumed hostesses, and idealized garden. Dow's work impressed many, including Henry Watson Kent, who would establish the American Wing at the Metropolitan Museum in 1926. As curators and preservationists competed with the likes of D. W. Griffith to make their forebears more alive, they turned to "living history," which originated at the Swedish folk museum Skansen (1891). Some New Englanders wanted their own Skansen to educate the public about the ills of industrialism and commercialism, but the first living history museum in the region opened in 1928. Depicting the Puritan settlers who arrived in Salem in 1628, Dow wanted his Pioneer Village (aka Colonial Village) to "show the roots of customs buried in the past" and how they were expressed in the crafts and community. Its shops were "filled with life" as busy, happy artisans worked in the vein of the Protestant ethic. He expected his staging to so contrast with "the monotony of an ordered museum" that it would "foster the best kind of national feeling." He admitted that he held no "purely sentimental aim" but strove "to increase the knowledge and love of one's native land." Presented during the Massachusetts tercentennial, Dow's imagination often got the better of him, however, as his reconstruction was conjectural and his depiction idealized. Initially a temporary attraction, the village became a permanent means to Americanize Salem's immigrant children, who ironically saw Yankees pay homage to folk traditions they themselves were sacrificing in the name of progress.[25]

Williamsburg more directly influenced Mystic Seaport in Connecticut. Begun as a small museum in 1929 by Carl Cutler, it expanded significantly with the 1941 acquisition of the century-old *Charles W. Morgan,* the nation's last wooden square-rigged whaler, and subsequent plans to re-create a seaport community that, according to the *New York Herald Tribune,* would be "a monument to the whaling era quite comparable, in its smaller way, to the Williamsburg restoration in Virginia." Cutler, a disillusioned Wall Street businessman who became a maritime historian, wanted his museum to rekindle the spirit of an old-time Yankee community, one that derived from puritanism, small towns, and the sea. The ideals of individual character, honest work, and personal responsibility had once been holy, he claimed, but they were being destroyed by big factories, cities, and money. While "Broadway Dudes" of the 1920s imitated "the fops and voluptuaries . . . of decadent Rome's ruling class," many other Americans were becoming no better than "human jellyfish." They simply could not understand his heroes, the stouthearted seafarers of the mid–nineteenth century. "Today's standards are [so] changed and shrunken," he said,

Fig. 4.9 Pioneer Village, Salem, Massachusetts, 1930. Conceived by George Francis Dow and built for the Massachusetts tercentenary, the invented village reflected Dow's belief that the first colonists has been strong, orderly, and productive. His colleague Appleton hoped to build his own Skansen, but his commitment to in situ preservation stood in the way. (The Yankee Publishing Collection. Courtesy of the Society for the Preservation of New England Antiquities.)

that "their deeds assume gargantuan proportions that baffle comparison."[26] He wanted his re-created seaport to give visitors the illusion of being transported back into the nineteenth century. Booming with the onset of the Cold War, Mystic Seaport expanded to twenty-two acres of re-created town and wharf by the early 1950s. In 1947, Congress had even given it the square-rigger *Joseph Conrad,* which the museum would use to "indoctrinate thousands of youngsters . . . with an inspirational vision of America's past."[27] Similarly, other open-air museums in New England, such as Plimoth Plantation, Sturbridge Village, and the Shelburne Museum, invented a lost community so as to re-create the spirit of a distant time.

During the 1930s, historic preservation was spurred by the entry of the U.S. government, primarily through the Historic American Buildings Survey and its sponsor, the National Park Service. Leicester B. Holland, who helped organize HABS in 1933, was most influenced by SPNEA.

Fig. 4.10 The *Joseph Conrad,* Mystic, Connecticut. The second windjammer acquired by Mystic Seaport, the *Conrad* had been launched in 1882 as the *Georg Stage,* a Danish training ship for young sailors. Purchased in 1934 by Alan Villiers, who sailed her around the world, she served the United States training mariners during World War II. Then and now, the *Conrad* has been used to teach youth the stalwart maritime tradition. (Photograph by Kenneth C. Barnes, c. 1950. Courtesy of the Society for the Preservation of New England Antiquities.)

Orienting the federal program to its professional standards, he regarded America's landmarks as symbols of the values necessary to rebuild the nation during the depression. Those buildings expressed, he said, "the sturdiness and the heroic spirit of the hardy early pioneers who had such great confidence in themselves and in the land which they loved, toiled for and peopled, and in which they laid the enduring foundations of the greater America of today."[28] At the same time, the federal government increasingly (but slowly) applied the Antiquities Act (1906) to the historic sites in the East. For example, Congress passed legislation in 1930 to create Colonial National Monument (with Jamestown and Yorktown). At the same time, the NPS picked up a cash-starved project to rebuild Wakefield, the birthplace of George Washington. Totally speculative in its architectural details, Wakefield became a patriotic memorial during the bicentennial of Washington's birth in 1932. Cabell humorously called it the "supreme gem" in Virginia's "bright treasury of paste jewels."[29]

Yet in Richmond, as many authentic landmarks fell to the wreckers in the late 1920s, Mary Wingfield Scott introduced a new spirit. After earning her Ph.D. in architectural history at the University of Chicago, where she became familiar with Jane Addams's Arts and Crafts museum at Hull House, she formed her own APVA chapter in 1935. Her activism was unique. Campaigning to preserve the Adam Craig House in the industrial Shockoe Valley, which was home to poor African Americans and recent Eastern European immigrants, she educated blacks about preservation and established a Negro Art Center at the Craig house. Grappling with the social realities of preservation, she said that saving the historic landscape was anything but "a stuffy museum job unrelated to the bitter world we live in." She urged preservationists to orient their work to human needs and "realize the close connection between mankind's dwellings of yesterday and his life today."[30] Too few city planners or preservationists were willing to do that, however, as the ominous clouds of urban renewal darkened overhead.

In the century after Mount Vernon's preservation, therefore, the preservation movement is best understood by examining the changing cultural politics of the time. With a perspective shaped by their social standing, property, and traditions, preservationists reacted to the unsettling changes by protecting buildings, artifacts, and sites that symbolized a respected, but often imagined, past. As was the case, the past had a purpose, one that generally reflected the political conservatism, social boundaries, and proper tastes of preservationists. As a result, their "past" did not generally include people of color, everyday women, and ordinary folk, unless they were acceptably cast in a traditionalist mold. While the practical methods that preservationists chose to implement their agenda did change gradually from that of amateur to professional, the belief that the past should "fire the imagination" of the living changed little.

Yet there were inklings of change. Some preservationists, like Appleton, were gradually motivated by as much scholarly curiosity as traditionalism. His budding interest in the construction of framed buildings and their archaeological investigation contributed significantly to the study of vernacular architecture. Others, like Scott, whose personalism was tied to social reform, keenly realized that preservation helped enliven modern communities. Moreover, much of the historical fabric that was preserved before 1950 is a resource ripe for reinterpretation. As in the case of the Sargent-Murray-Gilman House in Gloucester, Massachusetts, what was once appreciated for its finely carved woodwork and as the home of an important Universalist minister is now primarily presented as the home of Judith Sargent Murray, an early women's rights advocate.

In the last half of the twentieth century, preservationists in Virginia and New England showed more varied interests. Cultural politics still plays a hand. With the "new social history" and the civil rights struggles of the 1960s and after, some preservation work is geared toward defining the past more inclusively. For example, Strawbery Banke in Portsmouth, New Hampshire, opened to the public in 1965 as a traditional, Williamsburg-style enterprise. Established when the ten-acre "slum" was threatened by urban renewal in 1958, it did allow the demolition of Victorian buildings, but it has recently tried to present the gamut of Portsmouth's history. The Drisco House interprets the home of an Italian American shipyard worker in 1954, while Abbott's Little Corner Store shows a mom-and-pop grocery that served ordinary people during World War II. More remarkably, the Shapiro House uniquely exhibits the lives of Jewish immigrants in 1919; the museum hopes it "will serve as a catalyst for frank discussions of immigration, tolerance and cultural differences." Along those same lines, Mystic Seaport has reconstructed the slave ship *Amistad,* while Plimoth Plantation interprets a Native American homesite.[31] As a result, interpreting these historic sites is akin to the work of dendrochronology; while a tree's old rings tell of earlier eras, its structure is wrapped in the new.

NOTES

1. William A. R. Goodwin, *Bruton Parish Church Restored and Its Historic Environment* (Petersburg, VA: Franklin Press, 1907), 33; Goodwin, *Historical Sketch of Bruton Church, Williamsburg, Virginia* (Petersburg, VA: Franklin Press, 1903), 9, 166.
2. Charles B. Hosmer Jr., *Presence of the Past: A History of the Preservation Movement in the United States Before Williamsburg* (New York: G. P. Putnam's Sons, 1965), and *Preservation Comes of Age: From Williamsburg to the National Trust* (Charlottesville: University Press of Virginia, 1981). Hosmer's works are required reading, not for their interpretive emphasis on an emerging professionalism, which itself requires more significant analysis, but for their wealth of factual information. Finishing his Ph.D. dissertation at Columbia University in 1961, Hosmer's perspective was not only limited by the prevailing historiography of his day, but also shaped admittedly by his own New England, WASP background (Hosmer to author, 30 July 1984, in author's possession). No subsequent historian, however, has tried to match his chronicle of the "who, what, when, and where" of the mainstream preservation movement. For more analytical accounts, see Michael Kammen, *Mystic Chords of Memory: The Transformation of Tradition in American Culture* (New York: Alfred A. Knopf, 1991); Mike Wallace, *Mickey Mouse History and Other Essays on American Memory* (Philadelphia: Temple University Press, 1996).
3. For a brief overview, see James M. Lindgren, "Historic Preservation," in Paul Boyer, ed., *The Oxford Companion to United States History* (New York: Oxford University Press, 2001), 340–1.
4. Quoted in James M. Lindgren, *Preserving the Old Dominion: Historic Preservation and Virginia Traditionalism* (Charlottesville and London: University Press of Virginia, 1993), 43. See also Patricia West, *Domesticating History: The Political Origins of America's House Museums* (Washington: Smithsonian Institution Press, 1999), 1–37.

The saga of Mount Vernon even shaped the earlier preservation of the site where the nation had been born in 1776 and its laws codified in 1787 (Charlene Mires, *Independence Hall in American Memory* [Philadelphia: University of Pennsylvania Press, 2002).

5. For personalism, see James M. Lindgren, " 'A New Departure in Historic, Patriotic Work.' Personalism, Professionalism, and Conflicting Concepts of Material Culture in the Late Nineteenth and Early Twentieth Centuries," *The Public Historian* 18 (Spring 1996), 41–60.
6. Cunningham quoted in Lindgren, *Preserving the Old Dominion*, 44.
7. Lyon G. Tyler, *Virginia Principles* (Richmond, VA: Richmond Press, 1928), 1; Bryan quoted in James M. Lindgren, " 'First and Foremost a Virginian': Joseph Bryan and the New South Economy," *Virginia Magazine of History and Biography* 96 (April 1988), 161.
8. Bryan quoted in "Talk about Old Things," *Richmond Times*, 19 January 1890; [Joseph Bryan], "The Old Powder Horn," *Richmond Times*, 19 January 1890.
9. W. Gordon McCabe, "Proceedings," *Virginia Magazine of History and Biography* 19 (1911), xix; Lora Ellyson quoted in *Preserving the Old Dominion*, 208.
10. Mary Newton Stanard, *Richmond: Its People and Its Story* (Philadelphia: J. B. Lippincott, 1923), 3; Mary M. P. Newton, "The Association for the Preservation of Virginia Antiquities," *American Historical Register*, September 1894, 10, 19.
11. Coleman quoted in " 'For the Sake of Our Future': The Association for the Preservation of Virginia Antiquities and the Regeneration of Traditionalism," *Virginia Magazine of History and Biography* 97 (January 1989), 54; Charles Washington Coleman quoted in *Preserving the Old Dominion*, 193; [Bryan], "The Old Powder-Horn."
12. Quoted in James M. Lindgren, " 'Virginia Needs Living Heroes': Historic Preservation in the Progressive Era," *Public Historian* 13 (Winter 1991), 9–10; James Branch Cabell, *Let Me Lie: Being in the Main an Ethnological Account of the Remarkable Commonwealth of Virginia and the Making of Its History* (New York: Farrar, Straus, 1947), 46, 51; Kirk Savage, *Standing Soldiers, Kneeling Slaves: Race, War, and Monument in Nineteenth-Century America* (Princeton, NJ: Princeton University Press, 1997).
13. William M. DeMarco, *Ethnics and Enclaves: Boston's Italian North End* (Ann Arbor, MI: UMI Research Press, 1981), xiv, 2; Samuel Adams Drake, *Our Colonial Homes* (Boston: Lee and Shepard, 1893), 19. Edward Thompson Taylor of the Seamen's Bethel Church inspired Melville's depiction of Father Mapple in *Moby-Dick*. Emerson ranked him with Demosthenes and Shakespeare.
14. Appleton quoted in James M. Lindgren, *Preserving Historic New England: Preservation, Progressivism and the Remaking of Memory* (New York and Oxford: Oxford University Press, 1995), 3.
15. James Michael Curley, *I'd Do It Again: A Record of All My Uproarious Years* (Englewood Cliffs, NJ: Prentice Hall, 1957), 3, 11, 30–2; Bolton quoted in *Preserving Historic New England*, 34.
16. Charles Eliot Norton, "The Lack of Old Homes in America," *Scribner's Magazine* 5 (May 1889), 638, 640. Norton's romantic notion of the Yankee's earlier respect for the family home is qualified by a later SPNEA director; see Abbott Lowell Cummings, *The Framed Houses of Massachusetts Bay, 1625–1725* (Cambridge, MA, and London: Harvard University Press, 1979), 204. For Americanization, see William B. Rhoads, "The Colonial Revival and the Americanization of Immigrants," in Alan Axelrod, ed., *The Colonial Revival in America* (New York and London: W. W. Norton, 1985), 341–61.
17. Appleton quoted in James M. Lindgren, " 'A Constant Incentive to Patriotic Citizenship': Historic Preservation in Progressive-Era Massachusetts," *New England Quarterly* 64 (December 1991), 599.
18. Kelly quoted in *Preserving Historic New England*, 89, 119.

19. Appleton quoted in *Preserving Historic New England,* 82–3.

20. Quoted in *Preserving Historic New England,* 86–7.

21. See West, *Domesticating History,* 93–127; Melvin I. Urofsky, *The Levy Family and Monticello, 1834–1923: Saving Thomas Jefferson's House* (Charlottesville, VA: Thomas Jefferson Foundation, 2001); and particularly my review of the latter in *Virginia Magazine of History and Biography* 109:3 (2001), 343–4.

22. William J. Murtagh, *Keeping Time: The History and Theory of Preservation in America* (Pittstown, NJ: Main Street Press, 1988), 34, 80–2. For favorable assessments of Appleton, see also Jane Brown Gillette, "Appleton's Legacy," *Historic Preservation* 46 (July–August 1994), 34. For Morris, see " 'The Survival of Truly Mediaeval Mannerisms in Construction and Detail': Cultural Politics and New England Antiquities in the Early Twentieth Century," in Chris Miele, ed., *From William Morris: Building Conservation and the Arts and Crafts Cult of Authenticity, 1877–1939,* Studies in British Art: Vol. 10 (forthcoming: New Haven, CT, and London: Yale University Press for the Paul Mellon Centre, 2004).

23. See Lindgren, " 'A New Departure,' " 41–60.

24. Rockefeller quoted in C. Van West and Mary Hoffschwelle, " 'Slumbering on Its Old Foundations': Interpretation at Colonial Williamsburg," *South Atlantic Quarterly* 83 (Spring 1984), 161; Cabell quoted in *Preserving the Old Dominion,* 232. Within the past decade, many dissertations have been written on Williamsburg's restoration, but only one has been published as a monograph; see Anders Greenspan, *Creating Colonial Williamsburg* (Washington, D.C.: Smithsonian Institution Press, 2002). For an anthropologist's perspective, see Richard Handler and Eric Gable, *The New History in an Old Museum: Creating a Past at Colonial Williamsburg* (Durham, NC: Duke University Press, 1997).

25. George F. Dow, "Notes and Gleanings," *Old-Time New England* 21 (October 1930), 93; Dow, *Domestic Life in New England in the Seventeenth Century* (Topsfield, MA: Perkins Press, 1925), i, 22–3.

26. "The Morgan Comes to Mystic," *New York Herald Tribune,* 3 October 1941; Carl C. Cutler, *Queens of the Western Ocean: The Story of America's Mail and Passenger Sailing Lines* (Annapolis, MD: U.S. Naval Institute Press, 1961), 357; Cutler, *Greyhounds of the Sea: The Story of the American Clipper Ship* (New York: G. P. Putnam's Sons, 1930), xii–xiii. See also Lindgren, " 'Stout Hearts Make a Safe Ship': Individual and Community at Mystic Seaport, 1929–1959," in *Preserving Maritime America: Marine Museums and Cultural Politics in the United States* (forthcoming).

27. "Old Ships Find Haven in Maritime Museum," *Christian Science Monitor,* 13 August 1951; "Joseph Conrad, Famed Square-Rigger, to See Service Again," *New York Herald Tribune,* 27 July 1947; *The Log of Mystic Seaport* 3 (March 1949), quoted in "*The Log of Mystic Seaport* Turns Fifty," *The Log of Mystic Seaport* 50 (Autumn 1998), 38.

28. Holland quoted in Lindgren, *Preserving Historic New England,* 151; Hal Rothman, *Preserving Different Pasts: The American National Monuments* (Urbana: University of Illinois Press, 1989).

29. Cabell quoted in Lindgren, *Preserving the Old Dominion,* 189.

30. Quoted in Mary Wingfield Scott, "A.P.V.A. Tries to Save Old Richmond," *Journal of the American Society of Architectural Historians* 3 (1943), 31; see also Lindgren, *Preserving the Old Dominion,* 237.

31. Quoted in Lindgren, "Historic Sites and Preservation Movements," an essay in Burt Feintuch and David H. Watters, eds., *The Encyclopedia of New England Culture* (forthcoming; New Haven, CT: Yale University Press, 2003).

5

HISTORIC PRESERVATION, PUBLIC MEMORY, AND THE MAKING OF MODERN NEW YORK CITY

Randall Mason

Within the limits of our own city, in the dramas of the past, have been enacted tragedies that are inspirations to lofty undertakings, the memories of which are fast fading from mind and of which no visible memorials have yet been established. Such landmarks are too rapidly yielding to the obliteration of time, and to preserve them is a sacred duty, akin to that of teaching the children of our public schools or maintaining libraries for the education of our people.

Andrew Haswell Green, the "Father of Greater New York," 1901[1]

This chapter debunks two myths about the origins of historic preservation in New York City, and places preservationists' efforts to construct a usable past in the context of early twentieth-century urban modernization and reform. The first myth is that New York City preservation began in 1963, after the destruction of Pennsylvania Station. Contrary to this popular and heroic protest story, there was a thriving preservation field in New York City by the turn of the twentieth century. The creation of the Landmarks Preservation Commission in 1965 was an important, but not the original, chapter in the preservation history of New York City.

The second myth holds that preservation emerged in the nineteenth century as the marginal gesture of a dying elite, and has stayed that way.[2] On the contrary, by the 1900s preservation was thoroughly embedded in broader economic, cultural, environmental, and other social processes driving urbanization.[3] Preservation was among the several types of social-environmental reform that took hold under the rubric of the Progressive movement around the turn of the twentieth century. These reform movements fundamentally changed the trajectory

Fig. 5.1 This 1911 panoramic view of City Hall Park encapsulates the role of this place as both anchorage for the civic past and center of the modern metropolis. The image centers on City Hall itself, looking from the west. The Municipal Building, to the far right, is still under construction; the transit station at the foot of the Brooklyn Bridge stands before it. The southern tip of the park remains occupied with the post office (the Second Empire–style building on the far left); in the few years after this picture was taken, the Woolworth Building would rise—on Broadway, just behind the post office—to be the world's tallest building. (Courtesy of Library of Congress.)

of the urban development, in the same remarkable historical and geographical moment when New York City was becoming truly modern and metropolitan following the 1898 consolidation of the five boroughs. Like the myriad other reform movements, focused on housing, transit, public health, sanitation, playgrounds, settlement houses, and more, historic preservation was *part of* the modernization of New York, not simply a reaction against it.

Early twentieth-century preservation is easy to dismiss if measured against today's field. To be sure, preservation at its roots was patriarchal, genteel, and didactic. The 1960s and 1970s notion of preservation as a means of democratic, grassroots social change had barely begun to gel. And preservation was *not* institutionalized as a public-sector responsibility in the same way city planning or other reform movements were (or as preservation was to become after the 1960s). But early preservation in New York *does* merit close attention, because it began as a project of mainstream city builders and leading reformers, marshaling both private and public resources to imprint civic memory in the transforming urban landscape—it was not merely a hobby of the blue-blood ladies and stuffy antiquarians. Many of the leaders of New York's modernization—prominent public and civic leaders such as Andrew Haswell Green, George McAneny, Robert De-Forest, and a host of prominent architects and politicians—*also* were the leading lights of the burgeoning preservation field.[4]

This chapter characterizes the early-twentieth-century preservation field in New York City, and explores its goals, strategies, successes, and failures. After describing who the early New York preservationists were, and what they sought to preserve and remember, questions of *why* and *how* preservation was practiced are addressed. The preservation stories of a few particular buildings and sites are then recounted in some detail, illustrating a spectrum of situations in which preservation was manifest as one current in the broader stream of early-twentieth-century modernization in New York.

AN EMERGENT HISTORIC PRESERVATION FIELD

Civic patriotism . . . is an all important factor.[5]

George Kriehn

A great deal of preservation activity went on in New York City between the 1890s and 1920s. The name of preservationists' umbrella group—the American Scenic and Historic Preservation Society (ASHPS)—signified the marriage of "historic" and "scenic" values to be protected. A correspondingly broad range of objects and places were the objects of preservation. Efforts focused on individual buildings, historic sites, statues, and plaques, as well as parks, battlefields, and open spaces. Typical preservation projects included historic houses associated with "great white men," the American Revolution, or simply the city's oldest structures and finest remaining architecture. Examples included Fraunces Tavern, Morris-Jumel Mansion, Hamilton Grange, City Hall, Billopp House, and Dyckman House.[6] Just as notable, however, were efforts to create new memorials and preserve actively used park landscapes, such as Central Park, the Battery, and City Hall Park. These green spaces were seen as historical landscapes, commemorated as civic achievements in themselves, and of course were also actively used for such nonpreservation land uses as transportation facilities and recreation.

The sum of the era's preservation efforts was a scattered but substantial collection of "historic and scenic places" protected and held up as totems of civic memory—a "memory infrastructure." Many of these buildings and sites, in fact, remain today. What the early preservation field did *not* achieve was the kinds of public policy framework (laws, best-practices guidelines, financial incentives) and broad public support that are the measures of success today. But the preservationists of the early twentieth century did sustain a level of activity and a body of built or preserved projects constituting a substantial impact on the city's metropolitan landscape.

The preservation field of the 1890s through the 1920s was not as coherent or formalized as what we know today. Preservation efforts

Fig. 5.2 The Morris-Jumel Mansion, also known as "Washington's Headquarters," dates to the 1760s and is located in Upper Manhattan overlooking the Harlem River. It was highly valued by early-twentieth-century preservationists both for its association with Washington and as "an interesting specimen of Colonial architecture." It was preserved and opened as a house museum by patriotic groups led by the DAR; the city of New York aided in the preservation by acquiring the park and building in 1903. (Courtesy of Library of Congress.)

were ad hoc, for the most part. And like today, successes were as common as failures. However, a variety of individuals, organizations, and public agencies were involved in general historic preservation advocacy and dozens of projects during this time. Groups were organized specifically to pursue preservation as a public good, and individuals of great influence devoted themselves to preservation. A remarkable range of institutions were engaged in various kinds of preservation work, including nonprofit or charitable organizations (primarily the ASHPS), hereditary groups (Daughters of the American Revolution, Sons of the Revolution), government agencies (the Parks Departments of the city's boroughs, the Art Commission), professional associations (the Fine Arts Federation, the Architectural League of New York), and individual citizens.

The ASHPS was the clearest harbinger and vehicle of the early preservation field in New York. It was an umbrella and gathering point for the informal network of preservation advocates who comprised the preservation field. The Society—"A National Society for the Protection of Natural Scenery, the Preservation of Landmarks and the Improvement of Cities"—projected a holistic vision of a landscape in which towns and cities were enriched by the presence and preservation of historic landmarks and natural places. Its mission statement articulated what would be achieved by creating memory infrastructure:

> The activities of most historical societies deal with events of the past. But the American Scenic and Historic Preservation Society was organized to deal with the past, the present, and the future. The work of the Society is designed to minister to both the physical and spiritual well-being of the people. Parks and playgrounds and good civic conditions tend to promote the health and happiness of the community. The cherishing of our historical landmarks and the perpetuation of our patriotic traditions tend to make better citizens of our people and to stabilize our cherished political institutions.[7]

Andrew Haswell Green was the founder and leading light of the ASHPS until his untimely death in 1903.[8] The inspiration for the Society came from Green and kindred "disinterested" professionals and reformers; in line with Progressive ideology, the Society was also a creature of the state. ASHPS was chartered by the State legislature in 1895 and headquartered in New York City (downtown, in the Tribune Building). In an 1895 "Memorial to the Legislature," Green proposed creating an organization specializing in historic preservation and natural ("scenic") conservation issues, using private initiative backed by state sponsorship to transcend political interests and protect historical memory and historical landscapes.[9] The Society's mandate included powers to acquire and hold property; receive donations; hold and administer lands given it by New York State; act in concert with other states (for example, in organizing the Palisades Interstate Commission with New Jersey); and report bills and other recommendations directly to the legislature.

A number of trustees and members played active roles in the Society's various projects after Green's death, and the day-to-day work of maintaining the Society as an umbrella for these many projects fell to the full-time Secretary, Edward Hagaman Hall.[10]

From the outset, ASHPS integrated historic preservation and "scenic preservation." Preservation was about more than buildings; parks and open spaces were equally important to ASHPS. And its interests were pegged also to a range of scales: buildings, urban parks, individual sites and monuments and artworks, whole battlefields and natural areas. Implicitly, the ASHPS adopted a very holistic idea of the objects of preservation—what today would be called a "cultural landscape" perspective, especially in the combination of natural and cultural resources.

In its first thirty years, the Society pursued three kinds of work: First was administering places of scenic or historical interest as a public trustee. The Society acted as steward of five state-owned properties (battlefields and scenic parks) and successfully managed and fundraised for them.[11] Second, it promoted the beautification and improvement of cities—largely focused on New York—by various means (including preservation of historic buildings, erection of memorials, creation of parks, and the "landscape adornment" of open spaces and thoroughfares). This promotion was done in the general statement of principle, and also in support of particular projects. Third, it proselytized and educated decision makers and the public about the need for preservation to shape public memory and cultivated public support toward this end. This was accomplished by publishing campaigns, fund-raising, and lobbying public officials. (The Society also mounted public relations campaigns with the help of newspapers such as the *Times* and the *Evening Post*.[12]) ASHPS kept vigil over dozens of projects, spanning the country and the world but focused on New York State, and presented the results in voluminous annual reports to the Legislature.[13]

The Society envisioned itself as a "Bureau of Information" for the burgeoning preservation field. Members were encouraged to use the Society and its office, so that "efforts for local projects of a public nature find their effectiveness still further increased by their association with an influential body of advisers and colaborers [sic]."[14]

The publications of the ASHPS are the best expressions of preservation ideology as a sustained strategy for shaping public memory and public space. (This contrasts with the isolated projects that heretofore had characterized preservation.) The Society's self-conscious archive—extensive Annual Reports, pamphlets, and board minutes—presents a wealth of information on the early preservation field.

ASHPS played a role in the most prominent preservation debates transpiring in this period of the city's history, including St. John's Chapel, City Hall Park, the Morris-Jumel Mansion, and Central Park. Its role was often one of advocacy. In some cases, though, the Society sought to play a material role—for instance, in its decades of work to purchase and steward Hamilton Grange.[15] It sought to create actual sites of public memory, not by seeking the regulatory structures that characterize preservation today (and which were being pioneered by city planners in the 1910s) but by purchase and donation. "The idea, of course, is to get possession of the titles of things that are in danger."[16]

ASHPS was an agent for "civic patriotism," which built on the American, Founding Father, and Revolutionary War narratives, and layered narratives about colonists, the development of the city, the sanctification of natural scenery and parklands, and other place-specific associations.[17] The Society envisioned preservation doing more than saving the houses of the Founding Fathers, and lacked hereditary groups' singular ideological bias toward national patriotic and filiopietistic narratives as well as their hereditary requirements for membership. Their aim was broader vis-à-vis historical narratives, resting on the "positive environmentalism" values inherent in natural as well as historical places, and ultimately feeding the catholic goal of the "improvement of cities"—embracing an urbanistic, as opposed to simply antiquarian, approach to preservation.[18]

Officers, trustees, and active committee members represented a "new" elite of upper-middle-class professionals and artists, whose collective mission was enacting a whole range of Progressive, nonpartisan reforms.[19] Other reformer-professionals who led the Society's work included architect, housing advocate, and antiquarian Isaac N. P. Stokes; engineer, municipal reformer, and amateur archaeologist Reginald Pelham Bolton; gemologist and Tiffany executive George Frederick Kunz; sculptor Henry Kirke Bush-Brown; and artist Frederick Stymetz Lamb. They were allied with the more conservative branches of the Progressive reform movement, seeking to ameliorate the worst excesses of capitalist development and build a society of democratic culture as well as economic prosperity. For instance, the Society included housing reformers among its members—but it was the more conservative Robert DeForest, not the more radical Benjamin Marsh. Advocates for reform of poverty were absent from the Society. Other members included engineer Nelson Lewis, landscape architect Samuel Parsons, architects Arnold Brunner and Thomas Hastings, and even national experts such as Charles Mulford Robinson and Daniel Burnham. The membership overlapped substantially with the Municipal Art Society, Fine Arts Federation, National Arts Club, and other visual arts and reform societies.[20]

The Society had the tacit (and sometimes material) support of the city's financial elite, too. The most prominent was J. Pierpont Morgan (Sr. and Jr., who was longtime honorary president and, with partner George F. Baker, bought and donated Hamilton Grange to ASHPS in 1924); another prominent figure was Samuel P. Avery, art collector, philanthropist, and donor of Columbia's Avery Library. The board actively invited prominent people to become members, including John Rockefeller and Mrs. Russell Sage.

Women were allowed, but marginalized, in the ASHPS membership. A few women were subscribing members of the Society, but the active work was almost exclusively done by men. In 1900, ASHPS spun off a "sister" organization, the Women's Auxiliary—a "separate organization" in membership and management—as a vehicle for the interest of some New York women in preservation, to complement the DAR's preservation projects. For instance, the Auxiliary continued the work started by the Fraunces Tavern committee of the Mary Washington Chapter of the DAR. It raised money, and created and curated historic house museums, focusing on themes of patriotism and domesticity.[21] The Auxiliary successfully pursued at least three projects: Fraunces Tavern, Morris-Jumel Mansion, and Poe Cottage in the Bronx. Its activities were not widely reported in the ASHPS reports, though Auxiliary leader Melusina Fay Pierce formally presented them at the Society's annual meetings. What is clear from the archival records is that these women were very successful in selecting a few preservation projects and implementing them—which contrasted with the Society's strategy of advocating many things and implementing very little.[22]

The ASHPS was the most important early historic preservation organization because of its complex and continual involvement in preservation concerns in the first decades of this century. It sustained a public discourse on the value of preserving public memory, and tirelessly enlisted others in cultivating the memory embodied in historical and scenic places. A 1910 *Literary Digest* editorial noted, "No other so-called patriotic society is doing work quite so disinterested and intelligent."[23]

As represented by the ASHPS and these other groups, the preservation movement of the early twentieth century was led by the era's foremost city builders and civic reformers. Along with ASHPS, some other city institutions took up the cause of preservation. These included professional societies such as the Architectural League of New York and the Fine Arts Federation, and agencies of city government such as the Art Commission and the Parks Departments of the five boroughs. For these groups, preservation was more a background value—not an explicit goal—and was pursued because of their interest in a specific site. Nonetheless, many of city builders regarded preservation as one arrow in the quiver of urban reform. Surprisingly, New York's city government—a notoriously changeable affair in this era—played a fairly substantial role in the 1900s and 1910s, managing and even acquiring properties. Despite the participation of these agencies, the thrust of preservation work remained advocacy and proselytizing—the bailiwick of the ASHPS.

By the early 1910s, Andrew Green's generation gave way to that of George McAneny, cementing the ascendance of a new elite of professional reformers with few ties to old money or mercantile classes but an abiding support for reform politics and real-estate-fueled urban growth.

McAneny exemplified the connection made between historic preservation and other Progressive-tinged projects to rebuild, reform, and modernize New York. He was one of New York's leading city builders, planners, and public officials in the first decades of the twentieth century—he was also a dedicated and pioneering historic preservationist.[24] McAneny exemplified the cadre of professional, Progressive reformers who set out to modernize, rationalize, and remake the New York City landscape in the decades of breakneck growth and consequent disorder that followed the 1898 consolidation of the city. He was a pioneer in several aspects of urban reform—he played a key role in creating the 1916 zoning resolution and clearing downtown sidewalks of obstructions, lectured on reform of civic administration, and negotiated the enormous expansion of the subway system in 1913–15. Along with other reformers, public officials, architects, and philanthropists, McAneny formed the core of an emergent historic preservation field in the early decades of the twentieth century, with institutional support in both the government and philanthropic sectors. In the 1930s and 1940s, McAneny helped lead the nascent national historic preservation movement—he was one of the founders of the National Trust for Historic Preservation, after serving as president of the ASHPS in the early 1940s and taking a leading role in the preservation of Castle Clinton.

CURATORIAL AND URBANISTIC APPROACHES

Old landmarks are obliterated; historical monuments destroyed; buildings of national importance sold for second hand building material.

ASHPS trustee Frederick Stymetz Lamb, 1897[25]

In the midst of the many changes in our fluid city, we need some permanent landmarks to suggest stability.

ASHPS, 1912[26]

How was preservation accomplished? There was no unified approach or practice to preservation in this era. It was marked, however, by some important shared ideas about preservation and theories about how preservation would affect citizens and societies.

At a broad level, the fundamental, shared idea behind preservation was the generalized notion of *environmental determinism,* a theory widely held at this time among a broad spectrum of reformers, intellectuals, and others, spanning from housing reformers to beautifiers to eugenicists. The idea that the character of the physical environment—its beauty, cleanliness, historical associations—directly shaped individual and social behavior was a basis for many reform movements. The salutary effect of orderly environments was taken as a matter of faith in a "subtle and complex process of influencing behavior and molding character through a transformed, consciously planned urban environment."[27]

More specific to early preservationists was the notion of *spatializing memory*—preserving and expressing historical memory in material form. Spatializing memory was a particular branch of environmental determinism, rooted in eighteenth- and nineteenth-century aesthetic theories of associationism, in Transcendentalist notions of individual encounter with nature, and in Enlightenment philosophy. "[T]he power of historic memories," as ASHPS's Edward Hagaman Hall termed it, was believed to be an inherent quality of old buildings and historical places. Preservation activated this power. The result was a variety of memory sites: restored buildings, protected parks, stone monuments, brass plaques, and so on. Memory sites were seen as didactic instruments: "No matter how well a story may be told in words, there yet remains something unexpressed, which form and color alone can portray," wrote New York sculptor and ASHPS leader Henry Kirke Bush-Brown.[28] Further, site specificity—locating a memorial on the actual spot of a historical event, or preventing a preserved building from being moved—added strength to the power of historic memories. By giving historical memory lasting form in the built environment, it was thought, the particular memory was endowed with power to reform the public at large. The mere presence of memorial, monuments, and nature, would have a salutary effect on citizens.

The power of spatialized memory sites has always proceeded more as a matter of faith than of verifiable science, and early preservationists' faith in the social usefulness of spatializing memory had quasi-religious cast. Andrew Green, writing in 1901, explained that "visible historic memorials" and places of natural beauty tap into "the faculty of Memory, which lies at the bottom of all intellectual processes" and function as "books of history. . . . [T]o preserve them is a sacred duty."[29] A number of scholars have testified to the tight links between collective/social memory and geography, urban form, buildings—Halbwachs, Yates, Norberg-Schulz, Boyer, Tuan, and Hayden, to name a few.[30]

Given their faith in spatialized memory, how did preservationists decide which historical memories should be spatialized? And how exactly would this be carried out? Whose historical memories would be represented? The spatialization of historical memory was (and is) an intensely political process. Understanding the cultural politics of the day clarifies why the filiopietistic, patriotic, and civic patriotic narratives were chosen—immigration, urban disorder, battle between reformers and machine politicians, American imperialism, and economic ascendance all militated toward a celebration of unifying, celebratory American and New York memorial canons. Creating memory sites was sometimes a process of wholesale creation or unabashed destruction, not simply a matter of less intrusive "preserving and restoring" as we recognize them today. Architecturally, urbanistically, and culturally, the test of effective preservation was finding and making a past that was sensible (given lasting material and visible form; unambiguously interpreted) and usable (in terms of cultural reform, politics, and the representation of urban development as "improvement"), but not necessarily authentic vis-à-vis fabric or representative of different groups.[31] Authenticity and integrity of historical fabric, as we think of these concepts today, were only loosely considered—a powerful image was more important—and rarely presented any impediment to the creation of a memory site. Moving buildings was often countenanced; creative restoration and reconstruction were common approaches. More speculative restoration was gradually supplanted by more "scientific" methods of restoration architecture in the 1910s.

At the heart of the preservation's emergence in early-twentieth-century New York were two different and somewhat divergent approaches to carrying out preservation. Both were based on the strategy of spatializing memory. The *curatorial approach* is the traditional core of the preservation field. As with museum curators, it suggests an urge to celebrate, care for, and interpret individual monuments. It grew from the nineteenth-century antiquarian impulse to save historic artifacts because of their inherent value as witnesses to the past and the contrast they provided to the present. Curatorship also requires taking the valued historic artifacts or monuments out of the hands of those who would mistreat them—for instance, buying them to take them out of the real estate market. This approach is exemplified by the creation of isolated house museums stretching back even before 1850. Professionalization of historic preservation as a field goes hand in hand with the curatorial approach, because it presupposes a group of experts who know how to identify the valued artifacts or monuments and how to care for them. Indeed, this era witnessed the rise of curatorial preservation experts, as part of the broad cultural phenomenon of the rise of experts.[32] The curatorial approach to preservation remains a strong impulse in the field up to this day, waxing and waning according to new ideas and external forces, but never disappearing.

A second impulse emerged in New York in the 1900s and 1910s, pushing preservation in a direction different from the hermetic curatorial model: an "urbanistic approach" characterized by the engagement (not retreat) of preservation with the mainstreams of urbanization, urbanism, and urban reform. Practically, this meant that preservation concerns were woven together with other social-environmental reform issues, and that a clear "preservation field" and set of "preservation issues" were not easy to discern. The "preservationists" were not exclusively devoted to saving old things; they saw preservation as one aspect of their larger project of transforming the city and its citizens. Preservation was integrated with city planning, public art, civic architecture and other reform efforts. Transcending, yet not abandoning, the purist approaches to buildings as artifacts, urbanistic preservation led to more flexible strategies and negotiations. This signaled preservationists' awareness that the need for public memory and memory sites was driven by social forces external to the field but ever present in the city—the depredations of urban "disorder," the achievements of technological and economic "improvement," the cultural convulsions and politics of the era. As the ASHPS wrote in 1909, "There is little permanence upon which to fasten one's memories, affections and historical traditions. A city needs just such piles as old St. John's to give it some idea of firmness and stability in contrast with the fleeting changes around."[33]

Disorder was the watchword of reformers and the enemy of environmental-social reform efforts, including historic preservation. "Many of our cities have grown up wild in Topsy-like fashion," wrote Manhattan borough president and preservationist George McAneny in 1914. "I speak, for one, with frank admission that that is our trouble in the city of New York."[34] The urban disorder that inspired McAneny and his fellow reformers had many aspects—political corruption, the congestion of clogged streets and slum housing, poverty, immorality, economic inefficiencies, public health crises, ugly or dirty or otherwise aesthetically displeasing streets—adding up to a sense of cultural dislocation that led to the invention of a historic preservation field in New York City. McAneny and other city builders and preservationists pursued an overarching, holistic urban order premised on environmental determinism and spanning social, environmental, political, and economic concerns—as well as the cultural need for collective remembering. These several concerns were part and parcel of their vision of a modern city. Preservation was pursued as an urban reform movement to create order out of chaos, instilling in citizens a proper, dignified, celebratory civic memory in the form of stone, bronze, authentic buildings, and historical park landscapes. The search for a "usable past" to fix the cultural disorder of the modern city was the raison d'être of preservationists.[35]

CREATING MEMORY INFRASTRUCTURE

It would be impossible to characterize the early preservation field by talking only about the people and institutions and their goals and ideas. Describing some of the actual preservation sites and projects of the era adds a critical dimension. The history of two sites—St. John's Chapel and City Hall Park—are briefly described here to illustrate ways in which preservation of "historic and scenic places," in both its curatorial and urbanistic modes, was woven into the process of building and modernizing New York.

St. John's Chapel and City Hall Park are two particularly rich examples. The full spectrum of preservation projects in turn-of-the-twentieth-century New York would include a dozen other examples, many of them fairly straightforward curatorial preservation and restoration efforts but each with its own story of retaining historical fabric and creating a usable past. A short list of these would include:

• **Dyckman House:** Located in northern Manhattan, the farmhouse of the Dyckman family dates from 1785 and is said to be the last surviving Dutch colonial farmhouse in Manhattan. Built after the Revolution to replace a seventeenth-century farmhouse that had been burned by the British, it represents the deepest possible European roots in New York. It has a low-pitched gambrel roof and is built of fieldstone, brick, and wood. Threatened by apartment-house development fueled by subway construction, the house was purchased in 1915 by two sisters, well-to-do descendants of the last Dyckman to live in the house. It was creatively restored, furnished with family heirlooms, and presented in 1916 by Dyckman descendants to the city of New York as a public house museum and garden.[36] The Dyckman House was a project typical in its mission of creating a didactic museum of colonial life. More coveted by historic preservationists was the opportunity to celebrate civic patriotism in deeply rooted, place-specific narratives of the long-rooted but unfamous Dyckman family (in the vernacular farmhouse building) as well as national patriotism (in the reconstructed "Revolutionary War hut" built behind the house). It was also convenient that the civic patriotism of the Dyckman family connected the history of the site with the philanthropy of the Dyckman descendants.

Fig. 5.3 The Dyckman House, located in far northern Manhattan, represented the vestiges of the rural landscape of the city's Dutch settlers. Constructed in the 1780s on the site of an earlier farmhouse, Dyckman House was threatened by apartment-house development stimulated by subway building in the early twentieth century (see back left of photo). Descendants of the Dyckman family bought, preserved, and donated the house to the city in 1915–16. (Courtesy of Library of Congress.)

• **Fraunces Tavern:** The Long Room of Fraunces Tavern was the scene of George Washington's farewell to his officers in 1784, as he left New York at the end of the Revolutionary War to resign his commission and return to private life. As the site of this heroic act of patriotism, Fraunces Tavern became, beginning in the 1890s, the object of veneration of the hereditary groups: first the Mary Washington chapter of the DAR in 1894; later, the Sons of the Revolution. Lobbied by these groups, the city passed an ordinance to buy the tavern in 1903, but rescinded this in 1904.[37] With the occasional support of ASHPS and other preservation and hereditary groups, the Sons took the opportunity to create a memory site authentically tied to Washington. The early-eighteenth-century building had been much changed over the years, leading architect William Mersereau to carry out a radical restoration, removing a great deal of nineteenth-century commercial-building fabric and speculatively reconstructing the building as it would have been in the 1780s.[38] Further efforts to lobby the city to condemn and clear other buildings on the block to create a green park around the

Fig. 5.4 Fraunces Tavern, in Lower Manhattan, is shown pre-1907 restoration (top) and in the 1970s (bottom). The Sons of the Revolution hired architect William Mersereau to restore and reconstruct the Revolutionary War–period building in which Washington bade farewell to his officers. (Courtesy of Library of Congress.)

tavern failed. Since 1907, Fraunces Tavern has been operated as a private museum in the crowded precinct near the tip of Manhattan.

• **Morris-Jumel Mansion:** "This beautiful old Colonial and most historic Mansion in the city of New York" was built in 1765 on Harlem Heights and served as Washington's Headquarters. On filiopietistic, patriotic, and architectural grounds, the mansion was the most obvious object for early-twentieth-century preservationists—a memory site ready for anointing and already set aside on a small green patch of ground from the bustling development of the surrounding row house neighborhood.

The city government collaborated with patriotic societies to restore the house and open it as a museum. Four chapters of the DAR combined to form the Washington Headquarters Association, which lobbied the administration of Mayor Seth Low to purchase the house and its property in 1903 for $235,000.[39] A 1904 ceremony sanctified the place officially by placing a bronze tablet and hosting an oration by New York's Senator Chauncey Depew, with many patriotic and preservation groups in attendance. The WHA restored and operated Morris-Jumel Mansion, while the City Parks Department retained ownership.

St. John's Chapel

St. John's Chapel was a grand Episcopal church on Varick Street, just below Canal, built in 1803 as a new chapel of Trinity Church and destroyed in 1918. The ten-year debate over the preservation of St. John's Chapel is mostly forgotten, though it encapsulated important moments in the evolution of historic preservation in New York. Between 1908 and 1918, a variety of interests weighed in to save the building, and the waxing and waning of their efforts map an important shift in how collective memory was conceived and translated by preservationists into the bricks and mortar of a usable past.

The chapel was designed by John McComb, New York's leading architect of the early nineteenth century, to anchor St. John's Park—a residential square developed by Trinity as an elite residential neighborhood removed from the increasingly congested tip of Manhattan. The area changed drastically over the middle of the nineteenth century: Wealthy New Yorkers moved even farther uptown by the 1840s, the area was inhabited by English, Irish, and German immigrants, and the park was sold by Trinity in 1867 to Cornelius Vanderbilt, who built an enormous freight warehouse to the lot lines (Vanderbilt included in the new building a monumental frieze celebrating the city's commercial power and his considerable control of it). Located in a neighborhood undergoing yet more dramatic change in the early twentieth century,[40] the fight to preserve the chapel highlighted the emergence of

Fig. 5.5 When St. John's Chapel was built in 1803, on Varick Street below Canal, it faced its own park and upper-class residential square (top). By the late nineteenth century, the area and its buildings had changed drastically—an area of industrial lofts and immigrant tenements surrounded the chapel, and an enormous railroad freight warehouse replaced the park in 1867. (Courtesy Avery Library, Columbia University.)

Fig. 5.6 Efforts to save St. John's Chapel from destruction failed in 1918. (Courtesy Avery Library, Columbia University.)

preservation as both a foil for unfettered redevelopment and a collaborator of more thoughtful redevelopment.

The "St. John's Case," as contemporary newspapers called it, broke in November 1908. At first preservationist reformers and the working-class chapel congregation were pitted against the building's owner, Trinity Parish, one of the city's most powerful landowners. Trinity's plans to close and demolish the chapel sparked the interest of preservation advocates, city officials, architects, clergymen, and other citizens. All were responding to different values of the chapel landscape—the architectural-artistic value of the building, the symbolic value of one of the few remainders of "Old New York,"[41] the economic value of the real estate, the social value as a congregation's place of worship—but found common ground in wanting to resist Trinity's disposal of the building, its community, and its memories. For many reasons, St. John's seemed a place worth keeping.

From 1908 to 1914, a variety of arguments were posed for why and how the chapel should be preserved. Preservationists lobbied and generated newspaper coverage of the dispute, through the ASHPS and independently. Particularly noteworthy were the efforts of Isaac Newton Phelps Stokes to make passionate appeals to save the chapel for its historical and religious values, and to rally support among the richest and most powerful New Yorkers. No less interesting or less effective were the backroom mediations attempted by ex-mayor Seth Low.[42] Trinity Parish, meanwhile, asserted the site's economic value, dismissed its other values, and claimed sole right to declare the chapel a private property and not a public good. The chapel's congregation and clergy led the way with lawsuits, pursued in 1908–09, that failed ultimately to challenge Trinity's legal right to do as it wished with the chapel property. Worship was ended in 1908, and the congregants were sent to St. Luke's Chapel, a mile away in Greenwich Village.[43] The chapel was locked up tight, yet Trinity did not act to tear it down or sell it.

In just the two years of preservation debate, the chapel's values and memories had been transformed. Once the congregation was gone, preservationists helped turn St. John's from an old, living church to a dead historic landmark. The traditional memory of the congregation, tied to its continuous and ongoing use of the building for worship, its personal and interior connection to the building, was broken when it was evicted. As preservationists intervened—beginning with the first threat in 1908 but continuing long after the congregation was gone—a more modern form of memory was constructed around the chapel, tied to the more abstract, impersonal, distant notion of civic patriotism (in its "Old New York" aspect). This change paralleled the broad shift, between the 1890s and 1920s, in the rationales offered to support preservation. The values ascribed to buildings shifted from the associational and historical to the aesthetic and artistic—a shift in emphasis, not an abandonment of one value for another—which reflected the larger cultural transformations of modernity that distanced contemporary life from traditional connections with the past.

A second chapter in the St. John's preservation story began in 1913 with the city's announcement of a program of subway construction and road widening—a key part of the city's economic expansion and downtown's redevelopment. This directly threatened the chapel because it required a widening of Varick Street that would destroy the chapel's portico. Preservationists once again mobilized. This time the rationale was fully premised on modern memory. It had nothing to do with use, worship, or community surrounding the building, but rather the chapel as a totem of Old New York and a static artifact of colonial architecture. The modernization of St. John's collective memory was complete.

Remarkably, the city government in 1915 funded a preservation solution to meet this threat, saving the chapel by rebuilding the portico (with the sidewalk now carried underneath, according to a plan drawn by a young architect named Rawson Haddon) and winning a two-year agreement from Trinity not to sell the property. George McAneny, as

Manhattan borough president, directed this pioneering instance of public investment in historic preservation as part of a major infrastructure project. This is a classic instance of the "urbanistic approach" to preservation: The building's integrity and context were somewhat compromised, but it remained intact and useful, while other public needs were met by widening the street and building the subway. (Meanwhile, more curatorially minded preservationists produced measured drawings of the building.[44])

By 1917, the chapel still had no use, no new buyer, and no prospect of being saved from the wrecking ball. Trinity resisted requests to donate the chapel for reuse as a school or public building. And in the absence of a large philanthropic gift and sustained advocacy for preservation (scarce in the war years), Trinity demolished the chapel in 1918 and quickly sold the property for redevelopment as an industrial loft building.

The ten-year wrestling match over the chapel—involving an array of private citizens, public agencies, and nonprofit groups—testified to the public nature of preservation debates, to the complexity of building values contested in urban preservation debates, and to the ultimately ad hoc nature of preservation efforts of the period. Even when strong political support and public opinion seemed to back preservation, private property rights held sway.

The long debate over St. John's also revealed fault lines evident in historic preservation ideology then and now—shifts from an emphasis on the associational values of old buildings and a community's continuing use of a place toward focus on the aesthetic values of "architecture" and the emergence of a distinctly modern, "landmark" conception of historic preservation as spatialized memory. This abstraction of memory from continuous use to embodiment in static artifacts enabled the professionalization of the preservation field, and, later, its conversion to public policy rather than a reform idea.

City Hall Park

Even by 1900, City Hall and its park was remembered as a symbol of civic grandeur, wealth, and serenity—a mythic scene from the 1830s, dreamed again by reformers in the chaotic 1900s. "City Hall Park as it appeared before the Post-office was built, and as it should be restored," read Edward Hall's caption of 1910.

City Hall Park has long been New York's touchstone site of civic power, authority, and identity. By the end of the nineteenth century, the park was under threat of encroaching redevelopment and was also the pivot in the memory infrastructure being imagined in the early

Copyright, 1913, H. C. Brown

The City Hall Park as it Appeared about 1830

The present Post Office which spoils its appearance and greatly reduces its size will soon be removed.

Fig. 5.7 City Hall Park was the touchstone for civic memory around the turn of the twentieth century. Despite the modern infrastructure that had already been included in and around the park by the 1910s, the image in preservationists' minds gravitated more toward this 1830s engraving displaying the grandeur of City Hall amid its landscaped park. (Courtesy Avery Library, Columbia University.)

twentieth century. Skyscrapers, transit systems, and speculative development were transforming all of Lower Manhattan.[45] Protection of the park's status was a priority for historic preservationists and others in a time when city government was expanding dramatically and struggling to manage its new metropolitan scale. The growth of city government required ever-more office space. The park, old City Hall (erected 1811), and several other buildings continued to occupy this triangle that had once been the colonial commons.

From the 1880s through the 1920s, the park, City Hall, and buildings around it were threatened by myriad proposals to rebuild and reuse the area more intensively—proposals for large new civic buildings, appeals to preserve old buildings, defenses of the park's open space, efforts to compose a "Civic Center," improvements to transportation, and the renovation of old City Hall itself. These debates and competing proposals cast a bright light on the material and political realities of constructing civic memory in this most public space in New York.[46]

City Hall Park was the most challenging—but clearly the most important—place for preservationists to be creating memory infrastructure in the 1900s.[47] Competition for space and symbolism around the park was keen: transportation structures, office buildings for government agencies, recreational uses, political protests, and the primary symbols of civic patriotism jockeyed for space. It's not surprisingly, then, the myriad changes made in the City Hall Park landscape in the decades around 1900: New buildings were added (the New Hall of Records, north of the park on Chambers Street) and older buildings removed (the "old" Hall of Records, also known as the Martyr's Prison, in the park northeast of City Hall); park space was encroached upon and vigorously defended; new transportation works (the Brooklyn Bridge terminal, the IRT subway) were inserted into the park. A number of other changes were proffered but not realized: proposals were frequently made to move, destroy, or reuse City Hall; two large structures from the 1860s—the Tweed Courthouse and the post office—were targeted for demolition in order to restore the historic shape of the park.

The obvious political symbolism of the park as literal and metaphoric center of the city, as well as a rich layering of buildings and historical events on the site, made it fertile ground for preservationists. The historical value of the park drew on its use as the commons of the colonial town, site of numerous of Revolutionary War events, the building of grand City Hall in 1803–11, and a profusion of celebrations, monuments, and protests in the park thereafter. Here was one place where the fullest sweep of the city's history was represented in the layering of buildings, memorials, streets, and associations.[48]

Three kinds of powerful narratives rooted in City Hall Park were cultivated as part of civic memory: The first concerned the Revolutionary War (this was the site of symbolic protests against the Crown, of prisons in which patriots were jailed and martyred, and the public reading of the Declaration of Independence in the presence of Washington himself); second was the symbolism, continuity, and artistic value represented by City Hall itself, acclaimed as the country's finest work of civic architecture;[49] third, fundamental aspects of civic infrastructure were embodied and/or celebrated here, including the Croton water system, the buildings of city government (going beyond City Hall to include courts, offices, records storage, jails, and so on), and the maintenance of park space (valued variously for its recreational, healthful, or aesthetic aspects—as well as its historical value as the colonial commons).[50]

Being literally central to downtown New York, City Hall Park was also an object of desire for commercial and real estate interests, politicians, urban designers, and other reformers. Arguably, no site was more caught up in the struggles over how to rebuild the core of modern New York City and coax a modern civic center out of the eighteenth- and nineteenth-century downtown.

The two of the main "characters" in the preservation story of City Hall Park were the groups of city planning and historic preservation advocates. Each pushed distinctly different ways of remaking City Hall Park. Both sides agreed that the park must be "usable" in several respects—as symbolic power center, as office complex, as transportation node, and as representation of the city's past. Preservationists envisioned achieving this by cultivating site-specific memory: keeping historical buildings (such as City Hall and the Martyr's Prison) intact and in place; making memorials on the site of lost structures (including the Liberty Poles and the Bridewell). City Beautiful advocates sought to use the abstract power of Neoclassical urban design and decorative schemes: While keeping City Hall intact, they sought a cleared park around it, and a unified set of new, Neoclassical buildings surrounding it.

There were some common aspects of these two views: First was the preservation in situ of City Hall itself—an important principle given the proposals calling for the wholesale removal and replacement of City Hall; second, both called for the maintenance of the substantial open green space of the park; and third, both called for the removal of two buildings seen as architectural intrusions and affronts to civic memory—the post office and the Tweed Courthouse. These two buildings were anathema to civic patriotism, representing the corrupt machine politics against which reformers were mobilized. So, paradoxically, preservationists insisted on the destruction of these old buildings in the park while endeavoring to save other elements of the landscape. Clearly, it was political meaning—not age or architectural quality—that mattered most to preservationists.

Preservationist E. H. Hall neatly summarized the preservation issues surrounding City Hall in a 1910 map that accompanied his history of the park. The preservationist argument valued site specificity of particular memories, and held that authentic fabric ought to be preserved and restored. New uses could be accommodated in the park, such as subways, but fitted around such authentic landmarks as remained (say, the Martyr's Prison and City Hall). This contrasted with the strategies of City Beautiful reformers, who wished to create an aesthetically pure, symmetrical, abstractly symbolic civic center, with large new "headquarters" structures. Conflict between the two strategies arose from the different values each group saw taking precedence in using the park: historical values or aesthetic values. City Beautiful advocates found City Hall useful as part of the decorative scheme, and acknowl-

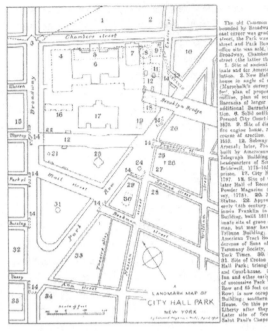

Fig. 5.9 In this map accompanying his 1910 history of City Hall Park, preservationist Edward Hagaman Hall represented the historical layers that contributed to the rich memorial value of the park, its buildings, and its surroundings. (Courtesy Avery Library, Columbia University.)

edged its value as a rare downtown survivor of history, but in their schemes it would be turned into a mere symbol, and the rest of the park was blank paper on their drawing boards. Preservationists, on the other hand, envisioned continuing use of City Hall—and in this use a continuous memorial connection with the city's past. As with St. John's Chapel, City Hall was threatened with becoming a modern landmark—an aesthetic marker, emptied of its former use and its connection with everyday life—though in this case, preservationists successfully advocated continuing use of the building as part of its preservation (see below regarding 1910s City Hall restoration).

City Beautiful clearance of the park endangered some historic buildings cherished by preservationists. For instance, the old Hall of Records sat in the northeast corner of the park and was valued by preservationists as "the Martyr's Prison"—the site where American patriots were imprisoned in deadly conditions by the British during the Revolution. But the Martyr's Prison stood in the way of an expanded transit station to serve the Brooklyn Bridge. The bridge emptied its crowds directly into this corner of the park, and there was great need for an expanded station. Over the protests of the ASHPS, the building was demolished—a simple stone marker preserved the memory of the prison.

Preserving civic memory was one part of the solution—especially when it came to the best embodiment of the civic narrative, City Hall itself. The other part of the solution was destroying buildings either in inconvenient places or with the wrong memory, as reformers did in the case of Tweed Courthouse (associated so strongly with the corrupt Democratic politics of Boss Tweed, the embodiment of machine politics reformers organized against) and the post office (its placement in front of City Hall and architectural dominance of the park was an affront to civic patriotism, and it was also associated with corrupt politicians who ceded the land for the post office to the federal government after the Civil War).

The question, for preservationists and planners alike, was not whether City Hall Park would be modernized, but how. This embodied the urbanistic impulse in preservation—engaging in compromise while asserting the primacy of historical values and memory goals. Efforts to construct the memory infrastructure were often merged with other kinds of projects. The justifications for saving City Hall, for example, routinely referred to the building's important historical associations *and* the economic wastefulness of tearing down or moving the building *and* the need for improving the transit flows around the park. Rarely was memory isolated, though preservationists per force gave it primacy. Civic memory was not conceived by preservationists as an independent, exclusive concern (a position too often taken today), but rather as one aspect of "improvement."

As with other preservation controversies of the time, a cadre of preservationist reformers sought to influence decision makers by suggesting compromises. No one solution ever was implemented wholesale, but the result of years of debate did largely satisfy preservationists' desire to spatialize civic memory by the selective preservation and destruction of buildings in and around this center of the civic and metropolitan orbit. The whole shape of the park was retained (and even recovered, in the late 1930s, with the demolition of the post office); City Hall was preserved and expertly restored; Tweed Courthouse remained; other historic buildings within the park were lost to new transportation infrastructure, but additional memorials were placed within the park.

The preservation of City Hall itself was another important moment in the development of early-twentieth-century preservation, of the more curatorial bent. By the turn of the twentieth century, City Hall, then about one hundred years old, was already among the city's oldest and most valued architectural and historic landmarks. As part of City Hall Park's story, the restoration of City Hall itself (between 1914–16)

Fig. 5.10 Architect, preservationist, and City Beautiful advocate Charles Rollinson Lamb drew this scheme for the preservation and redevelopment of City Hall Park (undated, probably drawn around 1899[51]). It is characteristic of efforts to bring together preservationist and development strategies to reassert the notion that City Hall Park—and City Hall itself—should remain the central civic space in Manhattan. (Courtesy Avery Library, Columbia University.)

speaks to the central role of architectural preservation in reshaping and asserting civic memory. Mrs. Russell Sage funded the restoration, at the behest of Robert DeForest and George McAneny. Architect Grosvenor Atterbury's work on City Hall marked the rise of scientific restoration as a privileged kind of preservation practice, and the onset of this kind of professionalization fundamentally changed the historic preservation field (well before Williamsburg).[52]

In the end, the park was reshaped in a way that privileged civic memory and resisted the overdevelopment of the park and its surrounds, while also accommodating transportation and office space needs. Today the park remains a place characterized by rich, chaotic layering of buildings from many periods. It is one of few open spaces in downtown Manhattan, a symbolic and literal crossroads.

City Hall Park's history is indispensable for understanding the ideology of historic preservation and "scenic conservation" as it wrestled to break free from antiquarian roots to become an urbanistic tool for reform.

CONCLUSIONS

Herbert Croly wrote in 1903 that New York City "still represents rather the formlessness and incoherence of our American past than the better defined and more fully rounded and proportioned creation of the future."[53] Preservationists saw their challenge as giving the civic past a form and, through form, endurance and reforming influence.

The substantial work and accomplishments of these early preservationists overturn the popular notion that historic preservation in New York (and indeed in the United States) was a post-1960s phenomenon. Preservation was seen by its proponents as an integral part of building the modern city—in keeping with the skyscrapers, subways, wide streets, clean sidewalks, green parks, and new suburbs, the project to improve and order the city extended to culture, and required a cultural infrastructure, new cultural institutions, and cultural ideals. Preservationists were the imagineers of a memory infrastructure serving the greater project of urban "improvement," and they considered City Hall Park among their most important works, and St. John's among their regrettable failures. Memory sites such as parks, preserved buildings, monuments, and so on, represented the cultural aspect of "improvement" ideal—opposed to the bugaboos of disorder and congestion—and provided New York with historical memory "commensurate with the dignity of the metropolis of the New World."[54]

The intended effect was that citizens would be faced with a memory-rich environment in which they could thrive and become engaged citizens and followers of the quasi-religion of civic patriotism. Through "The Teaching of Civic Patriotism," historian and preservationist Frank Bergen Kelley wrote, the city "becomes more than a mere collection of buildings, a despised place in which one must live, but for which there is no admiration, no love, no regard. Instead, it becomes a living organism with an interesting and honored past and a future to which every citizen ought to contribute, and for which every citizen should cherish great concern."[55]

Preservation, at its roots, was about an *engagement* with modernity, not a rejection of it. City Hall Park played a central role in how the city understood the past, how citizens accepted the need for expanding urban government, how people moved around the city—in short, here citizens could be shown, and could walk through, the reconciliation of a city that was changing quickly and drastically, while remaining rooted in the seemingly unchanging past. Culturally and aesthetically, one sees the jarring juxtapositions of this engagement in the Hudson-Fulton Celebration—a large public festival staged by civic boosters and preservationists in 1909, celebrating modern innovations such as electricity and airplanes under the umbrella of reverence for the civic past.[56]

The American Scenic and Historic Preservation Society and its allied groups spearheaded the creation of a vigorous historic preservation movement in New York in the early decades of the twentieth century. They imagined and (partially) realized an urban landscape studded with emblems of collective memory—a memory infrastructure of preserved buildings, naturalistic parks, new monuments, and other public art—as part of the modern city, along with the transit systems, tall buildings, and a geographical reach that was truly metropolitan.[57] They achieved this through personal, governmental, and ideological networks connecting preservation advocates to a plethora of other social-environmental reformers, city builders, and public officials emerging in the same era. ASHPS embodied the early-twentieth-century ideal of historic preservation as social reform. But as the era of Progressive reform waned in favor of more professionalized, bureaucratic City Efficient urban management, and a more professional-curatorial approach to preservation, ASHPS found itself on the sidelines.

NOTES

1. American Scenic and Historic Preservation Society, *6th Annual Report*, 1901, 52.
2. Advanced by Richard Hofstadter in *The Age of Reform*, and repeated by many thereafter.
3. This despite the desires of many preservationists to claim some quasi-religious status as a world apart from more prosaic concerns such as profit, modernization, social conflict, cultural change, and so forth.
4. McAneny wielded a great deal of influence in preservation, not only as a major civic figure in New York but also as one of the organizers of the National Trust for Historic Preservation in the late 1940s. Some aspects of his work are reported in Peter Derrick, *Tunneling to the Future: The Story of the Great Subway Expansion That Saved New York* (New York: New York University Press, 2001); Gregory F. Gilmartin, *Shaping the City: New York and the Municipal Art Society* (New York: Clarkson Potter, 1995); and Charles B. Hosmer Jr., *Presence of the Past* (New York: G. P. Putnam's Sons, 1965) and *Preservation Comes of Age: From Williamsburg to the National Trust, 1926–1949* (Charlottesville: University Press of Virginia/The Preservation Press, National Trust for Historic Preservation, 1981).
5. George Kriehn, "The City Beautiful." *Municipal Affairs*, volume 3, 1899.
6. The Annual Reports of the American Scenic and Historic Preservation Society are the best sources for understanding the scope and detail of preservation activities in this period.

7. American Scenic and Historic Preservation Society, *28th Annual Report,* 1923, 8.
8. Perhaps the most important reformer of the second half of the nineteenth century, known as "the Father of Greater New York" for his advocacy of consolidating the five boroughs into one city, Green held a number of public offices, was a political power broker and protégé of Samuel Tilden, and was also instrumental in creating Central Park, planning the development of the Bronx, and establishing the New York Public Library. See David Hammack, "Comprehensive Planning Before the Comprehensive Plan: A New Look at the Nineteenth-Century American City" in Daniel Schaffer, ed. *Two Centuries of American Planning* (Baltimore: The Johns Hopkins University Press, 1988); Kenneth Jackson, ed. *The Encyclopedia of New York City* (New Haven: Yale University Press, 1995), 505.
9. The group's original name was Trustees of Scenic and Historic Places and Objects in the State of New York. The precedent in Green's mind was the Trustees of Reservations in his native Massachusetts, formed for the patriotic mission of preserving the grounds on which patriotic deeds had been performed. See their *1st Annual Report,* 1895.
10. Hall was previously a newspaperman and writer of popular history.
11. There were no formal criteria for deciding which places, but working with donors and the state they focused on Revolutionary War battlefields.
12. With very mixed success; there were substantial victories, such as Morris-Jumel Mansion and Poe Cottage and some upstate properties; failures such as St. John's Chapel and Fraunces Tavern, and mixed results including City Hall Park. Frances Whiting Halsey, an active, longtime trustee of the Society, was editor of the *Times* Saturday Review section, and they actively recruited editors from around the state as members. Board Minutes for 1 December and 29 December 1900, American Scenic and Historic Preservation Society. Manuscript Papers. Rare Books and Manuscripts Collection, New York Public Library, New York, NY, Box 6.
13. See the ASHPS *Annual Reports,* 1895–1925.
14. ASHPS untitled promotional pamphlet, 1911, 13–4.
15. American Scenic and Historic Preservation Society. *The Grange: Relocation & Restoration, Two Hundredth Anniversary of Alexander Hamilton, 1757–1957* (New York : The Society, 1955).
16. George McAneny, *Reminiscences of George McAneny* (New York: Columbia University Oral History Project, Butler Library, Rare Books and Manuscripts, 1949), 86.
17. The ASHPS itself also became a sort of monument to Green, an act of civic filiopietism, preserving the memory of reform by lionizing the memory of a chief reformer. This was perpetuated by the constant retelling of Green's founding role, and by the A. H. Green Memorial Fund, endowed with ten thousand dollars from Green's estate for the benefit of the Society.
18. On positive environmentalism, see Paul Boyer, *Urban Masses and Moral Order in America, 1820–1920* (Cambridge: Harvard University Press, 1979). ASHPS supported city planning in general—endorsing the 1916 Zoning Ordinance, for instance—even though comprehensive, rational city planning ideas such as wider streets, expanded transit systems, and civic centers sometimes threatened the preservation of place-specific civic memory (for example, in City Hall Park and St. John's Chapel).
19. The emergence of this elite is described in David Scobey, *Empire City: The Making and Meaning of the New York City Landscape* (Philadelphia: Temple University Press, 2002).
20. The Society was a small organization, and it is something of a wonder that such a range and variety of work was sustained between 1895 and 1925, and that their annual reports and other products were so voluminous. In the first couple of decades, there were hints of financial need even for running the very small office. Subscribing membership hovered in the three hundred to five hundred range, while most of the activities were handled by a couple of dozen activist members who worked through a

large number of small committees. After two reorganizations in the first five years, the accumulation of some operating funds through subscriptions, and a small endowment from J. P. Morgan, Edward Hagaman Hall was hired in 1898 as full-time secretary. See American Scenic and Historic Preservation Society Manuscript Papers. Rare Books and Manuscripts Collection, New York Public Library, New York, NY; American Scenic and Historic Preservation Society, Annual Reports, 1895–1925.

21. Francesca Morgan. *"Home and Country": Women, Nation, and the Daughters of the American Revolution* (Ph.D. dissertation, Columbia University, 1998); Sarah Giffen and Kevin D. Murphy, eds., *'A Noble a Dignified Stream': The Piscataqua Region in the Colonial Revival, 1860–1930* (York, ME: Old York Historical Society, 1992).

22. The Auxiliary was quite successful in preserving and opening the Morris-Jumel Mansion and Poe Cottage. Their efforts on Fraunces Tavern—supported by the Society, which lobbied the Parks Department to acquire the property—were unsuccessful, though the building was later purchased and reconstructed by another patriotic group, the Sons of the Revolution. American Scenic and Historic Preservation Society, *5th Annual Report*, 1900.

23. *Literary Digest*, 1 January 1910.

24. In contrast with Green, whose private career was spent in the service of the traditional economic and political elite—lawyer to the Astor estate and protégé of Samuel Tilden—McAneny's professional roots were in the newspaper business, political reform, and public service.

25. *Municipal Affairs*, volume 1, 1897, 675.

26. American Scenic and Historic Preservation Society, *17th Annual Report*, 1912.

27. Boyer 1979, 221.

28. H. K. Bush-Brown, "New York City Monuments." *Municipal Affairs*, volume 3, 1899, 602.

29. American Scenic and Historic Preservation Society, *6th Annual Report*, 1901, 50–2.

30. Maurice Halbwachs, *The Collective Memory*. Trans. Francis J. Ditter Jr. and Vida Yazdi Ditter (New York: Harper & Row, 1980); Frances A. Yates, *The Art of Memory* (Chicago: University of Chicago Press, 1966); Yi-fu Tuan. *Space and Place: the Perspective of Experience* (Minneapolis: University of Minnesota Press, 2001); Christian Norberg-Schulz. "The phenomenon of place." *Architectural Association Quarterly*, v.8, n.4, 1976; Dolores Hayden, *The Power of Place: Urban Landscapes as Public History* (Cambridge: MIT Press, 1995); M. Christine Boyer, *The City of Collective Memory: Its Historical Imagery and Architectural Entertainments* (Cambridge: MIT Press, 1994).

31. This is a clear link between NYC's preservation history and the subsequent development of the historic preservation field throughout the twentieth century and across the country—"usability" has been the driving force in American preservation, not any purist sense of authenticity.

32. Hosmer 1965; Patricia West, *Domesticating History: The Political Origins of America's House Museums* (Washington: Smithsonian Institution Press, 1999). William Sumner Appleton is the best-known example of the pioneering preservation expert; see James Lindgren, *Preserving Historic New England: Preservation, Progressivism, and the Remaking of Memory* (New York: Oxford University Press, 1995). In New York, architects such as Grosvenor Atterbury and William Mersereau began to specialize in historic buildings early in the twentieth century.

33. American Scenic and Historic Preservation Society, *14th Annual Report*, 1909.

34. Response [to opening address] *Proceedings of the 6th National Conference on City Planning*, 1914. "Topsy," referring to a character in Uncle Tom's Cabin, describes something "that seems to have grown of itself without anyone's intention or direction" Oxford English Dictionary online: http://dictionary.oed.com/cgi/entry/ 00254614. See below for more detail on McAneny's varied, influential, and little-

known contributions to building and reforming New York in the first half of the twentieth century.

35.   Van Wyck Brooks's coining of "usable past" in 1918 referred to literature, but describes very well the attitude of McAneny and other advocates of urbanistic preservation—historical memory must be saved because society needs it. It is useful. "On Creating a Usable Past," *Dial* 64 (11 April 1918), 337–41.

36.   The project was designed by the husbands of the two sisters, architect Alexander McMillan Welch and museum curator Bashford Dean, as well as engineer and amateur historian-archaeologist Reginald Pelham Bolton (also an official of the ASHPS). Bashford Dean and Alexander McMillan Welch. *The Dyckman House: Park and Museum, New York City, 1783–1916* (New York: The Gilliss Press, 1916); American Scenic and Historic Preservation Society, *22nd Annual Report*, 1917.

37.   American Scenic and Historic Preservation Society, *6th Annual Report*, 1901 (Appendix B by Melusina Fay Pierce).

38.   Very little archival information was discovered to guide the restoration, decisions were therefore left to Mersereau's judgment.

39.   Reginald Pelham Bolton, *Washington's Headquarters, New York* (New York: American Scenic and Historic Preservation Society, 1903), 4; American Scenic and Historic Preservation Society, *15th Annual Report*, 1910, 57.

40.   Changing because of the new economic power of New York City: Downtown was expanding, the social geography of downtown neighborhoods being converted to industrial and shipping areas; new transportation infrastructure demanded more urban space (wider streets for trucks and subway construction). This dynamic is well-documented in Clara Cardia, *Ils ont construit New York: Histoire de la metropole au XIX siecle* (Geneva: Georg Editeur, 1987).

41.   Clifton Hood, "Journeying to 'Old New York': Elite New Yorkers and Their Invention of an Idealized City History in the Late Nineteenth and Early Twentieth Centuries." *Journal of Urban History* (September 2002): 699–716.

42.   As a leading citizen and an Episcopalian, Low had personal access to Trinity's influential vestry, but failed to broker a deal to save St. John's. St. John's chapel box, Diocesan Archives, Cathedral of St. John the Divine.

43.   The congregation removed several interior architectural elements when St. John's was closed, and took them to St. Luke's. Donald Gerardi, personal communication; "Historical Notes, 1820–1935, St. Luke's chapel, Trinity Parish, at Hudson and Grove Streets, New York, New York, and A Guide Book for its Interior, By a Curate" in George McAneny Papers, Box 127, Seeley Mudd Library, Princeton University.

44.   Rawson W. Haddon, (Measured drawings by F. L. Finlayson). "St. John's Chapel, Varick Street, New York City." *Architectural Record*, v.XXXV, n.V, May 1914.

45.   The Woolworth Building, tallest in the world, was built next to City Hall Park in 1911; some of the first "skyscrapers" were built in the 1870s along Park Row on the east side of the park. The first subway route terminated at City Hall Park, opening in 1904; the Brooklyn Bridge, having opened in 1883, had already made the area a transit hub.

46.   For further detail, see Gilmartin 1995; Randall Mason, *Memory Infrastructure: Preservation, "Improvement" and Landscape in New York City, 1898–1925* (Ph.D. dissertation, Columbia University, 1999); Max Page, *The Creative Destruction of Manhattan, 1900–1940* (Chicago: University of Chicago Press, 1999); Robert Stern, Gregory Gilmartin and John Massengale, *New York 1900: Metropolitan Architecture and Urbanism, 1890–1915* (New York: Rizzoli, 1983).

47.   Michele Bogart gives a detailed account of memorialization in City Hall Park in "Public Space and Public Memory in New York's City Hall Park." *Journal of Urban History*, v.25, n.2, 1999.

48. The sweep of history represented in preservation and other forms of public history was highly selective, and for the most part excluded mention of civil unrest, minorities, and disasters. Also see Hood 2002.
49. Montgomery Schuyler, "The New York City Hall: A Piece of Architectural History." *Architectural Record*, v.23, n.5, May 1908.
50. The Park was also the place where celebrations and protests were most often staged—from the 1863 draft riots to the mourning of Lincoln's death, from Lafayette's parade to ticker-tape parades. One of the best sources on the history of the Park remains Edward Hagaman Hall's article (ASHPS, *15th Annual Report*, 1910), 383–424; also see Bogart 1999.
51. Charles C. May. "[New York's City Hall] PART I—Historical notes." *Architectural Record*, v.39, n.4, April 1916; "[New York's City Hall] PART II—The Work of Restoration." *Architectural Record*, v.39, n.5, May 1916.
52. Herbert Croly. "New York as the American Metropolis." *Architectural Record*, March 1903, 198.
53. Hall 1910, 4.
54. Frank Bergen Kelley, "The Teaching of Civic Patriotism: The Work of the City History Club." *Municipal Affairs*, v.3, 1899, 61–5.
55. Especially the commercial aspects of New York's past—the "discovery" of Manhattan by Hudson, and Robert Fulton's successful steamboat, both of which paved the way for New York's commercial ascendance. See David Nye, *American Technological Sublime* (Cambridge: MIT Press, 1994), 153–65; Hudson-Fulton Celebration Commission, *Fourth Annual Report of the Hudson-Fulton Celebration* (Albany: J. B. Lyon Company, 1910).
56. The example of the Bronx River Parkway further illustrates the connections between the preservation/restoration of historical landscape and the construction of archetypally modern landscapes, and extends the idea of creating memory infrastructure beyond the explicit efforts of preservationists. The BRP was built between 1906 and 1925, as the first automobile parkway in the world, and it is not generally regarded as a historic preservation project. It is included in this sampling of early preservation efforts because it demonstrated an important instance of constructing the usable past in the service of modernizing without having an obvious connection to the institutions and terms of debates of "historic preservation" per se. However, the way the parkway's builders constructed and spatialized memory—through the design of the actual parkway landscape, and in their public communication strategies—clearly situates the parkway project as another means of spatializing memory, and therefore suggests stretching our definition of the roots of the preservation field. In the BRP, one glimpses very clearly the instrumental use of spatialized memory as infrastructure. Mason 1999.
57. The drawing is undated; Gilmartin 1995, 74, gives the clue.

6

MARKETING THE PAST

Historic Preservation in Providence, Rhode Island

Briann Greenfield

FROM THE **1940s** THROUGH the 1950s, architectural photographer Samuel Chamberlain recorded the historic homes of Providence, Rhode Island, in his popular New England picture book series.[1] Both the photos Chamberlain took and those he didn't spoke volumes about the state of Providence's historic buildings. Chamberlain recorded many homes on Providence's College Hill district, but he failed to publish images of buildings along northern Benefit Street, an area dense in colonial architecture. Chamberlain's careful editing of the historical landscape reflected his desire to portray the past as both elegant and refined—qualities northern Benefit Street severely lacked. Connected culturally and geographically to the poor African American community of nearby Lippitt Hill, northern Benefit Street was a slum. Many of its historic houses were tenements, often lacking sufficient heat, plumbing, and sanitary facilities.[2] Indeed, houses were in such disrepair that the Providence Redevelopment Agency considered the area for an urban renewal clearance project.[3] While many northern Benefit Street residents took pride in their community and their churches, their neighborhood was not the stuff of picture books.

Beginning in the late 1950s, historic preservationists rebuilt northern Benefit Street in the image of an idealized past. Middle-class white families remodeled and restored tarpapered colonials previously occupied by black families. They removed cheap siding, repointed chimneys, replaced windows, and turned junk-filled yards into urban

163

gardens. The movement spread quickly to southern Benefit Street and to the side streets of both neighborhoods. By 1967, city officials estimated that more than 150 buildings had been privately restored at a cost of approximately three million dollars.[4]

But Providence preservationists not only transformed a street; they also contributed to a larger transformation within the field of historic preservation. While market forces have always played a role in American historic preservation, early preservationists defined themselves in opposition to the market. According to historian Mike Wallace, America's antebellum ruling class disregarded historical properties, preferring to link their new republic to a classical past through the use of Greek and Roman architectural styles rather than constrain new construction by retaining actual historical properties. But as Wallace has found, between the 1880s and the 1940s—the height of American industrial capitalism—"a constituency emerged that questioned the prevailing dismissal of the past."[5] In the North, descendants of antebellum shipping merchants and industrialists, fearful of the influx of immigrants and the new moneyed classes, solidified their cultural authority by founding genealogical and historical societies. Joined by southern patricians, multimillionaire industrialists, and new professionals, these historically minded elites argued for the retention of historic buildings and against unconstrained growth. For the many preservationists who lived off previously accumulated wealth (whether their own or their ancestors'), sacrificing capitalist expansion for cultural cachet was a natural response to a booming economy that threatened to leave them behind. Often led by female benevolence workers, these advocates of the past pooled their financial resources to create house museums—historical shrines beyond capitalism's reach.[6]

With its founding in 1956, the Providence Preservation Society (PPS) became part of a new pro-market preservation movement. Rather than saving buildings by taking them off the market, these preservationists saved buildings by raising their market value. Managing real estate markets was an ambitious endeavor. To make it work, preservationists had to regulate the actions of private property owners and direct public opinion. But preservation innovations of the previous twenty years made such feats possible. As early as 1931, Charleston, South Carolina, developed the first historic zoning ordinance. Historic zoning gave preservationists control over aesthetic issues and exterior design. Charleston's 1931 ordinance lacked regulatory authority, but by the 1950s cities such as New Orleans, Philadelphia, Boston, and Alexandria were giving their architectural review boards stronger powers.[7]

Fig. 6.1 Northern Benefit Street before and after restoration. Providence preservationists used images such as these to illustrate the dramatic changes on College Hill. (Courtesy of the Providence Preservation Society.)

Equally important to the success of pro-market preservation was principle of city planning. Architectural surveys such as those conducted by Charleston; Savannah, Georgia; Winston-Salem, North Carolina; and Newport, Rhode Island, allowed preservationists to target specific communities and define their objectives.[8]

Building on the work of these innovators, Providence preservationists employed a variety of market-boosting strategies, including for-profit preservation companies, selective clearance, and historic district zoning. With the publication of its award-winning planning study and numerous magazine articles, Providence became a national model for pro-market preservation.[9] As Wallace argues, this approach became the dominant American preservation strategy in the 1970s and 1980s as historic preservation tax breaks, rising construction costs, and historical tourism combined to make preservation profitable.[10]

Pro-market preservation had an enormous impact on both the American landscape and the preservation movement. While earlier preservation efforts focused on creating individual house museums, only millionaires like Rockefeller and Ford could construct entire villages. In contrast, pro-market preservation was more inclusive. By attacking local real estate markets, the new preservation embraced whole neighborhoods. Also, by transforming preservation from a charity to an investment, pro-market preservation opened the field to the middle class who, in their zeal to acquire historical properties, embraced previously neglected Victorian buildings. But at the same time, pro-market preservation also reinforced some of the restrictive tendencies of earlier preservation movements. While the 1930s ushered in a more populist, government-sponsored form of preservation with such initiatives as the Historic American Buildings Survey (HABS), pro-market preservation valued private property over public resources. In this way, pro-market preservation appropriated large sections of American cities for exclusive residential use.[11]

EMBRACING THE MARKET

In Providence, pro-market preservation was built on profound economic and structural changes. Once one of the country's leading textile, machine tool, and metalwork producers, Providence had lost its industrial base by the late 1950s. Facing increasing competition from southern textile mills supplied with cheap labor and the latest technology, Rhode Island's cotton and woolen industries had gradually closed their doors. According to historian Gary Kulik, between 1948 and 1958, forty-four textile mills closed throughout the state.[12]

But while downtown businesses struggled, the three colleges on Providence's East Side, Bryant College, the Rhode Island School of Design (RISD), and Brown University, embarked on a program of expansion that continued unabated through the 1960s. Brown was the first to act. In 1951, Brown razed approximately fifty-one houses for the construction of Wriston Quadrangle, a walled dormitory complex bounded by Brown, Thayer, George, and Benevolent Streets.[13] Four years later, Brown began construction of the West Quadrangle (now Keeney Quad), a second dormitory complex that required the demolition of an additional eleven houses along two blocks of Charlesfield and Benevolent Streets.[14] The buildings destroyed included such local historic landmarks as the 1868 Thayer Street School, the Greek Revival Shepard Mansion, and the Victorian Powell House.[15]

Much as in earlier preservation movements, Providence's elites led the fight against Brown's expansion. As a descendant of the university's namesake, a member of its board of trustees, and a wealthy civic

Fig. 6.2 Site preparations for the construction of Brown University's West Quadrangle. With its expansion in the 1950s, Brown University demolished more than thirty nineteenth-century houses. Such actions enraged many old Providence families and encouraged the formation of the Providence Preservation Society. (Courtesy of Brown University, University Archives.)

leader, John Nicholas Brown believed it was his duty to redirect the school's expansion.[16] On February 20, 1956, Brown called the first meeting of the Providence Preservation Society. While the society immediately pledged to prevent further loss, it was not anti-growth. Speaking at the society's first meeting, John Nicholas Brown denied that the society's brand of preservation was a "sentimental antiquarian or archaeological project." Rather, he claimed, it would restore the "glory of our historic past" by "bringing an old and graceful section of the city back to economic stability."[17]

Brown's unusual attitude, that historic preservation could coexist with economic development, was a direct result of his city's industrial decline. Indeed, for men such as Brown whose reputation and power were tied to the city, Providence's well-being was a matter of personal pride. Undermining the city's economy by diverting funds to the reconstruction of historical reserves was out of the question. Instead, preservation leaders hoped to join cultural stewardship with economic expansion by redeveloping historic neighborhoods.

This pro-growth attitude made preservationists very popular with city officials. Largely composed of representatives from Providence's Irish and Italian communities, city officials were often at odds with the old Anglo-Saxon families of College Hill.[18] But in the wake of industrial decline and white flight, preservation offered city leaders a way to expand their dwindling tax base. Since the early 1950s, the Providence Redevelopment Authority had been looking for ways to transform the northern section of Benefit Street into a "high-value" neighborhood and had even proposed the demolition of historic houses on northern Benefit Street as part of the Lippitt Hill Slum Clearance Program. The founding of the PPS, however, provided agency officials with an alternative. With urban renewal coming under fire for its wanton destruction of historic buildings, the federal government began offering grants in 1954 to support alternatives to demolition. Shortly after the PPS's formation, the Providence City Plan Commission teamed up with the citizens' organization and successfully applied for a redevelopment study grant. The final report, *College Hill: A Demonstration Study of Historic Area Renewal,* looked in many ways like a traditional urban planning study, but it also incorporated historic preservation into future planning initiatives. To advance the careful use of historical properties, project staff member Antoinette Downing surveyed 1,350 of the approximately 1,700 buildings in the College Hill area, ranking each according to its historical significance, architectural quality, and physical condition.[19]

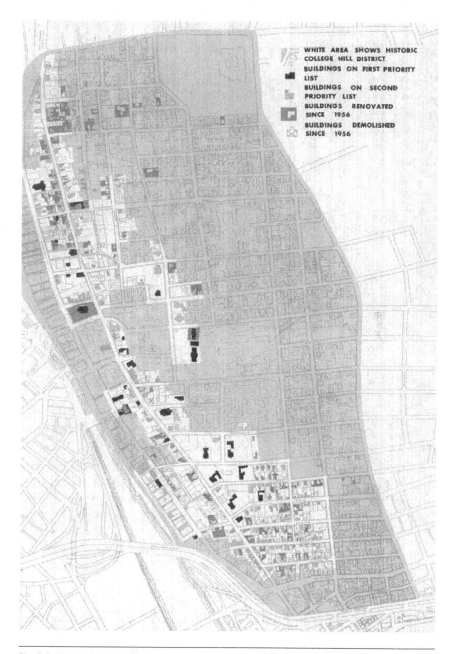

Fig. 6.3 Map of College Hill showing the historic preservation district highlighted in white. Benefit Street forms the preservation district's central spine. Published in the second edition of *College Hill,* this map also illustrates preservation activity from 1956 to 1965. Providence City Plan Commission in cooperation with the Providence Preservation Society and the Department of Housing and Urban Development, *College Hill: A Demonstration of Historic Area Renewal,* 2nd ed. (Providence: Charles G. Cowan Publishers for the Providence City Plan Commission, 1967.)

THE BUSINESS OF PRESERVATION

While the College Hill study included many recommendations to improve neighborhood amenities and promote historical resources, the crux of its proposal was a program of planned gentrification for northern Benefit Street. Preservationists supported gentrification, but making it happen required business savvy and a keen understanding of local real estate markets. From the beginning, preservationists realized that economic factors were in their favor. As architectural historian Antoinette Downing correctly observed at the PPS's first meeting, Providence had "a ready-made clientele for good small houses or for small apartments."[20] Indeed, while the city as a whole reported declining population, College Hill was growing at the rate of approximately 1 percent per year.[21]

While conditions were right for gentrification, previous restoration initiatives helped preservationists' understand the pitfalls of the market. In the early 1920s, future Rhode Island governor Theodore Francis Green and his brother Erik Green began "recouping the standing of the neighborhood" by buying and restoring old houses near their family home at 14 John Street.[22] By 1924 the two had formed the John-Thayer Company, named for the two streets where most of the buildings were located, and rented restored houses for profit.[23] But although the Greens owned fifteen buildings by 1929, they were not able to establish a self-sustaining community. Restoration was expensive and required homeowners to make investments in their property well above the initial purchase price. Yet when the property holders sold, they were often unable to recoup their investments because the presence of unrestored properties diminished the value of their renovated neighbors. Location determined the buildings' value.[24]

The lesson of Green Village was not lost on Beatrice Chace, who set out not only to restore individual properties, but also to transform the entire Benefit Street neighborhood.[25] Like John Nicholas Brown, Chace was the descendant of an old Providence family and had a personal stake in the city's architectural history. On the advice of her brother, who had worked in Historic Georgetown, Chace used her knowledge of real estate and personal wealth to transform College Hill.[26] Her first attempt was small scale. In June 1956, she purchased a single house on the corner of Thayer and Transit Streets. Located not far from Green Village, Chace's house also bordered deteriorated homes in the Fox Point district. Completing a dramatic restoration that included the removal of a false front, Chace explained that she was trying to "swing the balance," "reasoning . . . that if a key structure in such a block were rescued and restored it might have a good effect on its neighbors."[27]

In 1956, Chace also founded Burnside Company to buy and restore houses in the northern Benefit Street area. Operating Burnside out of her husband's Georgia-based real estate company, Chace first purchased seventeen houses on or near northern Benefit.[28] So successful were her efforts that Chace next acquired an entire city block of approximately twenty additional houses. For both projects, Chace's real estate brokers Roger Brassard and Robert Prescott Hall selected and purchased the houses while Brassard's contracting firm, Colonial Homes, did most of the restoration work.[29] Leaving interior decoration to their future occupants, Chace stipulated that Brassard should concentrate on the building's shell, updating electrical and plumbing systems, removing artificial siding, fixing roofs, repairing original clapboards, and replacing windows and decorative moldings with historically appropriate styles.[30] Protective covenants attached to the property deeds ensured that future owners would maintain the buildings' exterior appearance.

Burnside Company sold its properties at cost, but restoration expenses in the 1950s and 1960s drove the prices from $3,000–12,000 a house to $10,000–22,000. In addition, owners generally invested another $25,000–30,000 above the purchase price to complete the interior restoration.[31] Considering that the 1960 census reported the median price of houses in suburban Warwick as $12,100, purchasing a Burnside house was a luxury only the financially secure could afford.[32] To attract middle-class buyers, Chace painted the buildings with bright colors, orange, gold, and pink.[33] Literally bright spots in a drab neighborhood, Chace's houses were transformative.

Benefit Street's transformation was also reinforced by the construction of small, for-profit preservation companies. By the early 1950s, several such companies were already in operation elsewhere in the country. In the Mount Royal neighborhood in Baltimore, Maryland, residents founded Bolton Hill Inc., a for-profit real estate company organized to buy, renovate, and either sell or lease residential property in the city. Funded by stock sales, the company reinvested profits to support additional rehabilitation work. In its first year of operation, Bolton Hill rehabilitated thirteen separate properties and earned a 10 percent profit. Similarly, in Cincinnati, Ohio, Cincinnati Renewal incorporated to renovate residential buildings in the Avondale-Corryville section of the city. While not specifically targeting historical properties, Cincinnati Renewal provided another example of a private, stock-funded company raising "socially inclined capital" for investment in community projects. Best known was Historic Georgetown, Inc., a for-profit company that bought and rehabilitated historic buildings in the Thirtieth and M Street area of Washington, D.C. Like Bolton Hill and Cincinnati Renewal, Historic Georgetown raised money through stock subscription. Financially successful, the company's property rentals provided a "sizable surplus" above upkeep, taxes, interest, and preferred dividends.[34]

Following these examples, a number of preservation companies incorporated in Providence. Netop Restorations, Inc., Foxes Hill Corporation, The King Philip Company, and Hill Realty Company organized between 1959 and 1967 to buy and sell historical properties.[35] While diverse in both their size and level of activity, these preservation companies usually raised money by registering as corporate entities with the Rhode Island secretary of state and selling stock.[36] Purchasers then became shareholders in the corporation and elected a board of directors to run the day-to-day operations. While several companies employed prominent Rhode Island businessmen, many stockholders were Benefit Street homeowners with a vested interest in completing the area's restoration.[37]

Founded on business principles, for-profit preservation was rarely very profitable. The PPS realized the difficulties associated with restoration when it nearly lost its shirt financing the move of the Mawney Carpenter House (also known as the IBA House) from North Main Street to 16–18 Halsey Street.[38] The investment specialists did only slightly better. Netop, which usually sold houses in a more finished state than the other companies, aimed for a return of 6 percent but not atypically made no money on 20 Sheldon Street.[39] Likewise, Foxes Hill hoped only to break even on 40 Sheldon Street.[40] Having learned from the others' mistakes, Hill Realty was slightly more profitable. The company dispensed with paid staff, invested in one house at a time, and limited rehab work.[41]

But even when companies did make a profit, most chose to reinvest in the preservation market rather than pay dividends to stockholders. For them, the goal was not to make money on a single house but to strengthen the market by assuring the restoration of the entire neighborhood. In this regard, for-profit preservation companies accomplished an important function. While Burnside purchased large groups of houses, the smaller companies filled in the gaps. Foxes Hill, for example, worked to support preservation on southern Benefit Street, an area that retained several restored properties from the Green Village project but lacked more recent investment.[42]

While preservation companies helped raise area real estate values and complete the neighborhood's restoration, they also worked to control the direction of new development. Incorporated after the initial preservation boom, Hill Realty made filling empty lots a priority.[43] By the late 1960s, empty lots had become an important issue for preservationists. Armed with the power of eminent domain, Providence's Redevelopment Agency conducted what it termed "spot clearance," the demolition of individual buildings. Spot clearance did much to support the preservation agenda. By eliminating public buildings and commercial structures such as St. Dunstan's School (19 Benefit), Apoc Printers (38 Benefit), and the Jewish Community Center (65 Benefit), the Redevelopment Agency helped construct a quiet residential neighborhood that supported preservationists' efforts to raise area property values.[44] But spot clearance also posed dangers for preservationists. As area real estate prices increased, preservationists feared developers would use empty lots to build apartments and condominiums that would intrude on the neighborhood's historic character.[45]

To construct Benefit Street as an area of single-family homes, Hill Realty began moving properties to empty lots and providing low-cost loans to homeowners and developers for similar work. The latter service proved especially important, since banks rarely allowed mortgages to include moving expenses. By 1982, Hill Realty had contributed to six relocation projects: the Zachariah Allen House, moved from North Main to 1 Benefit Street; 46 Branch Avenue moved to 40 Benefit; a porticoed Greek Revival moved from the city's west side to the former site of the Jewish Community Center; and a Star Street house moved to Burr's Lane. Many of these buildings came from urban renewal districts around the city, making Benefit Street a repository for historical architecture.[46]

CONSTRUCTING HISTORY

For-profit preservation companies were the predecessors of today's nonprofit preservation revolving funds, a form of preservation financing pioneered in Charleston in 1957.[47] Both revolving funds and for-profit companies provided preservationists with a mechanism to direct funds into specific real estate markets, finance private restoration, and hold title to endangered properties until a suitable buyer could be found. But while money was essential to the preservation process, also important was the definition of what kind of buildings were considered historically valuable. This task fell to Antoinette Forrester Downing. Downing held many roles in the preservation movement. She encouraged John Nicholas Brown to organize the PPS, served as the organization's chief consultant, surveyed the architecture of College Hill for the City Plan Commission, and in 1968 became the

Fig. 6.4 House at 40 Benefit Street. This house was among several moved to Benefit Street under the sponsorship of Hill Realty, a company dedicated to filling empty lots with historic structures. (Courtesy of the Providence Preservation Society.)

first chairperson of the Rhode Island Historic Preservation Commission, a title she retained until 1995.[48] But Downing was more than an activist. As a scholar, she helped define Benefit Street's history.

Downing was an art history professional. Before coming to Providence with her husband, George, a professor of art history at Brown, Downing had graduated from the University of Chicago, completed a master's degree in art history at Radcliffe, directed the Fitchburg Art Museum, and written a book titled *Early Homes of Rhode Island*. Because of her background in art history, Downing began her career valuing historic buildings as aesthetic objects. This was an approach shared by the majority of preservationists in the 1950s, who argued that old buildings should be preserved because they are beautiful. But Downing also advocated an inclusive definition of *preservation*, one that embraced vernacular buildings as well as high-style ones, new buildings as well as old. Downing's strength was her catholic appreciation for many styles of architecture. While earlier preservationists favored either elite, high-style structures or those linked to the pre-immigrant social order, Downing found many buildings worthy of preservation. Because of her artistic training, she saw architectural design as a rightfully evolving art, reflecting the constantly changing na-

ture of society. In this way, Downing not only embraced Victorian
structures and early-twentieth-century homes but also promoted new
construction so that "this era's philosophy of architecture can take its
place among those of our forebears."[49]

In practice, while Downing appreciated buildings of many eras, she
did not find all appropriate to Benefit Street. Downing believed that
buildings belonged together if they "scaled" together—that is, if they
shared similar proportions.[50] The doctrine of scale helped preservationists define Benefit Street as a neighborhood of one- or two-family
homes and exclude apartment buildings and other large dwellings. But
the idea that a historic neighborhood could embrace multiple time periods also helped preservationists assemble a viable community. Indeed, if Downing had restricted the label *historic* to Benefit Street's few
high-style colonial homes, preservation companies would have been
hard pressed to assemble enough restored structures to reinforce area
property values. Instead, Downing's supported pro-market preservation by claiming the entire neighborhood as historically significant.

MARKET CONSEQUENCES

By the mid-1960s, for-profit preservation companies, zoning laws, and
spot clearance had transformed Benefit Street's real estate market.

Fig. 6.5 Preservation activist Antoinette Downing lecturing to a women's group in the 1950s.
(Courtesy of the Providence Preservation Society.)

While Burnside Company purchased properties for between five thousand and ten thousand dollars in the 1950s, ten years later prices had more than doubled. Restored properties regularly sold for more than $45,000 and in at least one case shot up to $125,000.[51] As a *Providence Sunday Journal* article reported, "Almost anyone on the street can cite cases of dramatic jumps in prices on individual dwellings. One resident told of a house that sold for six thousand dollars a few years ago going for twenty thousand dollars. Another said one owner wants twenty-four thousand dollars for a structure that will require another twenty thousand dollars to restore to its original beauty."[52] Encouraged by such national publications as *Reader's Digest, House Beautiful, House and Garden, Antiques, Yankee Magazine,* and *National Geographic,* prospective homeowners flocked to Benefit Street.[53] Nancy Fisher, a graduate student entering Brown University's program in American civilization, wrote Downing, "I had hoped . . . that I might find a small house, suitable to my needs and means, to restore. . . ."[54] But according to PPS executive director Frederick Chase, single-family homes were "scarce as hens teeth."[55] Indeed, Chace reported that he, too, had been unsuccessful in finding a house. "I have been looking for a house in this area for the past two years to buy. . . . Once in a while a restored old house does come on the market but is snatched up almost immediately at fantastic prices."[56]

Such real estate values worked to safeguard historic structures, but Benefit Street's popularity also put incredible pressures on its black residents. In only five years after moving to Benefit Street, Mr. and Mrs. Paul Cardoza, residents of 3 Jencks Street, witnessed five black families leaving the area. Only one family sold its property; the rest were renters, unable to profit from the preservation movement.[57] Effects of black displacement were also visible on the city as a whole. A 1962 *Providence Evening Bulletin* article reported that "the purchase of much property along Benefit Street by well-to-do whites interested in restoring the area has made living there by nearly all nonwhites an economic impossibility and thus has moved the color line both North (almost to Olney Street) and South (to Sheldon Street)."[58] Roger Brassard, a contractor for Chace's Burnside Company and owner of his own restoration business, was notorious for pressuring black families to sell. Virginia Williams, a former resident of 17 Benefit Street, recalled her mother referring to Brassard as "the cockroach" for his persistent solicitations.

Of course, real estate agents could not force blacks to sell. Wille Chapman, who remembered one real estate agent waiting at her front door all day, ignored all offers and retained her home at least into the 1990s. "I didn't sell," explained Chapman, "my father was a buyer and seller of property down in North Carolina and I could see what was going to happen."[59] But few blacks saw the potential that Chapman did. Faced with what they believed would be the highest prices they would ever receive for their property, most sold.

Many preservationists were dismayed by black displacement. Eric and Sally Godfrey, who purchased their Benefit Street property without the aid of a preservation company, told the *Providence Journal* that they enjoyed living in a "hodge podge" neighborhood, and didn't want the black family next to them to move out.[60] As displacement became more acute, some preservationists took action. In 1964, the Benefit Street Association, a group of homeowners organized to lobby city government on behalf of their neighborhood and the preservation initiative, listed among its goals "retention of the existing population characteristics with a minimum discomfort to and displacement of present inhabitants."[61] To further those goals, the association lobbied the Providence Redevelopment Authority to retain a variety of buildings in the area, including small multiple-family units accessible to blacks and other low-income groups.

But for the most part, such actions were too little, too late. Because of the initial investment that restoration required, preservationists were committed to a course of action that included redeveloping the area as a neighborhood of well-maintained single-family homes. In 1966, the PPS and the North Benefit Street Neighborhood Association joined forces to restrict rooming houses on North Benefit Street and petitioned the Redevelopment Authority to change the area's zoning from R-4, multifamily zoning, to R-2, two-family zoning. Such restrictions helped raise area property values, but also made it very difficult for blacks find affordable housing.

By the 1970s, prices had climbed so high on Benefit Street that even preservationists worried about their ability to hold on to the neighborhood. A *Preservation Newsletter* warned, "To a very real extent the success of the project has helped to jeopardize it even more. As the area becomes more attractive for residential use, the demand for bigger buildings becomes more and more real."[62] In 1971, preservationists encountered such a challenge. Seeking to expand the city's tax base, the Providence Redevelopment Authority proposed luxury town houses and condos for renewal areas on Burr's Lane, a side street off Benefit's northern end.[63] Preservationists successfully mobilized against the new development, but soon after, Beatrice Chace herself— the founder of the Burnside preservation company—sold developer Marc Lowenstein of Evolution Incorporated a twenty-one-thousand-square-foot parcel for condo development.[64] Located on Pratt Street and forming the western side of the block previously restored by

Fig. 6.6 Burnside Company's proposed redevelopment of an entire city block in the northern Benefit Street area. While the final project retained several structures omitted in this preliminary plan, Burnside Company created controversy within the preservation community by selling land along Pratt Street to developer Marc Lowenstein for the construction of modern condominiums similar to the ones pictured here. (Courtesy of the Providence Preservation Society)

Chace's Burnside Company, the parcel was just outside the limits of the historic zoning district. While unable to oppose the development on legal grounds, area residents were still divided over Lowenstein's proposed condominiums.[65] Some favored the condos for replacing a number of early-twentieth-century three-family residences, a building type often scorned by Providence's preservationists as unattractive. Others opposed the project on the grounds that it undermined the neighborhood's historical atmosphere.

Such developments made many preservationists rethink the value of old buildings. In the 1980s, much of the debate centered on the preservation of three-story tenements, commonly referred to as triple-deckers. Constructed in the late nineteenth and early twentieth centuries, these buildings served the needs of immigrants and other working-class families. As artifacts of working-class life, triple-deckers didn't live up to Downing's aesthetic vision. Indeed, Downing did not include triple-deckers on either of her two priority lists for historic zoning protection.[66] But by the 1980s, as Benefit real estate prices began to exclude all but the most well-to-do, preservationists started to value triple-deckers as both records of working-class life in the past and promoters of social diversity in the present. Frank Mauran III experienced firsthand this newfound interest in working-class housing.

A former PPS president, Mauran was also the owner of one of Benefit Street's most distinguished residences, the 1809 Sullivan Dorr House. When Mauran purchased the house, several early-twentieth-century triple-deckers bordered the property. Mauran soon began to purchase these buildings with the intention of razing them once he assembled title to the entire group.[67]

But while Mauran slowly enacted his plan, sentiment about the value of three-family residences began to change. In 1988, Mauran petitioned Providence's Zoning Board of Review, a board headed by Downing and designed to safeguard historic buildings by regulating demolition permits, to demolish six triple-deckers on Benefit, Bowen, and Wheaten Streets.[68] His request denied, Mauran appealed his case the following year, only to achieve similar results. To Mauran, the buildings' preservation was an absurdity. Not only did they lack architectural or aesthetic distinction, but triple-deckers were among the Providence's most common building type, dominating large areas of the city's West Side. Surely, such ubiquitous structures did not need protection.[69] But while the majority of residents speaking out at the appeal hearing agreed with Mauran, Downing believed the buildings' preservation was an essential step in expanding Benefit Street's historical scope. Speaking at the appeal hearing, Downing argued that the triple-deckers represented a "very important architectural statement for the early twentieth century."[70] Laura Bell of 56 Pratt Street also supported the buildings' retention, emphasizing that the rental units encouraged social diversity in the neighborhood. "We need places for young couples, places for little old ladies, even places for students."[71] While seemingly a debate over the historical and social value of a few early-twentieth-century structures, the triple-deckers' fate was wrapped up in the meaning of preservation itself.

With such high stakes, Mauran and Downing used every means possible to achieve their objectives. While acknowledging that she had not considered the triple-deckers historically or architecturally significant in the 1960s, Downing added the six buildings to the College Hill district priority list. Mauran countered by filing suit in superior court, a move that prompted city council members to remove the properties from the protected list. In the end, there was no absolute winner. Downing convinced Zoning Board Commission members to uphold the principle that twentieth-century working-class houses were historically significant, a precedent she hoped would guide the board in future cases. But the triple-deckers are no longer extant. Exercising his rights as a property owner, Mauran left the buildings vacant until a 1998 fire damaged them.[72] Allowed to demolish what remained, Mauran finally had his way.

CONCLUSION

In many ways, the debate over the triple-deckers is a reminder of how far the preservation movement has come. Pro-market preservationists were revolutionary in their desire to join aesthetic interests to economic growth. With their business savvy and keen understanding of real estate, they used history to construct a visually coherent and socially homogeneous neighborhood that raised property values and drew middle-class residents back to the city. The result was not only a restored street, but also new types of preservationists—educated middle-class whites with the financial resources and business acumen to transform preservation from a charity to an investment. In their effort to protect the neighborhood, these new preservationists expanded the boundaries of history to include previously neglected vernacular structures and Victorian homes as historically valuable.

But success had its price. While liberal preservationists congratulated themselves for reviving declining neighborhoods, they could not ignore the damage they had done to poor, often black, communities. Antoinette Downing herself became an activist in the movement to improve low-income housing through her involvement in SWAP (Stop Wasting Abandoned Properties). In the 1990s, preservationists became increasingly active in issues surrounding land use, the well-being of cities, social diversity, and the construction of an inclusive history.[73] But the question remains: Will preservationists be able to combine their socially responsible goals with economic growth, or will they, like their nineteenth-century predecessors, find themselves locked in a battle against the market?

NOTES

1. Chamberlain wrote more than forty New England picture books. For examples, see *Ever New England* (New York: Hastings House, 1944); *New England Doorways* (New York: Hastings House, 1939); *The New England Image* (New York: Hastings House, 1962).
2. Providence City Plan Commission in Cooperation with the Providence Preservation Society (hereafter cited as PPS) and the Department of Housing and Urban Development, *College Hill: A Demonstration of Historic Area Renewal*, 2nd ed. (Providence: Charles G. Cowan Publishers for the Providence City Plan Commission, 1967), 151.
3. Providence Redevelopment Agency, "Redevelopment Proposals for Central Areas in Providence, Rhode Island," November 1951, 121.
4. Providence City Plan Commission, *College Hill*, 225.
5. Mike Wallace, "Preserving the Past: Historic Preservation in the United States," in Mike Wallace, *Mickey Mouse History and Other Essays on American Memory* (Philadelphia: Temple University Press, 1996), 185.
6. Wallace supplies one of the most succinct explanations of preservation's formation. See "Preserving the Past," and "Visiting the Past: History Museums in the United

States," both in *Mickey Mouse History.* Other useful cultural histories of historic preservation include: Michael Kammen, *Mystic Chords of Memory: The Transformation of Tradition in American Culture* (New York: Vintage Books, 1991); James M. Lindgren, *Preserving Historic New England: Preservation, Progressivism, and the Remaking of Memory* (New York: Oxford University Press, 1995); Patricia West, *Domesticating History: The Political Origins of America's House Museums* (Washington, D.C.: Smithsonian Institution Press, 1999). For parallels in the English preservation movement, see Patrick Wright, *On Living in an Old Country: The National Past in Contemporary Britain* (London: Verso, 1985).

7. On Charleston's contributions to the preservation movement see Robert R. Weyeneth, *Historic Preservation for a Living City* (Columbia, SC: University of South Carolina Press, 2000).

8. Providence City Plan Commission, *College Hill,* 2–3.

9. The Providence City Plan Commission's preservation planning study, *College Hill,* was first published in 1959. A second printing was funded by the Department of Housing and Urban Development in 1967.

10. Wallace, "Preserving the Past," 200–3. For an example of how economics continues to influence preservation, see Arthur P. Ziegler Jr. and Walter C. Kidney, *Historic Preservation in Small Towns: A Manual of Practice* (Nashville: American Association for State and Local History, 1980).

11. I have benefited greatly from speaking with individuals who have worked in the Providence preservation movement and/or lived on Benefit Street. Those people include Melvin Feldman, Robert Goff, Karen Jessup, Frank Mauran III, Alfred Van Liew, Elizabeth Warren, and William McKenzie Woodward. I have also had valuable conversations on the history of Benefit Street with Robert Emlen, Richard Meckel, Joanne Melish, and Robert Lee. Finally, this article also owes a debt to Kathy A. Spiegelman for her senior thesis, "Architectural Renewal on College Hill" (honors thesis, Department of American Civilization, Brown University, 1974).

12. Gary Kulik and Julia C. Bonham, *Rhode Island: An Inventory of Historic Engineering and Industrial Sites* (U.S. Department of the Interior, Heritage Conservation and Recreation Service, Office of Archeology and Historic Preservation, Historic American Engineering Record, 1978), 24–5.

13. Benevolent Street was later closed so that Brown's residential buildings could extend uninterrupted to Charlesfield Street.

14. Antoinette Forrester Downing, "Historic Preservation in Rhode Island," *Rhode Island History* 35(1):20 (February 1976); William Collins, "College Hill Restoration 25 Years Old," *Providence Sunday Journal,* 3 May 1981, sec. B; Spiegelman, "Architectural Renewal," 4.

15. On the buildings destroyed for the two quadrangles, see Woodward and Sanderson, *Providence,* 158; City Plan Commission, *College Hill* 63; Cady, *Civic and Architectural Development of Providence,* 139, 275–6; John Hutchins Cady, *Walks around Providence* (Providence: Akerman-Standard Press, 1942), 20–1. Today a plaque marks the former location of the Goddard mansion at the corner of George and Brown Streets.

16. Downing, interview with Victoria Gianitsaris, 21 February 1992, Graphics Department, RIHS.

17. "Group Hopes to Save City's Old Buildings," *Providence Journal,* 21 February 1956. For further proof of the PPS's pro-market intentions, see Downing, "Historic Preservation," 20. Brown had employed a similar preservation strategy in 1945 when he helped the Rhode Island Association for the Blind secure an 1828 shopping arcade in downtown Providence for its headquarters. See Downing, "Historic Preservation," 15.

18. Melvin Feldman, interview by author, 11 March 1998.

19. For information about the behind the scenes work at the College Hill study, see Spiegelman, "Architectural Renewal," chap. 3.
20. Antoinette Downing, "Providence Preservation Society: Speech of Mrs. Antoinette Downing," PPS Papers, RIHS.
21. City Plan Commission, *College Hill*, 196.
22. " 'Green Village' Restores a Bit of Old Providence," *Providence Sunday Journal*, 31 January 1926. For a history of 14 John Street, see Francis M. G. Wayland, "An Account of 14 John Street Recorded by Francis M. G. Wayland, July 1916 for her Nephew, Theodore Francis Green," Francis Rogers Arnold Family Papers, RIHS.
23. " 'Green Village' Restores a Bit of Old Providence," *Providence Sunday Journal*, 31 January 1926; "The John Thayer Company," *PPS Newsletter*, June 1965, Rockefeller Library, Brown University; Downing, interview with Victoria Gianitsaris, 13 March 1992, Graphics Department, RIHS.
24. In the 1910s and 1920s, Charleston experienced a privately funded rehabilitation campaign similar to that conducted by the Green brothers. See Weyeneth, *Historic Preservation for a Living City*, 11; Sidney Bland, *Preserving Charleston's Past, Shaping Its Future: The Life and Times of Susan Pringle Frost* (Westport, CT: Greenwood Press, 1994).
25. Ibid.
26. Antoinette Downing to Frank Barnes, 18 October 1965, PPS Papers, RIHS.
27. "Rehabilitation," *Providence Sunday Journal*, 28 October 1956.
28. Spiegelman, "Architectural Renewal," 15; City Plan Commission, *College Hill*, 93, 225–6; "Old Houses Turned into Assets in Providence" *Worcester (Massachusetts) Sunday Telegram*, 10 December 1967.
29. "Plan to Restore Benefit St. Colonial Homes Launched," *Providence Sunday Journal*, 9 November 1958.
30. Spiegelman, "Architectural Renewal," 16.
31. City Plan Commission, *College Hill*, 97; Antoinette Downing to Frank Barnes, 18 October 1965, Providence Preservation Society Collection, RIHS.
32. Table 17, "Financial Characteristics and Duration of Vacancy for SMSA's, Places of 50,000 Inhabitants or More," *1960 Federal Housing Census*, U.S. Department of Commerce, Bureau of the Census.
33. Robert Goff, interview by author, 20 April 1998. Goff's family was one of the first to purchase a house from Burnside Company.
34. Providence City Plan Commission, *College Hill*, 13.
35. Foxes Hill Incorporation Papers, Foxes Hill Collection, RIHS; "Netop: A Business With a Mission" *Rhode Island's Magazine of Business Finance Industry*, supplement to the *Providence Sunday Journal*, 15 December 1963; Hill Realty Company, Incorporation Papers, Hill Realty Collection, RIHS.
36. "Hill Realty Continues Early Tradition," *PPS Newsletter*, March–April 1982, Rockefeller Library, Brown University; "Prospectus of the Hill Realty Company," Elizabeth G. L. Allen Papers, RIHS.
37. "Certificate of Foxes Hill Corporation," 11 July 1963, Foxes Hill Collection, RIHS; "Prospectus of the Hill Realty Company."
38. On the IBA House, see Box 5, PPS Papers, RIHS; "St. Dunstan's Site," *PPS Newsletter*, March 1975, Rockefeller Library, Brown University.
39. "Netop: A Business With a Mission."
40. "To the Stockholders of Foxes Hill Corporation," 16 May 1960, Foxes Hill Collection, RIHS.
41. "Hill Realty Continues Early Tradition," *PPS Newsletter*, March–April 1982, Rockefeller Library, Brown University; "A corporation will soon be formed to buy properties . . . ," untitled, undated document from Randall W. Bliss, J. K. Ott, Mrs. Phineas Sprague, Hill Realty Collection, RIHS.

42. Foxes Hill Incorporation Papers, Foxes Hill Collection, RIHS.

43. William Mackenzie Woodward, past president of Hill Realty, interview by author, 15 June 1998.

44. While spot clearance was conducive to the construction of a residential neighborhood, preservationists did not always agree with the Redevelopment Agency's decisions to tear down specific buildings. On the PPS's support for St. Dunstan's School, see Washington Irving to Mr. Stanley Bernstein, Providence Redevelopment Agency, 2 July 1964, PPS Papers, RIHS.

45. "Benefit Street Goals Remain Uppermost in Face of Constant Threats" *PPS Newsletter*, February 1970, Rockefeller Library, Brown University; Frank Mauran III to Edmund Mauro, chair, Providence Redevelopment Agency, 2 February 1971.

46. "Hill Realty Continues Early Tradition," *PPS Newsletter*, November–December 1982, Rockefeller Library, Brown University. For details on each of these projects, see "Minutes of the Board of Directors Meetings," Hill Realty Collection, RIHS.

47. On the origins of Charleston's revolving fund, see Weyeneth, *Historic Preservation for a Living City.*

48. Morgan McVicar, "Her Determined Efforts Preserved Providence," *Providence Journal*, 10 May 2001.

49. City Plan Commission, *College Hill*, 187. On Downing's appreciation for different architectural periods, see also Antoinette Downing, interview with George Goodwin, 27 October 1992, Graphics Department, RIHS.

50. City Plan Commission, *College Hill, 74. On the concept of scale, see also Antoinette Downing, interview with George Goodwin, 27 October 1992, Graphics Department, RIHS.*

51. "A Future in the Past," "Who's New on the Street," both *Providence Sunday Journal*, 2 February 1964.

52. "A Future in the Past."

53. For magazine articles, see "Benefit Street: 1756–1956," *Yankee Magazine*, January 1956, 34–41; Barbara Snow, "Preserving Our Cities," *Antiques Magazine*, October 1961, 355–7; Karl Detzer, "They Bring Back Magic Yesterdays," *Reader's Digest*, March 1966, 160–5; W. F. Lawrence, "Festival on College Hill," *Yankee Magazine*, May 1966, 54–9; Barbara S. Delaney, "Benefit Square, Providence," *Antiques Magazine*, April 1968, 512–3; Robert De Roos, "Rhode Island: New England's Lively Experiment," *National Geographic*, September 1968, 370–401.

54. Mrs. Nancy Fisher to Antoinette Downing, undated; Frederic Chase to Mrs. Michael Werthman, 24 January 1969; Frederick Chase to Mrs. Lester, 17 October 1969, all in PPS Papers, RIHS.

55. Frederic Chase to Mrs. Michael Werthman, 24 January 1969, PPS Papers, RIHS.

56. Ibid.

57. "A Future in the Past."

58. Bruce B. Van Dusen, "The East Side: Changes Threatening Its 'Rightful Destiny'?" *Providence Evening Bulletin*, 26 December 1962.

59. "Resident Is Glad She Stayed," *Providence Sunday Journal*, 3 May 1981, sec. B.

60. "Who's New on the Street."

61. "Benefit Street Association," Report for the 9 December 1963 Meeting, PPS Papers, RIHS.

62. "Benefit Street Goals Remain Uppermost in Face of Constant Threats," *PPS Newsletter*, February, 1970, Rockefeller Library, Brown University.

63. "Renewal Plan Stirs a Dispute," and "Foes Say Plan Not Suited for Area," both undated clippings, PPS Papers, RIHS.

64. "East Side Residents against Apartments," newspaper clipping dated 10 January 1974, PPS Papers, RIHS.

65. Ibid.; "Row Housing Stirs 'Historic' Protest," *Providence Journal*, 16 January 1974.

66. Chap. 1342, No. 345, Ordinance of the City of Providence, State of Rhode Island and Providence Plantations, Approved 5 August 1960.
67. Frederic L. Chase Jr., letter to unknown recipient, 21 April 1967.
68. Robert Corriea, "Historic Panel Goes to Bat for 3-Deckers," *Providence Journal,* 4 May 1989.
69. Frank Mauran III, interview by author, 27 April 1988.
70. Ibid.
71. Ibid.
72. Randall Richard, "College Hill Dispute Heats Up as Fire Damages Vacant Houses," *Providence Journal,* 25 May 1998.
73. On new directions in preservation, see Wallace, "Preservation Revisited."

7

PLACE OVER TIME

Restoration and Revivalism in Santa Fe[1]

Chris Wilson

IN THE EARLY 1980s, at the dawn of what we now call globalization, a wave of books and articles projected Santa Fe to the world as an exotic getaway—America's own Tahiti in the desert, bathed in the golden glow of sunset. By the early 1990s, readers of *Conde Nast's Travel* magazine were voting Santa Fe their favorite travel destination in the world. But Santa Fe was hardly an overnight success. Community leaders had consciously set out in 1912 to transform their city into a tourist mecca. Their initiation of a communitywide historic restoration—at a time when preservationists elsewhere concentrated on house museums—helped broaden the scope of the American historic preservation movement.

What most visitors take to be an authentic pre-industrial city is largely a creation of the twentieth century. The city government, Museum of New Mexico, and business boosters have chosen to emphasize the city's distinctive regional sense of place over a homogenized modern spirit of the times. Through speculative restorations, historical design review for new buildings, select preservation projects, and the removal of overt signs of Americanization, they have—depending on one's point of view—either transformed Santa Fe into a proto-Disney, Spanish-Pueblo fantasy, or sustained a vibrant regional architectural tradition in the face of modernism. In truth, they have done both while creating one of the most livable American cities of the past century.

This small community in the desert stood on the cutting edge of heritage tourism development in the 1910s and again in the 1980s. But

185

the desire for a refuge from a rapidly changing world (embraced by tourists and romantic residents alike) favors the mystification of these twentieth-century initiatives. And because post–World War II preservation orthodoxy prohibits the sort of free-wheeling restorations and historical revivalism that Santa Fe has favored, previous histories of preservation in America have overlooked the city's pivotal role.

Founded in 1610 as the capital for the isolated province of New Mexico, Santa Fe was a recognizable Spanish colonial city with a church fronting onto a plaza defined by flat-roofed adobe houses lined by *portales*—porches supported by log posts capped by carved double corbels. With some five thousand residents in 1848, it was the largest and most important town annexed into the United States following the U.S.-Mexican war.[2]

With the arrival of the railroad in 1880, the Anglo and Hispano business community avidly modernized the city with redbrick schools and Italianate business blocks lining three sides of the plaza. Images of these new buildings in territorial promotional literature sought to persuade a reluctant Congress that predominately Hispanic and Catholic New Mexico was Americanized enough to receive statehood. Despite

Fig. 7.1 South side of Santa Fe plaza, 1897. (Philip E. Harroun, Museum of New Mexico.)

this progressive spirit, Santa Fe was in trouble. Its mountainous terrain had caused the Santa Fe Railroad to bypass the city with its main line, leaving it stranded at the end of an eighteen-mile spur. As a result, the city's population dropped from roughly seven thousand residents in 1880 to five thousand in 1910—a 10 percent decline per decade. Yet even as Santa Fe simultaneously Americanized and declined, *Harper's*, *Frank Leslie's Weekly*, and other illustrated publications catered to the national fascination with the Pueblo Indians, and tourists began filtering through Santa Fe on their way to visit the pueblos.[3]

1912 CITY PLAN

The establishment of the joint Museum of New Mexico/School of American Archeology (later named the School of American Research) in 1909 put in place institutional resources, a visionary leader, and staff expertise that would power the city's revival. The new museum director, Edgar Lee Hewett, was born in 1865 to a prosperous Illinois farm family. By age thirty-three, he had risen through the bureaucracy of public education to become the first president of New Mexico Normal College in Las Vegas. A devotee of antiquities, he took a doctorate in archaeology at Geneva, Switzerland, before returning to campaign for the 1906 Antiquities Act, the first federal preservation legislation. Hewett cultivated institutional backing for his cultural campaign from the Archaeology Institute of America, headquartered in New York. Founded in 1879, the Archaeology Institute of America flourished through its field schools in Rome, Athens, and Jerusalem. When it began looking for a suitable home for an American field school, Hewett lobbied for Santa Fe over the other aspirants: Colorado Springs, Denver, and Los Angeles. The matter was settled in 1909 when the New Mexico Legislature offered an annual appropriation and use of the Palace of the Governors—the old capital building facing the plaza. Hewett soon assembled a network of local collaborators and museum staff that included archaeologists, photographers, writers, painters, and architects.[4]

When Santa Fe was finally released from the need to Americanize by the granting of statehood in January 1912, Mayor Arthur Seligman quickly created a city planning board and charged it with finding a way to stem the city's economic decline. Hewett and staff archaeologist Sylvanus Morley were appointed to the commission, and the museum's resources thrown into the effort. Chair of the Santa Fe planning board was forty-year-old Harry H. Dorman, the son of a New York textile manufacturer who had come to Santa Fe in 1901 for his health and established a successful real estate and insurance business. Dorman sent out dozens of letters requesting advice from large cities and nationally renowned experts such as pioneer city planner John Nolen and landscape architect Frederick Law Olmsted Jr. (son of Central Park's designer). Although the board could not afford to hire a professional planner, it received encouragement, planning treatises, and city plans from across the country, all steeped in City Beautiful rhetoric. City Beautiful proponents sought to reestablish a sense of order and refinement out of the commercial and industrial jumble of rapidly growing cities. Their aesthetic campaign emphasized the construction of parks, boulevards, and grand civic plazas ringed by Classical city halls, libraries, museums, and opera houses.[5]

"The City of Santa Fe is planning extensive improvements," wrote Dorman in true City Beautiful spirit, "that include the laying out of parks and boulevards, the extension of streets, the restriction of manufacturing plants to a suitable district, the elimination of bill-boards and the bringing about of some sort of architectural homogeneity." But while other City Beautiful plans employed Beaux Arts classicism to achieve visual unity, this style would be too costly for Santa Fe, and, according to board member Morley, would destroy "our most priceless possession, an individuality, which raises us above hundreds of other American Cities. . . ." Remarkably, not only was Santa Fe the smallest community with a City Beautiful plan, but that plan also broke significant new ground by combining the standard emphasis on architectural homogeneity with a local revival style based on the city's historical architecture—a Romantic/Arts and Crafts impulse. Cultivating a historic image became central to reversing economic decline by stimulating tourism, while also expressing civic pride in the achievement of statehood. Soon the chamber of commerce was promoting Santa Fe not as another City *Beautiful,* but as the City *Different.*[6]

The preparation of a supplement to the 1912 plan describing the Santa Fe style fell to Morley, the meticulous, twenty-nine-year-old museum archaeologist. People had not previously studied local vernacular architecture, and when Morley began, all he could see were "the hundred variations of the Santa Fe style." Jesse Nusbaum, the museum's photographer who had also learned construction from his building contractor father, conducted an extensive survey of Santa Fe, concentrating on the unimproved, Spanish-Mexican sections of town. Poring over Nusbaum's photographs, Morley drew inspiration for the architectural revival from this pre-1850 tradition. He prescribed flat-roofed, one-story adobe construction (or at least an adobe stucco appearance), but ignored the more irregular residences in favor of

Fig. 7.2 U.S. Forest Service building, designed by Jesse Nusbaum, 1912. (Nusbaum.)

formal houses with a room placed symmetrically on either side of a portal. This purely Spanish phase of the Santa Fe style produced a new Forest Service building, and Morley's restoration of a similar historic building as his own residence.[7]

Unlike their counterparts in the East and South, Santa Fe's restorationists did not open house museums to commemorate Revolutionary or Civil War heros, or their local equivalents—Pueblo patriots and Spanish conquistadors. The museum staff and civic leaders instead sought to remake the entire community as a romantic tourist destination. Toward that end, the 1912 plan asserted "that it should be the duty of all city officials to guard the old streets against any change that will affect their appearance. . . . We further recommend that no building permits be issued . . . until proper assurance is given that the architecture will conform exteriorly with the Santa Fe style." Noted landscape architect Frederick L. Olmsted Jr., who reviewed the plan, doubted "whether any court would hold it to be within the powers of . . . a City Council, to impose such an obligation upon the owner of private property . . . without provision for the payment of damages." In a time when cities with far greater resources struggled to establish land-use zoning, the political climate was not yet ready for historical design control. After lobbying the state legislature unsuccessfully for design review authority, planning board chair H. H. Dorman began to urge "that everything should be done to create a public sentiment so strong that the Santa Fe style will always predominate." Although the 1912 plan never became legally binding, by 1920 a communitywide consensus formed behind the revival style.[8]

RESTORING THE PALACE OF THE GOVERNORS

Beginning in 1909, Jesse Nusbaum also oversaw a general rehabilitation of the palace, and by the fall of 1912 turned his attention to its plaza facade. No sketches or photographs exist of the eighteenth-century Spanish portal, which had been replaced in the 1850s with a modest Greek Revival–style porch, and again in 1877–78 with heavier, milled posts with molding capitals, a classical balustrade, and stucco scored and painted to resemble stone. To create "a noble monument to the memory of the Spanish founders of the civilization of the Southwest," Nusbaum stripped away evidence of "the rush, the impatience, the progress" of the modern world—namely, the 1878 portal. The replacement was "designed to conform to the architectural style of the period when the building was constructed." Because the evidence available on the pre-1850 facade was sketchy and somewhat contradictory, the replacement portal would of necessity be a speculative re-creation. "In smaller buildings," Nusbaum would later write, "residences and the like, such projections of the house enclosing the ends are frequently present. . . . the Palace was no exception." Nusbaum thereby assumed that the palace was an oversized version of formal domestic type that Morley had just emphasized in his definition of the revival style.[9]

In the 1913 facade remodeling, the museum staff added masonry pavilions where they conjectured rooms may been stood historically. However, they opened these up to accommodate the flow of pedestrians. A long colonnade flanked by open pavilions was a common Beaux Arts facade treatment for public buildings—for instance, New York's Penn Station. The facade of the Palace of the Governors is best understood not as an example of Spanish colonial architecture but rather as a monument in the development of an eclectic revival style, and of Beaux Arts formality turned out in regional garb.[10]

By the fall of 1913, the museum's journal, *El Palacio*, claimed that the work had "progressed sufficiently to give an adequate idea of the unity and massiveness of this historic old structure." To create this massive appearance, Nusbaum installed tree-trunk posts far thicker

Fig. 7.3 Palace of the Governors, 1913 restoration.

than typical Spanish-era columns, necessitating huge corbel capitals, roughly twice the size of a model corbel bracket found inside the palace. To make "the whole building uniform," he also applied a contemporary, pebble-dash cement stucco "simulating as nearly as possible the original finish." Formed by throwing a slurry of pebbles and cement stucco onto walls, pebble-dash provided a rustic surface quite unlike earthen plaster applied by hand. This stripping of recent accretions followed by speculative reconstruction to achieve stylistic unity reveal the museum staff as aggressive practitioners of the scrape restoration approach.[11]

INTERPLAY OF RESTORATION AND REVIVAL STYLE

In 1915, the museum staff drew inspiration from Zuni and Taos Pueblos for their design of the Painted Desert, a midway attraction at the 1915 Panama-California Exposition in San Diego. This multistory, lathe-and-plaster pseudo-Pueblo, and the accompanying dances and crafts demonstrations, proved highly popular with fairgoers. As a result, Santa Fe's boosters realized that prospective tourists were far more fascinated with exotic Pueblo Indians than with the Spanish-speaking population of New Mexico.

Jesse Nusbaum's work as the Museum of New Mexico's director of "Architectural Reconstruction and Photography" beginning in 1909 demonstrates the fluid interplay of research, restoration, and revival-style design. Nusbaum stabilized Ancestral Puebloan ruins at Mesa Verde and reconstructed a ceremonial kiva in Frijoles Canyon (now Bandelier National Monument). His photographic survey of old Santa Fe supported Morley's first definition of the revival style and the restoration design for the Palace of the Governors. Nusbaum also oversaw construction of the Painted Desert exhibit at San Diego and the 1916 Fine Art Museum in Santa Fe—an eclectic assemblage of Spanish mission and Pueblo forms.[12]

Back in Santa Fe after the San Diego fair, the museum infused its promotional material with Pueblo imagery and added terraced, multistory Pueblo forms to the Santa Fe revival style. Here, for the first but no means the last time, Santa Fe's identity and cultural life were adjusted to satisfy tourists' expectations. Although the style draws equally from Spanish and Pueblo sources—and is most accurately termed the Spanish-Pueblo Revival style—people began to call it simply the Pueblo style, and even to ignore the Spanish contribution altogether.

One-story Spanish- and Mexican-era courtyard houses around the plaza were likewise demolished to make way for revival-style buildings that emphasized terraced Pueblo forms, such as the 1920 tourist hotel, La Fonda. This increasing veneration of Pueblo Indians rankled Span-

Fig. 7.4 La Fonda Hotel, designed by Rapp, Rapp & Henderickson, 1919. (Cross Studio.)

ish American leaders, and few participated in the museum's early cultural revivals. As late as the mid-1950s, when Santa Fe was still more than two-thirds Hispanic, only twelve of the four hundred members of the city's leading preservation group had Spanish surnames. Concha Ortiz y Pino, grande dame of the Spanish American elite, for instance, remarked in 1990 apropos of Anglo-Americans remodeling historic houses that "I am happy my ancestors built of adobe, so that rather than have them desecrated by ignoramuses, they have, for the most part, gone back to the earth." Few are were outspoken as Ortiz y Pino, but she expressed a deep-seated resentment about Anglo-American manipulation of historical identity.[13]

As the community began to reverse the "ill-conceived Americanization" of Santa Fe, Anglo-American traditionalists also resolved to preserve the ancient missions that had become prototypes for the revival style. During its active years from 1922 to 1932, the Society for the Restoration and Preservation of New Mexico Missions restored churches at Acoma, Laguna, Santa Ana, and Zia Pueblos, and the Spanish village church of Las Trampas. The society sought to purify the missions of modern accretions and to restore historical appearances based on typically sketchy evidence. The society's architect, John Gaw Meem, for instance, undertook an addition to La Fonda in 1926 while also supervising restoration of the Acoma mission towers. He first designed

Fig. 7.5 La Fonda Hotel addition, deigned by John Gaw Meem, 1926. (T. Harmon Parkhurst.)

Fig. 7.6 Acoma Mission, facade restoration by John Gaw Meem, 1927. (T. Harmon Parkhurst.)

a tower for the hotel addition based on his conception of the historical appearance of the Acoma mission. The proportions and details of the hotel tower design in turn informed the Acoma restoration.[14]

In 1930, a competition for the redesign of the plaza was sponsored by Cyrus McCormick Jr., Chicago heir to the McCormick reaper fortune, who was then building a Meem-designed summer house north of the city. Meem won the competition with a plan to add unifying Spanish-style portals on the east and west sides and remake all building facades in either the Spanish-Pueblo or the Territorial Revival style (the latter based on the frontier hybrid of the Greek Revival with the adobe vernacular). The plan was not immediately executed for lack of resources and legal authority, but Meem would receive private commissions to remodel the facades of nine plaza buildings between 1937 and 1954.[15]

Elsewhere in America after World War I, the house museum approach broadened to the type of preservation pioneered by Santa Fe—the re-creation of large historical environments. Most notable was John D. Rockefeller Jr.'s restoration of Williamsburg, the colonial capital of Virginia. Rockefeller acquainted himself with Santa Fe's 1912 restoration plan when he visited the city in the summers of 1924 and 1926, just before beginning work at Williamsburg. Likewise, other pivotal figures in the history of preservation, such as William Sumner Appleton of the Society for the Preservation of New England Antiquities and those who spearheaded Charleston, South Carolina's, groundbreaking historic preservation district, were well aware of developments at Santa Fe.[16]

RESPONSES TO MODERNISM

Santa Fe's unwritten restoration consensus continued between the world wars, but was violated in the mid-1950s by a generation of young, modernist-trained architects. Their designs employed flat-roofed adobe and rustic stone forms in keeping with the local tradition, but suppressed historical ornament and included cantilevered forms and floor-to-ceiling windows in true modernist fashion. In February 1956, the *New Mexican* issued a call for a city ordinance mandating the Santa Fe style: "Our chief danger lies in the fact that we are fast becoming less and less unique, and more and more like any southwestern community of comparable size." City councilor Leo Murphy seized the issue, stating "this situation is going to get out of hand one of these days, if we don't get busy and draw up a code and a systematic plan for orderly growth which also will preserve Santa Fe's distinctiveness." "Relying as we do upon the tourist dollar for a substantial part of our economy," editorialized the *New Mexican* in support of Murphy, "Santa Fe can not afford to allow even occasional architectural misfits to slip by."[17]

The foremost spokespersons for the traditionalists were Pulitzer Prize–winning novelist Oliver La Farge and local architect Irene Von Horvath. They drafted a design-review ordinance requiring that a "historic Style Committee shall judge any proposed alteration or new structure for harmony with adjacent buildings, preservation of historic and characteristic qualities, and conformity to the Old Santa Fe Style." This encompassed "the so-called 'Pueblo,' or 'Pueblo-Spanish' or 'Spanish-Indian' and 'Territorial' styles." The ordinance described the Spanish-Pueblo Revival as Morley had in the teens, even paraphrasing passages from his writings. Flat roofs and adobe-colored walls complemented projecting vigas, canales, buttresses, and portales. The ordinance also allowed a "Recent Santa Fe Style" that adapted historic forms to modern needs, but nevertheless employed materials, colors, proportions, and details similar to historic buildings. It prohibited cantilevered forms and limited doors and windows to not more than 40 percent of a building's facades, and to no closer than three feet from the corner of a building.[18]

As the council vote on the ordinance neared in the fall of 1957, opposition coalesced behind the newly founded Southwest Design Council, consisting primarily of young architects and architectural historians. "We are not opposed to—we are in fact heartily in favor of—the preservation of historic buildings and areas," observed council president John Conron. "The Ordinance, as proposed, outlines no procedure for the maintenance and preservation of valued historical buildings. Instead the ordinance stresses the importance of limiting future buildings . . . to mimicked copies of historical landmarks." Indeed, council members would prove themselves staunch historic preservationists over the years; they simply doubted that good design could be legislated. At a final public forum, the "amount of frequent applause" indicated strong support for the ordinance. Two nights later, the city council adopted it unanimously.[19]

The deep spatial structure of the Spanish colonial town with its plaza and informal grid leading quickly to winding lanes was fixed by property-ownership boundaries and guaranteed much of Santa Fe's distinctiveness. The historic design review ordinance emphasizing stylistic details would add to visual harmony, but addressed only one spatial pattern: the Spanish tradition of portales lining the plaza and commercial streets. Santa Fe's portales had been removed in the 1890s with the construction of Italianate business blocks set back at the sidewalk's edge. The museum staff called for the return of the portales in the teens, a sentiment reiterated by the 1930 plaza design competition. Finally, in 1966, Meem drafted an economic revitalization plan that argued that the plaza area "must counteract the parking handicaps by being so attractive in itself that it will draw not only tourists, but high-class business as well." Central to increasing its attractiveness was the return of the "portales, unify all the business, faced [on] the Plaza." Meem and fellow architect Kenneth Clark designed the new ten-and-a-half-foot-tall portales, which offered "the required spaciousness and dignity." (Compare figures 7.1 and 7.7.) Forty-two years after the 1912 plan, the ill-conceived Americanization of the railroad era had finally been reversed.[20]

The adoption of the design review ordinance also stimulated interest in Santa Fe's historic architecture and in historical preservation as distinct from restoration. When the planning commission surveyed the city to identify significant buildings in 1956, "to its utter amazement, it found that only some twenty-five buildings comprised the great antiquity of this world-renowned tourist mecca!" Those who

Fig. 7.7 South side of Santa Fe Plaza, with restored portal by John Gaw Meem and Kenneth Clark, 1967. (Chris Wilson.)

had rallied behind the design review ordinance now turned to the preservation of these key buildings and, in the late 1960s, to the fight against urban renewal plans to level a skid row and working-class district west of the plaza.[21]

As in Santa Fe, the grassroots preservation groundswell of the 1950s and 1960s nationally reacted against the homogeneous International Style, and the modernist remaking of inner cities (through urban renewal clearances and interstate highway construction) by fighting to preserve historic buildings and districts. The reaction against modern placelessness was often cast as a call for a greater sense of place. Uses of that concept have ranged from the relatively shallow appreciation of aesthetic character or as tourism advertising images to the more spatially rooted creation of public spaces for social and civic identity by Charles Moore and Christopher Alexander, or the cultivation of place-based identity through grassroots public history, historic preservation, and participatory public art chronicled by Dolores Hayden and Lucy Lippard.[22]

But even as the very notion of preservation involved an intent to capture and cherish a particular place in an earlier time, preservation theory and federal initiatives resulting from this movement embraced a central modernist concept. In the nineteenth century, historians had observed that the art and architecture of a particular period expressed the spirit of that time—in German, its *zeitgeist*. Modernist theorists turned this after-the-fact observation into the moral imperative that contemporary architects must express the zeitgeist of the industrial, technological era. For preservationists, this meant that additions to historic buildings should embody the contemporary spirit; it would be false for them to adopt the style of historic buildings. Amid the pervasive modernist sensibility of the era, the spirit of the time became more important than the sense of place.

Of course, the preservation of historic buildings has done much to sustain the spirit of place. But as preservationists have increasingly acknowledged in recent years, freezing buildings as historic artifacts ignores and, in some cases, works against the living cultures that are also essential to local vitality. The requirement that structures be at least fifty years old to be eligible for the National Register of Historic Places, and the denigration of later construction as noncontributing, even intrusive to historic districts, opens a gulf between history and the present, while many preservationists lose sight of the value of ongoing regional design traditions. If regional revival styles, speculative restoration, and preservation intertwined before World War II, the postwar preservation orthodoxy—codified in the Secretary of the Interior's Standards for Rehabilitation in 1976—effectively prohibited historical revivalism and strongly discouraged speculative restoration. Not surprisingly, perhaps, the leading historian of preservation during these years, Charles Hosmer, retrospectively justified the postwar preservation orthodoxy by downplaying, criticizing, and often omitting examples of the earlier synergies among revivalism, restoration, and preservation. In the 1,547 pages of his three volumes, for instance, he makes no mention of the 1912 Santa Fe plan.[23]

THE REGIONAL PARADOX OF GLOBALIZATION

In many ways, globalization represents an intensification of the social, technological, and economic modernization of the past two centuries. The term *globalization*, coined in the mid-1970s, describes the lowering of international trade barriers to permit the freer movement of goods and capital, which favored the growth of multinational corporations. In the early 1980s, at the behest of these corporate interests, Ronald Reagan and Margaret Thatcher led the move to downsize national governments by deregulating everything from banking to air travel, and rolling back social welfare programs, labor rights and environmental laws. Globalization penetrated our everyday lives in the form of the communications revolution—in the fax modem, cellular telephones, personal computer, Internet, and increasing personal mobility from our daily automobile rounds to the regularization of business air travel.[24]

Many assume that these developments lead inexorably to cultural homogenization. But paradoxically, for a variety of reasons, globalization has also meant the resurgence of regionalism. Resistance to social dislocations caused by globalization has fostered traditional and local associations as diverse as ethnic and fundamentalist religious renaissances, the anti-globalization movement with its consciousness of regional ecological differences, and calls for the revitalization of local democratic control. With the declining power of nation-states and the free movement of capital, local governments and business elites have also formed new alliances in the ruthless competition to attract corporate investment.

The globalization of the consumer economy also has made regional difference an increasingly valuable commodity. The cultivation of the sense of place increasingly challenges the modernist emphasis on the spirit of the time. Cultural products for export or for a local tourism market, and the income they generate, can also help revitalize local languages and cultures. Cheaper air travel combined with the need to counter deindustrialization and regional economic stagnation has led many state and local governments to turn to heritage tourism development. Similarly, with the mobility afforded by air travel and the communications revolution, many with flexible occupations or increased wealth from the reduction of tax rates on upper income brackets (under Reagan's 1981 Economic Recovery Tax Act) have increasingly built second homes in places with a salubrious climate, stunning landscapes, and a variety of historical and cultural amenities.[25]

EFFECTS OF THE VOGUE OF SANTA FE

In this context, the 1980s vogue of Santa Fe turns out to have been an early manifestation of globalization. With its then-seventy-year history of heritage tourism development, Santa Fe offered an already commodified regional culture adaptable as a style of interior decoration, as a proven tourist destination, and a magnet for the new subculture of amenity migrants. Million-dollar residences, time-share condominiums, and tourist hotels were built in abundance; hotel receipts jumped from twenty-five million dollars in 1985 to eighty-six million in 1992. Art galleries and Indian goods shops nearly tripled from 107 to 295 during the 1980s, while gourmet restaurants, chic clothing stores, bookstores, and tour businesses multiplied. Santa Fe's million-plus tourist visitors annually, combined with several thousand amenity migrants who came and stayed, were more than a city of sixty thousand could comfortably absorb. Globalization has had three major impacts on the preservation of Santa Fe's community character: the gentrification of working-class neighborhoods, the construction of larger, out-of-scale buildings in the plaza area, and the revitalization of regional urban design traditions.[26]

Growing numbers of amenity migrants increased residential real estate speculation by the mid-1980s. In effect, the entire community began to be gentrified—notably the Hispanic, working-class West-side/Guadalupe neighborhood. A few nineteenth-century houses in the neighborhood stand side by side at the street's edge, and oriented toward private courtyards. As the neighborhood grew after 1920, however, Hispanic residents built more compact, freestanding houses, situated ten or fifteen feet back from the sidewalk, in part emulating bungalows and suburban ranch houses. But most also enclosed the sides and rear of their lots with tall walls and defined the sidewalk's edge with low masonry walls or masonry piers linked by picket fences, wrought iron, chain link, or decorative block. The vibrant aes-

Fig. 7.8 Mercer Street, Westside neighborhood, 1991. (Chris Wilson.)

thetic of textured stucco, polychromatic brickwork, wrought iron, ornamental stone veneers, and vivid colors in the Westside contrasted
sharply with the muted, Arts and Crafts, earth-tone palette of the
tourist plaza and the wealthy, predominantly Anglo Eastside neighborhood.[27]

As rents and property values escalated in the 1980s, many working-
class residents could no longer afford Santa Fe's cost of living, and they
moved thirty miles north to Española trailer parks or sixty miles south
to the Albuquerque suburbs, from which they commuted to their min-
imum-wage service jobs or state government work. As property values
escalated elsewhere in Santa Fe, the Westside became attractive to
young, primarily Anglo-American, but also Hispanic professionals. By
1990, it was not uncommon to see a banged-up, black '76 Chevy in
front of an owner-built house, and next door to glimpse a BMW and
an Isuzu Trooper in the compound of a recently remodeled Santa Fe
revival house. Gentrified properties typically have a new six-foot-tall,
adobe-colored wall or pole fence (in real estate parlance, a coyote
fence) at the sidewalk—the better to create a romantic Spanish courtyard within. Longtime residents complained that this was destroying
the face-to-face interaction and sense of community fostered by the
low walls.[28]

Fig. 7.9 De Fouri Street, gentrified portion of Westside neighborhood, 1991. (Chris Wilson.)

Just as real estate speculation heated up in 1983, the city's historic design review process was extended to the eastern half of the Westside neighborhood. The ordinance establishing the Westside district specified "browns, tans, local earth tones and soft pastels" but prohibited the painting "of buildings with a color that causes arresting or spectacular effects or bold repetitive patterns." It also prescribes "brick, adobe, masonry, rock, wood, and coyote fencing," and prohibits unpainted concrete block and chain link—the predominant vernacular choices. Although some owner-built projects evade the design review process, the most vibrant examples of the contemporary Hispanic vernacular are now illegal in the eastern half of the Westside barrio. "It is probably no coincidence," wrote architect Beverly Spears in 1990, "that the creation of the Westside/Guadalupe Historic District and its design controls coincided with a period of sharply escalating property values and real estate speculation in the area." The suppression of the working-class Hispanic aesthetics goes hand and hand with their displacement from the neighborhood.[29]

Escalating commercial property values likewise encouraged a jump in the scale of new construction surrounding the plaza. Two massive five-story buildings erected in the 1980s—the First Interstate Bank and the El Dorado Hotel—precipitated a crisis in the design review process. In contrast to the picturesque composition of earlier Spanish-Pueblo Revival buildings, the long, repetitious porches of the Interstate building and the symmetrical facade of El Dorado betrayed the regimentation of large-scale financing and a formal grandeur at odds with the style's vernacular origins. With the construction of these and other massive buildings, the community realized that detailed historical style regulations alone would not protect their image of Santa Fe. In response, the city planning department produced a handbook defining fifteen townscape districts, and tying the height and density of new buildings to the existing architectural scale in each. This contextual sensibility insisted that buildings have a responsibility to help define the edges of streets and public spaces.[30]

But large buildings per se were not the problem. John Gaw Meem's locally admired 1929 addition to La Fonda Hotel, for instance, is taller and more densely developed than the 1980s buildings. Yet Meem suggested the piecemeal accretion of a terraced Pueblo village when he made a six-story tower the off-center focus of the addition, and broke the massing into asymmetrical yet carefully composed forms (see figure 7.5). Architects of Meem's generation learned the uses of historical evocation and picturesque composition. Despised by modernists as illegitimate concerns in the modern machine age, these skills, which had been so essential to the development of Santa Fe's character in the 1920s and 1930s, disappeared from architectural education after World War II.

Santa Fe persisted as a significant enclave of regional historicism through the modernist 1950s and 1960s, and found validation in the postmodernist turn to popular iconography in the 1970s and the rise of New Urbanism in the 1990s. New Urbanists criticize single-use zoning and automobile sprawl for wasting land and nonrenewable resources, and for fragmenting communities. They seek to update preautomobile design patterns—especially higher-density, mixed-use building types, and pedestrian-oriented settlement patterns—that create greater opportunities for face-to-face community. New Urbanists study classic main street and plaza pedestrian spaces, and adapt these to new town designs. The New Urbanist revitalization of historical precedents complements the commodification of regional difference under globalization.[31]

The suburban neighborhood village of Aldea (originally named Frijoles Village) was initiated by a partnership of Santa Fe investors and designed in 1998 by the leading New Urbanist firm of Duany Plater-Zyberk, with later refinements by Moule and Polyzoides. (The principal partners of these two firms made up four of the six founding members of the Congress for the New Urbanism.) Marketed primarily to newcomers, recent brochures nostalgically suggest that "Aldea is reminiscent of a time when people built harmonious villages where they lived, worked, shopped and socialized." The design adopts Santa Fe's architectural mystique as a marketing image, while also cloning the most desirable aspects of the city's urban fabric. The new village center echoes the old plaza, while the twenty lots surrounding it are zoned for two-story buildings that mix stores and home offices on the ground floor with residences above—an echo of the railroad-era business block. Small parking courts tucked behind the buildings accommodate the automobile, while apartments around the plaza give way gradually to courtyard houses and compounds inspired by Spanish-Mexican and Anglo art-colony traditions, which yield residential densities roughly double surrounding subdivisions.[32]

Avant-garde modernist architects may think Santa Fe's ongoing regional historicism violates the spirit of the age, while those who adhere to the preservation orthodoxy of the Secretary of the Interior's standards dismiss the free-wheeling restoration approach that has prevailed in Santa Fe. And yet the preservation of select streets and building, the fostering of a regional style, and the revitalization of a vocabulary of courtyard houses, compounds, and plazas have helped

Fig. 7.10 Forecourt Houses from Frijoles Village Plan (now Aldea de Santa Fe) by Duany Plater-Zyberk & Co., town planners. (Courtesy of Duany Plater-Zyberk Company.)

sustain the city's distinctive sense of place, its economy, and its cultural life. The intensified commodification of history and cultural difference under globalization since 1980 and the related rise of New Urbanism have revitalized regional architecture and urban design not only in Santa Fe, but increasingly across the country as well. The future vitality of the preservation movement—and the vitality of communities dependent on heritage tourism—hinges, in part, on a critical reexamination of the modernist underpinnings of preservationist values to permit the balancing of the expression of the spirit of the time with a dynamic sense of place. It may also hinge on a more sympathetic appreciation of the synergies of preservation, restoration, and revivalism at Santa Fe, and in the larger preservation movement before World War II.

NOTES

1. I would like to thank Virginia Scharff, Lynée Busta, and Max Page for their valuable editorial suggestions. This piece is adapted in part from my book *The Myth of Santa Fe: Creating a Modern Regional Traditions* (Albuquerque: University of New Mexico Press, 1997), with the permission of the publisher. I note secondary sources and the sources for direct quotes below, but rather than reiterate all of the primary source materials cited in the endnotes of *The Myth of Santa Fe,* I cite only the appropriate sections of that book here.

2. Wilson, *Myth,* chap. 1.
3. Wilson, *Myth,* chap. 2, 3.
4. Wilson, *Myth,* 117–21; Beatrice Chauvenet, *Hewett and Friends: A Biography of Santa Fe's Vibrant Era* (Santa Fe: Museum of New Mexico Press, 1983).
5. Wilson, *Myth,* 121–2; M. Christine Boyer, *Dreaming the Rational City: The Myth of American City Planning* (Cambridge, MA: MIT Press, 1983).
6. Wilson, *Myth,* 122. Quotes: H. H. Dorman to Honorable Mayor of Chicago, 18 March 1912, Wiess-Loomis Collection (WL) History Library, Museum of New Mexico (MNM), Santa Fe. "Proceedings of the City Council," *Daily New Mexican (DNM),* 24 November 1912, 7, reproduces the text of the 1912 city plan. "Planning the City," Bulletin No. 4 of the National Conference on City Planning (Boston: Wood, Clark Press, 1913), WL-MNM, lists fifty-nine U.S. cities with city plans or organizations to promote planning. Of the five with populations less than 25,000, Santa Fe was smallest in the 1910 census with 5,072, and Boulder, Colorado next smallest with 9,539.
7. Wilson, *Myth,* 122.
8. Wilson, *Myth,* 236–7; Santa Fe City Plan, undated TS, probably 1912, under subheading "Ancient Streets and Structures," WL-MNM; Frederick L. Olmsted to H. H. Dorman, 7 July 1913, WL-MNM; "Notes of Interest on City Planning," *DNM,* 5 March 1912, 3.
9. Wilson, *Myth,* 124–5; Archeology Institute of American (AIA), "Second Annual Report of the Managing Committee of the School of American Archeology, 1908–09," 180; "Restoration of the Palace," *El Palacio (EP)* 1:1 (November 1913), 5; Rosemary Nusbaum, *The City Different and the Palace . . . Including Jesse Nusbaum's Restoration Journals* (Santa Fe: Sunstone Press, 1978), 48.
10. Wilson, *Myth,* 126.
11. Wilson, *Myth,* 125; "Restoration of the Palace," *EP* 1:1 (November 1913), 5; Letter to Dear Sir [outlining work accomplished on the palace and arguments for further funding from upcoming state legislative session], 1 February 1912, Hewett Collection (H), MNM, Box 23, Folder 4.
12. Wilson, *Myth,* 120, 235.
13. Membership list for Old Santa Fe Association, undated but probably about 1956 judging from the other materials in the file, Cassidy Family Papers, Bancroft Library, University of California, Berkeley; interview with Concha Ortiz y Pino de Kleven, 10 March 1990.
14. Wilson, *Myth,* 237–44.
15. Wilson, *Myth,* 251.
16. Wilson, *Myth,* 252–553; "Western Trip 1924," and "Western Trip 1926" files, Rockefeller Family Papers, Rockefeller Archives Center, Tarrytown, New York; William Sumner Appleton, "Destruction and Preservation of Old Buildings in New England," *Art and Archeology* 8:3 (May–June 1919), 130–83 at 180; Robin E. Datel, "Southern Regionalism and Historic Preservation in Charleston, South Carolina, 1920–1940," *Journal of Historical Geography* 16:2 (1990), 197–215 at 209.
17. Wilson, *Myth,* 253–53; "A Time for Action," editorial, *DNM,* 10 February 1956, 4; 23 February 1956, 1; "Murphy Plugs for Return to Santa Fe Style," *DNM,* 4 March 1956, 1; "Santa Fe Style," editorial, *DNM,* 23 February 1956, 4.
18. Wilson, *Myth,* 255–6; Ordinance No. 1957–18, City of Santa Fe, Sections 3.A, 7.F (republished *DNM,* 25 October 1957, 12).
19. Wilson, *Myth,* 256–7; John Conron, letter to the editor, *DNM,* 30 October 1957, 4.
20. Wilson, *Myth,* 259; John G. Meem, "Phase II: Santa Fe Plaza Renewal Project," TS, 22 April 1970, General Files, Correspondence F File, Meem Collection, Zimmerman Library, University of New Mexico, Albuquerque.
21. Wilson, *Myth,* 260; Oliver La Farge and Irene Von Horvath, "Excerpt from City Planning Commission, Committee on Preservation of the Santa Fe Character, October 4,

1956, Addendum to Report of August 30, 1956," Box 6, Folder 8n, Bunting Collection, Zimmerman Library, University of New Mexico, Albuquerque.

22. Donlyn Lyndon, Charles W. Moore, Sim Van der Ryn, and Patrick J. Quinn, "Toward Making Places," *Landscape* 12:1 (Autumn 1962), 31–41; Christopher Alexander et al., *A Pattern Language: Towns, Buildings, Construction* (New York: Oxford University Press, 1977); Dolores Hayden, *The Power of Place: Urban Landscapes as Public History* (Cambridge, MA: MIT Press, 1995); Lucy R. Lippard, *The Lure of the Local: Senses of Place in a Multicentered Society* (New York: The New Press, 1997).

23. Charles B. Hosmer Jr., *Presence of the Past: A History of the Preservation Movement in the United States Before Williamsburg* (New York: G. P. Putnam's Sons, 1965); Charles B. Hosmer, *Preservation Comes of Age: From Williamsburg to the National Trust*, 2 vols., (Charlottesville: University Press of Virginia, 1981).

24. David Harvey, *Justice, Nature and the Geography of Difference* (London: Blackwell, 1996), esp. 420–4; Nicholas Lehmenn, "No Man's Town," *The New Yorker*, 5 June 2000, 42–8.

25. Michael Keating, *Nations Against the State* (New York: St. Martin's Press, 1996).

26. Wilson, *Myth*, 263.

27. Wilson, *Myth*, 269–70.

28. Wilson, *Myth*, 272, 375–76, note 71.

29. Wilson, *Myth*, 271–3; City of Santa Fe, "Bill no. 9, 1983, Establishing a Westside-Guadalupe Historic District ...," 1, 4; Beverly Spears, "Santa Fe's Westside/Guadalupe Historic District: Hispanic Vernacular Versus Pueblo Revival," *New Mexico Architecture* 31:5–6 (September 1990), 9–13 at 9.

30. Wilson, *Myth*, 262–5.

31. Peter Katz, *The New Urbanism: Toward an Architecture of Community* (New York: McGraw-Hill, 1994); Congress for the New Urbanism, *Charter of the New Urbanism* (New York: McGraw-Hill, 2000).

32. "Criticism of Frijoles Village Illustrates Need for Dialogue," *New Mexico Designer/Builder*, March 1995, 5–7; Duany Plater-Zyberk & Company, "Draft Master Plan of Frijoles Village" (Santa Fe: author, 1997); "Invitation to a Lifestyle: Aldea de Santa Fe," promotional brochures, 2002, author's files.

8

CHICAGO'S MECCA FLAT BLUES[1]

Daniel Bluestone

CHICAGO'S LATE-NINETEENTH-CENTURY apartment buildings helped to dramatically transform the urban landscape. They provided architects with novel design problems and accommodated tens of thousands of residents. Nevertheless, architectural historians have more readily focused on other Chicago subjects, including the downtown skyscrapers and an alluring group of stylistically notable single-family houses dotting the suburban prairie.[2] In contrast to these structures, neatly categorized as either commercial or residential, the city's apartment houses represent an uneasy combination of public space and private realm, commerce and residence. These early apartment houses formed something of a hinge between the skyscraper and the single-family house, adopting skyscraper models for accommodating people at high density while navigating strong ideological commitments to the single-family residence. By their hybrid nature, they confounded the order that some observers believed appropriate to turn-of-the-twentieth-century urban social life.

This essay explores the Mecca (figure 8.1), one of Chicago's largest nineteenth-century apartment houses. Designed in 1891 by Willoughby J. Edbrooke and Franklin Pierce Burnham, the Mecca reflects broader architectural developments, in particular the role of natural light and landscape in shaping turn-of-the-twentieth-century Chicago architecture. Yet the Mecca, like many apartment buildings, differed from other urban structures in its unusually cosmopolitan combination of social and spatial elements. The Mecca's extraordinary twentieth-century history reveals many urban planners' intolerance for that openness intrinsic to

Fig. 8.1 Edbrooke & Burnham, The Mecca, Chicago, 1891–1892. Exterior perspective, looking north into courtyard. Detail from 1893 advertisement. The Mecca provided hotel accommodations during the Columbian Exposition. ICHi-29342. (Courtesy of the Chicago Historical Society.)

some apartment-house designs. It also suggests the need for historians to pursue architectural history well beyond the tidy nexus of meaning that exists between original patrons, forms, and civic purpose. Over time, race intersected with urban space to alter the history and fragment public perceptions of the Mecca. These changing perceptions stood at the center of a decade-long preservation struggle. Although the early preservation movement generally adopted prevailing notions of Chicago School aesthetics as its point of departure, the Mecca campaign emphasized housing and neighborhood. In place of an aesthetic model for preservation efforts, the Mecca's story recovers a series of alternative priorities.[3] Its narrative enriches our understanding of American urbanism, architectural history, and preservation practice.

Apartment living vexed late-nineteenth-century Chicagoans. In 1891, the astute editors of *Industrial Chicago* argued that the economic depression of the 1870s had "banished the idea of a permanent home from many hearts." Apartment buildings took the place of small homes by grouping between ten and forty units under one roof. Reflecting contemporary cultural concerns, the editors inquired: "What if the flat would destroy home life?"[4] Similar questions dogged apartment designers and profoundly shaped building design. Architectural historian Carroll William Westfall has summed up the problem confronting Chicago residents: "Although the house became less practicable for the lives they found themselves living, they continued to equate the house with home. The result was a conundrum: civil manners forbade what utility required."[5]

The romanticized image of middle-class, nuclear-family domesticity hovered over apartment-house debates. A 1905 *Chicago Tribune* editorial, capturing the tone of contemporary critiques, reported that physicians in London had found that the "monotony" of apartment living was "driving an alarming number of women mad. . . . Her husband leaves for business early in the morning and usually doesn't return until evening. Between the janitor and the maid she has little housework to do. . . . The greater the number of the people living in the building with her the fewer she knows. . . . Race suicide or the rules of the flat deprive her of the luxury of children." Though the editors identified "avenues of escape," including reading, art, charitable work, and even business occupations, the editorial gave credence to the fear that apartment living would lead Anglo-American couples to stop raising large families, further tipping the demographic balance toward immigrants.[6] To the extent that women were charged with the moral stewardship of the family and the nation, the notion of the deterioration of their privacy and their possible jettisoning of family altogether troubled social commentators. This critique framed apartment-house design at the turn of the twentieth century.[7]

The Mecca's size combined with the originality of its design to capture attention in the 1890s. Projected as a Mecca for "flat-seekers," the building would require a large population, since the six-hundred-thousand-dollar structure included ninety-eight flats and occupied a site that cost two hundred thousand. Built four miles south of downtown, the four-story building stretched 234 feet along State Street and 266 feet west along Thirty-fourth Street to Dearborn. The Mecca's simple Romanesque style elevations, with their arched entrances and round-arched top-floor windows rippled with projecting window bays and the play of shadows cast by the cornice and stringcourses. The style and composition reflected the popular forms of numerous commercial and residential structures built by leading Chicago architects during the 1880s. What struck reporters as unusual was that each floor covered nearly one and a half acres. The Mecca's density contrasted sharply with the more familiar patterns of organizing domestic space in the growing city. The *Chicago Tribune* reported that the anticipated population of nearly five hundred residents would approach that of a "fair-sized village. Ninety-eight cottages would cover each lot in two five-acre blocks, and with twelve stores [the Mecca] would outrank many a rising suburb."[8]

Many late-nineteenth-century Chicago architects actually fostered associations with the suburbs and disguised flats as houses in order to diffuse the hostility toward apartment living. In multifamily dwellings with from two to six units, architects could give apartments the appearance of single mansions. In larger buildings, varied fenestration patterns, pitched gables, ornamental details, and choice building materials helped blend apartments into the broader residential landscape. When the size of apartment buildings stretched beyond that of the house or mansion, architects appropriated hotel and club models to maintain domestic associations.[9] Although homeowners in single-family neighborhoods often complained of the "flat invasion," apartment-house builders in these areas proudly pointed to the exclusive character of the neighborhood.[10]

Beyond formal stylistic strategies for blunting the prejudice against flats, architects developed site plans that incorporated the cherished images of single-family suburbs. Landscaped courtyards proved central to the effort. When the *Tribune* calculated that the Mecca's ninety-eight units would require ten acres of land if configured as suburban cottages, it implied that nearly eight and a half acres of trees, yards, and gardens would be jettisoned in the transit from suburb to Mecca. Some apartment buildings actually stood back from their lot line in order to incorporate a modest landscaped setting. The Mecca did not do this. Instead, Edbrooke & Burnham gave the Mecca an unusual U-shaped plan centered on a landscaped courtyard that opened south onto Thirty-fourth Street. On the way into the Mecca's main entrance, residents and visitors traversed the apartment equivalent of a suburban lawn, a "miniature park" measuring 66 by 152 feet (figures 8.1, 8.2).[11]

The Mecca's exterior courtyard, with its handsome fountain, provided the first local example of the low-rise courtyard apartment building that proliferated in Chicago and its suburbs from 1900 through the 1920s.[12] In Chicago, small residential parks had earlier provided a focus for single-family row-house developments such as Aldine Square, built in 1876 at Vincennes Avenue between Thirty-seventh and Thirty-ninth Streets (figure 8.3). Beyond the landscaped court, the Mecca's plan also provided a bay window in nearly every parlor, increasing light and air circulation through the apartments. In subsequent Chicago courtyard designs, the concern for natural light expanded to include sunrooms, balconies, and individual porches. For a given-sized lot, the courtyard configuration created a much longer embellished front facade than was possible in a building massed on the front lot line. In the Mecca, walls of high-quality Roman brick lined the courtyard and the three street facades. Cruder common red brick appeared only on the rear alley wall. In contrast to apartments built around interior light wells, these designs also opened a greater percentage of interior spaces to prime prospects over landscaped

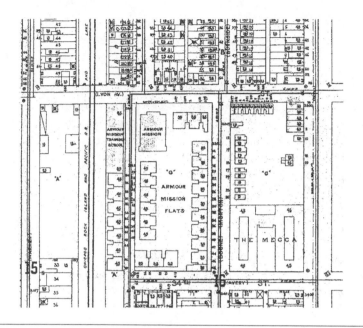

Fig. 8.2 Map plan of the Mecca and its context. Street at right is State Street, Dearborn Street is marked Boone, Armour Street, later named Federal Street, runs to the left of the Armour Mission. The five-story Armour Mission Training School was the first building of the Armour Institute. It is now occupied by the successor institution, the Illinois Institute of Technology, see figure 15. From Greeley-Carlson Company, *Second Atlas of the City of Chicago, Volume Two*, Chicago, 1892. (Courtesy of Library of Congress.)

courts and to the street.[13] These elements compressed suburban forms for apartment tenants.

Courtyards also addressed another critical issue in the debate over apartment houses—that of domestic privacy. Large apartment buildings that relied upon central stairs and elevators concentrated building residents and visitors at single main entrances, in lobbies, around stairs and elevators, and in common corridors linked to the circulation core. In contrast, courtyards diffused the building's density before people actually entered. As the courtyard form developed in Chicago, numerous entrances opened onto the courtyard. Each entrance gave access to a stair that generally reached only two apartments on each landing (figure 8.4). Thus only six to eight families, as opposed to all of the building's tenants, used each entrance. Architectural critic Herbert Croly argued that Chicago courtyard buildings could "wear a domestic aspect," "obtain a certain amount of propriety," and "suggest the privacies and seclusion of Anglo-Saxon domestic life."[14]

Yet unlike Chicago courtyard apartments constructed later, the Mecca turned both outward toward its exterior courtyard and, most un-

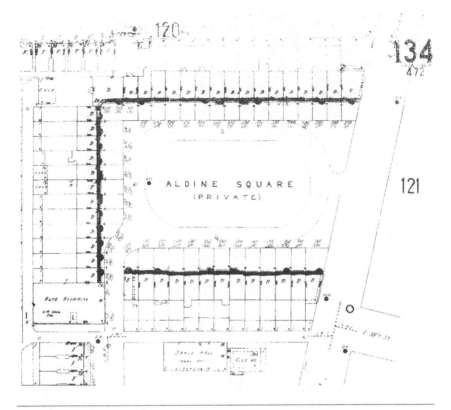

Fig. 8.3 Map plan of Aldine Square, Chicago, built 1876, demolished c. 1935. Single-family row houses faced a landscaped park. From Sanborn Map Company, *Insurance Maps of Chicago, volume 4,* New York, 1912. (Courtesy of Library of Congress.)

usually, inward toward extraordinary interior atria. Edbrooke & Burnham planned each of the two primary wings of the Mecca around an enormous interior skylit atrium, each one measuring 33 by 170 feet (figures 8.2, 8.5). In each wing, a ground-story lobby, stairs, and heavily foliated ornamental balconies, cantilevered from the atrium's walls, provided access to the individual apartments. Each apartment's interior rooms had windows opening onto the atrium courts and received natural light from the gabled skylights. The atria provided the Mecca with two expansive interior spaces flooded with light that expressed in monumental form a pervasive cultural concern for light and air. Although suburban landscapes reflected this same desire for light, they rarely captured it in the monumental architectural forms that emerged as middle-class residents started living and working at much higher densities.

The Mecca's exterior courtyard helped establish a Chicago precedent for courtyard buildings; however, the atria distinguished it in im-

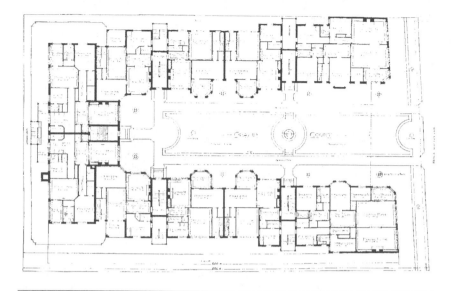

Fig. 8.4 Andrew Sandegren, Oak Ridge Apartments, Evanston, Illinois, 1914. Plan shows the diffused circulation provided by five separate courtyard entrances. From A. J. Pardridge and Harold Bradley, *Directory to Apartments of the Better Class Along the North Side of Chicago,* Chicago, 1917. (From author's collection.)

Fig. 8.5 The Mecca, 1891–1892. Interior atrium served as a "Ladies Parlor" when the Mecca provided hotel accommodations during the Columbian Exposition. Detail from 1893 advertisement. ICHi-29342. (Courtesy of the Chicago Historical Society.)

portant ways from subsequent courtyard buildings. The Mecca had two entrances on State, two on Dearborn, three in the courtyard, and one on the rear alley. The multiple entrances conformed to the general pattern of later courtyard buildings that discreetly diffused the building's density. Yet the Mecca's atria made a spectacle of the comings and goings of residents, of the concourse of daily human life. In the atria, on the balconies, at interior doors and windows, the massing of people in the Mecca clearly manifested itself. With their "promenade balconies," the atria developed as public places where people would see and be seen.[15] The atria thereby negated the potential for privacy made possible with courtyard entrances. Thus the Mecca design contained two rich but contrary tendencies. One tendency, captured in the exterior courtyard and separate entrances, responded to entrenched fear over the compromise of single-family living and familial privacy; the other tendency, represented in the skylit atria, cultivated the possibilities of a gregarious and cosmopolitan gathering of five hundred people under a single roof. It took only a few years for the more private model to completely rout the cosmopolitan one in the work of Chicago apartment architects.

The Mecca's novel courtyard followed the general logic evident in the downtown commercial landscape, where architects had learned to sacrifice space for light, "leaving out of doors everything that cannot be perfectly lighted."[16] Successful commercial architects warned that dark rooms would not be rented and should not be built. The Mecca atria (figure 8.6) enjoyed specific local precedents among some of Chicago's notable skyscrapers. The *Chicago Tribune* compared the Mecca's atria to the prominent skylit atrium in Baumann & Huehl's thirteen-story Chamber of Commerce Building, constructed in 1888. That building incorporated a 35-by-108-foot skylit atrium rimmed by galleries and ornate balustrades that provided access to the offices on every floor (figure 8.7). Describing the Mecca plan in terms of the Chamber of Commerce Building, the *Tribune* settled on a model known for its prominent two-hundred-foot-high atrium. Moreover, it singled out a building that the Mecca's architects knew well; Edbrooke & Burnham maintained their architectural offices at the very top of the Chamber of Commerce atrium.[17] George W. Henry, the Mecca's developer, had a real estate office opening onto the atrium two floors below Edbrooke & Burnham.

Beginning in the 1870s, many leading Chicago architects had developed great architectural effect by flooding the interiors of their increasingly massive buildings with natural light. In the 1880s, the modern light-court atrium became an integral and monumental part of skyscraper architecture. In 1881, for example, Burnham & Root de-

Fig. 8.6 The Mecca, 1891–1892. Interior atrium with detail of foliated metalwork of the promenade balcony rail. Photograph by Wallace Kirkland, 1951. ICHi-29352. (Courtesy of the Chicago Historical Society.)

signed the six-story Chicago, Burlington & Quincy Railroad's office building around an atrium measuring more than one hundred by fifty feet. Iron galleries encircled the light court, giving access to the offices (figure 8.8). Wheelock & Clay adopted a similar plan for the Open Board of Trade Building in 1884. Burnham & Root's 1893 Masonic Temple Building contained a central light court that ran 302 feet to a rooftop skylight. Other Chicago office buildings incorporated central

Fig. 8.7 Baumann & Huehl, Chamber of Commerce Building, Chicago, 1888–1890, demolished. View of balconies and interior skylit atrium where the developer and architect of the Mecca had offices. (Courtesy of the Avery Library, Columbia University.)

light courts without fully developing such dramatic architectural effects. Burnham & Root's 1885 Rookery Building, for example, enclosed a central light court at the level of its two-story lobby rather than at the top of the building and relied upon an internal double-loaded corridor system rather than galleries for access to offices.[18]

Fig. 8.8 Burnham & Root, Chicago, Burlington & Quincy Railroad Building, Chicago, 1881–1882, demolished. Perspective of interior skylit atrium and balconies. From *New York Daily Graphic* (26 February 1883). (Courtesy of Library of Congress.)

Chicago's skylit commercial and residential interiors drew upon a broad nineteenth-century building tradition. Technological developments in the manufacture of both glass and metal permitted the expansive lighting of interior spaces, which proved especially important given the increasing size and complexity of nineteenth-century buildings. Skylit retail arcades, with shop-lined pedestrian corridors, opened in major cities throughout Europe and the United States. The arcades, with central skylights and multistory galleries, included key features of the atrium system at the Mecca. Art galleries, train stations, conservatories, prisons and asylums, department stores, and office buildings all used skylights to great effect. Buildings such as J. B. Bunning's Coal Exchange, London (1846–49), had offices open onto galleries around a circular court topped by a glass-and-metal skylight. Many retail arcades provided housing on the floors above the shops.

The purely residential application of the arcade found formative expression in early-nineteenth-century utopian plans for phalansteries made by French social reformer Charles Fourier. It is notable that Fourier's vision of collective housing communities of two thousand residents incorporated an interior "street gallery" to give access to apartments on several floors. It also included enclosed skylit passages between different parts of the community. The architecture of the phalanstery highlights the gregarious and collective basis of the residential atrium with its gallery corridor system. Indeed, the preferences for domestic privacy in Chicago contrasted sharply with Fourier's conception of communities as well as with prison atria used for better supervision of inmates. The Chicago structures extended the disparate uses of the building type.[19]

The Mecca's atria also reflected aspects of a broader European and American tradition of central-courtyard apartment buildings. Central courtyards provided a semipublic space with possibilities for weaving the fabric of community. In some notable model tenements, such as Alfred Treadway White's 1890 Riverside Apartments in Brooklyn, designers established courtyards as protected areas of leisure for both children and adults. Courtyards also undoubtedly accommodated informal patterns of social life. Making a cultivated virtue out of the need to provide light to interior rooms, some developers planned handsome courtyard gardens, lawns, and carriage driveways. Nevertheless, most central courtyards functioned in the same way that exterior courtyards did: They distributed tenants into separate stairways and elevators located inside the walls of the building, giving access to only a few apartments per floor. Placing the entire circulation system outside in the courtyard space was far more unusual. The Ashfield Cottages, built in 1871 by the Liverpool Labourers' Dwelling Company, included exterior stairs and continuous balconies to reach apartments on the three upper stories. In 1895, Frank Lloyd Wright's two-story Chicago model tenement, Francisco Terrace, provided access to second-story units along a continuous balcony ringing a central courtyard. These unusual designs shared with the Mecca a level of spectacle and gregariousness lacking in more common courtyard buildings. In the United States, in general, domestic ideology deterred developers of central-courtyard buildings from promoting or exploiting their potential for collective activity.[20]

The Mecca rose as the first Chicago residential building to appropriate the atrium. In 1892, local architects constructed two other Chicago apartment buildings around skylit atria. John T. Long designed the Yale, an apartment building at the corner of Yale Avenue and Sixty-sixth Street. The seven-story, Romanesque-style building had a six-story skylit and galleried atrium measuring twenty-five by eighty-two feet (figures 8.9, 8.10).[21] Like the Mecca, the Yale's fifty-four apartments had interior rooms with windows opening onto the atrium. Built on its lot line, the Yale stood as a striking anomaly in its suburban neighborhood of Englewood, where two-story wood-frame houses, set on landscaped lots, dominated the local streetscape. Nevertheless, the flood of light entering the Yale's atrium evidenced a shared concern for light and air that characterized the area's development. In 1892, in a somewhat denser urban neighborhood on Chicago's North Side, Enoch Hill Turnock designed the city's third skylit-atrium residential building (figures 8.11, 8.12). The eight-story Brewster Apartments at the corner of Diversy Boulevard and Pine Grove Avenue was initially planned in 1892, but it was not completed for several years. The Brewster's central light court was narrower than the courts in the Mecca and the Yale. Glass-decked bridges extended across the center of the interior court on each floor, while short gangways extended to the doors of the building's forty-eight units.[22]

Developers constructed the Mecca, the Yale, and the Brewster during the building boom that accompanied the 1893 World's Columbian Exposition. In 1894, the boom yielded to a deep depression that lasted until the turn of the century. When apartment building resumed, forms established in the Mecca quickly became clear. At the turn of the century, developers constructed more than ten thousand apartment units in Chicago every single year. The number was usually four to five times higher than the number of single dwellings.[23] Looking back to the period of intense experimentation with building plans, developers built hundreds of apartment buildings with exterior courtyards like the one at the Mecca. They built no buildings with skylit, galleried atria; the interior skylight turned out to be a road not taken in Chicago residential design. Instead of atria, high-rise apartment buildings that

Yale Building, Englewood, Ill.

Fig. 8.9 John T. Long, The Yale, Chicago, 1892–1893. Photograph by C. R. Childs, c. 1909. (Collection of LeRoy Bommaert.)

concentrated tenants and visitors at main entrances and around eleva- tors often included quite ornate lobbies that similarly provided grand interior public spaces. These elevator apartment buildings tended to cluster in a narrow geographical strip along the Lake Michigan shore. The effort to take advantage of the lake's scenic and recreational re- sources pushed land values higher and encouraged designers to orient

Fig. 8.10 The Yale, 1892–1893. View of interior skylit atrium, stairs, and elevator core. Photograph by Mildred Mead, 1953. ICHi-24351. (Courtesy of the Chicago Historical Society.)

floors toward prime views. In these high-rise areas, developers appeared less willing to make the generous allotments of space required for an interior light court when the real amenity of the location existed in exterior views of the lakeshore. Cultivation of views in high-rises and continuing efforts to foster images of domestic and suburban privacy in low-rises spurred alternative apartment arrangements at the turn of the century.

Fig. 8.11 Enoch Hill Turnock, The Brewster, Chicago, 1892–1896. Photograph by C. R. Childs, c. 1909. (Collection of LeRoy Bommaert.)

Fig. 8.12 The Brewster, 1892–1896. View of interior skylit atrium, glass block hallway bridges, stairs, and elevator core. Photograph by Bob Thall, 1982. (Courtesy of the Commission on Chicago Landmarks.)

In the absence of architectural emulation, continued public and historical recognition of the Mecca's grand atria and innovative plan was more dependent on the fate of the building itself than on the structures it inspired. The Mecca's history thus became bound up with the dynamics of urban change that drastically altered both public and private perceptions of the building. In the mid–nineteenth century, few people had built or settled in the area around the future South Side site of the Mecca. When the railroads extended lines through the area in the 1850s, they brought in their wake various factory operations and block after block of working-class residences. The Mecca's site stood just a block east of the Chicago, Rock Island & Pacific Railroad. A major industrial belt opened on the far side of the track, where the sprawling Union Stockyards opened in 1865. In the area east of the Mecca's future site, Stephen A. Douglas established a seventy-acre suburban lakeshore subdivision in the early 1850s and provided land there for the campus of the first University of Chicago. Between the suburban residences to the east and the stockyards to the west rose a large neighborhood of modest working-class homes—one- and two-story wood-frame and brick houses standing on twenty-five-foot-wide lots.[24]

Situated on an emerging commercial artery and surrounded by rather modest homes, the lot at the corner of State and Thirty-fourth Streets did not seem to provide fertile ground for investing hundreds of thousands of dollars in a building intended for middle-class residents. The construction of monumental buildings in the 1880s and early 1890s on the single block immediately west of the Mecca's site undoubtedly encouraged the Mecca's developers. On this block, the meatpacking Armour family made a substantial philanthropic investment in middle-class domesticity. In 1886, with a fund of more than two hundred thousand dollars, the Plymouth Congregational Church opened its Armour Mission. Occupying a handsome Romanesque-style building designed by Burnham & Root, the mission provided spiritual, educational, and recreational programs for the neighborhood's poorer residents (figure 8.13). In 1886, in an effort to establish a system of perpetual support for the mission, Philip D. Armour constructed the Armour Flats, twenty-nine three- and four-story buildings with 194 large middle-class apartments. The profits from rentals would support the mission. Patton & Fisher, architects of the Armour Flats, took advantage of the whole-block site to disguise the dense apartment development in the formal elements of single-family row houses. Rusticated Marquette sandstone fronts, with pressed brick and terra-cotta, conspicuous placement of chimney stacks and corner turrets, bay windows, varied massing, and variable design treatment of adjacent sections adopted the general forms of the city's recent single-family architecture (figure 8.14).[25] Armour encouraged middle managers and other employees in his company to rent apartments in the Armour Flats.[26]

In 1891, Armour laid the cornerstone for a massive five-story building designed by Patton & Fisher. Built to house the Armour Institute,

Fig. 8.13 Burnham & Root, Armour Mission, Chicago, 1886, demolished. From Irene Macauley, *The Heritage of Illinois Institute of Technology.* (Courtesy of the Illinois Institute of Technology.)

Fig. 8.14 Patton & Fisher, Armour Flats, Chicago, 1886–1890, demolished. Armour Flats at the right, the Mecca stands in left background. The modest character of the wood-frame rowhouses was typical of surrounding neighborhood; view taken c. 1909. (Collection of LeRoy Bommaert.)

Fig. 8.15 Patton & Fisher, Armour Institute Main Building, Chicago, 1891–1893. From Irene Macauley, *The Heritage of Illinois Institute of Technology.* (Courtesy of the Illinois Institute of Technology.)

chartered with one million dollars from Armour, the impressive structure accommodated a college for training industrial technicians and engineers. The building added a final note of monumentality to the block it filled just west of the Mecca's site (figure 8.15). By the time the institute opened its doors, the Mecca was nearing completion on State Street. The connections between Armour and the Mecca intensified in the coming decades; simple geography and complex urban dynamics increasingly enmeshed their institutional and architectural histories.

When the Mecca opened, it provided apartments for Chicago residents; however, hoping to cash in on World's Columbian Exposition business, the owners rented hotel rooms. The Mecca stood midway between the fair and the downtown "business and amusement" area. State Street cable cars ran by the door, and the Thirty-third Street station of the recently completed South Side elevated train stood a block away. The Mecca hotel offered special advantages to families, who could stay in five- to seven-room furnished suites with bathrooms. The hotel also rented single rooms for seventy-five cents to two dollars per day, with corner and bay-window rooms costing slightly more. Patronage by visitors to the fair passed quickly and was followed by a deep national economic depression. The Mecca failed to establish a solidly middle-class tenant population. In fact, its initial owners lost the building in foreclosure. Paul J. Sorg, an industrialist from Middletown, Ohio, who had purchased and leased the Mecca's site to the developers for twelve thousand dollars a year, ended up owning both the land and the building. Sorg subdivided some of the flats; renters could obtain two- to seven-room apartments for between ten and thirty-five dollars per month. These rents were generally lower than those charged for middle-class South Side apartments located both east and south of the Mecca.[27]

When the U.S. government's census taker visited the Mecca in June 1900, he found 107 units occupied by 365 people. There were blue-collar and white-collar employees and relatively few middle-class professionals. The Mecca accommodated carpenters, electricians, house painters, dry-goods, railroad, and grocery clerks as well as clerks in insurance and other business offices, traveling salesmen, egg inspectors, day laborers, several bartenders, waiters, cooks, tailors, bookkeepers, a typesetter, machinists, a butcher, a packing-house foreman, an architect, a physician, an optician, a musician, locomotive engineers and firemen, railroad and elevator conductors, music teachers, a watchman, a postal clerk, a glass cutter, a freight checker, janitors, a real estate agent, a coachman, a teamster, a decorator, a retired capitalist, and a frog dealer. Some families made the rent by taking in boarders. No family had live-in servants. The vast majority of Mecca residents in 1900 were born in the United States; many had parents born in the United States. Some residents had Scottish-, Irish-, German-, Canadian-, or Polish-born parents. All of the Mecca's residents were white.[28]

The surrounding neighborhood was not nearly as uniform. During a time in which the black population of the city was expanding rapidly, poverty and racial exclusion in housing had spurred an increasingly concentrated black settlement pattern. South Side blacks settled in an area known as the Black Belt, a narrow strip of land along the railroad and industrial land just west of the Mecca, from the downtown southward. It extended east of the Mecca to Wabash Avenue, which after the early 1890s suffered from the blighting effects of the elevated transit line running down the alley between Wabash and State Streets. In 1900, blacks occupied many houses in this area, stretching from the Loop south to Thirty-ninth Street. They lived in some of the more modest houses on the north end of the block occupied by the Mecca and pursued many of the same occupations as their white neighbors in the Mecca—housepainter, day laborer, cook, paper hanger, and porter. Set in an integrated neighborhood, the internalized atria in the Mecca constituted a more exclusively white realm.[29]

The racial disparity between the Mecca and its neighborhood increased over the next decade. In 1910, the Mecca's residents were still white, while blacks occupied many adjacent houses and apartments. Like the Mecca apartments, the Armour Flats continued to have only white tenants. In 1910, native-born Americans still predominated in the Mecca, though there were also German, Swedish, Austrian, Canadian, Irish, Scottish, English, and Russian immigrants living in the building. Russian-born Israel Goldman, for example, the fifty-year-old sexton of a local synagogue, lived in a Mecca unit with his wife, Golda, and three of his four children, including a son who worked as a tailor and a daughter who was a dressmaker. In 1910, the Mecca housed porters, cooks, waiters, hatmakers, actors, journalists, day laborers, piano movers, elevator operators, and many other people with occupations similar to those who had lived in the building in 1900.[30]

In 1911, the Sorg estate sold the Mecca for four hundred thousand dollars—half the amount it had cost to build twenty years earlier. With a gross annual rent of $42,000 and a $170,000 mortgage at 5½ percent, the Mecca investment looked attractive. In 1912, Franklin T. Pember, a banker, fur trader and commission merchant, agricultural-implement manufacturer, and prominent naturalist and philanthropist, and his wife, Ellen J. L. W. Pember, of Granville, New York, purchased the Mecca for four hundred thousand dollars.[31] The Pembers' investment came just a few years before a massive migration of African Americans from the rural south to Chicago industrial jobs, spurred by World War I production. As Chicago's black population more than doubled in the 1910s, from 44,103 to 109,458, the neighborhood around the Mecca received an influx of new residents. Real-estate interests and many white Chicagoans greeted African American residential expansion with alarm and hostility, ranging from threats and broken windows to house bombings. Racial violence encouraged a more concentrated settlement pattern among blacks than had previously existed. It also created both economic and social pressure for the conversion of white-occupied residential buildings within and adjacent to the already established Black Belt neighborhood. In the months after their purchase of the Mecca, the Pembers' rental agent began to advertise in the *Chicago Defender* and to rent apartments to African Americans. The advertisements declared that the Mecca was for "first-class people only"; however, there was no mistaking the fact that the twenty-year-old building now stood as a monumental addition to Chicago's South Side Black Belt.[32]

In July 1919, racial tensions on Chicago's South Side burst into a full-scale riot. A group of whites stoned a black youth swimming in Lake Michigan, who drowned as a result. The incident sparked more than a week of mob action that took a huge toll, including thirty-eight people killed, 537 injured, and more than a thousand people displaced from their homes. Some of the most serious rioting occurred up and down State Street both north and south of the Mecca.[33] The building had completely changed over from white to black tenants before the riot.[34] In 1920, it was occupied by people with many of the same occupations as those who had previously lived in the building. There were porters, foundry molders, machinists, upholsterers, tanners, tailors, mattress, mantle, shade, dress-, and cigar makers, butchers, bakers, cooks, laundresses, janitors, maids, bellboys, hairdressers, manicurists, day laborers, switchmen, steelworkers, musicians, chauffeurs, postal clerks, shipping clerks, and peddlers. Nearly all of the residents were born in the United States, and the majority were born outside Illinois, largely in southern states. The census takers counted 148 occupied units with 510 residents. Many families took in boarders to help pay the rent. Mecca households were now large and complex. Thomas McClure, for example, a thirty-one-year-old native of Alabama, worked as a chauffeur for the Nash Motor Company and lived with his wife, Lula, a twenty-eight-year-old native of Tennessee, who was not employed outside the home. The McClures accommodated a forty-eight-year-old uncle, Nobles Clark, a native of Tennessee, who worked as a packing-company butcher; Jesse Walker, a twenty-nine-year-old packing-house laborer from Alabama, and Mattie Pierson, a twenty-one-year-old restaurant waitress from South Carolina, also lived with the McClures.[35]

When the Mecca turned from white to black, the spectacle of public life played out in the exterior courtyard and around the atria became more closely patterned after life in the immediate neighborhood (figure 8.16). In the late 1910s, the Mecca stood just a block north of what emerged as Chicago's African American business and retail center. Around Thirty-fifth and State Streets, business buildings, many constructed by African Americans, housed banks, real estate and insurance offices, retail stores, fraternal lodges, and newspaper offices. In the 1910s and 1920s, this area also accommodated a dynamic nightlife, including many of Chicago's leading jazz clubs, featuring such musicians as King Oliver, Louis Armstrong, and Jelly Roll Morton. The Pekin Theater at Twenty-seventh and State Streets led the way when it opened in 1905; other clubs included the De Luxe, a block south of the Mecca; the Dreamland Cafe, two blocks south; and the Elite Club, three blocks north. The Royal Gardens on Thirty-fifth Street and the Sunset Cafe on Thirty-fifth Street shared local nightlife with other clubs such as High Life and the Entertainers.[36]

Links between the Mecca and jazz were immortalized when local bands began to play and record improvised blues tunes titled the

Fig. 8.16 Keith Elementary School students crossing the intersection of Thirty-fourth Street and Dearborn Street in front of the Mecca. Photograph by Wallace Kirkland, 1951. ICHi-29353. (Courtesy of the Chicago Historical Society.)

"Mecca Flat Blues." In August 1924, pianist and composer James "Jimmy" Blythe recorded "Mecca Flat Blues" with jazz singer Priscilla Stewart. Two years later, Blythe followed with "Lovin's Been Here and Gone to Mecca Flat." In 1939, pianist Albert Ammons also recorded "Mecca Flat Blues," and musicians have continued to record versions of the music down to the present. Jimmy Blythe and Priscilla Stewart's version of the song gave dramatic personae to the "Mecca Flat Man" and the "Mecca Flat Woman," who led sensual and adulterous lives, causing no end of heartbreak to their partners. Local "extemporizing troubadours" continually added episodes to the "Mecca Flat Blues," charting the "trials, tribulations, and tragedies" of the residents. One observer speculated that if collected and printed, the verses would "make a book."[37]

The musicians were doing more than simply punning on musical notations when they seized upon the Mecca "Flat." By referring to the local people and landmarks, they could root their blend of New Orleans, St. Louis, and other jazz expressions into a distinct Chicago idiom. Tales of heartbreak and adultery, the stuff of the blues, were perhaps more apparent at the Mecca because of the urban spectacle captured around the atria; these tales seemed to confirm the nineteenth-century critique of apartment-house living. Here, according to the songs, were concentrated the temptations and evils of high-density living and the obvious intrusions on familial privacy and domestic virtue. Nevertheless, the public space of the atria helped give the Mecca a sense of place and a comprehensible identity that few other "private" buildings enjoyed. The public permeability of the domestic realm that had made the design problematic in its conception now contributed to its fame, or notoriety, in Chicago culture. In the 1960s, Chicago poet Gwendolyn Brooks expanded the Mecca canon in verse. Her work "In the Mecca" follows family members in search of a lost child, visiting flat after flat and making inquiries along the balconies. The poem nicely captures the cosmopolitanism of a building with an array of alluring, fascinating, as well as repulsive characters.[38]

Simple geography had always united the Mecca and the Armour Mission, Institute, and Flats. On the face of it, the shifting racial composition of the neighborhood should not have affected Armour, with its ecumenical and racially inclusive vision. The mission was established to be "broad and wholly non-sectarian, without any restrictions whatsoever as to race, creed, and color." Armour Institute was an integrated school since its founding in the 1890s. Nevertheless, Armour officials were troubled by the expansion of the Black Belt, as they found it increasingly difficult to persuade company employees and Armour Institute faculty to live in the Armour Flats. Mission and institute officials responded curiously to the housing crunch caused by the migration of African Americans to Chicago: They demolished the Armour Flats. Between 1917 and 1919, 131 of the 194 apartments were torn down, and many of the remaining units were converted to offices, laboratories, and classrooms (figure 8.17).[39]

In demolishing the Armour Flats, the officials eliminated vestiges of the middle-class residential landscape that had provided the context for construction of the Mecca. Despite creating a physical buffer between its academic buildings and the surrounding residences, Armour actively tried to relocate the campus altogether. There had been some

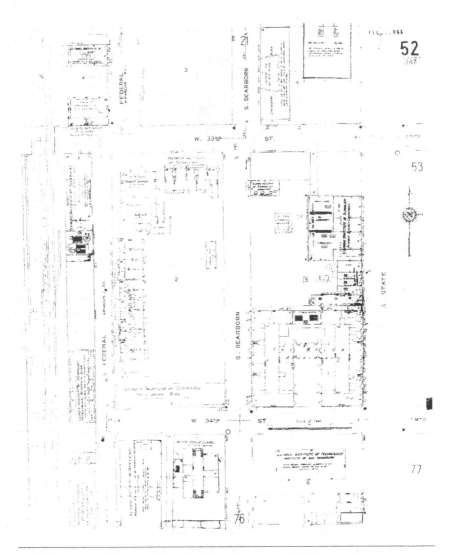

Fig. 8.17 Map plan of Mecca and Illinois Institute of Technology, 1949. The vacant land along Dearborn is where a section of the Armour Flats stood before being demolished, 1917–1919. "Chapin Hall," fronting on Federal, adapted part of the Armour Flats as a physics laboratory. The Armour Mission has been converted into the Student Union. From Sanborn Map Company, *Insurance Maps of Chicago, volume 4,* New York, 1912–1949. (Courtesy of Chadwyck-Healey/Library of Congress.)

discussion as early as 1902 of becoming affiliated with the University of Chicago. In 1920, J. Ogden Armour paid a million dollars to purchase an eighty-acre tract of land in South Shore, a growing suburban neighborhood of Chicago, five miles south of the institute. Subsequently experiencing financial difficulties, Armour sold the South

Shore site in 1922, stating that it had grown too valuable to hold while awaiting the resources to fund the institute's relocation.[40]

Armour Institute persisted in efforts to raise an endowment and leave its historic campus. In the 1920s, it attempted to affiliate with Northwestern University, and in the 1930s Armour considered a move into an eleven-story building on Lake Shore Drive, north of downtown. The depression heightened the distress with which institute officials viewed their location and at the same time diminished the possibility of amassing resources for relocation. In 1937, a committee of the institute's board of trustees intensively studied Armour's prospects. Board president James Cunningham insisted that the institute had a bright future as a leading school of scientific and engineering education, governed by a board of industrial leaders who "think straight," in one of the world's largest industrial centers.[41]

In 1937, the board clearly viewed the institute's fate as tied to its location. After spending months looking at sites in the Loop, on the North Side, on the West Side, as well as in suburban locations, a board committee advocated remaining at the existing location. Cunningham reported, "This will undoubtedly shock some of you out of your chairs. The present site, at Thirty-third and Federal, was, and I say 'was' advisedly, in the heart of the Black Belt, but it got too dilapidated and run down for the Negroes so they have moved further south. They have left a totally devastated area in their wake, to be sure. It is axiomatic that when anything has gotten to the very bottom the only direction it can go is up, and this is just the conclusion of the Committee. The present Institute occupies a site of nine acres. It is proposed to purchase about thirty acres of property adjoining the nine acres. . . . Wrecking of the buildings in the entire area could be accomplished, I think, by a moderate wind storm, so dilapidated are the structures. . . . There is a possibility of having State Street boulevarded from the Loop south, which, of course, would greatly influence the trend of this entire district. Many students of real estate are definitely committed to the development of this area from the Loop south, as a so-called white collar community."[42]

The board then mapped out a strategy for quietly purchasing the necessary parcels, including the Mecca, to control the area from Thirty-first Street south to Thirty-fifth Street, from State west to the Rock Island tracks.

The institute modeled its plans on slum-clearance precedents of the 1930s. Federal legislation enacted in 1934 and 1937 supported massive assembly and clearance of urban tracts. Starting in the mid-1930s, planners proposed numerous South Side clearance projects. In 1934, the federal government selected a forty-seven-acre tract at Thirty-seventh

Street and South Park Avenue for the Ida B. Wells Homes. Opened in 1941, the project provided 1,662 units of public housing on a site that had previously contained nineteenth-century brownstone row houses and single-family detached houses. Landlords had subdivided many of these buildings into more modest units, occupied primarily by African American tenants.[43] These land-clearance programs provided some institutions with an alternative to suburbanization; they might choose to stay in their historic locations, buffered from neighborhoods in decline by cleared land and renewed neighborhoods.

Departing from prevailing approaches to Chicago urban renewal, the institute initially adopted a plan for pursuing renewal through the private real estate market. Newton C. Farr, a Chicago Realtor who directed the board's campaign to purchase property for the institute, reported that the Mecca, with 178 apartments "occupied by colored," was one property that "has caused us some concern in the expansion." Farr thought that the building, with a gross annual income of $38,881 and a net income of $9,739, could be purchased for $85,000. In 1938, the board's secretary, Alfred L. Eustice, acting as a private citizen, bought the Mecca from Franklin Pember's estate for eighty-five thousand dollars.[44] Meanwhile, the institute's land-acquisition program secretly continued for several years and involved dozens of purchases.

People deliberating the institute's future proved acutely sensitive to the landscape and racial character of the surrounding neighborhood. In 1940, the institute's president, Henry Townley Heald, wrote that it had been "beset" by the "increasing deterioration of its neighborhood."[45] The board saw the "morale" of both faculty and students decline. For years, through all of the various relocation plans, people openly worried that the institute's immediate urban context might frustrate its effort to rival national institutions such as the Massachusetts Institute of Technology and California Institute of Technology.[46] These concerns intensified when Armour merged with the Lewis Institute to form the Illinois Institute of Technology in 1940. The next year, the institute went public with its plans for a new campus, with modern buildings on a site cleared of its Black Belt identity. Even with the central site under control, the board continued to worry about the approaches to the campus; it had hoped for a boulevard from the Loop, but also wanted to control the frontage of all streets approaching the future campus.[47]

In 1941, when Alfred Eustice deeded the Mecca to the institute, the building quickly crystallized the racial and class calculus that governed the board's view of its neighborhood's people and buildings. By the early 1940s, the Mecca accommodated more than a thousand residents. The combination of a decade of depression, the onset of further war-induced migration, and continuing white hostility toward the expansion of black housing resulted in the Mecca's having far more residents than the building was designed to accommodate. The sheer density and visibility of the people who resided there had made the place an object of cultural interest in the 1920s. As the institute pursued its campus plans, that same density and visibility came to symbolize all that the board deplored about its location. By the same token, the fact that so many people called the Mecca home presented a problem for the institute's clearance plans. The board hoped that the mere act of purchase would let it tidily clear a monument of neighborhood "blight" from one of its approaches. It soon became clear that local residents had not, in fact, moved farther south and that it would require more than a "moderate wind storm" to clear the site.[48]

When the institute took control of the Mecca in 1941, it aimed to demolish the structure as quickly as possible. The board resolved to wait until Mecca leases expired in September 1942 to vacate the building. A sense of urgency hung over the Mecca deliberations, because Chicago's Fire Prevention Bureau had brought suit against the institute to force it to install a fire sprinkler system required by the local building code.[49] The sprinkler for the Mecca was estimated to cost as much as twenty-six thousand dollars. The institute stalled on the sprinkler litigation, hoping that either tenant leases would lapse or the court would order it to demolish the building immediately. By 1942, however, the war had exacerbated the housing crisis, and the proposed demolition took on a very different meaning. As the leases began to expire, the institute tried vacating the building. This stirred public debate, as the Metropolitan Housing Council, Chicago Urban League, Chicago Welfare Administration, and local politicians joined with Mecca's tenants to protest. The Metropolitan Housing Council professed no great affection for the Mecca, which it considered old, overcrowded, unsanitary, and a fire hazard; nonetheless, it reported: "There's a war on, and it looks as if there'll be little more new building, if any, in Chicago. And the Negro community is beyond the saturation point."[50]

In 1942, Newton Farr expressed some sympathy for the plight of Mecca tenants. As long as the war limited campus building, the twenty-two thousand dollars in net rental income seemed attractive as a means of funding institute real estate purchases. President Heald was unmoved by Farr's arguments. Ignoring the number of boarding families, he insisted that surely it would be possible to "absorb" 175 families "somewhere in the total colored population." Giving voice to entrenched distaste for the Mecca and the appearance of the institute's neighborhood, Heald concluded: "As long as it stands, it is a distinct handicap to our efforts to clean up our campus area and, even though it produces an income, I really believe that it is worth more to us torn down than in its present state."[51] Despite this view, the pressure of the civic organizations as well as a direct appeal from Alderman Lindell, chair of the Chicago City Council's Housing Committee, persuaded the institute to defer demolition of the building.

In 1943, the Mecca preservation battle moved to the Illinois House and Senate. State senator Christopher Wimbish, an African American graduate of Northwestern University Law School, effectively galvanized a huge coalition against the Mecca's impending demolition. His bill barring the demolition passed in the House 114 to 2 and in the Senate 46 to 1. The legislative debate featured impassioned appeals to patriotism. Advocates of the bill pointed out that more than forty residents of the Mecca were fighting abroad "for democracy they did not enjoy at home," and yet the institute proposed to tear down the roof over the heads of their families. One delegate charged that the bill's interference with private property rights was "un-American." This claim met a harsh rejoinder from one of the bill's supporters: "You who refuse to vote to prevent the eviction of these women, children, and war workers, the lame and the sick, from the Mecca flats; you who vote 'No' on this roll call, you are un-American, you are vicious."[52] Beyond patriotism, the bill's supporters hoped to prevent "trouble" that could be expected when Mecca tenants searched for housing in adjacent white neighborhoods.[53] Despite broad support, Governor Dwight Green vetoed the Mecca bill as unconstitutional.[54]

After the governor's veto, Senator Wimbish pushed the battle forward in Chicago Municipal Court, where he represented tenants threatened with eviction. Wimbish argued that the case involved "property rights versus human rights." He pointed to the difficulties faced by blacks in finding housing in a city where "restrictive covenants and neighborhood clannish-ness prohibits normal expansion"; the tenants were "hemmed in by an American ghetto system." Institute lawyers had to admit that the site could not be rebuilt until after the war; but they argued that the building was unsafe and should be torn down immediately. In his ruling, Judge Samuel Heller barred the evictions and ordered the institute to abide by all municipal building and safety codes.[55] The institute hired a watchman rather than install sprinklers. It also sent a letter to tenants demanding that they move out, stating, "ALL PERSONS WHO CONTINUE TO REMAIN IN THE BUILDING DO SO ON THEIR OWN RESPONSIBILITY AND AT THEIR OWN RISK."[56] These developments added a dimension of political history to the building's significant architectural and cultural history.

Just a few months after failing in its effort to demolish the Mecca, the institute sought to put some distance between itself and the building. In July 1943, the U.S. War Department decided to sell the Stevens Hotel, purchased at the outset of World War II to serve as a training school and barracks. The twenty-five-story building on Michigan Avenue between Seventh and Eighth Streets, designed between 1922 and 1927 by Holabird & Roche, had three thousand rooms, myriad public meeting spaces, a convention hall seating four thousand, and kitchen and dining facilities. With more than a million and a half square feet of space, the building could easily be converted to house the institute's dormitories, laboratories, offices, classrooms, library, auditorium, and gymnasium. When the board heard about the availability of the Stevens, it jumped at the chance to move from the "heart of the Black Belt" to the "heart of Chicago's cultural center." One board member insisted that the move would have a positive "psychological effect" on faculty and students.[57] The board reported that dormitory space with a view across Grant Park to Lake Michigan would help the institute cultivate "national importance." Proximity to the Art Institute, the Field Museum, the Planetarium, the Chicago Public Library, and other institutions would add a "humanistic-cultural background" to the institute's "scientific-technological education."[58]

The institute lost the Stevens with a cash bid that was $581,000 less than that of an investor who planned to reopen the building as a hotel.[59] The institute then revived earlier plans to clear a space for itself in and around its original campus. President Heald vigorously advocated clearance and redevelopment of broad tracts well beyond the institute's immediate bounds. In 1946, at a Chicago housing forum, Heald termed the existence of fifteen thousand acres of blighted land in Chicago "intolerable." "Blight is a deadly disease which attacks and destroys cities and devours the property and investments in them," he stated. He advocated eminent domain to assemble large tracts and subsidies to encourage developers to rebuild in urban areas rather than in expanding suburbs. He declared that institute officials "had only two choices—run away from the blight or to stand and fight. I submit that this is everybody's choice—and that behind the principle of 'Stand and Fight' is where we must all be counted."[60] After years of flirting with running away, the institute would stand. Fighting meant, among other things, fighting to demolish the Mecca. It also meant that the institute would become a key partner in the massive postwar South Side urban renewal program. In 1946, the institute and Michael Reese Hospital joined forces to establish the South Side Planning Board, a not-for-profit organization advocating a new vision for the area. The planning board, with Heald serving as its first chairman, focused on a large area from Roosevelt Road to Forty-seventh Street, the Rock Island tracks to Lake Michigan, maintaining that this seven-square-mile tract was the minimum planning area needed for successful redevelopment. The board advocated the South Expressway construction, which involved demolition of a huge area of very modest housing just west of the campus. It also quickly identified 333 acres for public clearance, including the entire neighborhood between the institute and the lake.[61]

Despite advocating construction of private and public housing, the institute did not want low-income housing just anywhere, and continued its efforts to transform the immediate campus area into a middle-class, white-collar community. In 1944, when the institute's board learned that the Chicago Housing Authority was planning a low-income housing project just north of the campus, toward the Loop, it lodged a strong protest. Heald had envisioned neighborhood housing for students and faculty "unhampered by the construction of low-cost housing. . . . We believe that with a great Center of Technology as a stimulus, a large area of the South Side can be completely rehabilitated and once again become a really important commercial, residential, and cultural area of the City."[62] The institute failed to keep public housing away. Just to its north, the Dearborn Homes, the first high-rise public housing in the city, opened in 1950. With sixteen elevator buildings, six and nine stories high, and including eight hundred units, the Dearborn Homes took the form of modernist towers spread across expansive greenswards.[63] Modernizing neighborhood form and style, the buildings did not alter the area's racial or class character.

As plans for South Side renewal and the institute's campus developed, it became obvious that the Mecca represented more than a social and political challenge. The building stood in stark contrast to the palette of modern architecture envisioned as a key to a new urbanism and a changed neighborhood. The arrival in 1938 of Ludwig Mies van der Rohe to head the institute's Department of Architecture boosted the vision of a new architecture for the area. Mies used a number of early studio classes to design a new campus and then opened a private office to develop the plans more fully.[64] Proposing a radically different architectural expression, Mies's plan called for demolition of the Romanesque-style Armour Mission and Armour Institute. In their place, Mies, who eventually designed twenty-two buildings for the institute, proposed strikingly modern-styled buildings in brick, glass, and welded steel. Clean, abstract lines and carefully proportioned spaces resonated with the broader agenda of "cleaning up" the neighborhood.

Fig. 8.18 Photo collage of model for Illinois Institute of Technology's campus expansion and aerial view of South Side of Chicago, Ludwig Mies van der Rohe lead architect and planner for campus expansion, 1942. (Courtesy of the Illinois Institute of Technology.)

Mies's style also reinforced the vision of a radical break with the historical and, in the minds of institute officials, the blighted character of the neighborhood. Photocollage techniques used to present the campus plan underscored the institute's effort to establish a unified stylistic and urban form. The visual representations effectively placed a photo of an architectural model of the proposed campus on top of an aerial photograph of the South Side. Order and harmony confronted the hodgepodge of high and low, wide and narrow, wood and brick, commercial and residential buildings (figure 8.18). Since the campus plan aimed to demolish the adjacent neighborhood, it adopted a dominant low-rise, low-density form that sprawled across a landscaped site made up of cleared land and vacated alley and street rights-of-way of the earlier urban grid. In place of older buildings pressed to the lot line (figure 8.19), the new campus would move buildings away from street fronts and surround them with grass (figure 8.20). The Mecca, built on its lot line on both State and Dearborn Streets and including patches of terracotta ornament, obviously frustrated the stylistic and urban intentions of the early campus plans, disposed symmetrically around an axis running along Thirty-third Street (figures 8.18, 8.21). Planners also hoped that the campus would "have a harmonious relation to its environment," which they felt would be built up with "well planned housing developments surrounded by large park areas."[65] In fact, Skidmore, Owings & Merrill, Walter Gropius, Reginald Isaacs, and other noted modern designers who consulted on South Side planning shared Mies's commitment to a radical break with historic architectural and urban forms.[66] Modern urbanism generally eschewed historic patterns of retail spaces oriented to streets and pedestrians. These older patterns,

Fig. 8.19 The Mecca, 1891–1892. View looking west along 34th Street with the Armour Flats visible in background. Mecca stands on its lot line. Two of the Mecca's State Street stores are visible. A large fence separates the exterior courtyard from the street in this c. 1909 view. (Collection of LeRoy Bommaert.)

Fig. 8.20 At left is Ludwig Mies van der Rohe, Institute of Gas Technology Building, Chicago, 1947–1950. Building sits on grass plot, away from lot line. Mecca is in the background standing on its lot line. Photograph by Wallace Kirkland, 1951. ICHi-29349. (Courtesy of the Chicago Historical Society.)

Fig. 8.21 Ludwig Mies van der Rohe, Illinois Institute of Technology Campus Model, Chicago, c. 1942, view includes faculty member James Clinton Peebles (right), Mies van der Rohe (center), Institute President Henry T. Heald (right). From Irene Macauley, *The Heritage of Illinois Institute of Technology.* (Courtesy of the Illinois Institute of Technology.)

exemplified by the Mecca's twelve stores fronting on State Street, ran counter to the single-use zoning and specialized patterns advocated by modern planners.

Campus plans and Mies's aesthetic ideals contained little room for accommodation with the fifty-year-old Mecca. The rigid ideal of campus symmetry did eventually give way to incorporate the institute's earliest building, designed by Patton & Fisher, but the inclusion of this historic structure memorializing the institute's origin in philanthropic support undoubtedly proved easier than preserving neighborhood narratives associated with the Mecca. A more complicated form of campus planning that might have incorporated the Mecca and other existing buildings did not take place. Moreover, the institute never considered using the Mecca as a dormitory for students, even though its atria could have ideally accommodated the many students who reveled in the gregariousness of campus social life. Using the Mecca as a student residence hall would have compromised part of the institute's rationale for displacing the Mecca's black tenants—that the building had to be demolished because it failed to meet building codes.[67]

In the mid-1940s, Skidmore, Owings & Merrill made a plan for institute student and faculty housing, reporting that, beyond a few old residences on Michigan Avenue that could be temporarily used as fraternity houses, none of the neighborhood buildings was suitable for housing.[68] Failing to view existing buildings, such as the Mecca, as a resource for campus expansion entailed steep costs. The institute's housing program adopted a high-rise model that led it to spend more than a million dollars apiece for ten-story apartment buildings, such as Gunsaulus Hall designed by Mies, that accommodated many fewer residents than had lived in the Mecca in the 1890s. The institute and its planners saw little value in neighboring buildings. Leaders of the African American community, including realtor Oscar C. Brown, president of the Chicago Negro Chamber of Commerce, advocated a planning approach that would identify the numerous dwellings that should be "left standing and integrated into the larger redevelopment program." More concerned with decent housing opportunities for African Americans than with developing buffers between South Side institutions and their neighbors, Brown urged a less radical, more preservation-oriented vision of South Side renewal.[69] Yet planners were determined to carve out a single-purpose academic campus where engineering students would be insulated from the very society they were being educated to serve.

After the war, the institute started construction of its modern campus. In February 1950, the board noted an easing of South Side housing and renewed its push to demolish the Mecca.[70] President Heald again insisted that the building was unsafe.[71] Mecca tenants responded with mass protests (figures 8.22, 8.23). Again Senator Wimbish advised them of possible legal and administrative remedies. Lillian Davis, a Mecca tenant, argued that it was "unconstitutional" to evict rent-paying tenants: "It's a law of life that a person has to have a place to live."[72] Ward aldermen filed proposals to bar issuance of wrecking permits until tenants had been legally evicted and a program initiated to alleviate their hardships. These proposals went to the City Council's Committee on Housing, which failed to take action.[73] Despite the echoes of earlier arguments, the dynamics of the preservation campaign had changed. Tenants did not argue against demolition so much as insist upon expedited assistance in locating alternative space in private or public housing.[74] The institute had sapped the energy of the preservation movement by continually lowering rents and filling the building with poorer and poorer people while refusing to put money

Fig. 8.22 Mecca tenants organizing meeting, 1950. Photograph by Charles Stewart, Jr. ICHi-25338. (Courtesy of the Chicago Historical Society.)

into maintenance and repairs. The exterior courtyard deteriorated into an unkempt dirt patch and graffiti-covered interior walls. When the courts permitted relocations and evictions to proceed, squatters quickly moved into the Mecca apartments, furthering the building's reputation as "a prime example of the worst slum tenements."[75]

In the early 1950s, these renewed efforts to demolish the Mecca were framed by a distorted historical narrative. A Mecca myth arose that embodied a classical story of a fall from grace. In this rendering of Mecca history, the "last word in show apartments" had fallen into a "slum tenement," brought on by "deterioration" that originated when blacks moved into the building.[76] Built during "Chicago's golden age" for "fat cats" and the "rising rich," the Mecca was once a "showplace because of its floors of Italian tile, its rising tiers of balconies overlooking enclosed courtyards where fountains played." Then "the rich tenants moved out; and the not-so-rich who replaced them gave up the Mecca's elegance to underprivileged Negroes", the Mecca became "Chicago's most notorious . . . slum."[77]

Fig. 8.23 Mecca tenants filing legal motions in the Illinois Institute of Technology's eviction proceedings, 1950. Photograph by Charles Stewart, Jr. ICHi-24830. (Courtesy of the Chicago Historical Society.)

Author John Bartlow Martin extended the Mecca myth in a long essay on the building titled "The Strangest Place in Chicago," which was published in *Harper's Magazine* in 1950.[78] Martin developed the story of a "splendid palace," a "showplace" that had dazzled people as the "finest apartment building in Chicago if not in America." Then came the fall, providing a "showplace but of a very different sort . . . one of the most remarkable Negro slum exhibits in the world." Martin's article, illustrated by haunting line drawings by Ben Shahn, absolutely captured the building's gregarious life that centered on the interior atria (figure 8.24). Here the disorder of the place appeared. Martin wrote of men and women spitting from the balconies to the floor below. The noises of the building's tenants always filled the atria. A toddler urinated from the balcony to the floor below. People reported the time when a pimp threw a prostitute from the balcony and when a man murdered the building's janitor in a struggle over a woman. Martin's essay recognized the same public massing of humanity around the atria that versions of the "Mecca Flat Blues" had captured. In the view of the institute and other South Side planners, the

Fig. 8.24 Ben Shahn, Mecca tenants on balcony. From *Harper's Magazine,* (December, 1950).

Mecca's fall from grace crystallized and rendered inescapable the logic of urban renewal and the need for inaugurating a new "golden age."

Martin's essay contrasted the institute's modern campus of "sleek brick-and-glass buildings surrounded by new trees and new grass" with the Mecca, a "great gray hulk."[79] The conceptual tropes of traditional style and materials giving way to the modern, of novelty gone stale, high gone low, white gone black all supported the institute's demolition plan. The overall treatment of the Mecca presented it as a building unworthy of a longer life, a building that had slipped so far from its intended social station that it failed to stir a sense of historic veneration. Yet the tenants anticipated loss. Jesse Meals, who had lived in the Mecca for thirty-one years, told a reporter, "You watch, a lot of people who lived here, they gonna die from grief."[80]

A year after the *Harper's* essay appeared, *Life Magazine* reworked Martin's narrative in captions for a photo essay by Wallace Kirkland titled "The Mecca, Chicago's Showiest Apartment Has Given Up All but the Ghost"[81] (figure 8.25). The building's social standing had undoubtedly declined, but the decline was not nearly so precipitous as commentators suggested; the building had remained a largely working-class place throughout its entire history. The myth carried a note of truth only in relation to the Columbian Exposition promotion that had heralded the richness of the "elegantly furnished" rooms and fine dining available at the Mecca "Hotel." Nevertheless, this portrayal of decline into blight strengthened the case for demolition. In 1950, Jim Hurlbut presented a radio commentary on WMAQ that celebrated the institute's plans for demolition, stating, "Undoubtedly there are those in the city who will sigh regretfully over the passing of the once fabulous apartment house. . . . Even a few may be listening who lived in its richly appointed suites,

Fig. 8.25 The Mecca, 1891–1892. Tenants in hats hanging out at balcony. Photograph by Wallace Kirkland, 1951. ICHi-29354. (Courtesy of the Chicago Historical Society.)

when residence there was a sign of opulence and social position. Now, of course, residence at the Mecca is more a sign of desperate poverty." In Hurlbut's view, demolition would help the institute develop "a beauty spot in the center of one of the city's worst slum areas. . . . It will be one of the city's most attractive sections."[82] For both planners and the institute, the demolition of the Mecca stood at the center of this vision.

Fig. 8.26 The Mecca, 1891–1892, demolished January, 1952. Photograph by Bernice Davis, 1952. ICHi-29350. (Courtesy of the Chicago Historical Society.)

The institute hired social workers to help relocate tenants and to co-ordinate the effort with housing agencies. It took nearly eighteen months to empty the building. In early January 1952, the Speedway Wrecking Company demolished the Mecca (figure 8.26). The *Chicago Sun-Times* reported the event under the headline FABULOUS S. SIDE SLUM REACHES END OF ROAD. In what soon became a tradition in the culture of Chicago architecture, some people salvaged architectural bits of the

Fig. 8.27 Groundbreaking ceremony for Ludwig Mies van der Rohe, Crown Hall, Illinois Institute of Technology, Chicago, 2 December 1954. Groundbreaking took place of the site of The Mecca, among those present are James D. Cunningham, first from left and Henry Crown, fourth from left. From Irene Macauley, *The Heritage of Illinois Institute of Technology*. (Courtesy of the Illinois Institute of Technology.)

Mecca. The distinctive foliated balcony panels that had lined the building's atria proved popular among collectors of local architectural fragments. This method preserved forms and memories of the building while leaving the economic and social program of urban renewal advocates largely unfettered.

Nearly three years after the demolition of the Mecca, the institute's board, led by Cunningham, gathered on the Mecca's original site to break ground for a new building (figure 8.27). Crown Hall, designed by Mies, would house the architecture department and at the same time assume the Mecca Flats' old street address. In its program and formal elements, Crown Hall sharply contrasts with the Mecca. The roof is suspended from four exposed plate girders that project from the simple facade of plate glass and steel. Taking the form of a glass pavilion (figures 8.28, 8.29), Crown Hall appears as a huge but relatively simple one-room glass box floating above the ground.[83] Mies

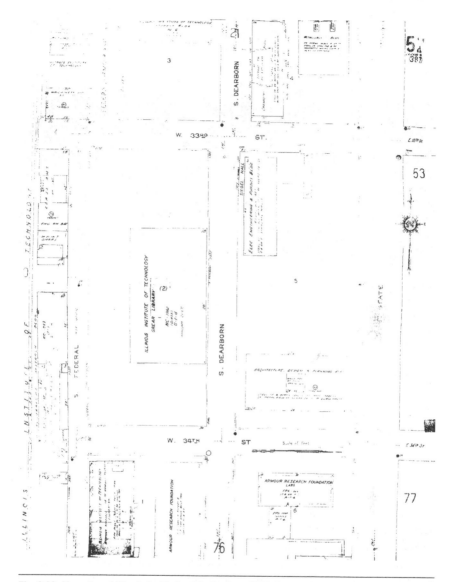

Fig. 8.28 Map plan of Illinois Institute of Technology, 1970. The Architecture, Design & Planning Building is Crown Hall and occupies the site formerly occupied by the Mecca. The campus's large open spaces and low buildings are evident. The only buildings remaining from the nineteenth century is the "class rms." building at the corner of Federal and 33rd. From Sanborn Map Company, *Insurance Maps of Chicago, volume 4,* New York, 1912–1970. ICHI-18506-M3. (Courtesy of the Chicago Historical Society.)

Fig. 8.29 Ludwig Mies van der Rohe, Crown Hall, Illinois Institute of Technology, Chicago, Illinois, 1950–1956. Photograph by Hedrich-Blessing, c. 1955. ICHi-18506-M3. (Courtesy of the Chadwyck-Healey/Library of Congress.)

used modern materials and forms to monumentalize an interior space, flooded with natural light and enlivened by the spectacle of people coming and going. Ironically, Edbrooke & Burnham had incorporated similar elements in the Mecca's atria.

Upon completion, Crown Hall was quickly assigned its own set of myths. Architect Eero Saarinen, who participated in the Crown Hall dedication ceremony, insisted that Mies's work established him as the third great Chicago architect after Louis Sullivan and Frank Lloyd Wright, ensuring the city's position as the "center of the universe in modern architecture." "This same bold spirit that created the Chicago architectural tradition [motivated] the creation of this campus. . . . Because Chicago is a place of courageous thinking, a slum gives way to a brand new campus—crisp and clean and beautiful and harmonious—a model of a total environment."[84] This connection between Sullivan and Mies (figure 8.30) omitted, among other things, Sullivan's abundant and often foliated ornament, his sense of the vital connection between buildings and the street, and his knowledge of how to build urban density. These qualities are more akin to the Mecca than to Crown Hall. The institute's new buildings cultivated a myth of connection to Chicago's historic architecture even as they destroyed the physical basis for taking the measure of the architectural continuities and changes represented in Mies's designs.

Fig. 8.30 Louis Sullivan Exhibit in Mies's Crown Hall, c. 1965. (Courtesy of the Illinois Institute of Technology.)

In many ways, the South Side "slum" created a lens of race through which institute officials had viewed the Mecca for decades, failing to see the building's architectural innovations. They failed to appreciate the tenants' efforts to preserve housing and to define a neighborly domestic realm in a market hedged by racism, violence, and a domestic ideology that spun on the axis of single-family housing. Moreover, the critical enthusiasm for Mies's teaching and his designs fostered a narrative of Chicago history and preservation that, on the face of it, viewed buildings such as the Mecca as largely irrelevant.[85] Certainly, the Mecca's exterior courtyard represented a precedent of great relevance for Chicago domestic architecture. The extraordinary interior spaces, with their massing of tenants, failed to win broad emulation. In fact, the intensity of the institute's efforts to demolish the Mecca turned upon the visible massing, around the atria, at the windows, in the courtyards, of an African American cultural presence. The cultural vitality evoked in the "Mecca Flat Blues" and the strength of the Mecca preservation campaign usefully underscore the value of an architecture and an urbanism that could embrace rather than jettison the possibilities of human density and public life in the city. Such spaces would undoubtedly enrich rather than detract from any "total environment." Capturing the richness of the Mecca's changing meaning and history necessarily involves following its story beyond the circumstances of its origin to those of its use and ultimate demolition.

NOTES

1. Revised version of an essay originally published in the *Journal of the Society of Architectural Historians* 57, 4 December 1998. This essay originated in 1997 when my friend Philip Krone, a keen advocate of historic cities, called to discuss strategies for preserving the Yale, a distinguished but abandoned apartment building in Chicago. As the project developed, the Mecca provided a rich context for approaching the problem of the Yale. The Yale was restored and re-opened for residential purposes in 2003 by developer John Luce. Many people have my special thanks. They made contributions that ranged from sharing information to opening inaccessible archives, from making cogent criticisms of a first draft to digging through dumpsters looking for misplaced research notes. I would especially like to thank Timothy Barton, Eve Blau, LeRoy Blommaert, Robert Bruegmann, Diane Dillon, Gordon Field, Scott Meacham, Joan Powell, Timothy Samuelson, Barbara Clark Smith, and Carroll William Westfall.

2. William H. Jordy, "The Commercial Style and the 'Chicago School,' " *Perspectives in American History* 1 (1967), 390–400. Focusing on the work of a single yet prolific firm, architectural historian Robert Bruegmann has recently offered a more nuanced and insightful view of Chicago architecture and urbanism in his book *The Architects and the City: Holabird and Roche of Chicago, 1880–1918* (Chicago: University of Chicago, 1997). See also essays collected in John Zukowsky, ed., *Chicago Architecture, 1872–1922: Birth of a Metropolis* (Munich: Prestel-Verlag, 1987).

3. Richard Cahan, *They All Fall Down: Richard Nickel's Struggle to Save America's Architecture* (Washington, D.C.:Preservation Press, 1994); Daniel Bluestone, "Preservation and Renewal in Post–World War II Chicago," *Journal of Architectural Education* 47 (May 1994), 210–23; Theodore W. Hild, "The Demolition of the Garrick Theater and the Birth of the Preservation Movement in Chicago," *Illinois Historical Journal* 188 (1995), 79–100.

4. *Industrial Chicago: The Building Interests* (Chicago: Goodspeed Publishing Company, 1891), 240.

5. Carroll William Westfall, "Chicago's Better Tall Apartment Buildings, 1871–1923," *Architectura* 21 (January 1992), 178; see also idem, "From Home to Towers: A Century of Chicago's Best Hotels and Tall Apartment Buildings," in Zukowsky, *Chicago Architecture*, 266–89.

6. *Chicago Tribune*, 13 March 1905.

7. Elizabeth C. Cromley, *Alone Together: A History of New York's Early Apartments* (Ithaca, NY: Cornell University Press, 1990); Gwendolyn Wright, *Building the Dream: A Social History of Housing in America* (New York: Pantheon Books, 1981), 96–113, 135–51.

8. *Chicago Tribune*, 12 September 1891; see also building note in *Industrial Chicago*, 591–2; and Carl W. Condit, *The Chicago School of Architecture: A History of Commercial and Public Building in the Chicago Area, 1875–1925* (Chicago: University of Chicago Press, 1964), 156–7.

9. Westfall, "Chicago's Better Tall Apartment Buildings," 184.

10. Apartment-house advertisements championing "exclusive" suburban areas often appeared in the *Chicago Tribune*. For example, advertisements for Chicago's Pattington Apartments declared, "This beautiful property is located in the exclusive residence section of the north shore" (*Chicago Tribune*, 17 March 1905). Advertisements for a Clarendon Avenue apartment declared that its apartments were "overlooking large private lawns" of adjacent single-family residences (*Chicago Tribune*, 21 April 1907).

11. *Chicago Tribune,* 12 September 1891.

12. In 1898, upon completing the Richmond Court Apartments in the Boston suburb of Brookline, Ralph Adams Cram and Bertram Grosvenor Goodhue declared that the courtyard plan was "quite unusual in this country, though frequently found abroad." With the "effect of a large English Manor," Richmond Court took on the "qualities of strength, dignity and repose, while the court is not forced into fulfilling the ignominious function of a mere light well." Quoted in Douglass Shand Tucci, *Built in Boston: City and Suburb, 1800–1950* (Boston: New York Graphic Society, 1978), 118–9.

13. E. S. Hanson, "As the Editor Sees It," *The Apartment House* 1 (January 1911), 18.

14. Herbert Croly, "Some Apartment Houses in Chicago," *Architectural Record* 21 (February 1907), 119–30.

15. "The 'Mecca' Hotel," advertisement, published on the back of McNally & Company's *Standard Map of the Columbian Exposition and City of Chicago* (Chicago, 1893), refers to the balconies as "promenade balconies." Copy in Chicago Historical Society.

16. *Chicago Tribune,* 15 July 1888.

17. Ibid., 12 September 1891.

18. Daniel Bluestone, *Constructing Chicago* (New Haven, CT: Yale University Press, 1991) 105–51.

19. Johann Friedrich Geist, *Arcades: The History of a Building Type* (Cambridge: MIT Press, 1983), 3–114.

20. Cromley, *Alone Together,* 48, 55, 61, 129, 145, 148, 164, 195, 200; Elizabeth Hawes, *New York, New York: How the Apartment House Transformed the Life of the City (1869–1930)* (New York: Knopf, 1993), 134–5, 161–7; Iain C. Taylor, "The Insanitary Housing Question and Tenement Dwellings in Nineteenth-Century Liverpool," in Anthony Sutcliffe, ed., *Multi-Storey Living: The British Working-Class* (London: Croom Helm, 1974), 41–87; Devereux Bowly Jr., *The Poorhouse: Subsidized Housing in Chicago, 1895–1976* (Carbondale, IL: Southern Illinois University Press, 1978), 1–4; Cristina Cocchioni and Mario De Grassi, *La Casa Popolara a Roma* (Rome: Edizioni Kappa, 1984); Johann Friedrich Geist and Klaus Kurvers, *Das Berliner Mietshaus, 1862–1945* (Munich: Prestel, 1984).

21. *Chicago Tribune,* 21 August 1892; *Economist* 25 (15 June 1901), 775.

22. "Synopsis of Building News," *Inland Architect and News Record* 20 (December 1892), 58; Condit, *Chicago School of Architecture,* 157–8; see also C. W. Westfall, "The Civilized 2800 Block on Pine Grove Av.," *Inland Architect* 18 (July 1974), 13–8. The Sanborn Fire Insurance Map for 1894 records only foundations for the Brewster, suggesting that it was still incomplete in 1894; the Blue Book does not record residents until 1897.

23. Frank A. Randall, *History of the Development of Building Construction in Chicago* (Urbana, IL: University of Illinois Press, 1949), 298.

24. Glen E. Holt and Dominic A. Pacyga, *Chicago: A Historical Guide to the Neighborhoods; The Loop and South Side* (Chicago: Chicago Historical Society, 1979), 49–57.

25. "[Flats for the Armour Mission]," *Inland Architect and Builder* 8 (January 1887), 101.

26. Harper Leech and John Charles Carroll, *Armour and His Times* (New York: D. Appleton-Century Company, 1938), 211–2.

27. *Chicago Tribune,* 12 September 1891, 21 April 1901; "The 'Mecca' Hotel," advertisement; Cook County Deed Books, Chicago, Illinois.

28. Manuscript Population Schedule, Twelfth Census of the United States, 1900, Chicago, Cook County, Illinois, Enumeration District No. 84.

29. Allan H. Spear, *Black Chicago: The Making of a Negro Ghetto, 1890–1920* (Chicago: University of Chicago Press, 1967); Thomas Lee Philpott, *The Slum and the Ghetto: Immigrants, Blacks and Reformers in Chicago, 1880–1930* (New York: Oxford University Press, 1978).

30. Manuscript Population Schedule, Thirteenth Census of the United States, 1910, Chicago, Cook County, Illinois, Enumeration District No. 214.

31. *Chicago Tribune*, 8 April 1911, 2 February 1912; see "Franklin T. Pember," in Greshan Publishing Company, ed., *History and Biography of Washington County and the Town of Queensbury, New York, with Historical Notes on the Various Towns* (Richmond, IN: Greshan Publishing Company, 1894), 287–91.

32. Advertisements capture the transition of the Mecca from white to black, see *Chicago Tribune*, 9 April 1911 and *Chicago Defender*, 11 May 1912. On racial transition in the Black Belt, see Commission on Chicago landmarks, *Black Metropolis Historic District* (Chicago: Commission on Chicago Landmarks, 1994), 45.

33. Philpott, *The Slum and the Ghetto*, 177–19; *Chicago Tribune*, 29 July 1919; Chicago Commission on Race Relations, *The Negro in Chicago: A Study of Race Relations and a Race Riot* (Chicago: University of Chicago Press, 1922).

34. Secondary accounts vary on when the first black tenants moved into the Mecca; *Life* magazine reported, correctly, in 1951 that the first blacks moved in "by 1912"; see "The Mecca: Chicago's Showiest Apartment Has Given Up All But the Ghost," *Life* 31 (19 November 1951): 133, this account is consistent with the 1912 change in the advertising venue for Mecca rentals from the *Chicago Tribune* to the *Chicago Defender*. *Harper's* quoted a tenant in 1950 as saying that in 1917 "white people hadn't been gone so long": see John Bartlow Martin, "The Strangest Place in Chicago," *Harper's Magazine* 201 (December 1950): 89. These accounts and local newspaper stories all agree that by World War I, African American tenants filled the apartments in the Mecca.

35. Manuscript Population Schedule, Fourteenth Census of the United States, 1920, Chicago, Cook County, Illinois, Enumeration District No. 84.

36. Commission on Chicago Landmarks, *Black Metropolis*, 5–6.

37. *Chicago Tribune*, 29 March 1943.

38. Gwendolyn Brooks, *In the Mecca* (New York: Harper & Row, 1968), 5–31.

39. Irene Macauley, *The Heritage of Illinois Institute of Technology* (Chicago: Illinois Institute of Technology, 1918), 36.

40. Ibid., 39–40.

41. "A Sketch of James D. Cunningham, Head of Republic Flow Meters," in Philip Hampson, *The Road to Success* (Chicago: Chicago Daily News, 1953), 37–9.

42. Mames Cunningham Report to the Board of Trustees, 17 May 1937, in Armour Institute of Technology Board of Trustees' Minutes, 1934–40; this report and other manuscripts cited are located, unless stated otherwise, in the Illinois Institute of Technology Archives, Paul V. Calvin Library, Illinois Institute of Technology, Chicago.

43. Bowly, *The Poorhouse*, 27–32; Arnold R. Hirsch, *Making the Second Ghetto: Race and Housing in Chicago, 1940–1960* (Cambridge: Cambridge University Press, 1983).

44. Minutes of Annual Meeting of the Board of Trustees, 11 October 1937, in Armour Institute of Technology Board of Trustees' Minutes, 1934–40.

45. Henry T. Heald, "President's Report, for the Year Ended August 31, 1940," in Illinois Institute of Technology Board of Trustees' Minutes, vol. 1, 1940–41.

46. See, for example, Illinois Institute of Technology, Minutes of the Special Meeting of the Board of Trustees, 9 July 1943, Illinois Institute of Technology Board of Trustees' Minutes, vol. 2, 1942–43.

47. Buildings and Grounds Committee Minutes, 17 May 1944, Board of Trustees of Illinois Institute of Technology, 1943–47, Box HB 12; see similar concern in original campus proposal, in James Cunningham, Report to the Board of Trustees, 17 May 1937, in Armour Institute of Technology Board of Trustees' Minutes, 1934–40.

48. James Cunningham, Report to the Board of Trustees, 17 May 1937, in Armour Institute of Technology Board of Trustees' Minutes, 1934–40.

49. Illinois Institute of Technology, Executive Committee of the Board of Trustees, Minutes of Meeting, 24 September 1941, Box HB 4, 1941–44.

50. Metropolitan Housing Council, "The Case of the Mecca Building," *Housing News* 2 (August 1942), 1–2; typescript newsletter in Board of Trustees of Illinois Institute of Technology, Box HB 2; see also City Council of Chicago, Committee on Housing, "Report of the Subcommittee to Investigate Housing Among Colored People," *Journal of the Proceedings of the City Council of Chicago*, 19 June 1941, 4982–7; Hirsch, *Making the Second Ghetto*, 20, 22.

51. Newton C. Farr to Henry T. Heald, 31 July 1942; Henry T. Heald to Newton C. Farr, 31 July 1942, Board of Trustees of Illinois Institute of Technology, Box HB 2.

52. *Chicago Defender*, 1 May 1943.

53. Ibid., 15 May 1943.

54. Ibid.; Newton Farr, "Report on the Mecca," Minutes of the Regular Meeting of the Board of Trustees, Illinois Institute of Technology, 12 April 1943.

55. *Chicago Defender*, 5 June 1943; draft of "Petition for Mandamus," Board of Trustees of Illinois Institute of Technology, Box HB 2.

56. Illinois Institute of Technology to the Tenants of the Mecca Building, May 1943, Board of Trustees of Illinois Institute of Technology, Box HB 2.

57. Illinois Institute of Technology, Minutes of the Special Meeting of the Board of Trustees, 9 July 1943, 9 August 1943, Illinois Institute of Technology Board of Trustees' Minutes, vol. 2, 1942–43; "Black Belt" reference is from James Cunningham Report to the Board of Trustees, 17 May 1937, in Armour Institute of Technology Board of Trustees' Minutes, 1934–40.

58. "Additional Considerations Which Should Be Given Weight by the War Department in Determining Acceptable Bid," Board of Trustees of Illinois Institute of Technology, Box HB 1.

59. Henry T. Heald to Henry I. Stimson, 7 September 1943; Henry T. Heald to Sydney G. McAllister, 6 September 1943, in Board of Trustees of Illinois Institute of Technology, Box HB 1.

60. Henry T. Heald, *Reclaiming Chicago's Blighted Areas* (Chicago, 1946), Metropolitan Housing Council pamphlet without pagination located in Chicago Historical Society.

61. Wilford G. Winholtz to members of the Chicago Land Clearance Commission, 26 January 1948, South Side Planning Board Files, July 1947–April 1950, Board of Trustees of Illinois Institute of Technology, Box HB 12.

62. Henry T. Heald to Chicago Housing Authority, 4 October 1944, in Minutes of the Illinois Institute of Technology, Board of Trustees Buildings and Grounds Committee, 1943–47, Box HB 12.

63. Bowly, *The Poorhouse*, 61–5.

64. Kevin Harrington, "Order, Space, Proportion—Mies's Curriculum at IIT," in *Mies van der Rohe: Architect as Educator, Catalog for Exhibition, 6 June–12 July 1986* (Chicago: Illinois Institute of Technology, 1968), 49–68.

65. Skidmore, Owings & Merrill, "Outline of Preliminary Report, Illinois Institute of Technology Housing Report," c. 1945; see also Illinois Institute of Technology, 4 October 1944, Board of Trustees Buildings and Grounds Committee Minutes, 1943–47, Box HB 12.

66. "Illinois Tech Replans 16 City Blocks," *Architectural Forum* 85 (September 1946), 102–3.

67. Skidmore, Owings & Merrill, "Outline of Preliminary Report."

68. Ibid.

69. See Oscar C. Brown to Milton Mumford, 9 February 1948; Wilford C. Winholtz to Oscar C. Brown, 13 February 1948; President Henry T. Heald Papers, South Side Planning Board Files, Box HB 63; Oscar C. Brown, *Some Facts and Factors on Housing*

for Negroes in Chicago (Chicago, 1953); Oscar C. Brown Corporation pamphlet, no pagination, located in Chicago Historical Society.

70. Board of Trustees Buildings and Grounds Committee Minutes, 17 February 1950, in Illinois Institute of Technology Buildings and Grounds Committee Minutes, 1943–55.
71. *Chicago Tribune,* 23 May 1950.
72. Quoted in *Chicago Daily News,* 14 August 1951.
73. *Journal of the Proceedings of the City Council of Chicago,* 24 March 1950, 5998; 25 October 1950, 7057.
74. *Chicago Defender,* 27 May 1950.
75. *Chicago Tribune,* 23 May 1950.
76. See *Chicago Tribune,* 23 May 1950; "The Mecca's End," *Newsweek* 39 (14 January 1952), 23–4.
77. "The Mecca's End," 23–4; *Chicago Sun Times,* 30 December 1951.
78. John Bartlow Martin, "The Strangest Place in Chicago," 86–97.
79. Ibid., 86.
80. Quoted in "The Mecca's End," 24.
81. "The Mecca, Chicago's Showiest Apartment Has Given Up All but the Ghost."
82. Jim Hurlbut, "WMAQ Radio Script, June 6, 1950," President Henry T. Heald Papers, Box HB 40.
83. Kevin Harrington, "S.R. Crown Hall," in Alice Sinkevitch, ed., *AIA Guide to Chicago* (New York: Harcourt Brace, 1993), 376–7; Commission on Chicago Landmarks, *S.R. Crown Hall, Illinois Institute of Technology, 3360 S. State St., Preliminary Staff Summary of Information* (Chicago: Commission on Chicago Landmarks, 1996).
84. Eero Saarinen, quoted in Macauley, *Illinois Institute of Technology,* 78.
85. Bluestone, "Preservation and Renewal in Post–World War II Chicago."

9

ANCESTRAL ARCHITECTURE
The Early Preservation Movement in Charleston

Robert R. Weyeneth

Essay reprinted from *Historic Preservation for a Living City: Historic Charleston Foundation, 1947–1997*, by Robert Weyeneth with permission from University of South Carolina Press.

TO UNDERSTAND THE ESTABLISHMENT of Historic Charleston Foundation in 1947 and its evolution over the following five decades, it is useful to examine the historic preservation movement in Charleston prior to the 1940s. As in so many other cities, the first stirrings of the preservation impulse were stimulated by the destruction—or threatened destruction—of landmark buildings, structures closely linked with community history whose presence on the cityscape often fostered a sense of civic identity for residents. Charleston faced loss of landmark buildings a number of times in the first years of the twentieth century, and these threats galvanized heritage groups to action and even inspired the creation of a new organization, the Society for the Preservation of Old Dwellings. But in one revealing way, the early preservation movement in Charleston was unlike the experience of any other American city: Charleston was the first city in the country to use the zoning process to encourage historic preservation. Through its zoning ordinance of 1931, municipal officials and preservationists sought to marshal public authority to protect historic architecture. The origins of Historic Charleston Foundation in 1947 were rooted in this vibrant local context that spawned both the private campaigns to rescue landmark buildings and municipal government's pioneering preservation ordinance of 1931.

In the twentieth century, Charleston became synonymous with historic preservation, and the new century had barely begun when, in

Fig. 9.1 The Powder Magazine (c. 1713), pictured about 1903. Early preservation efforts in Charleston focused on saving landmarks of the colonial period such as the Powder Magazine, purchased in 1902 by the National Society of Colonial Dames. Under a long-term lease with the Colonial Dames, Historic Charleston Foundation restored this early-eighteenth-century storehouse and reopened it as a museum in 1997. (Courtesy of HCF.)

1902, the National Society of Colonial Dames in the State of South Carolina purchased a small structure known as the Powder Magazine to save it from demolition. The Powder Magazine had long been viewed as an important link with South Carolina's colonial past, having been built in the early eighteenth century along one of the walls of the fortified city to store gunpowder. Shortly after acquiring the historic structure, the Colonial Dames restored it and used the building as the headquarters for the statewide chapter. Subsequently, it was opened to the public as a museum.[1] The Daughters of the American Revolution played a similar early role in preserving the architectural legacy of colonial South Carolina when it acquired the Old Exchange Building, a former customs house and city hall erected in the mideighteenth century. The local Rebecca Motte chapter of the Daughters had worked since 1899 to save this imposing building situated at the foot of Broad Street near the Cooper River waterfront, and its campaign proved successful in 1913 when Congress authorized the transfer of the structure from the federal government to the nonprofit organization. The local chapter set up offices in the Old Exchange, and soon after that it was opened as a museum.[2] Both of these early preservation campaigns in Charleston had focused on public buildings dating to the colonial era, and the Society of Colonial Dames and the Daughters of the American Revolution had sought to rescue the landmarks for their educational potential as museums to teach about history, especially the beginnings of American nationalism.

By the 1920s, threats to residential architecture, as well as to public buildings, attracted the attention of Charlestonians worried about the pace of change on the cityscape. Two threats loomed largest: the rise of the gasoline filling station and the dismantling of historic homes for their architectural details. To accommodate the growing number of automobile owners in Charleston, oil companies began constructing filling stations in convenient locations around the city, sometimes razing existing structures to make room for the requisite pumps, repair facilities, and rest rooms. Standard Oil in particular sought to break into the Charleston market, and the company quickly found itself at odds with residents concerned about its construction program. In one of the great paradoxes of American preservation history, during the 1920s the Standard Oil Company became the nemesis of Charleston preservationists at the same time that one of its major stockholders and the son of its founder, John D. Rockefeller Jr., was embarking on his ambitious restoration of Virginia's colonial capital, Williamsburg.

Out-of-town art collectors represented a different kind of threat to Charleston's residential architecture. Wealthy individuals wishing to furnish town houses and country homes in an early American style as well as museums inspired by the vogue for re-creating their galleries as period rooms found a ready supply of fine interior paneling and ornate exterior ironwork in Charleston.[3] For their part, Charlestonians were willing to sell the architectural detailing of their old homes for a variety of reasons: They needed the money to pay taxes, a building was being demolished anyway, their property was in a deteriorated area occupied by African American tenants, and the prices being offered were simply too tempting to resist.[4] A network of local antiques dealers sprang up to identify potential sources of paneling, mantels, and balconies for these individual and institutional collectors. For architect Albert Simons, whose voice became one of the most vociferous raised to protest the export of Charleston's architectural legacy, the antiques dealer even more than the oil company was "the greatest menace to the preservation of old buildings."[5]

The first public campaign in Charleston to rescue a private residence from demolition was waged on behalf of the Joseph Manigault
House. The three-story brick mansion was built on Meeting Street
about 1803 in a Neoclassical style for planter Joseph Manigault by his
brother, Gabriel Manigault, who designed a number of important
Charleston buildings, including the South Carolina Society Hall, the
Orphan House Chapel, and probably the Bank of the United States,
which serves today as city hall. By the early twentieth century, the
Manigault property had passed through a number of hands; the mansion itself had been subdivided into a tenement, and a dry-cleaning
firm operated on the grounds.[6] Despite this ragged appearance, the
impending demise of the building for a Ford automobile dealership
inspired a handful of citizens to organize themselves into what became
the city's first historic preservation organization. The new group called
itself the Society for the Preservation of Old Dwellings, a name that reflected both its immediate concern (saving the Joseph Manigault
House) and a prediction of its future role of preserving residential architecture.[7] Its founder and first president was Susan Pringle Frost—a
dynamic and unorthodox real estate agent, suffragist, and feminist—
who had already established credentials as a preservationist through
some of her earlier real estate transactions.[8]

The Society for the Preservation of Old Dwellings was able to rescue the Joseph Manigault House by purchase in May 1920, but ownership of the property proved burdensome and eventually unsustainable
for the fledgling organization. The house had been purchased through
a bank loan, with pledges of financial support from the society's
founding members, most significantly from Susan Frost's cousin Nell
McColl Pringle. Even with energetic fund-raising appeals over the next
two years and attempts to locate suitable tenants for the Manigault
House, the society was unable to meet expenses. In 1922, Nell Pringle
and her husband came to the rescue a second time, assuming a personal debt of some forty thousand dollars. To reduce the size of this financial commitment, the Pringles reluctantly sold the Manigault
garden to the Standard Oil Company for a filling station and agreed to
rent the house to African American tenants. Beginning in 1928, they
tried, briefly, to open the house as a museum. But these measures
could not stave off foreclosure on the Pringle mortgage. Despite several years of efforts to find a new owner and ongoing concern that the
spectacular interiors of the Manigault House would be dismantled
and sold, the mansion was put up for sale at auction in 1933. It was
rescued—for a third time—when a South Carolinian who owned a
plantation in the vicinity of Charleston and was the heiress to a major

Fig. 9.2 Joseph Manigault House (c. 1803). The Joseph Manigault House was the first private residence in Charleston saved through a public campaign, and its rescue was an important initial victory for the city's oldest historic preservation organization, the Society for the Preservation of Old Dwellings, now called the Preservation Society of Charleston. (Courtesy of the Charleston Museum.)

northeastern grocery store fortune purchased it for three thousand dollars and donated it to the Charleston Museum.[9] Shortly thereafter, in 1937, the Standard Oil Company was persuaded to deed its filling station in the former garden to the museum, effectively reassembling the Manigault property.[10]

The Charleston Museum continues to own the property today and operates it as a house museum, one of several in the city that are furnished and interpreted as the homes of important antebellum Charlestonians. The Joseph Manigault House is unique, though, from one perspective: its place in the history of the local historic preservation movement. It was the first private residence in Charleston saved through a public campaign, and its rescue represented an important first victory for the city's oldest preservation organization, the Society for the Preservation of Old Dwellings.

Even before it accepted the donation of the Manigault House in 1933, the Charleston Museum had been playing a significant role in preserving Charleston's architectural legacy. As concern mounted in the 1920s about the sale and export of woodwork and ironwork from old Charleston houses, the museum became an architectural repository of last resort with the support of its director, Laura M. Bragg.[11] Remnants from buildings scheduled for demolition often came to the museum through the intercession of Albert Simons, who seemed always to be on the watch for new construction projects and imminent demolitions. Simons, a Charlestonian trained at the University of Pennsylvania, had studied in Europe and would become the city's leading preservation architect well into the 1970s. Typically, the young architect would communicate with the property owner, arrange to inspect a site personally, and then compile an inventory of features he considered "worthy of salvaging."[12] Simons had no special stake in building the museum collections as such; rather, the salvage effort was a partial solution to what seemed to him an assault on the civic heritage: "It distresses me painfully to see our fine old building[s] torn down and their contents wrecked or what is more humiliating sold to aliens and shipped away to enrich some other community more appreciative of such things than ourselves."[13] Sometimes the Charleston Museum sought to purchase architectural features from vacant buildings that were falling into decay. In some instances the museum was successful in these negotiations, and at other times private collectors were able to offer higher prices. The museum also learned to be wary of local citizens marketing architectural features from buildings in no danger whatsoever. As Albert Simons warned, "many of our own people . . . are only too ready to sell anything provided enough is of-

Fig. 9.3 In the garden of the Joseph Manigault House, 1936. Following the acquisition of the Joseph Manigault House by the Charleston Museum in the 1930s, the Standard Oil Company was persuaded to donate the filling station it had operated since the 1920s in the former garden. Pictured here are E. Milby Burton, Dick Lewis, and Burnet Maybank. (Courtesy of the Charleston Museum.)

fered."[14] Such salvage work on the part of the Charleston Museum was clearly not a substitute for preserving whole buildings in place, but in the context of the 1920s and the thriving Charleston antiques trade, it seemed a reasonable stopgap measure for a problem that did not entirely recede with the coming of the Depression in the following decade.[15]

Perhaps the most visible role for the Charleston Museum in the city's nascent preservation movement was its participation in the campaign to save the Thomas Heyward House. Planter Thomas Heyward, who would become one of the South Carolina signers of the Declaration of Independence, built this brick structure on Church Street as his city residence about 1771. Because President George Washington stayed in the town house for a week during a visit to Charleston in 1791, it has become known as the Heyward-Washington House. By the late 1920s, the first floor of the mansion was in commercial use as a bakery, and rumors were circulating that art collectors were interested in acquiring the contents of the residence. In response, the Charleston

Fig. 9.4 Heyward-Washington House (c. 1771), with bakery. By the late 1920s the home of Thomas Heyward, one of the South Carolina signers of the Declaration of Independence, was in commercial use as a bakery, and rumors were circulating that art collectors were eyeing the interior architectural details. With support from the Society for the Preservation of Old Dwellings and Mrs. William Emerson of Boston, the Charleston Museum purchased the property and opened it in 1931 as the city's first historic house museum. Historic Charleston Foundation helped pay off the outstanding mortgage in 1953. (Courtesy of the Charleston Museum.)

Museum agreed to take an option on the Heyward House in 1928, making use of a generous contribution from Mrs. William Emerson of Boston. Frances W. Emerson had become interested in preserving Charleston architecture as a result of a recent visit to the city with her architect husband, Dr. William Emerson of the Massachusetts Institute of Technology. In following years, the Boston couple became important backers of preservation initiatives in Charleston. In 1929, a fundraising campaign in tandem with the Society for the Preservation of Old Dwellings generated half of the purchase price, and the Charleston Museum exercised its option to buy the mansion. Following a major restoration of portions of the house supervised by the architectural firm headed by Albert Simons and Samuel Lapham Jr., the Heyward-Washington House opened its doors to the public in 1931. It is usually considered Charleston's first historic house museum, despite the earlier, abortive effort by the Pringles to open the Joseph Manigault House as a museum. Even with the income from museum admissions, though, the Heyward House remained a constant financial drain on the Charleston Museum. At one point it was seized for nonpayment of taxes but was rescued again by the generosity of Mrs. Emerson, and in 1933 the state legislature exempted both the Heyward and Manigault Houses from further taxation.[16] The mortgage on the Heyward-Washington House was finally paid off in the early 1950s with the assistance of Historic Charleston Foundation.

In the campaigns to save the Joseph Manigault and Heyward-Washington Houses, preservationists in Charleston came to realize that local resources were usually insufficient for projects that involved the purchase of historic properties and their operation as house museums. Despite the harsh rhetoric about the culpability of northern museums, winter tourists, and other wealthy aliens vandalizing Charleston's architectural patrimony, the reality was that out-of-town money was crucial for saving the city's old buildings. And of course it was also true that Charlestonians themselves shared some responsibility for the export trade in which many seemed to participate willingly. In a pattern that would come to characterize the history of preservation efforts in twentieth-century Charleston, local preservationists sought out northern capital time and again to rescue historic buildings. In part, the need to seek funds elsewhere reflected demographic and economic shifts in the nineteenth and twentieth centuries that had bypassed Charleston and located centers of growth and prosperity in other regions of the United States. But the reliance on such benefactors also reflected the fact that many Americans, not just South Carolinians or southerners, could attach significance to the uniqueness and beauty of the city's architectural heritage.

It was to this potential national audience that local preservationists tried to turn when they approached the American Institute of Architects (AIA) in 1930. The AIA had previously commissioned and published a work on the city's historic architecture by Albert Simons and Samuel Lapham Jr. titled *Charleston, South Carolina* (1927). At the suggestion of Mrs. William Emerson, and with her considerable financial backing, the AIA consented to establish an ad hoc committee to publicize the necessity of preserving Charleston's historic architecture. This blue-ribbon committee was composed of both nationally prominent figures in the world of fine arts, whose responsibilities included spreading the word about the threats facing Charleston, and knowledgeable local citizens, whose own efforts over the next couple of years emphasized the ongoing work on behalf of the Heyward-Washington and Joseph Manigault Houses, attempts to discourage Standard Oil from constructing filling stations in historic areas, and the promotion of municipal planning and zoning.[17] In a nod to the situation in Charleston, in 1932 the American Institute of Architects went on record urging museums to avoid the practice of incorporating historic interiors into exhibits, except for those from buildings legitimately on the verge of demolition.[18]

The triumphs and tribulations of the struggle to save the Manigault and Heyward residences during the 1920s and 1930s have become familiar benchmarks in the history of the city's early preservation movement, even as they illustrated the pitfalls of the "museum solution" to historic preservation. There had been prior preservation campaigns in Charleston by the Society of Colonial Dames and the Daughters of the American Revolution, of course, and their efforts had targeted civic rather than residential architecture.[19] But their understanding of historic preservation resembled that of the Society for the Preservation of Old Dwellings and the Charleston Museum: Preservation was an educational enterprise carried out with the ultimate goal of establishing museums for the teaching of history. However, saving buildings through purchase and conversion into museums was an enormously expensive undertaking, as the Manigault and Heyward campaigns vividly demonstrated. Use of this strategy could rescue only a handful of the most important landmarks in a community, unless of course one had the resources of a Rockefeller and the drive to create a restored museum village on the scale of Colonial Williamsburg in Virginia.

As crusades to rally public support on behalf of landmark buildings went forward, some Charlestonians had already been exploring other ways to preserve the city's architectural legacy: through keeping historic buildings in use as living and working spaces. As early as the 1910s, real estate agent Susan Pringle Frost—who would go on to found the Society for the Preservation of Old Dwellings in 1920—had begun her own efforts to buy, stabilize, and resell modest homes among the slums of St. Michael's Alley and eastern Tradd Street, with an eye to encouraging rehabilitation in the area as a whole. Although by the 1920s and 1930s she was chronically overextended financially, Frost continued to buy and hold properties, restoring them to a livable condition when necessary and often trying to beautify them by adding balconies, gates, and mantels. Her imaginative remodeling efforts took full advantage of the supply of doorways, wrought-iron balconies, and other architectural remnants that she had salvaged over the years. Susan Frost's campaign of targeting a succession of houses in a single neighborhood anticipated the modern "area" approach to preservation, which became a potent strategy when linked to the financial mechanism of a revolving fund by Historic Charleston Foundation in the 1950s and 1960s. Her purchases and renovations continued in subsequent decades on Tradd Street, Bedon's Alley, and East Bay Street, almost up to her death in 1960. Dorothy Haskell Porcher Legge was another preservation pioneer who worked privately and effectively to inspire the revitalization of a block of deteriorated eighteenth-century mercantile structures on East Bay Street, beginning with the purchase and restoration of her own residence at No. 99–101 in 1931. Her notion of a nonhistorical pastel color scheme for the exteriors subsequently inspired the name Rainbow Row for the picturesque collection of buildings restored in the 1930s, 1940s, and 1950s. In 1936, Mr. and Mrs. Reynolds Brown rehabilitated a kitchen building and courtyard on Church Street at Cabbage Row into a landscaped winter residence for themselves, inaugurating a trend to renovate former outbuildings into substantial private residences.[20] By the end of the decade, Frederick Law Olmsted Jr., a keen observer of the American urban scene, was struck by the scale and pace of these private efforts. He was impressed by "the rehabilitation and refurbishing of a considerable number of fine old dwellings and the adaptation of other interesting old structures and their surviving accessories to new uses," developments that seemed to offer "a strong and very encouraging counter-current" to the forces of deterioration and intrusion that were transforming twentieth-century Charleston.[21]

Public agencies were sometimes able to follow the example set by the private sector in adapting historic structures to fresh contemporary uses. With federal funds available through the New Deal in the 1930s, municipal officials undertook two significant "adaptive use" projects: Dock Street Theatre and the Robert Mills Manor public housing project. Throughout the 1920s and 1930s, preservationists had worried about the fate of the nineteenth-century Planter's Hotel, but not until Mayor Burnet Rhett Maybank was able to arrange funding through the federal Works Progress Administration was it possible to implement a novel idea for the old hotel: reconstruction of the eighteenth-century theater that had once occupied the site. Between 1935 and 1937, under the supervision of Albert Simons, the interior was fitted with a period-style theater, using woodwork from the Thomas Radcliffe-Mitchell King House, which was demolished by the College of Charleston in 1938.[22] Equally innovative was the effort to preserve and integrate historic buildings into the plan for a public housing complex also erected with New Deal assistance. The architectural firm of Simons and

Fig. 9.5 Planter's Hotel/Dock Street Theatre, pictured about 1900. With federal funds available through the New Deal, the city undertook a significant adaptive-use project at the nineteenth-century Planter's Hotel in the 1930s. The eighteenth-century theater that had once occupied the site was reconstructed within the hotel. The theater opened under the management of the Carolina Art Association, and it provided early office space for Historic Charleston Foundation. (Courtesy of the Charleston Museum.)

Lapham, working with architect Douglas Ellington and landscape architect Loutrel W. Briggs, constructed thirty-four multiunit brick homes in 1939–41 adjacent to several existing historic structures: two antebellum residences on Beaufain Street, the former city jail, and the so-called Marine Hospital built for ailing merchant seamen. The modern housing project was named for Robert Mills, the early federal architect who had added a wing to the city jail in the 1820s and designed the Marine Hospital in the 1830s. Today the Marine Hospital provides offices for the city's housing authority.[23]

Without doubt, the most significant governmental action taken to promote historic preservation in the 1920s and 1930s was the adoption in 1931 of the zoning ordinance, which had an innovative provision to encourage "the preservation and protection of historic places and areas of historic interest."[24] This ordinance was the culmination of seven years of municipal attempts to think systematically about the causes and consequences of urban change in Charleston. Typically,

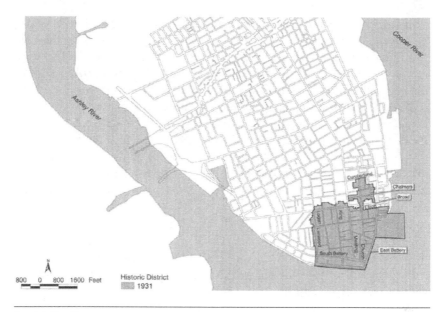

Fig. 9.6 The "Old and Historic Charleston District," established in 1931.

Susan Pringle Frost had been one of the first citizens to wonder how the authority of local government might be used to preserve the city's architectural heritage. In the mid-1920s, she had approached Mayor Thomas P. Stoney about drafting a municipal ordinance to prohibit the removal of old ironwork and woodwork from Charleston. But the city attorney could find no legal basis for restricting the rights of private property owners in this way, and nothing came of Frost's proposal. Zoning, on the other hand, seemed to hold out a number of possibilities, particularly since the state legislature had recently authorized municipal governments to enact zoning ordinances if they wished.[25]

It was at the initiative of the chamber of commerce in December 1924 that city council was first urged to implement planning and zoning for Charleston. Both the chamber and city council studied the issue for several years until April 1929, when a temporary City Planning and Zoning Commission was established. The commission proceeded in fits and starts, unsure how to meet its dual responsibilities for devising a zoning ordinance and evaluating requests for new commercial construction in the historic city, such as the petitions from the Standard Oil Company to build filling stations. The mandate was clarified in October 1929 when city council established a Special Committee on Zoning, separate from the interim City Planning and Zoning

Commission, to draft a proposed ordinance. The special committee, under the chairmanship of Alston Deas, who had recently succeeded to the presidency of the Society for the Preservation of Old Dwellings, was able to cobble together a temporary ordinance that prohibited filling stations, automobile repair shops, and factories in a portion of the city south of Broad Street.[26] The committee also recommended professional assistance to prepare a fully adequate ordinance. In October 1930, the city council abolished the interim zoning commission, reconstituted it with new legal authority, and named as the new commissioners the former members of the special committee. At the same time, the council agreed to seek professional planning assistance from the Morris Knowles firm of Pittsburgh, Pennsylvania.[27]

Staff members of Morris Knowles were dispatched to Charleston in 1930–31, charged with developing both a comprehensive zoning ordinance and recommendations for a city planning document. The consulting firm eventually suggested a set of use and height districts, as well as a "historic district." To formulate ideas for the latter, the Morris Knowles engineers worked with knowledgeable citizens such as Albert Simons to survey and map the location of buildings constructed before the mid–nineteenth century. Simons and the planners assumed that these colonial, Federal, and antebellum structures were "practically all that is of historic and architectural interest."[28] One of the Morris Knowles reports, presented to the City Planning and Zoning Commission in July 1931, offered predictions about population trends and assessments of where new schools, parks, playgrounds, and transportation routes should be constructed to accommodate orderly growth consistent with "the purposes of the Zoning Ordinance and the City Plan."[29] Special attention was devoted to the future racial distribution of the population and how civic improvements, such as schools and parks, might be used to maintain or direct patterns of residential segregation. "In the South, where separate schools are established for white and negro children," the report observed, the careful placement of public buildings and playgrounds can operate as "an effective influence for the desirable development of the surrounding territory."[30] Despite its disturbing deference to contemporary racial attitudes, the Morris Knowles report represented one of the earliest attempts in Charleston to consider long-term urban growth from a proactive planning perspective.

Charleston did not adopt a full-scale city plan as a result of the recommendations, but the city council formally ratified a general zoning ordinance in October 1931 that included a small but significant section on historic preservation. While many American cities had been

Fig. 9.7 Gas station, 108 Meeting Street. Public outrage about the demolition of three residences on Meeting Street near Chalmers Street by the Standard Oil Company helped Mayor Thomas P. Stoney gain approval for the zoning ordinance of 1931. Standard Oil tried to bolster its public image by employing Albert Simons to design a "colonial revival" filling station with salvaged architectural details. It is shown here in the 1970s. (Courtesy of HCF.)

experimenting with both city planning and zoning for some time by the 1930s, Charleston's zoning ordinance was novel for provisions that sought to protect historical architecture. Article X of the ordinance designated a portion of the city as the Old and Historic Charleston District and established a Board of Architectural Review (BAR) with authority over certain types of architectural changes to all buildings in this district. As originally constituted, the BAR was to consist of five members drawn from organizations that offered useful institutional expertise for the new municipal body: the City Planning and Zoning Commission, the local chapters of the American Institute of Architects and the American Society of Civil Engineers, the Charleston Real Estate Exchange, and the Carolina Art Association, a long-established fine-arts society that managed the local art gallery. Part-time staff support was provided by the city engineer.[31]

Under the zoning ordinance, the Board of Architectural Review had potentially significant regulatory authority over changes to exterior features of buildings in the Old and Historic Charleston District that were "subject to public view from a public street or way."[32] In practice, though, the BAR sought to play an "advisory rather than disciplinary" role, in order to gain acceptance for itself and its mandate.[33] Instead of seeking to impose rulings on citizens sensitive about the rights of private property owners and thereby inciting hard feelings and possibly court challenges to its authority, the BAR operated like "a free Architectural Clinic," dispensing sketches of appropriate alterations and tips on paint colors, for example.[34] While its statutory authority was fairly broad, at least by the standards of the time, the geographical extent of its jurisdiction was actually rather limited compared with the size of Charleston's historic districts today. The Old and Historic Charleston District established in 1931 consisted of a small portion at the tip of the peninsula, generally south of Broad Street and roughly bounded by East Bay Street, South Battery, and Lenwood and Logan Streets on the west.[35] What was significant about the ordinance was not the size of the historic district but that Charleston sought to target a whole neighborhood, not just individual buildings. This area approach to protection of historic architecture would come to define the modern preservation movement.

From the vantage point of the 1931 ordinance, it is instructive to look back over the preservation concerns of the previous decade in Charleston. Despite all the clamor in the 1920s about the exodus of Charleston paneling and mantels, the 1931 ordinance did not give the Board of Architectural Review any jurisdiction over interior details of a building. The BAR had jurisdiction only over exterior features—if they were visible from a public right-of-way and, of course, if the building was located in the Old and Historic Charleston District. While the Heyward-Washington House was within these boundaries, the Joseph Manigault residence was well outside, and consequently the 1931 ordinance offered the Manigault House no protection in the perilous years prior to its donation to the Charleston Museum. One of the most contentious preservation issues of the 1920s had been the razing of historic structures for the construction of filling stations. Indeed, public outrage about the demolition by the Standard Oil Company of three residences on Meeting Street near Chalmers Street had helped Mayor Thomas P. Stoney gain approval for the zoning ordinance.[36] Nevertheless, even after 1931 property owners remained free to raze historic buildings anywhere in the city, including those located within

Fig. 9.8 Frances R. Edmunds Center for Historic Preservation. Historic Charleston Foundation acquired the gas station at Meeting and Chalmers Streets in the 1980s and converted it to the Frances R. Edmunds Center for Historic Preservation. (Courtesy of HCF.)

the Old and Historic Charleston District. Not until 1959 did the Board of Architectural Review gain the power to delay demolitions, and not until 1966 did it have authority to prohibit demolitions. As novel as the zoning ordinance was for its inclusion of a section on historic preservation and its focus on an entire neighborhood, it did not fully address the threats that had emerged previously in Charleston.

One measure of the genuine success of Charleston's pathbreaking approach to historic preservation in the 1930s was that so many other cities chose to follow its example in subsequent years. The list included cities as far flung as New Orleans, Louisiana (1937); Alexandria, Virginia (1946); Winston-Salem, North Carolina (1948); Santa Barbara, California (1949); Georgetown, Washington, D.C. (1950); Natchez, Mississippi (1951); Annapolis, Maryland (1952); St. Augustine, Florida (1953); Santa Fe, New Mexico (1953); Tombstone, Arizona (1954); and Boston, Massachusetts (1955). By one estimate, by the 1970s more than two hundred American cities had enacted municipal ordinances to preserve historically or architecturally significant private property. Many of these borrowed heavily from the

Fig. 9.9 Dedication of the Frances R. Edmunds Center for Historic Preservation. Located in a former Standard Oil gas station, this unusual monument to the early preservation movement in Charleston was opened by the Historic Charleston Foundation in 1986.

wording of Charleston's original statute, and some even called their efforts "Charleston ordinances." By the 1990s, the number of historic preservation ordinances in the United States was estimated at more than eighteen hundred.[37]

One question that might be posed is: Why Charleston? What was it about the city that produced this pioneering zoning ordinance, as well as the flurry of campaigns on behalf of landmark buildings? Three reasons come to mind: the city's unique architectural environment, the web of family linkages associated with this historic architecture, and the romanticization of the local scene through the Charleston Renaissance. All of these help to explain the origins and vitality of the early preservation movement.

Paradoxically, the urban environment inherited by twentieth-century Charleston reflected both the city's historic wealth and its historic poverty. The slave-based economy of plantation agriculture had made the port one of the wealthiest cities in the English colonies before the American Revolution, and its affluence continued into the first decades of the nineteenth century. The style and construction of Charleston's early buildings reflected the material success of this planter and merchant aristocracy.[38] The poverty that descended on the city following the Civil War persisted well into the twentieth century and had the unintended effect of preserving much of this distinctive cityscape. Because progress and prosperity largely bypassed the city for an extended period of time, Charlestonians did not have the resources to follow the lead of Americans elsewhere who were rushing to replace the old with the new as quickly as possible. It was not until the 1920s that the intrusions of the automobile and the influx of wealthy visitors seemed to pose significant threats to the architectural inheritance.[39]

When early activists took up the preservation banner in response to the pace of urban change, it was often in the hope of protecting places with strong ancestral associations. In a small and parochial community such as Charleston in the first decades of the twentieth century, preservation of local heritage was frequently inseparable from preservation of family history. Many early preservationists had a personal identification with the old buildings they wanted to save, and in this way preservation could be a form of celebrating family lineage. The author of an essay about the restoration of the Joseph Manigault House, for example, was described as "one of Charleston's most active and enthusiastic preservationists" by virtue of her "inheritance, interest, and experience."[40] The collective memory of civic conservators inspired their efforts just as it informed their ideas of what constituted meaningful history.[41]

Appreciation of the city's distinctive architecture and history was also fostered by a cultural reawakening in the 1920s and 1930s that has come to be called the Charleston Renaissance. Like regional artistic and literary revivals elsewhere, it drew primary inspiration from the local scene. The books and paintings of Alice Ravenel Huger Smith celebrated the beauty of the historic city and the surrounding Low-country, as did the etchings and drawings of Elizabeth O'Neill Verner, whose work often emphasized the aesthetic contributions of vernacular buildings, portraying poverty and dilapidation as picturesque. Alfred Hutty's prints were inspired by the city's grand architectural monuments, scenes of African American street life, and rural vistas that evoked the Old South. In the opening passage of his novel *Porgy*, a story about the lives of African Americans on the fictional "Catfish Row," DuBose Heyward characterized Charleston as "an ancient, beautiful city that time had forgotten before it destroyed."[42] Artists and writers alike discovered a sentimental charm in the crumbling structures of the old city, and they created images that promoted a powerful, nostalgic aesthetic. The sense of place articulated by the Charleston Renaissance helped to fuel early preservationist sentiment in general and even to motivate several individuals to become active and committed preservationists.[43]

It was against this backdrop of preservation in the 1920s and 1930s that Historic Charleston Foundation emerged in the 1940s. Although the foundation was a completely new organization, a number of the people who served as its trustees in the 1940s, 1950s, 1960s, and even into the 1970s had been deeply involved in efforts to preserve Charleston in the 1920s and 1930s. These men and women had participated in the implementation of the original zoning ordinance, provided leadership for the Charleston Museum and the Society for the Preservation of Old Dwellings in their initial preservation campaigns, and been associated with the Charleston Renaissance.[44] While fresh faces would join these experienced hands to establish Historic Charleston Foundation in 1947, the institutional agenda of the new organization reflected the legacy of the first generation of Charleston preservationists. In the decades following its creation, the foundation would build upon this early record of success through efforts to refine the operation of the zoning ordinance, experiment with an area approach to preservation, capitalize on the vitality of the private sector, and address ongoing issues of planning and development. In time, Historic Charleston Foundation would also seek to broaden the meaning of historic preservation beyond a reverence for ancestral architecture to a concern for the urban welfare of diverse groups of citizens.

The Bottle Man

Elizabeth O'Neill Verner

Fig. 9.10 Elizabeth O'Neill Verner, *The Bottle Man*. Appreciation of the city's architecture and history was fostered by a cultural awakening in the 1920s and 1930s known as the Charleston Renaissance. Elizabeth O'Neill Verner was among those who found artistic inspiration in the local scene, often emphasizing the aesthetic contributions of vernacular buildings and portraying scenes of poverty and dilapidation as picturesque. (Courtesy of the Charleston Museum.)

NOTES

1. Martha Zierden, "Charleston's Powder Magazine as a Symbol of Cultural Change" (paper presented at the Southeastern Archaeological Conference, Birmingham, Alabama, 1996); Laurence Vail Coleman, *Historic House Museums* (Washington, D.C.: American Association of Museums, 1933), 152. As part of a strategy to stabilize and restore the structure, the Colonial Dames leased the Powder Magazine to Historic Charleston Foundation in the 1990s.
2. On the acquisition and subsequent use of the Old Exchange Building, see Jana Lynn Trapolino, "The South Carolina Daughters of the American Revolution and Historic Preservation" (M.A. thesis, University of South Carolina, 1995), 78–84.
3. These collectors included museums in Minneapolis and St. Louis, as well as individuals such as Francis P. Garvan of New York, who made significant donations of his collections to the new American Wing of the Metropolitan Museum of Art. Perhaps the best-known loss was the dismantling of the Mansion House (71 Broad Street) in 1928.
4. Albert Simons to Mrs. William Emerson, 28 April 1928; Schuyler L. Parsons to [William Adams Delano], 18 October 1930. Unless otherwise indicated, correspondence cited in this chapter is located at the South Carolina Historical Society (SCHS) in the Albert Simons Papers.
5. Albert Simons to Leicester B. Holland, 9 November 1931.
6. Jonathan H. Poston, *The Buildings of Charleston: A Guide to the City's Architecture* (Columbia: University of South Carolina Press, 1997), 26, 612–3.
7. When the group reorganized itself in 1956, it changed the name to the Preservation Society of Charleston, to suggest the breadth of the institutional agenda as it actually developed after 1920.
8. For a biography of Frost as well as an informative history of the early preservation movement in Charleston, see Sidney R. Bland, *Preserving Charleston's Past, Shaping Its Future: The Life and Times of Susan Pringle Frost,* 2nd ed. (Columbia: University of South Carolina Press, 1999). For a recent general history of the Preservation Society, see the narrative by Robert P. Stockton and the chronology compiled by Trina South and Ward Reynolds in *Preservation Progress* 38 (Spring 1995), 4–11; 38 (summer 1995): 11–24; 38 (Winter 1996), 3–20. See also Michael Kevin Fenton, " 'Why Not Leave Our Canvas Unmarred?': A History of the Preservation Society of Charleston, 1920–1990" (M.A. thesis, University of South Carolina, 1990); and William Henry Hanckel, "The Preservation Movement in Charleston, 1920–1962" (M.A. thesis, University of South Carolina, 1962).
9. Harriett Pollitzer, the Princess Pignatelli, was the anonymous benefactor.
10. Bland, *Preserving Charleston's Past,* 64–83; Poston, *Buildings of Charleston,* 612–3; Charles B. Hosmer Jr., *Preservation Comes of Age: From Williamsburg to the National Trust, 1926–1946,* 2 vols. (Charlottesville: University of Virginia Press, 1981), I:236–8, 242–50.
11. For a recent assessment, see Louise Anderson Allen, *A Bluestocking in Charleston: The Life and Career of Laura Bragg* (Columbia: University of South Carolina Press, 2001).
12. Albert Simons to Mills B. Lane, 11 May 1928.
13. Albert Simons to Mr. Rivers, 8 May 1928.
14. Simons to Emerson, 28 April 1928.
15. In a similar vein, Susan Pringle Frost undertook her own private campaign to salvage architectural remnants, filling storerooms at the Miles Brewton House with her acquisitions. Curiously, histories of the Charleston Museum do not seem to recognize the important preservation role that the museum has played as an architectural repository. See, for example, Caroline M. Borowsky, "The Charleston Museum, 1773–1963," *Museum News,* February 1963, 11–21.

16. Bland, *Preserving Charleston's Past*, 73–4; Poston, *Buildings of Charleston*, 77–9; Hosmer, *Preservation Comes of Age*, I:242–50; *Charleston News and Courier*, 18 May 1929; Albert Simons to Mrs. Victor Morawetz, 2 February 1931; Thomas R. Waring to Mrs. William Emerson, 9 October 1931.

17. The members of the blue-ribbon committee included Franklin O. Adams, Leicester B. Holland, Fiske Kimball, Alfred L. Kocher, Robert D. Kohn, Everett V. Meeks, and Horace Peaslee representing the AIA; and Mrs. Cesare Andreini, Alston Deas, Julian Mitchell, Harrison Randolph, Albert Simons, and Thomas R. Waring from Charleston.

18. Mrs. William Emerson to Albert Simons, 23 April 1928, 3 May 1928; [Robert D. Kohn] to Franklin O. Adams, et al., 9 December 1930; Albert Simons to Mrs. William Emerson, 2 February 1931, 28 September 1931; Albert Simons to Alfred Huger, 7 March 1931; Albert Simons to Thomas R. Waring, 2 April 1931; Albert Simons to George W. Bacon, 15 April 1931; *Charleston News and Courier*, 10 April 1932; Hosmer, *Preservation Comes of Age*, I: 245–50.

19. Some commentators trace the origins of historic preservation in Charleston to the nineteenth century, pointing to decisions to restore damaged buildings to their earlier appearance rather than rebuild in the current architectural idiom. Robert P. Stockton makes this case in "Charleston's Preservation Ethic," *Preservation Progress*, special edition (spring 1993), 11–2, and in "The Preservation of Charleston: The Origin of a Tradition," *Preservation Progress* 38 (Spring 1995), 4–7.

20. Bland, *Preserving Charleston's Past*, 46–63; Poston, *Buildings of Charleston*, 51, 52, 54, 76, 79–80, 99, 100–2, 104–5, 138, 193–4. See also Robert P. Stockton, "The Evolution of Rainbow Row" (M.A. thesis, University of South Carolina, 1979).

21. Frederick Law Olmsted Jr., "Central Considerations" (unpaginated typescript report to the Carolina Art Association, located in the Olmsted Associates Records, Job File 2326 (microfilm edition) at the Library of Congress, Washington, D.C., and in the Albert Simons Papers at the South Carolina Historical Society). Olmsted visited Charleston in January 1940 to consult for the Carolina Art Association, and his recommendations were formative in the establishment of Historic Charleston Foundation in 1947.

22. Because the historic appearance of the theater is not known, the "reconstruction" is entirely hypothetical.

23. Poston, *Buildings of Charleston*, 179–80, 345, 351–2, 392–3, 439–40; Bland, *Preserving Charleston's Past*, 71; Hosmer, *Preservation Comes of Age*, I.250–4.

24. City Council of Charleston, *Proceedings*, Regular Meeting of 13 October 1931, 697–711. See also Stephen Neal Dennis, " 'The Genius of the Place': Charleston Discovers How to Protect 'The Circumstances and the Locality,' " *Preservation Progress*, special edition (Spring 1993), 21.

25. Thomas P. Stoney to John I. Cosgrove, 27 May 1925, and John I. Cosgrove to Thomas P. Stoney, 29 May 1925, file 30–25–5, SCHS; A. J. Tamsberg to Albert Simons, 22 April 1957. In *Euclid v. Ambler* (1926), the U.S. Supreme Court affirmed the validity of zoning as a proper use of the municipal police power.

26. Alston Deas continued to play an important role as a member of the first Board of Architectural Review and as author of *The Early Ironwork of Charleston* (Columbia, SC: Bostick & Thornley, 1941), a study of the city's decorative wrought iron.

27. Tamsberg to Simons, 22 April 1957; Hosmer, *Preservation Comes of Age*, I: 238–40. The first members of the permanent City Planning and Zoning Commission established in October 1930 were M. B. Barkley, Louis Y. Dawson Jr., Alston Deas, J. Ross Hanahan, Burnet R. Maybank, Cotesworth P. Means, James O'Hear, Albert Simons, and Walter B. Wilbur.

28. Albert Simons to Mrs. Victor Morawetz, 2 February 1931.

29. Morris Knowles, Inc., *Report of the City Planning and Zoning Commission upon a Program for the Development of a City Plan with Specific Studies of Certain Features*

Thereof (2 July 1931), 34, located in the Olmsted Associates Records, Job File 2326 (microfilm edition), Library of Congress.

30. Morris Knowles, *Report of the City Planning and Zoning Commission,* 17.

31. Debbi Rhoad, "The Board of Architectural Review in Charleston, 1931–1993," *Preservation Progress,* special edition (Spring 1993), 13–8; Civic Services Committee, *This Is Charleston* (Charleston: Carolina Art Association, 1944), 134–6. The first members of the BAR, who assumed their duties in November 1931, were Alston Deas, Albert Simons, E. D. Clement, Stephen F. Shackelford, and Thomas R. Waring, who served as chairman.

32. Quoted in Dennis, " 'The Genius of the Place,' " *Preservation Progress,* special edition (spring 1993), 21.

33. Albert Simons, quoted by Hosmer, *Preservation Comes of Age,* I:241.

34. Albert Simons to Delos H. Smith, 10 December 1946; Albert Simons to Leicester B. Holland, 18 March 1932.

35. Rhoad, "The Board of Architectural Review in Charleston, 1931–1993," *Preservation Progress,* special edition (spring 1993), 13–8; Hosmer, *Preservation Comes of Age,* I:238–42. Only a portion of Broad Street itself was included in the original district.

36. In response, the Standard Oil Company sought to make amends by employing Albert Simons to design a "colonial revival" filling station on the site, using brick, columns, and balusters salvaged from the Gabriel Manigault House, which was then being demolished at 279 Meeting Street. The gas station closed in 1981, and Historic Charleston Foundation acquired it, converting it into the Frances R. Edmunds Center for Historic Preservation, which was dedicated in 1986. This unusual monument to the early preservation movement in Charleston is located at 108 Meeting Street. See Poston, *Buildings of Charleston,* 188.

37. Jacob H. Morrison, *Historic Preservation Law* (New Orleans: Pelican Publishing Company, 1957), 80–5, rev. ed. (1965), 129–86; Hosmer, *Preservation Comes of Age,* I:231–77; Civic Services Committee, *This Is Charleston,* rev. ed. (Charleston: Carolina Art Association, 1976), 134–6; Dennis, " 'The Genius of the Place,' " *Preservation Progress,* special edition (spring 1993), 22.

38. On early Charleston architecture, see Poston, *Buildings of Charleston;* James R. Cothran, *Gardens of Historic Charleston* (Columbia: University of South Carolina Press, 1995); Kenneth Severens, *Charleston Antebellum Architecture and Civic Destiny* (Knoxville: University of Tennessee Press, 1988); Beatrice St. Julien Ravenel, *Architects of Charleston* (Charleston: Carolina Art Association, 1945); as well as earlier "classics," including Alice Ravenel Huger Smith, *Twenty Drawings of the Pringle House, on King Street, Charleston, S. C.* ([Charleston]: n.p., c. 1914); Alice Ravenel Huger Smith and Daniel Elliott Huger Smith, *The Dwelling Houses of Charleston, South Carolina* (Philadelphia: J. B. Lippincott Company, 1917); Albert Simons and Samuel Lapham Jr., eds., *Charleston, South Carolina* (New York: American Institute of Architects, 1927); and Samuel Gaillard Stoney, *Plantations of the Carolina Low Country* (Charleston: Carolina Art Association, 1938).

39. Robert P. Stockton has questioned the "preservation through poverty" thesis by pointing to evidence of commercial, residential, and industrial expansion in the decades after the Civil War; see his paper "Charleston: The Preservation of a City" in C. Edward Kaylor Jr., ed., *A Consideration of Growth in the Trident Area: From the Academy to the Marketplace* (Charleston: South Carolina Committee for the Humanities, 1982), 13–31.

40. Beatrice St. Julien Ravenel, "The Restoration of the Manigault House," *Journal of the American Society of Architectural Historians* 2 (October 1942), 30–2.

41. Don H. Doyle argues that the early preservation movement in Charleston reflected the backward-looking conservatism of the city's upper class and its fascination with

genealogy, custom, and family heirlooms; see Doyle, *New Men, New Cities, New South: Atlanta, Nashville, Charleston, Mobile, 1860–1910* (Chapel Hill: University of North Carolina Press, 1990), 159–88, 226–45.

42. DuBose Heyward, *Porgy* (New York: George H. Doran Company, 1925), 11.

43. The Charleston Renaissance is receiving growing study, particularly through the work of Martha R. Severens. See, for example, her *The Charleston Renaissance* (Spartanburg, SC: Saraland Press, 1998); *Alice Ravenel Huger Smith: An Artist, a Place, and a Time* (Charleston: Carolina Art Association, 1993); and "Pride of Place and Artistic Renewal," *Preservation Progress*, special edition (spring 1993), 4–7. See also Michael C. Scardaville, "Elizabeth O'Neill Verner: The Artist as Preservationist," in Lynn Robertson Myers, ed., *Mirror of Time: Elizabeth O'Neill Verner's Charleston* (Columbia: McKissick Museum of the University of South Carolina, 1983), 17–25, and Scardaville's "The Selling of Historic Charleston," *Preservation Progress* 30 (March 1986), 1, 6–11; Boyd Saunders and Ann McAden, *Alfred Hutty and the Charleston Renaissance* (Orangeburg, SC: Sandlapper Publishing Company, 1990); Pamme Lynn Eades, "Alice Ravenel Huger Smith and the Development of Charleston Regionalism" (M.A. thesis, University of South Carolina, 1994); Marjorie Elizabeth Peale, "Charleston as a Literary Center, 1920–1933" (M.A. thesis, Duke University, 1941). For a recent, general study of regionalism, see Robert L. Dorman, *Revolt of the Provinces: The Regionalist Movement in America, 1920–1945* (Chapel Hill: University of North Carolina Press, 1993). For a useful case study, see Robin Elisabeth Datel, "Southern Regionalism and Historic Preservation in Charleston, South Carolina, 1920–1940," *Journal of Historical Geography* 16 (April 1990), 197–215.

44. Albert Simons (1890–1980) was arguably the most important figure in the early preservation movement whose role continued into the postwar years. He was a preservation architect, urban planner, and civic leader; a founding trustee of Historic Charleston Foundation, serving until 1962; and a member of the Board of Architectural Review from its establishment until his resignation in 1975. To date, though, he has not been the subject of a book-length biography despite the richness of the Albert Simons collection at the South Carolina Historical Society. The College of Charleston also has a small collection on Simons. For a sampling of information on Simons, see "Architects in Profile: Albert Simons," *Preservation Progress* 8 (March 1963), 4–5; *Charleston News and Courier*, 16 June 1975; Kenneth Severens, "Toward Preservation Before 1931: The Early Career of Albert Simons," *Preservation Progress*, special edition (Spring 1993), 8–10.

10

MAKING HISTORY

Historic Preservation
and Civic Identity in Denver

Judy Mattivi Morley

Dean was the son of a wino, one of the most tottering bums of Larimer Street, and
Dean had in fact been brought up generally on Larimer Street and thereabouts. . . .
He used to beg in front of Larimer alleys and sneak the money back to his father,
who waited among the broken bottles with an old buddy.

Jack Kerouac, *On the Road*[1]

Standing in Denver's Larimer Square today, a visitor would hardly recognize the world of Dean Moriarty, described by Jack Kerouac in *On*
the Road. Larimer Street, once one of Denver's seediest districts, now
boasts fancy boutiques, upscale restaurants, and plazas with park
benches and lighted trees. The bums and winos disappeared in the
1970s when historic preservation transformed Larimer Street into
"Larimer Square." Twenty years after Larimer Square's transition, historic preservation turned the rest of Denver's skid row, called lower
downtown, into one of the city's most desirable neighborhoods and
home to Denver's largest entertainment district. The story of the
preservation of these two districts exemplifies trends in city planning
and historic preservation typical of post–World War II western cities.

After World War II, the West was the most urban region in the nation, containing more than half of the United States' fastest-growing
cities between 1950 and 1980.[2] The war transformed the West from a
region dependent on eastern capital to the center of an urban-based,
global economy. As western cities grew, they became more architecturally and culturally similar to the East.[3] Western tourism also increased after World War II, and postwar travelers expected to find
the "Wild West" of popular culture.[4] In this era of overwhelming

expansion and increasing tourism, western cities faced the problem of defining a regional identity. Although regional character is usually taken for granted, the combination of growth, economic and architectural standardization, and tourism potential led western citizens, business leaders, and city planners to attempt to define unique civic identities.[5]

One tool these groups used to create civic identities in the postwar period was historic preservation. Historic preservation changed the look of cities nationwide during the 1960s and 1970s, creating new urban landscapes out of old buildings. Although historic districts were a national phenomenon, their appearance in western cities was out of character with western city planning history. While preservation had a tradition in the East, the West's boom-and-bust economy promoted development, not preservation. After World War II, however, western city planners used local historic designation to protect the city's heritage and create an asset marketable to tourists.[6]

Historic preservation as a city planning strategy began as a reaction to urban renewal. In the traditional parlance of city planning, *urban renewal* connoted comprehensive strategies that rebuilt central business districts into functionalist, modern systems.[7] Urban renewal emphasized efficiency and modernity, and sought to promote investment and economic revitalization in decaying inner cities. Urban renewal generally created an impersonal, homogenized landscape of office buildings, skyscrapers, and parking lots. Conversely, *historic preservation* connoted a civic service, usually sponsored by upper-class women wanting to save a piece of history, generally of national significance.[8] In Denver, the traditional notions of these two concepts merged, thanks to a woman named Dana Crawford, who showed that historic preservation could be profitable. By developing old buildings, Crawford used historic preservation to revitalize Denver's central business district and, in the process, defined a unique civic identity for Denver.

The first settlement in Denver came in 1858 after prospectors found gold in the South Platte River. General William Larimer, a town promoter from Leavenworth, Kansas, started the city, naming the settlement for the governor of the Kansas Territory, James W. Denver, and the main street for himself.[9] Denver became the supply center for the entire Pikes Peak mining region, and the frontier town boomed.[10] The depression of 1893, the First World War, the Dust Bowl, and the Great Depression took their toll, however. By 1940, Denver fell from its position as third largest city west of the Missouri River to fifth largest, following Los Angeles, San Francisco, Houston, and Seattle.[11]

As in most of the West, World War II changed Denver's fortunes. During the 1940s and 1950s, the growing defense industry boosted the economy, bringing federal money and high-technology workers to Denver. The metro area's population surpassed the one million mark in 1961, nine years earlier than growth analysts predicted.[12] The population growth did not come to the central business district, however. Small farming and mining communities surrounding Denver, such as Littleton and Golden, suddenly became suburbs of the metropolis. The new suburbs featured housing subdivisions constructed by national builders who shunned the traditional "Denver Square" bungalow for standardized styles.[13] Additionally, highways transformed traditional shopping patterns. Between 1960 and 1970, Denver's retail activity moved out of downtown to suburban shopping areas such as Cinderella City and Cherry Creek. The historical downtown, now known as lower downtown,[14] became a notorious skid row, filled with crumbling buildings, abandoned warehouses, seedy bars, flophouses, and bums.[15]

Denver's economy also changed after World War II. Traditionally "western" industries, such as mining, logging, and cattle ranching, lost their prominence to computer industries and defense installations.[16] Economic power moved out of the hands of the conservative native elite, and into the hands of out-of-state developers.[17] Investors such as New Yorker William Zeckendorf and Dallas oil millionaires Clinton and John Murchison used their wealth to buy downtown real estate and build high-rises that dwarfed Denver's familiar landmarks.[18] The economic changes convinced Denver's mayor, Quigg Newton, to focus on economic development, especially tourism. Between 1948 and 1968, tourism surpassed mining as the state's third largest industry, following value-added manufacturing and agriculture. Revenue from tourism increased 418 percent during those twenty years, and visitors to the state increased 303 percent.[19]

As a reaction to growth, standardization, and tourism potential, Denver's city council, planners, and business elite searched for ways to restore Denver to a place of prominence in the western economy and landscape and compete with Los Angeles, Dallas, Houston, Seattle, and Phoenix.[20] Their solution to Denver's declining fortunes was urban renewal. Denver planners outlined urban renewal strategies that called for leveling entire city blocks, increasing warehouse and manufacturing space in lower downtown, and building highway access through the city's oldest areas.[21] The Denver Urban Renewal Authority (DURA) focused on a 117-acre project, named Skyline, to eliminate "skid row, a major blighting influence in the area."[22] Skyline necessitated the clearing of thirty blocks of historic buildings downtown. The plan's borders missed most of lower downtown, although Larimer Street fell within the boundaries.[23] The planning board adopted Skyline in 1963, but voters did not approve funding until 1967.[24]

At this point, Dana Crawford offered a different solution for renewing downtown Denver. Crawford had a bachelor's degree from the University of Kansas, and she graduated from a business management program at Radcliff. In 1954, Crawford moved to Denver with hordes of postwar immigrants from the East and Midwest. After working for a public relations firm, Crawford married John W. R. Crawford III and had four boys. Although she was a newcomer, Crawford quickly became a member of Denver's social elite, joining the Junior League and serving as a volunteer at the Denver Art Museum.[25]

Crawford was more than the upper-class housewife persona she portrayed, however. She was a shrewd businesswoman looking for an investment. In 1963, Crawford read about Gaslight Square in St. Louis and began scouting for a location to create a similar district in Denver. According to Crawford, she wanted to create a place "where people of all backgrounds could celebrate their history and community."[26] She frequently visited Larimer Street to shop for antiques, and it occurred to her that the buildings themselves were antiques worthy of preservation.[27] After looking at a few other locations, Crawford decided that the 1400 block of Larimer Street could create the atmosphere she wanted.[28] That block fell under the jurisdiction of DURA, however, as the northwestern edge of the Skyline project. When Crawford approached the directors of DURA with her ideas, they were skeptical, but did not immediately impede the plan. Because Skyline was still in the initial approval phases, Crawford was able to begin buying and restoring buildings on Larimer Street with DURA's benign neglect. Although her initial inclination was to structure the project as a non-profit corporation, her business background convinced her that the buildings in Larimer Square would be more likely to be preserved if the project was profitable.[29]

To begin acquiring the buildings on the 1400 block of Larimer Street, Crawford organized the corporation Larimer Square Associates (LSA) in August 1964 with herself as president. The mission of the corporation was to acquire "the property on Larimer Street between 14th and 15th Streets; subsequently, to develop this property in an 'Historic Denver' motif, and to create an 'after 5' recreation center for Denver residents and visitors."[30] Many of the initial investors in LSA were property owners on Larimer Street who traded equity in their buildings for shares of stock. Future congresswoman Patricia Schroeder and her husband, James, also invested in LSA.[31] By the beginning of 1965, the corporation had acquired control over fifteen of the eighteen buildings on the 1400 block of Larimer, valued between sixteen thousand and fifty thousand dollars each. Most of the valuation was for the land—the appraisers found the structures to be virtually worthless, although they were structurally sound.[32]

Initially, Crawford publicly linked the profit motive and the civic service she performed in Larimer Square. In an interview in May 1965, a reporter for the *Denver Post* asked Crawford if her motivation in Larimer Square was preservation or profit. In her response, Crawford tied the two concepts together. She replied, "This is definitely a for-profit corporation. . . . The people who are involved wanted a sound investment, of course. But our first motive is preservation. After all, this belongs to the people of Denver."[33] In an interview with the *Christian Science Monitor,* Crawford again linked the financial and cultural benefits of preservation on Larimer Street, saying, "We think Larimer Square will be here 100 years from now and paying both cultural and financial dividends to the city and to investors."[34]

Because Larimer Square was within Skyline's boundaries, Crawford realized she would need support from the mayor and city council to implement her development plans. To get their support, Crawford emphasized the benefits that preserving Larimer Square provided for the city. In 1965, Crawford told the *Denver Post,* "Founders of Larimer Square are motivated to do something for the people of Denver to help them retain some of the frontier city's heritage."[35] Also in 1965, Crawford took the audacious step of calling a mayoral press conference to unveil Larimer Square before inviting the mayor. Despite the unorthodox tactics, Mayor Tom Currigan endorsed Larimer Square, and agreed that preserving Larimer Square would benefit the city.

> Before the turn of the century, Denver was a gay and boisterous city, and its spirit was typified by Larimer Street. Recapturing that spirit of youthful Denver in this fashion and at the same time preserving some of our historic buildings is a marvelous concept. In addition, this plan, when it comes to fruition, will help stabilize the lower downtown area, improve the tax base, and become a source of pride for all Coloradoans.[36]

The benefit of preserving Larimer Square came from the block's connection to Denver's heritage. In the last twenty years, cultural historians such as David Lowenthal and Michael Kammen have argued for a distinction between *history* and *heritage. Heritage* differs from *history* in that it celebrates only those aspects of history agreed upon and valued by a group, leaving out any problematic information. Thus heritage is nostalgic, re-creating the past as a time of innocence and consensus. Heritage is mythic, using symbols rather than facts to convey historical meaning.[37] Historian David Lowenthal compares heritage to religious faith: People have no real proof that the events occurred, but accept them based on a feeling that they must be true.[38] Heritage also forms shared memories, and in this capacity facilitates identity formation.[39]

In order to emphasize Larimer Square's role in Denver's heritage, Crawford used propaganda to invent a tradition for it.[40] She launched a media campaign extolling Larimer Street's importance to Denver's frontier heritage. Crawford wrote most of the press releases for Larimer Square herself, and what she did not write she edited before release.[41] According to these materials, Larimer Street was the most famous street in the West, a claim that is questionable at best. In a history of Larimer Street that went into the first marketing packets published for Larimer Square Associates, the author, most likely Crawford, wrote:

> Denver has one of the most colorful, raucous, fascinating histories in America. Its rugged early days of gold and silver, boom or bust, rags to riches, will always capture the imagination of man. The antics of its now legendary city founders, the furtrappers [sic], gold seekers, and adventurers, have inspired much of America's greatest folklore. Larimer Street in Denver was the most famous street in the West. The restaurants and hotels of its heyday were world-renowned. Stories of what happened when the greats and near-greats of the West strode up and down the streets filled volumes. And tales of what went on behind closed doors in the neighborhood shocked a nation.[42]

The language from this initial promotional packet was repeated for years in flyers, economic feasibility reports, tourist maps, and marketing proposals. For example, an undated marketing packet described Larimer Square:

> Larimer Square is a city block of 17 buildings on facing sides of Larimer Street—the most famous street in the west. Here are the sites and buildings where early Western outposts began and events stretching through the gold boom of the '50's and '60's, the silver boom of the '70's and '80's and the subsequent panic of the '90's wove the very fabric which makes Denver the city it is today.[43]

Similarly, a 1969 economic feasibility report compiled for Larimer Square Associates began:

> In the last half of the 19th century Larimer Street in Denver was the most famous street in the West. The restaurants and hotels of its glamorous

past were world-renowned. Stories of what happened when the great and near-greats [*sic*] of the West strode down the streets filled volumes, and tales of what went on behind closed doors in the neighborhood shocked a nation.[44]

Finally, a tourist brochure for Larimer Square from between 1966 and 1968 read:

> Denver has one of the most colorful, raucous, fascinating histories in America. Everyone who lives or visits here knows of the city's rugged early days of boom or bust, rags to riches in the eager search for gold and silver. At the heart of Denver's history, on the most famous street in the frontier west, stands Larimer Square. . . . It's a fashionable place to browse and sip and dine in an atmosphere that faithfully [!] reflects the elegance and gayety of Denver's heyday. . . . The street is paved with stories of the nineteenth century.[45]

The Denver media soon picked up the rhetoric used by Crawford and Larimer Square Associates, reinforcing the images of Denver's heritage. After Crawford unveiled the concept of Larimer Square in 1965, both the *Denver Post* and the *Rocky Mountain News* praised her attempts to revitalize Denver's glory days. The *Rocky Mountain News* exclaimed that the "joyous spirit that characterized busy, brawling Larimer Street in frontier Denver a century ago is about to be revived."[46] The *News* went on to quote Crawford, who showed off her gift for hyperbole, claiming that Larimer Square Associates would recreate "the excitement that made Larimer Street the talk of the nation in yesteryear."[47]

The one heritage that no one in Denver was interested in preserving for Larimer Street was its heritage as skid row. Unlike the original Skid Road in Seattle, a historic district that reveled in its seediness, with Crawford's hard work, a completely "rehabilitated" Larimer Street was disassociated from its derelict phase. In an investors' package from 1965, the proposal addressed Larimer Street's blighted reputation, but downplayed the presence of any bums or slums. Although the proposal acknowledged that Larimer Street had deteriorated, LSA admitted only to having "marginal businesses" such as plumbing contractors' shops, a used commercial-equipment dealer, and a saddle-and-harness store. LSA also stressed that the 1400 block of Larimer was situated "two long blocks" from the skid row district, and presented no problems of "human rehabilitation or policing."[48] This statement was misleading, because in 1965 the 1400 block of Larimer Street had two bars, a mission, three low-rent hotels that also provided housing, and seven

Fig. 10.1 Larimer Street looking north from 14th street, circa 1895, Denver, Colorado. (Courtesy of Colorado Historical Society, from a photo by W.H. Jackson.)

vacant, boarded buildings along with the saddle-and-harness store and the commercial-equipment dealer.[49] Clearly, LSA wanted nothing to do with the mystique of a skid row identity.

Because the propaganda used by LSA and the media created an identity for Denver based on a glorified "Wild West" heritage, the restoration of the buildings had to reinforce that identity. The buildings became symbols of the tradition Crawford had created. In her initial media announcement of Larimer Square, Crawford celebrated the buildings and the "real west" architecture they represented.[50] When describing the architecture in investors' packages, LSA acknowledged that the buildings were vital to the creation of an "Early Denver" motif.[51] Thus, the renovations of the buildings created a faked authenticity characteristic of invented traditions.[52] Although the founders of the historic district claimed that the buildings represented a previous era, Larimer Square in the 1970s looked considerably different from the block of the nineteenth century. From the late nineteenth century until the advent of Larimer Square, buildings on Larimer Street looked like part of any big city. They sat right next to the street. Fire escapes prominently adorned the fronts of buildings, and signs were painted on the side of the building or placed on the roof.[53] By the time Larimer Square was created ninety years later, however, the buildings no longer

Fig. 10.2 The 1400 block of Larimer Street, circa 1960, as "skid row." (Photo courtesy of Denver Public Library.)

sat near the street. The first floor was recessed, creating sunken entrances and arched, covered sidewalks that gave the block an atmosphere reminiscent of Old West wooden sidewalks. The fire escapes disappeared, and some upper floors of buildings sported flower boxes. The historic district ordinance required business signs to be small, hanging directly over entrances as they do on small-town main streets.[54]

Larimer's streetscape also changed with the creation of the historic district. In the 1880s, the block was unmistakably urban. Utility wires ran overhead, and large utility poles dotted the sidewalk. Streetcar tracks ran down the middle of the street, and carriages and cars parked along the curb. After 1920, parking meters lined the street. The sidewalks were narrow, crowded, and bustling. Tall, overhead lights brightly lit the block. Horse manure, coal dust, and the fluid results of chewing tobacco filled the streets and sidewalks. No vegetation grew at all along Larimer Street.[55] The Larimer Square Historic District, however, removed the trappings of big-city life. Antique-looking gas-style lamps replaced the overhead streetlights. The city removed the parking meters, and banners similar to those welcoming visitors to small towns hung across the block, announcing upcoming events. Large clocks reminiscent of courthouse lawns resided at either end of Larimer

Fig. 10.3 Vibrant Larimer Square today. (Photo courtesy of the author.)

Square. Antique-looking wrought-iron signs marked where visitors entered and exited the historic district. Larimer Street lost one full lane of traffic as the city widened sidewalks to make room for benches and trees along the block, giving Larimer Square both the look and the feel of a town square rather than a bustling city street.

As Larimer Square took shape, Crawford and LSA found themselves in repeated conflict with the Denver Urban Renewal Authority. Although DURA director Robert Cameron claimed that the urban renewal authority was receptive to historic preservation, DURA's directors scrutinized everything Larimer Square Associates did, and frequently impeded renovations.[56] In order to continue building Larimer Square unbothered, Crawford and LSA approached the Denver Landmark and Preservation Commission (DLPC) for historic district designation in 1971. Crawford was not initially an advocate of historic designation. She was wary of the design review process in the historic district, which made her fear that she could not rebuild the structures as she chose. She allied with the DLPC primarily for protection against DURA, but waited until most of the major renovations were done before approaching the Landmark Commission so that it could not stop her plans. Ultimately, however, she realized that historic designation would make Larimer Square more appealing to tourists, and thus more profitable.[57] The DLPC unanimously voted to designate Larimer Square Denver's first historic district on June 21, 1971.[58] Larimer Square became a National Register–designated historic district two years later, on May 7, 1973.[59]

To ensure the economic success of the venture, Crawford ran Larimer Square like a shopping mall. She volunteered to run Denver's Belcaro Shopping Center to gain experience in mall management.[60] Crawford patterned LSA leases after mall leases, and retained control over hours of business and aesthetics such as displays, restaurant menus, and ads. Crawford justified these stipulations as a way to keep the historical integrity of the block, but she also desired a degree of commonality that would ensure profits.[61] Crawford's business practices angered some tenants, however. According to one merchant, "She [Crawford] is a very good businesswoman, and you have to be a callous witch to be a very good businesswoman."[62] Small businesses that could not profit under LSA's stringent guidelines left Larimer Square and moved into lower downtown, starting a small retail community there.

Crawford understood that Larimer Square's profits had to come from both tourists and residents. To appeal to tourists, Crawford advertised Larimer Square as one of the major attractions of the city. In market analyses and investors' packages, Crawford compiled figures on tourism and recreation in Denver, and estimated that half of Larimer Square's traffic came from tourists. According to Crawford, two and a half million visitors went to Larimer Square in 1968.[63] To attract residents of the metro area, Crawford analyzed traffic patterns and planned for parking spaces around Larimer Square. In order to provide adequate parking, LSA purchased six lots on the 1400 block of Market Street, directly behind Larimer Square, and, ironically, tore down historic buildings to put up a parking garage.[64]

Crawford was careful to pick the type of tenants that could prosper on Larimer Square. Initially, she courted high-end, "quality" retailers that would enhance the project's "cultural, historical atmosphere," such as art galleries, bookstores, flower shops, boutiques, tea and spice outlets, jewelry and watch shops, candy stores, and restaurants.[65] The first businesses to open on Larimer Square were the Gay Nineties–themed restaurant Your Father's Mustache, Gusterman Silversmiths, Blue Bottle Stained Glass, Poor Richard's Leather Goods, Le Chocolat Candy, and The Criterion Christmas Store.[66] Single-point businesses struggled on Larimer Square, however. Perhaps it was the strict lease terms, or perhaps it was competition from other downtown developments that opened in the late 1970s and 1980s, but many of the small businesses on Larimer Square folded or moved. By 1980, Crawford actively courted national chains to fill space on Larimer Street. Between 1983 and 1986, Williams-Sonoma, Ann Taylor, Talbots, and Laura Ashley opened shops on Larimer Square, adding to the shopping mall atmosphere.[67]

Despite the struggle of small businesses, Larimer Square was a hugely profitable real-estate venture. In 1973, New York Life Insurance granted Larimer Square Associates a twenty-year long-term conventional loan for improvements and renovations, making Larimer Square the first historic district approved for such a conservative financing agreement in the business community.[68] Twenty years after Larimer Square Associates incorporated, property values had risen exponentially. The fifteen properties that Crawford and LSA purchased in 1965 individually for between sixteen thousand and fifty thousand dollars, plus two other buildings purchased later, were collectively worth fifteen million dollars by 1985. In 1965, buildings on Larimer Street leased for eleven cents per square foot. In 1985, that figure jumped to twenty dollars per square foot.[69]

Realizing that she had taken Larimer Square as far as she could, Crawford and Larimer Square Associates sold the property in 1986. The Hahn Company, a real estate developer from San Diego, bought it for $14.5 million.[70] After the sale, Crawford got involved with real-estate development in lower downtown and the Central Platte Valley. In 1983, the *Denver Post*'s *Empire Magazine* speculated that Crawford was the most powerful woman in Denver, and her control over property on Larimer Street and lower downtown made her one of the city's most influential developers. Crawford's reputation as a historic preservationist did not fare so well, however. Initially, she was nationally recognized as an authority on historic preservation, becoming involved with the National Trust for Historic Preservation in 1968, and helping to found Historic Denver, Inc., in 1970.[71] Although Colorado Preservation, Inc., still sponsors the annual "Dana Crawford Awards" for preservation projects, Crawford has been described as "more of a preservation-minded developer than a development-minded preservationist."[72]

Despite the criticism, Crawford's fusion of preservation and development had a tremendous impact on Denver's city planning policy. Whereas Crawford fought against city agencies to establish Larimer Square, her influence changed the policy of those same agencies. By the mid-1980s, Denver's city government, planners, and business leaders accepted historic preservation as a powerful development strategy,

Fig. 10.4 Warehouses on Wynkoop Street in lower downtown. (Photo courtesy of Denver Public Library.)

so much so that planners and preservationists believed that establishing a Lower Downtown Historic District, adjacent to Larimer Square, would revitalize the central business district. These groups followed Crawford's example, using rhetoric connecting lower downtown with Denver's heritage to overcome objections from property owners and establish a historic district.

Whereas Larimer Street had been the center for Denver's retail commerce, lower downtown, sitting near the railroad tracks, was the warehouse, shipping, and manufacturing district. Like the rest of the central business district, lower downtown's fortunes fell at the turn of the twentieth century. Because lower downtown depended on rail traffic, construction of the interstate highway system after World War II led to a further decline, causing many of the old warehouses to be abandoned. The city built viaducts through lower downtown to facilitate truck traffic to and from the warehouses. These viaducts created a dark no-man's-land, and the streets under the raised roadways became havens for bums and transients. Homeless people took up residences in the empty warehouses, frequently vandalizing the buildings and causing fires.[73]

Lower downtown escaped demolition in the 1960s because the Skyline Urban Renewal Project's boundaries missed it. By the time city planners started to consider revitalizing lower downtown, Larimer Square's success caused them to look at rehabilitation options besides urban renewal.[74] In fact, the city planning office changed lower downtown's zoning in 1974 to "provide for and encourage the preservation and vitality of older areas that are significant because of their architectural, historical, and economic value."[75] The district had been zoned for industrial and manufacturing businesses, which prohibited any other uses, but Larimer Square's popularity and pressure from a few property owners led the city to change the area's zoning to B-7, mixed use, allowing for commercial, retail, and residential development.[76]

The 1974 rezoning prompted private investment in lower downtown. A few pioneer developers, impressed with the increase in property values in Larimer Square, saw opportunities for adaptive reuse of the old commercial structures. As the Skyline Urban Renewal Project tore down historic buildings along Lawrence and Larimer Streets to revitalize downtown commerce, more sensitive developers used neighboring historic buildings to achieve the same purpose. According to an article in the *Denver Post's Empire Magazine,* "The alley that divides central downtown from lower downtown Denver is a Royal Gorge. On one side rise the towers of the Skyline Urban Renewal Project. . . . Northwest of that alley, construction is just as vigorous. But instead of tall towers being raised, two- and three-story antiques are being restored."[77]

Like Dana Crawford in Larimer Square, the people driving the earliest restoration projects in lower downtown did not come from Denver. Locals were too prejudiced against lower downtown to see any value in the neighborhood, but transplants recognized the potential in the run-down old warehouses.[78] One of the earliest developers, William Saslow, came to Denver in 1971 after living in Boston and Philadelphia. In 1974, after lower downtown's rezoning, Saslow renovated Market Street Mall at 18th and Market Streets, gutting the building to provide twenty-eight thousand square feet of office space. Saslow also developed the Blake Street Bath and Racquet Club in the 1700 block of Blake Street, which contained second-floor condominiums and ground-floor office and retail space. Saslow's partner, Allan Reiver, a transplant from Houston who arrived in Denver in 1970, developed Market Center, an office complex at 17th and Market. By 1981, a vice president of First Denver Mortgage Company estimated that private developers were responsible for rehabilitating 865,000 square feet of office space in lower downtown at an estimated cost of more than twenty-nine million dollars.[79]

The early developers of lower downtown also saw potential for the old warehouses to be living space. By the 1970s, loft living was becoming a fashionable housing option. Beginning in the 1950s, artists nationwide began moving into former manufacturing buildings in inner cities to take advantage of the large studio space and cheap rent. Within twenty years, urban living gained popularity with portions of the middle class, as well. Moving into lofts was a proclamation of an unconventional lifestyle, a way to associate with the aesthetics of the urban art community. Communities patterned after Soho, New York, spread through post-industrial cities across the nation, and lofts became a trademark of upper-middle-class urban chic.[80] The developers of lower downtown realized that Denver's old warehouses could create a community complete with housing, retail businesses, and commercial investment.

Although not the pioneer in lower downtown, Dana Crawford joined the effort to revitalize the area in the early 1980s. In 1981, Crawford and developer Charles Callaway bought the Oxford Hotel at 17th and Wazee. The Oxford was one of lower downtown's architectural jewels, designed by Frank Edbrooke, the architect who later built the famous Brown Palace Hotel at the other end of downtown. The Oxford had closed for remodeling in 1979, but the project stalled for lack of funds until Crawford and Callaway got involved and shepherded the $6.7 million restoration through to completion.[81] Crawford also joined a partnership to buy the Ice House, once a warehouse and storage facility for a local dairy. Crawford and partners restored the Ice House into a design center that became the artistic anchor of lower downtown.[82]

Despite private investments and zoning changes, lower downtown witnessed a blitzkrieg of demolitions in the early 1980s. Denver's oil boom of the late 1970s inspired speculators to buy property and tear down the buildings to make way for new office space and parking lots. In 1982, the city council amended lower downtown's zoning ordinance, giving owners of historic buildings a chance to sell their unused development rights to someone wanting to put up a higher-density building on vacant land.[83] The zoning amendment failed to slow down demolitions, however, and 20 to 25 percent of the buildings in the district met the wrecking ball between 1981 and 1988.[84] Historic preservationists and downtown business activists realized that incentives to private developers were not enough motivation to save the old buildings. In 1981, a preservation organization called Historic Denver joined a group of business leaders called Downtown Denver, Inc. (DDI), to campaign for a historic district in lower downtown to protect the area's "critical mass" of historic structures.[85]

DDI and Historic Denver did not make much progress, however, until 1983, when Denver voters elected mayor Federico Peña, who came into office with an ambitious revitalization agenda for the city. His campaign slogan, "Imagine a great city," set the tone for his administration.[86] Peña's priorities included a convention center for Denver, a new airport, and a downtown residential neighborhood. His civic agenda and willingness to make substantial changes inspired journalists and politicians to talk about programs to enhance Denver's *livability*, a term they used to mean uniqueness, accessibility, safeness, and friendliness.[87] One aspect of Denver's livability was creating a historic district in lower downtown. When Peña ordered the creation of a Downtown Area Plan in 1985, the preservation of lower downtown was one of the cornerstones.[88]

The authors of the Downtown Area Plan envisioned lower downtown as an urban neighborhood and artistic anchor. The plan proposed art galleries, public art projects, a design center at the Ice House, architects' offices, and downtown housing, using the old warehouses for lofts. The residential component of lower downtown would give Larimer Square and the central business district a twenty-four-hour community.[89] The Downtown Area Plan also called for demolition control in lower downtown. Preservationists, supported by Mayor Peña, insisted that a demolition moratorium in lower downtown had to be part of planning policy so that no more historic structures could be destroyed.[90]

In 1986, the city council approved the Downtown Area Plan, but a separate ordinance still needed to pass the council to ensure lower downtown's preservation. To solidify support, Historic Denver and the preservation community had to convince Denver citizens that the old skid row district was worth preserving. Since Denverites had a bias against the dilapidated old warehouses, proponents of the historic district needed to make the area appealing to people accustomed to avoiding it. Business leaders with DDI, now called the Downtown Denver Partnership, and preservationists with Historic Denver echoed Dana Crawford's public relations strategy in Larimer Square, arguing that lower downtown's connection to Denver's heritage made the area vital to the city's future.[91]

Supporters of a historic district in lower downtown argued that the district provided Denver with a unique asset. Denver's post–World War II sprawl had standardized the city architecturally and commercially, and thus diluted the city's civic identity.[92] According to Denver City Planning Director Jennifer Moulton, "Denver has no point of difference other than [lower] downtown. Everything else we've done in the last twenty years looked like it could have been done anywhere . . . we have no identity other than lower downtown."[93] Activist Lisa Purdy echoed this sentiment, saying, "Lower downtown is what separates us from the suburbs. It is a unique asset. If it gets wiped out, we've got nothing. We're like anywhere else."[94] Bill Mosher of the Downtown Denver Partnership agreed, claiming that "[d]owntown needs to be unique and different from the suburbs . . . if part of your advantage is being unique and different, that means capitalizing on your historic heritage."[95]

According to preservationists, lower downtown's unique identity gave Denver an economic asset that would spark revitalization of the entire central business district. During city council hearings on lower downtown, Peña's aide Tom Gougeon informed council members that creating a historic district in lower downtown was more important to Denver's economy than either a convention center or a new airport. He told the council, "I've never told you any of those is the single most important issue for the city, but I'm telling you that historic designation for Lower Downtown is."[96] According to Peña, historic designation for lower downtown was "the best opportunity to kick off the revitalization of downtown Denver."[97] The Downtown Area Plan claimed that the district was a "market asset," and advocated the preservation and development of the district because it would "stimulate new economic demand in Lower Downtown."[98] Finally, the urban design plan for lower downtown claimed the district gave Denver a "market niche" to attract visitors.[99]

The past Denver needed to preserve in lower downtown was *not* warehouses and manufacturing plants, however. In order for lower downtown to promote the revitalization of the central business district, city planners, the mayor's office, preservationists, and business interests had to create a new identity that maintained a link to Denver's past without promoting the historical uses of the district. According to Dick Flemming of Downtown Denver, Inc., people should think of downtown Denver "as they do Faneuil Hall in Boston, an urban remake that draws more customers than Disneyland."[100] The "urban remake" Flemming proposed was an invented tradition, outlined by the Downtown Area Plan.[101] Following Larimer Square's example, the authors of the Downtown Area Plan outlined an invented tradition that used lower downtown's warehouses to invoke nostalgia for Denver's frontier heritage while designing other elements of the district to create a livable urban neighborhood and "unified overall image."[102] Like

Larimer Square, lower downtown sought to re-create a small-town atmosphere in the middle of the city. The Downtown Area Plan proposed historical landscaping, street furniture, and light fixtures that reinforced the "urban village" image.[103] The urban design plan suggested keeping the alleyways intact, not to facilitate deliveries or trash removal, but rather to "maintain the rhythm of buildings" and prevent development of entire blocks, thus ensuring "unique pedestrian passages" between structures.[104]

Despite the promises of economic revitalization, the invented tradition in lower downtown met with stiff opposition from the district's property owners. The crux of the opposition was the design review and demolition restrictions, which pioneer William Saslow called "draconian."[105] Most of the property owners felt that the threat of demolition was minimal. Developers such as Saslow and Allan Reiver argued that they were the first to see the potential in the old buildings, so were not likely to tear them down. The property owners felt that the moratorium on demolitions carried preservation too far, and infringed on their property rights.[106] Ironically, one of the most outspoken opponents of the historic district was Dana Crawford. Although Crawford advocated maintaining the historical character of the district, she disagreed with the demolition restriction, and her experience with DURA in Larimer Square made her wary of any design review guidelines. Crawford also was promoting a development on the edge of the district, and feared that design review guidelines would hinder the construction of that project.[107]

The condition of the state's economy exacerbated opposition to the establishment of a historic district in lower downtown. The Rocky Mountain states witnessed a deep recession during the late 1980s.[108] Speculators had overbuilt downtown office space during the oil boom of the early 1980s, and when the market busted five years later, entire high-rises sat vacant. Downtown land prices declined as much as 80 percent, and office vacancies exceeded 25 percent by 1987.[109] Lower downtown developers experienced foreclosures, repossessions, and bankruptcies, and some property owners felt they needed the freedom to sell the development rights to their buildings just to stay solvent. Demolition restrictions and design guidelines imposed by the historic district ordinance dramatically decreased the value of development rights.[110]

Knowing that opposition from lower downtown property owners would be hard to overcome, preservationists went directly to the public to ensure the city council's approval of the historic preservation ordinance.[111] Preservation activists spent more than a year stumping for the creation of the Lower Downtown Historic District, using the district's importance to Denver's heritage as the key factor to creating a community in lower downtown.[112] Property owners fought back, signing petitions protesting the formation of the district and hiring lawyers to try to declare the ordinance unconstitutional on the grounds that it was tantamount to a taking of property.[113] The debate over implementing the Lower Downtown Historic District ordinance deteriorated into a "bloodletting."[114] Preservationists' efforts paid off, however, and after four months of hearings, the city council passed the Lower Downtown Historic District ordinance in 1988.[115]

Once the historic district went into effect, Historic Denver, the Downtown Denver Partnership, the mayor's office, and the Office of Planning and Community Development implemented programs to defuse the property owners' dissatisfaction. The city planning office agreed to sponsor an economic impact study in the district every two years. To jumpstart investment, the Downtown Denver Partnership opened the Lower Downtown Business Support Office, which marketed the area to potential investors and administered a revolving loan program for building improvements.[116] The Office of Planning and Community Development provided infrastructural improvements such as benches, flower pots, and trash containers.[117] The Department of Transportation removed the viaducts, adding tunnels, bridges, and new streets.[118] The Lower Downtown Historic District also got support from an unlikely source—the Denver Urban Renewal Authority. DURA had changed its stance on historic preservation since the battles with Crawford over Larimer Square, and became one of the most important proponents of historic preservation in Denver. As of 1996, DURA had played a critical role in thirteen major rehabilitations in the district that totaled $174 million.[119]

Soon after the establishment of the historic district, Lower Downtown took on a new identity—"LoDo." Coined by *Denver Post* columnist Dick Kreck, *LoDo* was, of course, a play on the name of the artists' colony of SoHo in New York City. The new nickname perfectly symbolized the identity that Historic Denver, the Downtown Denver Partnership, Mayor Peña, and the planning office sought to create for Lower Downtown.[120] Envisioned as an urban village, LoDo symbolized Denver's new standard of livability, as residents dwelled in the middle of an offbeat, artistic urban neighborhood. Creators of LoDo believed that the district's combination of bohemian businesses, urban residences, and art galleries, literally built on foundations of Denver's heritage, would define a new kind of lifestyle in Denver.[121]

LoDo took on a life of its own, however. Historic designation led to a boom in the district that even preservation supporters did not imagine. In the two years after designation, LoDo's twenty blocks were home to fourteen significant new construction projects and 114 new businesses.[122] Contrary to the fears of property owners that historic preservation would deflate property values, the establishment of the historic district stabilized real estate in the district. Brad Segal, coordinator of the Lower Downtown Business Support Office, estimated that in the first year that LoDo was a historic district, forty million dollars in new investments came into the district, along with forty new businesses and 150 new jobs.[123] Economic impact statements in 1990 and 1992 showed that Lower Downtown prospered better than the rest of downtown Denver.[124]

One factor in LoDo's economic success was its popularity as a residential district. During the 1980s, only 5 percent of Denver's workforce lived downtown, well below the national average of 20 percent, signaling that there was a strong market for housing close to the central business district.[125] Lower Downtown was the logical place for urban housing, since the historical character of the buildings made it desirable for a neighborhood, the scale of the buildings promoted a pedestrian-friendly environment, and it was close to downtown.[126] Lofts became the preferred type of housing in LoDo, reinforcing the initial vision of Lower Downtown as a center for the arts. Lofts were popular with people other than artists, however, and the market boomed. Between 1990 and 1996, LoDo's resident population grew more than 20 percent.[127] The popularity of lofts caused property values in Lower Downtown to soar dramatically.

In 1995, Coors Field, home of the expansion major-league Colorado Rockies baseball team, opened on the edge of the historic district, prompting property values to rise even higher. The stadium proved to be a mixed blessing for Lower Downtown, however. Economically, it brought a rush of business to LoDo, almost doubling sales in the district its first year.[128] Some observers attributed the economic boom in LoDo to the arrival of the stadium, but preservationists countered that the revival of LoDo began with the establishment of the historic district, and Coors Field merely accelerated a trend already in place.[129] The stadium did, however, change the character of the historic district. Sports bars, nightclubs, upscale restaurants, and bistros inundated the blocks nearest Coors Field.[130]

The increasing number of entertainment establishments created a district very different from the one envisioned by the preservationists who fought to establish Lower Downtown. Instead of a center for the

Fig. 10.5 The Brecht Candy Company, circa 1900, in lower downtown. (Photo courtesy of Denver Public Library.)

arts, Lower Downtown became the city's hottest nightspot, with more than fifty bars and restaurants by 1995.[131] The changes in LoDo led *Denver Post* columnist Dick Kreck to observe,

> This is not the way we envisioned it. Lower Downtown was supposed to be an urban village, a place where residents would live in renovated ware-houses and stroll to small shops, galleries, and boutiques. What we have is a party-hearty zone full of sports bars, restaurants, and coffee filling sta-tions. It is beginning to wear.[132]

Because the sports bars, many national chains, were willing to pay top dollar for space near the stadium, small businesses and independent art galleries could not compete. The artistic and design center of the city slowly moved out of Lower Downtown.[133]

The high concentration of bars and restaurants led to tension be-tween the owners of entertainment establishments and residents. Residents grew tired of dealing with rowdy baseball fans. Suburbanites coming to Lower Downtown to watch a game did not always realize that people lived in some of the old warehouses. LoDo dwellers told horror stories of drunken baseball fans urinating on cars and vomiting

Fig. 10.6 The Brecht Candy Building, reincarnated as Acme Lofts, 2002. (Photo courtesy of the author.)

Fig. 10.7 Coors Field helped revitalize lower downtown. (Photo courtesy of the author.)

in the entrances of million-dollar lofts.[134] When a huge entertainment complex called Planet LoDo tried to enter the neighborhood in July 1996, residents lobbied the city to deny the liquor license. The city denied the license, giving residents hope that they could achieve a favorable balance among residential, retail, and entertainment.[135] The dispute represented the conflict happening nationally between loft dwellers who came to the city for a bohemian lifestyle and the consumer forces driving the spread of downtown entertainment.

Despite the lingering tension between residents and entertainment establishments in LoDo, the historic district succeeded in revitalizing Denver's central business district. In the late 1990s, Six Flags Elitch Gardens amusement park and the Pepsi Center, home of the Denver Nuggets and Colorado Avalanche, established themselves on the edge of LoDo. Lofts are currently under construction in the Central Platte Valley, and the Regional Transportation District (RTD) extended its light-rail service to Union Station to accommodate the area.[136] LoDo and Larimer Square were consistently in Denver's top ten tourist attractions from 1997 to 2001, with LoDo beating the Colorado Rockies, Buffalo Bill's Grave, the Denver Mint, and Coors Brewery.[137] LoDo owes its success to the "historic development" strategy pioneered by Dana Crawford in Larimer Square.

Historic preservation addressed the problems of growth, homogenization, and tourism potential in postwar Denver, and exemplified a national trend in urban living. The process of historic preservation in both Larimer Square and Lower Downtown also created a civic identity for Denver. In Larimer Square, Crawford used propaganda and the media to connect the district to Denver's heritage, inventing a "Wild West" tradition. In Lower Downtown, city planners, preservationists, and business leaders built on Crawford's tradition, and used the old buildings as symbols to connect Denver's heritage with a new standard of livability and urban chic in the central business district. Tourism commodified and disseminated Denver's identity to visitors and residents alike. Today visitors to Larimer Square and LoDo find a twenty-first-century city built on the foundations of its frontier past.

NOTES

1. New York: Penguin Books, 1955, 38–9.
2. Carl Abbott, *The Metropolitan Frontier: Cities in the Modern American West* (Tucson: University of Arizona Press, 1993), 191.
3. Gerald D. Nash, *The American West in the Twentieth Century: A Short History of an Urban Oasis* (Albuquerque: University of New Mexico Press, 1973). See also Abbott,

Metropolitan Frontier; Christopher Tunnard and Henry Hope Reed, *American Skyline: From Log Cabin to Skyscraper—How the American City Is Shaped By, and Shapes, American Life* (Boston: Houghton Mifflin, 1953).

4. Robert G. Athearn, *The Mythic West in the Twentieth Century* (Lawrence: University Press of Kansas, 1986), 1–10.

5. David M. Wrobel and Michael C. Steiner, eds., *Many Wests: Place, Culture, and Regional Identity* (Lawrence: University Press of Kansas, 1997), 8–9. See also Richard W. Etulain, *Re-Imagining the Modern American West: A Century of Fiction, History, and Art* (Tucson: University of Arizona Press, 1996).

6. Athearn, *Mythic West,* 1–22. See also John M. Findlay, *Magic Lands: Western Cityscapes and American Culture After 1940* (Berkeley: University of California Press, 1992).

7. David Harvey, *The Condition of Postmodernity: An Enquiry into the Origins of Cultural Change* (Cambridge, MA: Blackwell, 1990), 66–98. See also Carl Abbott, "Five Strategies for Downtown: Policy Discourse and Planning Since 1943," in Mary Corbin Sies and Christopher Silver, eds., *Planning the Twentieth-Century American City* (Baltimore: Johns Hopkins University Press, 1996).

8. Barbara J. Howe, "Women in Historic Preservation: The Legacy of Ann Pamela Cunningham," *Public Historian* 12 (winter 1990), 31–61.

9. For a history of Larimer Street, see Thomas J. Noel, *Denver's Larimer Street: Main Street, Skid Row, Urban Renaissance* (Denver: Historic Denver, Inc., 1981).

10. For a comprehensive history of Denver, see Stephen J. Leonard and Thomas J. Noel, *Denver: Mining Camp to Metropolis* (Niwot: University Press of Colorado, 1990).

11. Ibid., 236.

12. Donna McEncroe, *Denver Renewed: A History of the Denver Urban Renewal Authority, 1958–1986* (Denver: The Denver Foundation, 1992), 102.

13. Leonard and Noel, *Mining Camp to Metropolis,* 296.

14. The term *lower downtown* was usually not capitalized until after the area became a historic district. I have followed these same guidelines.

15. W. A. Peterman, "Changing Commercial Patterns in Metropolitan Denver, Colorado: 1960–1970," Ph.D. dissertation, University of Denver, 1971.

16. Nash, *American West in the Twentieth Century,* 191–263. See also Abbott, *Metropolitan Frontier;* Richard M. Bernard and Bradley R. Rice, eds., *Sunbelt Cities: Politics and Growth Since World War II* (Austin: University of Texas Press, 1983).

17. Leonard and Noel, *Mining Camp to Metropolis,* 240.

18. Ibid., 248.

19. "Larimer Square Market Analysis, Mid-1969" in Larimer Square Associates Papers, Colorado Historical Society, Denver. The numbers compiled for this analysis came from the U.S. Department of Commerce, *Census of Manufacturers* and *Census of Business.*

20. Leonard and Noel, *Mining Camp to Metropolis,* 235–50. See also Edward W. Soja, *Postmodern Geographies: The Reassertion of Space in Critical Social Theory* (London: Verso, 1989), 157–89.

21. Denver Planning Office, Bulletin CAP-1: "A Demonstration Plan for Central Denver" (Denver, 1958).

22. Denver Urban Renewal Authority Papers, Denver Public Library Western History and Genealogy Department, Denver.

23. Minutes of the Denver Planning Board, 9 September 1963, Denver Public Library.

24. Denver Urban Renewal Authority Papers, Denver Public Library.

25. For a biography of Dana Crawford, see Dan William Corson, "Dana Crawford: From Larimer Square to LoDo, Historic Preservation in Denver," M.A. thesis, University of Colorado at Denver, 1998.

26. Dana Crawford, interview with the author, Denver, 29 October 2000. See also Corson, "Dana Crawford," 30–1.

27. Noel, *Denver's Larimer Street*, 38.
28. Crawford interview. See also Noel, *Denver's Larimer Street*, 38.
29. Corson, "Dana Crawford," 7.
30. "Larimer Square Incorporated Market Analysis," December 1965, in Larimer Square Associates Papers, Colorado Historical Society.
31. Investor Package Report and Annual Stockholders Minutes, 22 June 1967, Larimer Square Associates Papers. See also Corson, "Dana Crawford," 42–3.
32. Ibid., 42–3.
33. Dana Crawford quoted in *Denver Post*, 31 May 1965, 29.
34. *Christian Science Monitor*, 16 September 1975, 30.
35. Dana Crawford quoted in the *Post*, 23 May 1965, 1, 3.
36. Mayor Tom Currigan quoted in the *Post*, 23 May 1965, 3. See also *Daily Journal*, 25 May 1965, in Larimer Street clipping files, Denver Public Library.
37. David Lowenthal, *Possessed by the Past: The Heritage Crusade and the Spoils of History* (New York: Free Press, 1996); Michael Kammen, *Mystic Chords of Memory: The Transformation of Tradition in American Culture* (New York: Vintage Books, 1991).
38. Lowenthal, *Possessed by the Past*, 2.
39. Clyde A. Milner II, "The View from Wisdom," in William Cronon, George Miles, and Jay Gitlin, eds., *Under an Open Sky: Rethinking America's Western Past* (New York: W. W. Norton, 1992), 209–15; Kammen, *Mystic Chords*, 10.
40. For more on invented traditions, see Eric Hobsbawm and Terence Ranger, *The Invention of Tradition* (Cambridge: Cambridge University Press, 1983).
41. The boxes of Larimer Square Associates Papers are filled with press releases and promotional essays that Crawford wrote, edited, or made comments on before release. See also Corson, "Dana Crawford," 72–81.
42. "Larimer Square Incorporated Market Analysis," December 1965, Larimer Square Associates Papers.
43. Undated marketing proposal, Larimer Square Associates Papers.
44. Van Arket Report, November 1969, Larimer Square Associates Papers.
45. Tourism brochure for Larimer Square, Larimer Square Files, Office of Planning and Community Development, Denver.
46. *Rocky Mountain News*, 23 May 1965, 3.
47. Dana Crawford quoted in ibid.
48. "Investors Package 1965," in Larimer Square Associates Papers.
49. *Denver City Directory* (Denver: Gazetteer Publishing, 1965).
50. *Daily Journal*, 25 May 1965, found in Larimer Street clipping file, Denver Public Library.
51. "Investors Package 1965," Larimer Square Associates Papers.
52. Hobsbawm and Ranger, *Invention of Tradition*, 1–14.
53. Larimer Street photo collection, Denver Public Library.
54. Ordinance 739, Series of 1974, found in Larimer Square Files, Office of Planning and Community Development.
55. Larimer Street photo collection, Denver Public Library.
56. Crawford interview. See also Corson, "Dana Crawford," 23–5.
57. Corson, "Dana Crawford," 23–5.
58. Minutes of the Denver Landmark Commission, 21 June 1971, Larimer Square File, Office of Planning and Community Development.
59. National Register Designation Form, Larimer Square Associates Papers. See also Corson, "Dana Crawford," 118–21.
60. Crawford interview. See also Corson, "Dana Crawford," 6.
61. Corson, "Dana Crawford," 72–3. See also *News*, 30 June 1974, 3–4.
62. Fred Thomas quoted in ibid.
63. "Larimer Square Market Analysis," mid-1969, Larimer Square Associates Papers.
64. Corson, "Dana Crawford," 122–3.

65. "Larimer Square Incorporated Market Analysis," December 1965, Larimer Square Associates Papers.

66. Corson, "Dana Crawford," 75–6. See also *Denver City Directory,* 1969–70; Larimer Square Associates Papers.

67. Corson, "Dana Crawford," 80–1. See also Crawford interview.

68. *Christian Science Monitor,* 16 September 1975, 30.

69. *Post,* 3 June 1985, found in Larimer Street clipping file, Denver Public Library.

70. *Post,* 31 December 1986, 1B. See also *News,* 22 August 1986, 6; Corson, "Dana Crawford," 139–40.

71. Crawford interview. See also Corson, "Dana Crawford," 91.

72. Richard Moe and Carter Wilkie, *Changing Places: Rebuilding Community in the Age of Sprawl* (New York: Henry Holt and Co., 1997), 186. See also Thomas J. Noel, interview with author, Denver, 3 December 1999; Corson, "Dana Crawford," 144–57.

73. Noel and Leonard, *Mining Camp to Metropolis,* 446–58. See also Barbara Gibson, *The Lower Downtown Historic District* (Denver: Historic Denver, Inc., 1995), 6–7.; Denver Streets Photo Collection; *Denver City Directory,* 1956.

74. Corson, "Dana Crawford," 148. See also Jennifer Moulton, interview with author, Denver, 14 September 2000; *Post Empire Magazine,* 12 July 1981, 16.

75. Zoning ordinance quoted in *Post,* 12 July 1981, 16. See also William Saslow, interview with author, Denver, 2 July 2002.

76. Article in "Seventeenth Street West," October 15, 1980, in Denver Downtown Urban Renewal Clipping File, Colorado Historical Society.

77. *Post Empire Magazine,* 12 July 1981, 11. See also Saslow interview.

78. Ibid.

79. Ibid., 11–2, 16. See also Saslow interview; Corson, "Dana Crawford," 148.

80. Sharon Zukin, *Loft Living: Culture and Capital in Urban Change* (New Brunswick: Rutgers University Press, 1982). See also David Brooks, *Bobos in Paradise: The New Upper Class and How They Got There* (New York: Simon and Schuster, 2000).

81. *Post Empire Magazine,* 12 July 1981, 16.

82. Corson, "Dana Crawford," 153–4.

83. Moe and Wilkie, *Changing Places,* 184–5. See also "Economic Impact of Historic District Designation," 1990, in Lower Downtown District File, Office of Planning and Community Development; Lisa Purdy, interview with author, Denver, 3 July 2002.

84. Corson, "Dana Crawford," 151. See also Purdy interview.

85. Moe and Wilkie, *Changing Places,* 185–6. See also Purdy interview; *Post,* 13 December 1995, in Historic Denver clipping file, Denver Public Library.

86. Leonard and Noel, *Mining Camp to Metropolis,* 404–5.

87. Denver Partnership, Inc., and the Denver Planning Office, "Downtown Area Plan: A Plan for the Future of Downtown Denver," 1986, i. See also Bill Hornby, *Post,* 11 January 1987, 9G.

88. "Downtown Area Plan," 38–72. See also Purdy interview.

89. Ibid., 46–50.

90. Ibid., 46. See also Purdy interview; Moe and Wilkie, *Changing Places,* 185–6.

91. Purdy interview. See also Hornby, *Post,* 28 February 1988, 4F.

92. Moe and Wilkie, *Changing Places,* 198.

93. Moulton interview.

94. Purdy quoted in Moe and Wilkie, *Changing Places,* 185.

95. Bill Mosher quoted in Moe and Wilkie, *Changing Places,* 199.

96. Tom Gougeon quoted in Moe and Wilkie, *Changing Places,* 188.

97. Peña quoted in Moe and Wilkie, *Changing Places,* 189.

98. "Downtown Area Plan," 46–8.

99. "Lower Downtown Urban Design Project," in Lower Downtown Historic District File, Office of Planning and Community Development, 4.

100. Dick Flemming quoted by Sam Maddox in *Denver Magazine*, June 1981, 32–6, in Denver Downtown Urban Renewal Clipping File, Colorado Historical Society.
101. Hobsbawm and Ranger, *Invention of Tradition*.
102. "Downtown Area Plan," 48.
103. Ibid., 48.
104. "Lower Downtown Urban Design Project," 17.
105. Saslow interview.
106. Saslow interview; Purdy interview; Moulton interview. See also Hornby, *Post*, 28 February 1988, 4F; Moe and Wilkie, *Changing Places*, 186–7; Kathleen Brooker, interview with author, Denver, 14 February 2001.
107. Corson, "Dana Crawford," 150–1.
108. *New York Times*, 26 June 1988, in Larimer Square Associates Papers.
109. Leonard and Noel, *Mining Camp to Metropolis*, 425.
110. Saslow interview. See also Barbara Norgren, interview with author, Denver, CO, 2 February 01; Moe and Wilkie, *Changing Places*, 186; Leonard and Noel, *Mining Camp to Metropolis*, 407–27.
111. Purdy interview.
112. Ibid.
113. *Post*, 2 March 1988, 3. See also Saslow interview; Purdy interview; Barbara Gibson, interview with author, Denver, 22 July 2001.
114. Purdy interview.
115. *Post*, 2 March 1988, 3.
116. Purdy interview. See also Brooker interview; Moe and Wilkie, *Changing Places*, 189; Gibson interview.
117. Moe and Wilkie, *Changing Places*, 190. See also "Lower Downtown Urban Design Project," 5–17; Moulton interview.
118. "Lower Downtown Urban Design Project," 6–17.
119. Purdy interview. See also Moe and Wilkie, *Changing Places*, 192.
120. Moe and Wilkie, *Changing Places*, 192. See also Noel interview.
121. *Block by Block: Reclaiming Neighborhoods by Design,* video, American Architectural Foundation, 2001. See also Hornby, *Post*, 28 February 1988, 4F; Zukin, *Loft Living*, 111–48.
122. Corson, "Dana Crawford," 151–2.
123. *Post*, 6 June 1988, 1A, 6A.
124. Purdy interview. See also Moe and Wilkie, *Changing Places*, 189–90.
125. Moe and Wilkie, *Changing Places*, 193. See also Purdy interview.
126. "Downtown Area Plan," 47. See also Moulton interview.
127. *News*, 17 August 1997, 6G–7G. See also Zukin, *Loft Living*, 111–48.
128. *LoDo News*, April 1996, 1, 26.
129. Purdy interview; Brooker interview; Gibson interview; Noel interview; Saslow interview.
130. *Post*, 2 March 1998, 2A.
131. Moe and Wilkie, *Changing Places*, 193. See also Brooker interview.
132. Dick Kreck, *Post*, 2 March 1998, 2A.
133. Ibid.
134. *Post*, 4 February 1996, 7B.
135. *Post*, 4 August 1996, 1A; *News*, 18 July 1996, 3B.
136. *Post*, 21 November 1998, 1C; *Post*, 5 March 2000, 33A. See also Moe and Wilkie, *Changing Places*, 198.
137. Longwood International Survey for the Denver Metro Convention and Visitor's Bureau Survey, 1997–2001.

IV
Conclusion

MOVING FORWARD
Futures for a Preservation Movement

Ned Kaufman

PRESERVATION PROFESSION PICKS PRUDENCE OVER PASSION. Or so one might summarize Antoinette Lee's account of preservation's last forty years.[1] Once upon a time, historic preservation was a passionate protest. Now it's a prudent profession. The question is: Could this careful, practical, well-organized profession of historic preservation once again give rise to a *movement*—a passionate effort to change, in profound ways, how society imagines, preserves, and inhabits its heritage?

To ask this is not to indict the preservation profession. On the contrary, hundreds of landmarks commissions, of state and federal and local laws, of government offices to implement them, of cultural resource studies and of consultants to carry them out—all these are signs of health, not sickness. It is good that preservation is buttressed by laws and procedures and implemented by well-trained professionals.

And there is more to celebrate. Because of the preservation movement, we have an active network of citizen groups that know how to mobilize and are prepared to do so. Even more valuable, we have a language in which to oppose the destruction of place and heritage.

Still, it is hard to avoid the conclusion that we are losing ground. Listen to Ronald F. Lee, a senior official of the National Park Service, addressing a conference of planners in 1964, just before passage of the New York City Landmarks Law and the National Historic Preservation Act. Calling for a "major new effort to preserve our 'total environment,'" Lee draws on some of the most eloquent voices of his time, describing the condition of the American environment as a "quiet crisis" (Secretary of the Interior Udall), "God's Own Junkyard" (Peter Blake), "the most affluent slum on earth" (network news anchor Eric Sevareid), and "Silent Spring" (Rachel Carson).[2] One could hardly argue with this dire assessment . . . except that, in the intervening forty years, things have gotten so much worse—*despite* the great successes of the preservation and environmental movements. How many millions of acres of farm and forest have given way to suburban sprawl since 1964; how many sturdy old industrial cities gutted and abandoned; how many villages overrun; how many miles of rural roadway turned into strip malls; how many Grecian row houses, Gothic churches, Moorish movie palaces bulldozed for parking; how many wetlands paved over, old-growth forests cut, streams polluted; how much acid rain dropped and how many greenhouse gases lofted into the ozone layer? Surely things would have gotten much worse without the environmental and historic preservation movements; but does anyone really believe we are *better* off? That we no longer need a movement?

Despite its successes, in short, the movement has not stopped, or even measurably slowed, the destruction of the environment and the obliteration of history. It is as if the line of battle has simply swept over the preservation movement's troops. While we are fighting skirmishes, the front lines have moved so far beyond us that it is doubtful whether we can catch up.

It is worth asking whether the reasons for this failure lie in some shortcoming of the preservation movement's message: Perhaps people don't care all that much about history, heritage, architecture, urbanism? I do not believe this is so. People of all kinds, in places all across America, are deeply troubled by the loss of places they love: loss of character, access, enjoyment, historical memory. Preservationists have spoken well for their constituents. All the same, amateurs and professionals do not always worry about the same things. While preservationists debate problems of authenticity, integrity, architectural quality, stylistic purity, and significance, citizens seem to worry more about the loss of character, pleasure, or usefulness in the places they inhabit and love, of the ability to recall the past in them, of being forced to leave them. Many worry also about the loss of cultural identity associated with them.

Preservationists could legitimately claim all of these concerns as central themes. The difficulty is that the field increasingly defines professional competence in rather narrow terms that do not easily accommodate such big, emotional, and socially complex issues. It may be comforting to note that preservationists are hardly alone in missing the brass ring here: Both the environmental movement and the historical museums *could have* addressed the cultural dimensions of the environment but, until recently, largely haven't. Still, these big issues are really preservation's turf, and preservationists must decide whether to defend or concede it.

To concede it will be the cautious, professionally prudent course. To fight for it will require preservationists to move beyond the profession's internal discourse and acknowledge the full scope of popular concern over the loss of places and heritage. To fight for it opens up the possibility of an invigorated movement.

There are grounds for hope. In the last few years, a broad, humane language of place has taken hold in many quarters, a language subtly yet significantly distinct from the first language of the preservation movement. When people speak in this new language, they are able to take in historic landmarks, species habitat, favorite views or picnic spots, people's feelings about places—sometimes in a single sentence. This language lacks the precision of preservationists' professional discourse, but it expresses how human communities experience places, and how they feel about them.[3]

Adopting this language of place can help preservationists rebuild a movement out of what risks becoming a profession pure and simple. In the essay that follows I suggest a few other prescriptions: a new dedication to the power of history; courage to stand up to sacred cows such as economic growth and the real estate market; vision to imagine an order of things different from the current one; boldness to make seemingly impractical proposals; and patience to see them through.

GROWTH IS NOT GOOD FOR US

Let us begin boldly, then, by taking exception to the ideology of growth. American society is dominated by what John Logan and Harvey Molotch have called the "growth machine," an alliance of real estate developers, business interests, government, and news media that promote the belief that progress equals growth[4]—meaning more people, more economic activity, new and bigger buildings. Preservationists have assumed an awkward posture toward the growth machine, at once fearful and flattering. They fear, and with good reason, that standing up to growth will cause them to be marginalized: They will lose their seat at the table. Better to be seen as loyal supporters, even when it is painful: "I am wholeheartedly for growth . . . just not this *particular* growth, threatening this *particular* building." This stance has worked well, enabling preservationists to negotiate the retention of hundreds if not thousands of buildings.

Still, an underlying problem must be confronted. Growth is not the ally of historic preservation but its implacable enemy. How could it be otherwise? The ideology of growth prescribes constant change, disruption, ratcheting up of economic activity, density, people, production, and consumption. It has undergirded the theft of Indian lands and the destruction of Indian communities over three centuries, the smashing of African American neighborhoods after World War II, and the smothering of towns, fields, and forests under a spreading mat of suburbs in our own time. Not that all of the symptoms of growth are experienced equally everywhere. On the contrary, while growth happens in one place, shrinkage may be taking place in another. That is because, in the capitalist system, money is supposed to flow freely toward profit. So while one neighborhood of nineteenth-century row houses confronts developers' visions of thirty-story towers, a similar one struggles with the drying up of mortgage financing and insurance coverage, physical deterioration, and abandonment . . . all caused by the migration of capital toward growth opportunities in the first neighborhood. This is not a flaw in the growth machinery. This is how it is designed to operate.

Growth is a wonderful thing. It has brought us (or many of us) great blessings. It is hard to see how the social mobility and individual opportunities that so many Americans have enjoyed could have happened without growth. Yet while the machinery continues to clank away, there are signs that social mobility is declining. Apparently growth does not guarantee opportunity, at least not for everyone. On the other hand, growth *as we know it* does guarantee that the social fabric of many communities will be continuously threatened with disruption, their physical fabric by destruction—either the sudden death of development or the slow sickening of disinvestment and deterioration.

Growth has other consequences: the steady exhaustion of resources (including old buildings) and the fouling of the environment with ever-broadening waste streams. Those who maintain that growth on the planet can continue indefinitely base their belief on little more than blind faith. Since fixes have emerged unexpectedly for past problems, they will conveniently appear for the problems of growth. Perhaps. But the problems are real. There are currently many ingenious efforts to solve or mitigate some of them, from hybrid cars to wind farms, and these efforts deserve support. But we should be looking beyond them, to the larger question of whether growth (and the imbalances that it seems to produce) can continue indefinitely. The answer we seek will probably not be a simple yes or no. Rather, it will emerge from a thoughtful exploration of whether a society, or a network of global societies, could provide and broadly distribute social benefits without cranking up the engine of growth—without relying on relentless increases in economic activity, intensity of land use, desire for products, consumption of resources, generation of waste, and increase of population. Or alternatively, whether growth *in some form,* perhaps quite different from what we are familiar with, could provide and broadly distribute social benefits without constantly threatening the stability and heritage of communities.

These are among the most profound questions of our time, and the answers we propose will determine the success of the preservation venture in fundamental ways. Preservationists must grapple with them if they intend to win more than a skirmish in a steadily retreating line of battle. They should contribute their special knowledge and ways of looking at the world toward solving them. This can only happen if they dare to take the first and most difficult step: to publicly question the ideology of growth.

THE MARKET WILL NOT SOLVE OUR PROBLEMS

Closely linked to growth is the ideology of the market: the faith that market forces will solve all problems and resolve all questions of value or policy. This is absurd on its face: The market, quite evidently, has not solved all problems, certainly not those having to do with the preservation of buildings, communities, and cities, though it has undeniably dominated the development of policy. Like belief in growth, faith in the market is an ideology that preservationists have not much questioned. Yet they must if they are serious about turning the tide of destruction.

Preservation's market posture mirrors its stance on growth: "I support the free and unfettered operation of the market . . . just not in this particular instance." *Here* we need a little regulation, a little subsidy, but only to help out the market: in fact, to increase its profits. The preservationist sees herself as David with a black belt, harnessing Goliath's immense market strength to achieve preservation victories in the form of National Register listings or rehabilitated buildings. The tactic has worked well. The problem is that Goliath gets up from each encounter unweakened and undeterred. Real estate judo does not and cannot ever do more than manage a tactical retreat, as the market continues to move capital around at will, disinvesting here and overdeveloping there, following instincts rooted in profit rather than in community character, social equity, quality of life, historical memory, architectural connoisseurship, or any of the other values in which historic preservation trades.

318 • Ned Kaufman

There are other problems with the preservationist stance. It forces preservationists to play the capitalist's game, with rules that the capitalist controls and probably understands better. This can be a false position, with preservationists defending profit when the important values at stake are nonmonetary; and it can be a weak one, when their arguments fail.[5] None of this is to gainsay the real estate accomplishments of preservationists, to question the value of the professional skills that have been built up in the course of achieving them, or to suggest that preservationists should abandon the real estate arena anytime soon. However, while preservationists elect for tactical reasons to play the market game, they should never forget that their most enduring strategic strengths are cultural, historical, aesthetic, and communitarian; and that broad, lasting success can come only from them.

Unfortunately, loyalty to the market makes the effective deployment of these powerful assets less likely, because it constrains preservationists from asking the strategic question of whether a better alternative to the market might be devised—one whose rules might be more favorable to preservation's broad goals, the conservation of historic architecture, neighborhoods, and cultural heritage. Casting preservation as the handmaiden to capital anchors the imagination in the here-and-now of a familiar battlefield on which we are almost as comfortable losing as winning, foreclosing many interesting possibilities for cultural action. And it dims the prospects for an energetic campaign that could push back the lines of engagement and perhaps even transform its rules.

WE CAN CHANGE THE RULES OF THE GAME

At a recent environmental conference, a listener asked what could be done to solve an environmental problem that had just been described in some detail. The speaker counseled voluntary action: buying soap instead of detergent, cleaning up after washing the car, and so forth. I found this an appalling answer. Was it truly the best that the environmental movement had to offer? Was this indeed the same environmental movement that brought us the Clean Air Act, the Clean Water Act, the Wilderness Act? That took the lead out of the air and the PCBs out of the water? That achieved these huge advances not by appeals to voluntarism but by laws and regulations—democratically enacted rules that are backed up by the full force of society's legal machinery?

I said something of the sort. By way of a reply, the speaker advised me to consider the current political climate: Did I not think this was a bad time to be talking about new laws and regulations?

On the contrary, it is *precisely* the time to be talking about new laws and regulations, and not only laws and regulations but a broad program to advance preservationist values. Not timid tactical gestures but grand programmatic sweeps, bold assertions of value, improbable visions, laws, regulations, and perhaps even taxes that cannot possibly be enacted in today's climate: That is what we need now.

Our society's antipathy to law is truly tragic. We seem to have been remolded from citizens into consumers; to have accepted the lie that consumer choice constitutes the fullest expression of our values as individuals and as a society. But we are not only consumers. We are also friends, colleagues, family members, neighbors, volunteers, and citizens. In each of these roles, we make choices. Laws, binding expectations, rules and regulations can be profound expressions of the values that we, as citizens, choose to live by. Though not perfect, they are among the best instruments we have to mold the society that, as citizens, we want. Preservationists should not fear legislation as an expression of community values.

Of course, no ambitious program of new preservation legislation can be enacted now. But that is no reason to defer thinking, designing, advocating, and preparing for the time when it may become possible. That may be ten, twenty, or thirty years in the future. But without preparation now, it will never come; or if it does, the opportunity will be missed. What is needed is a beginning, a bold imagining of things that many will dismiss as impossible simply because they are impossible *today*.

There are many good legislative ideas within the preservation profession today, in stages ranging from energetic advocacy to wishful thinking. Many preservationists, including National Trust president Richard Moe, have pointed out that current tax laws tip the economic scales in favor of demolishing rather than reahabilitating old buildings, constructing new suburbs rather than investing in existing centers: Why not level the playing field by changing them?[6] Back in the fuel shortage of the 1970s, important studies were done on the energy embodied in the materials of old buildings—energy that is wasted and must be duplicated when they are torn down rather than reused:[7] Why not anticipate the next spike in energy prices by preparing measures to encourage the conservation of embodied energy? The National Trust has launched an important campaign against suburban sprawl: There are dozens if not hundreds of measures that could control sprawl. In New York State, organizations including the New York Landmarks Conservancy and the Preservation League of New York State have taken the lead in advancing a legislative proposal for a homeowners' tax credit that would encourage homeowners to invest in maintaining their houses. Preservationists have never abandoned the legislative arena. What is needed now is to marshal big ideas, to paint bold pictures of a better society founded on preservationist values. Legislative proposals on their own are good: Coupled with big ideas, they can be even better.

What might big ideas for a preservationist society look like? In a preservationist society, pieces of property would be treated as places where people live, work, or play, and only secondarily as real estate commodities to be traded for profit. People would have not only a language but also legal tools with which to express their intentions for their own places. In a preservationist society, communities settled in places would be able to determine their own destinies. People would still be able to choose change, but they would be able to choose it on their terms, and they could *also* choose stability. They would no longer be at the mercy of free-flowing capital and the market. In a preservationist society, communities would be able to provide and protect the shared resources through which their members express their cohabitation in place—public libraries, subways, favorite fishing holes, informal routes through fields or forests. In a preservationist society, resources would be cherished, reused, maintained, kept in service . . . not thrown away like gnawed bones. A preservationist society would recognize the tremendous investments that communities make in their places—investments of memory, tradition, and hard work—as a form of wealth to be carefully increased, not an obstacle to gain. In a preservationist society, historic sites, markers, and museums would present the experience of all groups in the land—of immigrant farm workers, African American slaves, homemakers, great musicians, and former presidents.

There is no dearth of ideas, no shortage of goals to be met. What is needed is the courage to propose them, and the patience to pursue them.

THINKING, TALKING, ORGANIZING

Enacting them will also demand immense inputs of energy and organization, and it is not easy to see where they will come from, given the chronically underfunded and understaffed condition of most preservation agencies, their tendency to focus on short-term goals (putting out fires and raising funds), and their organizational structure, which entrusts policy development to wealthy and well-placed trustees whose interests are generally better served by the status quo than by most alternatives that might replace it. Nevertheless, a way forward must be found.

One way or another, the preservation movement must devote a larger share of its resources to thinking and planning on a ten-, twenty-, or thirty-year horizon. That means putting resources into undertakings that have no immediate application. It also means thinking expansively, abstractly, and politically; researching, writing, publishing, debating; and always relentlessly enlarging the public space onto which big preservation ideas can be projected. In twenty years, it is possible that ideas dismissed as politically absurd today may be debated and even enacted—but only if preservationists are willing to devote current resources to future returns that could be substantial but are far from certain.

A reasonable mechanism through which to do this would be a preservation policy institute or think tank—or several. Professional schools could also play an important role. Currently in the United States, there are twenty-six professional degree programs in historic preservation. Mostly they teach the tools of the trade, and appropriately so. They train students to deal effectively with questions of mortar analysis, architectural design, historical interpretation. But in the "real world," by the time these decisions need to be made, the most important issues have already been settled, many of them at the level of assumption or underlying policy. In short, the schools are training professionals to act competently within the confines of a game whose rules others have already established. They are not training leaders to grasp the full complexities of the game, much less to rewrite its rules.

This is not a failure of the curriculum so much as it is the loss of an opportunity to go beyond the curriculum, to use the schools' tremendous thinking, convening, organizing, fund-raising power to float the preservation enterprise far beyond where the curriculum could take it. Why teach only preservation professionals? The schools could also teach lawyers, journalists, real estate developers, and government officials—all people with a capacity to influence outcomes. They could supplement the professional discourse with proposals that engage policy and values at a profound level. They could convene working groups to debate and advance these proposals. They could publish them. They could form partnerships with foundations or other research institutes to create hatcheries for big preservation ideas.

Unfortunately, it is hard to believe that our corrupted system of national politics could ever become the engine for progress toward a more democratic and preservation-minded society, one in which greed is curbed, scarce resources are conserved, and communities of place have some control over their destinies. Some faith in this possibility would seem to be a prerequisite for action. Fortunately, however, there are other arenas in which to work. National elections, after all, are not so much the content of democracy as its most formal expression. In a vibrant democracy, they would stand atop a robust foundation of civic activism. America has a tradition of such activism, and the preservation movement has been a vital part of it. While there is some evidence that America's tradition of citizen engagement is ailing, it is far from dead,[8] and the sickness of our national politics should not discourage preservationists from working at the local level.

There could not be a better time to do so. There is a ferment of ideas and energy in community planning: new planning techniques, a growing field of community economic development, creative ventures in community cultural development.[9] To participate in this unfolding movement, preservation will not have to do anything dramatically new, but it may have to do things a little differently. For while preservation can point to a history of great campaigns pursued at the community level, these campaigns have sometimes merited the accusation of being elitist or narrow in scope. Not that preservation groups have refused to embrace racially, ethnically, or economically diverse citizens. But it is one thing to welcome diverse adherents to your cause, another to craft a cause that is broadly inclusive of diverse needs and values. The former requires only goodwill; the latter also demands willingness to bend and enlarge one's thinking, to move beyond professional discourse and embrace the full scope of what communities enjoy and expect in places. How fortunate would communities be if the insights of preservation could be merged with those of community economic and cultural development in a single coherent movement for the nurturing of place and community. And how great the gain for preservation!

HISTORY IS IMPORTANT, AND IT IS NOT OVER

One would think that the oldness of places would be one of preservation's proudest arguments. Yet how timid preservationists are, how apologetic, in standing up for oldness! How readily they concede this crucially important territory. You are right, they say to the apostles of growth, newness is better than oldness, but please make an allowance for *this* old building, for there is something special about it, something exceptional. Yet perhaps this special old building is not such an exception; perhaps there are positive values that are inherent in oldness and are to be found only in old buildings.

Societies have long recognized that old people have certain forms of wisdom that come from living a long time. Relationships with them take on a distinct character by virtue of their duration, another manifestation of age. People recognize intrinsic value in the oldness of plants, too. A mature stand of trees has environmental qualities that younger trees lack. And even in the oldness of rocks: It takes a long time to make coal or oil. For that matter, it takes a long time to make rock. The very dirt we stand on, and which nourishes our trees, corn, rice, and flowers, is old, and nothing can substitute for time in the making of good soil. Though the scales by which we certify the quality of oldness vary tremendously—three-score-and-ten with people, ten-to-the-ninth with rocks—we live in a world in which oldness carries special qualities. Are buildings, then, valuable only when new, or unless they possess some special, exceptional quality that redeems their oldness?

Though one should not push analogies too far, oldness in buildings does have distinct cultural value: It preserves evidence of past skills (or sometimes lack thereof), anchors sense of place, provides testimony to past events. Oldness also has practical value. As Donovan Rypkema explains, ". . . you cannot build old buildings, and the cost of constructing new buildings is such that they provide only a narrow range of rental options."[10] A thriving local economy will include "small businesses, non-profit organizations, start-up firms, bootstrap entrepreneurs" who cannot pay the high rents commanded by new construction. Old buildings provide ecological niches for essential activities. Without them, settled communities cannot thrive.

One often hears the argument that we are a young society and therefore prone to overlook the values of oldness and indeed of history. This is an excuse, and it is time to debunk it. If we choose to see the United States as an offshoot of European civilization, its roots are old indeed. If we prefer to focus on its debt to Indian lands and cultures, its roots are yet older. Even if we pretend that American history started with the arrival of the first Europeans, we can now look back at five hundred years or so of history, which is surely enough to claim a past. Americans of many kinds are trying to do just that: From many quarters, the desire to delineate and belong to a history is being heard. And not just an abstract history but a vital and immediate one that can anchor people in communities and communities in places. A revitalized preservation movement can provide these histories.

Preservationists have never ignored history. On the contrary, while academic historians have largely ignored place, preservationists have nurtured the insight that the character and spatial relationships of places are the very stuff of historical experience and sometimes of causation. But preservationists' energy has occasionally been diverted into side streams. While it is good to know the construction chronology of each house in a historic district, good to chart the stylistic evolution of each of its architectural components, it is better to understand how the relationships between people and places have evolved. Though many preservationists appreciate this line of thinking, its power as an organizing tool has hardly begun to be explored. The history of communities in place, of the habitation of places, can be the foundation for preservation as a movement aimed at broad social change. It offers a robust intellectual lever for lifting up an inclusive, humane conception of place and heritage.

Many Americans can afford to take their heritage, or history, more or less for granted. An increasing number cannot and will not. African Americans, for example, whether descendants of southern plantation slaves or of free blacks in seventeenth-century New York, have a stake in the accurate presentation of American history, one that records both their sufferings and contributions, and sometimes that simply acknowledges their presence. Many other groups in American society have a similar interest, not in order to complain (or boast) but because history offers a way to establish a presence within the public space of political and cultural discourse—and without presence, one can hardly hope for leverage. History can't provide adequate housing, end discrimination, or prevent redevelopment, but it can contribute to the debate that is necessary to achieving these goals. It must be said, too, that the history of suffering as well as achievement, of the presence of society's most overlooked as well as its most celebrated actors, is also likely to be far more interesting than the narrow technical reports that preservationists must often write, or the flat and declaratory statements that pass for history at many historic sites.

There is no more important surface on which to project this history than the physical places of American society, which constitute not only historical documents but also a critically important dimension within the space of public discourse. Because places are the physical space that Americans cohabit, they register history's impact in extraordinary ways: slavery on the southern landscape, Mexican and Filipino migrant farmworkers on California's, Spanish land grants on the Southwest, English colonists on New England, clashes with Native Americans, Hawaiians, and Alaskans everywhere, the garment trade and the international art market on New York, Hollywood on Hollywood. It is a mistake to think that the American landscape has been homogenized by fast food and strip malls: Though it may be fast becoming so, American places still show their history in powerful ways. And because, again, they constitute the physical space that Americans cohabit—a sort of tablet that everyone can read—it is crucial that they preserve and present that history accurately, engagingly, passionately.

History is never mere declaration. It is an argument, and a revitalized preservation movement could do more to harness its persuasive power on behalf of communities and peoples—not by slanting but by presenting the full truth of profoundly complex and often painful relationships among people and between people and the land. In so doing, preservation can become a vital and progressive force in the struggle toward a more just society based on preservation values.

Preservationists, of all people, should be inclined to support the claims of historical presence that so many groups are eager to stake out through historical markers, sites, museums, and stabilized communities. True, they may differ in where they wish to place the emphasis: Where their constituents may wish to assert, "*We* were here," preservation professionals may prefer the less assertive formulation, "We were *here*." But the concept of *here* is surely vital to a preservation outlook. And its companion, the equally modest *were*, amplifies it in ways that go far beyond the implication of mere presence. Those who have been present in the American landscape the longest, American Indians, Native Hawaiians, and Native Alaskans, have also evolved the most profound understanding of what it means to be in place.[11] Their conceptions of the sacredness of places, of their power to instruct as well as sustain, of people's responsibilities toward them, of the consciousness that emerges with habitation in a place, may seem irrelevant to the experiences of more recent immigrants. Yet they are anything but. A deep reverence for the act of inhabitation, manifested in presence and history, is a powerful corrective to the excesses of growth and the market. Against the view of places as commodities to be traded or thrown away in a pitiless game of growth, preservation can argue a view of place based on history: history of presence, struggle, inhabitation.

And preservationists can do more than argue it. Preservationists have opportunities beyond those of most historians to be actors as well as chroniclers of history. They take sides in the struggles over place and heritage, using every available means to advance their side's interests, from grassroots organizing to sophisticated legal maneuvering, financial deal making to legislative lobbying. This is as it should be, though not all historians would agree. Many academic historians, indeed, see history as something enacted by *other* people: According to this view, historians should stand aside and watch. Some go farther, arguing that the only genuine historical actors are those who promote growth in some way. According to this view, almost everyone should stand aside and watch. To these historians, history is a chronicle of newness. To cheer on their relentless march to modernism, some paradoxically fall back on a tired notion: that each age possesses a mysterious spirit peculiar to itself, and that it is the responsibility of historical actors to manifest this spirit—a spirit, moreover, that resides only in new developments and new anxieties, never in love of place. These historians do not acknowledge the preservers of places and buildings as legitimate historical actors. They see them rather as trespassers on the stage; they accuse preservationists of obstructing history's rightful evolution.

Nothing, of course, could be more false. The custodians of place and heritage express the desires of millions to wrest some control over the places they inhabit, while nurturing a connection with tradition. Are these feelings not a crucially important facet of our age? Have these millions not as much right to act on history's stage as the builders, financiers, and publicists of growth?

Without preservationists, the evolving story of our places would be a sadly one-sided affair—not so much a history as one half of a telephone conversation. A revitalized preservation movement is needed to speak for the possibility of a society founded in values of place, habitation, history, citizenship, and equity. This is no revolutionary declaration but a call for return—return to the origins of the preservation movement, which lie in social commitment, not remedies for wood rot. I ask preservationists not to throw professionalism overboard but rather to put it in the service of passion—and by that I do not mean the kind of agitation that exhausts itself in looking busy, but rather a precise, prudent commitment to deep-rooted change in the world outside the profession. I do not ask preservationists to return to the social vision that guided the movement's pioneers—all white, all well-to-do, none either immigrant or native—for that would be inconceivable. I do ask preservationists to commit themselves and their practice to a social ideal appropriate to the dawn of the twenty-first century: a revitalized notion of citizenship within an equitable society, a public policy based in values of place, an invigorated concept of history, and a healthy skepticism toward growth and market forces. In short, to a passionate struggle to change how society imagines, preserves, and inhabits its heritage—a preservation movement.

NOTES

Though each may disagree with parts of this essay, the inspiration of four colleagues should be recorded: Daniel Bluestone, Roger Lang, Antoinette Lee, and Anthony C. Wood.

1. Antoinette Lee, "From Tennis Shoes to Sensible Pumps: How Historic Preservation Went from a Passion to a Profession," *History News*, 2002.
2. Speech by Ronald F. Lee, February 4, 1964, to the New Jersey State Planning Conference, Trenton, NJ: typescript, Records of the Northeast Field Office, National Park Service, General Correspondence 1952–66, entry 414B, National Archives, Philadelphia.
3. For further thoughts on how this sense of place might be applied to historic preservation, see Ned Kaufman, "Places of Historical, Cultural, and Social Value: Identifica-

tion and Protection," *Environmental Law in New York*, November–December 2001; idem, *History Happened Here: A Plan for Saving New York's Historically and Culturally Significant Sites* (New York: Municipal Art Society, 1996); and idem, "Is Westchester Some Place? Storyscape and Sense of Place in Westchester County," in *Land Use: Planning for a Just and Sustainable Future*, Pace Institute for Environmental and Regional Studies Proceedings (2003). An eclectic, personal, and incomplete selection of sources for this nascent understanding of place would include, in addition to the works cited in notes 9 and 11 below, the following: Irwin Altman and Setha M. Low, eds., *Place Attachment* (New York and London: Plenum Press, 1992); Robert N. Bellah et al., *Habits of the Heart: Individualism and Commitment in American Life* (Berkeley: University of California Press, 1985); Wendell Berry, *The Unsettling of America: Culture & Agriculture* (San Francisco: Sierra Club Books, 1977); Philip Brick, Donald Snow, and Sarah van de Wetering, eds., *Across the Great Divide: Explorations in Collaborative Conservation and the American West* (Washington, D.C.: Island Press, 2001); Robert D. Bullard, ed., *Confronting Environmental Racism: Voices from the Grassroots* (Boston: South End Press, 1993); Sue Clifford and Angela King, eds., *Local Distinctiveness: Place, Particularity and Identity* (London: Common Ground, 1993); Michael Conzen, ed., *The Making of the American Landscape* (New York and London: Unwin Hyman, 1990); Larry R. Ford, *Cities and Buildings: Skyscrapers, Skid Rows, and Suburbs* (Baltimore and London: Johns Hopkins University Press, 1994); Paul Groth, "Frameworks for Cultural Landscape Study," in Paul Groth and Todd W. Bressi, eds., *Understanding Ordinary Landscapes* New Haven, CT: Yale University Press, 1997); Dolores Hayden, *The Power of Place: Urban Landscapes as Public History* (Cambridge, MA, and London: MIT Press, 1995); Tony Hiss, *The Experience of Place* (New York: Vintage Books, 1991); Mary Hufford, ed., *Conserving Culture: A New Discourse on Heritage* (Urbana: University of Illinois Press, 1994); John Brinckerhoff Jackson, *Discovering the Vernacular Landscape* (New Haven, CT: Yale University Press, 1984); idem, *Landscape in Sight: Looking at America*, ed. by Helen Lefkowitz Horowitz (New Haven, CT: Yale University Press, 1997); Chris Johnson, "What Is Social Value? A Discussion Paper" Australian Heritage Commission Technical Publications, Series No. 3 (Canberra: Australian Government Publishing Service, 1992); Daniel Kemmis, *Community and the Politics of Place* (Norman: University of Oklahoma Press, 1990); William Kittredge and Annick Smith, eds., *The Last Best Place: A Montana Anthology* (Seattle: University of Washington, 1991); James Howard Kunstler, *The Geography of Nowhere: The Rise and Decline of America's Man-Made Landscape* (New York: Simon & Schuster, 1993); John R. Logan and Harvey L. Molotch, *Urban Fortunes: The Political Economy of Place* (Berkeley: University of California Press, 1987); Peter Marquis-Kyle and Meredith Walker, *The Illustrated Burra Charter: Making Good Decisions about the Care of Important Places* (Canberra: Australian Heritage Commission, 1992); Aldo Leopold, *A Sand County Almanac* (New York: Oxford University Press, 1949); J. E. Lovelock, *Gaia: A New Look at Life on Earth* (Oxford and New York: Oxford University Press, 1987); John Hanson Mitchell, *Trespassing: An Inquiry into the Private Ownership of Land* (Reading, MA: Addison-Wesley, 1998); Richard Moe and Carter Wilkie, *Changing Places: Rebuilding Community in the Age of Sprawl* (New York: Henry Holt & Co., 1997); Bud Moore, *The Lochsa Story: Land Ethics in the Bitterroot Mountains* (Missoula, MT: Mountain Press Pub., 1996); Myron Orfield, *Metropolitics: A Regional Agenda for Community and Stability* (Washington, D.C., and Cambridge, MA: Brookings Institution Press, Lincoln Institute of Land Policy, 1997); Clare Walker Leslie, *Into the Field: A Guide to Locally Focused Teaching* (Great Barrington, MA: Orion Society, 1999); Patricia F. Parker and Thomas F. King, *Guidelines for Evaluating and Documenting Traditional Cultural Properties*, National Register Bulletin No. 38, U.S. Department of the Interior, National Park Service; Matthew Potteiger and Jamie Purinton, *Landscape Narra-*

tives: Design Practices for Telling Stories (New York: J. Wiley, 1998); Michael H. Shuman, *Going Local: Creating Self-Reliant Communities in a Global Age* (New York: Routledge, 2000); Wallace Stegner, *Beyond the Hundredth Meridian: John Wesley Powell and the Second Opening of the West* (Boston: Houghton Mifflin, 1954); Carter Thomas and Carl Fleischhauer, *The Grouse Creek Survey: Integrating Folklife and Historic Preservation Field Research* (Washington, D.C.: Library of Congress, 1988); "Towards a Common Method for Assessing Mixed Cultural and Natural Resources: A Case Study Approach, A Cross-Disciplinary Conference. Conference Report" (White Oak: Howard Gilman Foundation and World Monuments Fund, n.d.); and Yi-Fu Tuan, *Topophilia: A Study of Environmental Perception, Attitudes, and Values* (Englewood Cliffs, NJ: Prentice-Hall, 1974).

4. John R. Logan and Harvey L. Molotch, *Urban Fortunes: The Political Economy of Place* (Berkeley: University of California Press, 1987).

5. I am influenced in this argument by the insights of Daniel Bluestone, expressed in conversation.

6. Richard Moe and Carter Wilkie, *Changing Places: Rebuilding Community in the Age of Sprawl* (New York: Henry Holt & Co., 1997).

7. Advisory Council on Historic Preservation, *Assessing the Energy Conservation Benefits of Historic Preservation: Methods and Examples* (Washington, D.C.: Advisory Council on Historic Preservation, 1979); National Trust for Historic Preservation, *New Energy from Old Buildings* (Washington, D.C.: Preservation Press, 1981).

8. Robert D. Putnam, *Bowling Alone: The Collapse and Revival of American Community* (New York: Simon & Schuster, 2000).

9. See, for example, John P. Kretzmann and John L. McKnight, *Building Communities from the Inside Out: A Path toward Finding and Mobilizing a Community's Assets* (Chicago: ACTA Publications, 1993); Ted Jojola, "Indigenous Planning and Community Development," *Traditional Dwellings and Settlements Review* (forthcoming); Edward J. Blakely and Ted K. Bradshaw, *Planning Local Economic Development: Theory and Practice* (Thousand Oaks, CA, London, and New Delhi: Sage, 2002); Don Adams and Arlene Goldbard, *Creative Community: The Art of Cultural Development* (New York: Rockefeller Foundation, 2001).

10. Donovan D. Rypkema, *The Economics of Historic Preservation: A Community Leader's Guide* (Washington, D.C.: National Trust for Historic Preservation, 1994), 61.

11. See, for example, Keith Basso, *Wisdom Sits in Places: Landscape and Language among the Western Apache* (Albuquerque: University of New Mexico Press, 1996); Andrew Gulliford, *Sacred Objects and Sacred Places: Preserving Tribal Traditions* (Niwot, CO: University Press of Colorado, 2000); Klara Bonsack Kelly and Harris Francis, *Navajo Sacred Places* (Bloomington: Indiana University Press, 1994); *Keepers of the Treasures: Protecting Historic Properties and Cultural Traditions on Indian Lands: A Report on Tribal Preservation Funding Needs Submitted to Congress by the National Park Service* (Washington, D.C.: U.S. Department of the Interior, National Park Service, Interagency Resources Division, 1990); Patricia F. Parker and Thomas F. King, *Guidelines for Evaluating and Documenting Traditional Cultural Properties,* National Register Bulletin No. 38, U.S. Department of the Interior, National Park Service; Jan Becket and Joseph Singer, *Pana O'ahu: Sacred Stones, Sacred Land* (Honolulu: University of Hawaii Press, 1999); Thomas R. Berger, *Village Journey: The Report of the Alaska Native Review Commission* (New York: Hill and Wang, 1985); Ted Jojola, op.cit.

CONTRIBUTORS

EDITORS

Max Page is an associate professor of architecture and history at the University of Massachusetts, Amherst, and a 2003 Guggenheim Fellow. He is the author of *The Creative Destruction of Manhattan, 1900–1940* (University of Chicago Press, 1999), winner of the Spiro Kostof Award of the Society of Architectural Historians, and co-author with Steven Conn of *Building the Nation: Americans Write About Their Architecture, Their Cities, and Their Landscape* (University of Pennsylvania Press, 2003). He writes for a variety of publications about New York City, urban development, and the popular uses of history.

Randall Mason studied geography, urban planning, and history and holds a doctorate from Columbia University. Since 2000, he has been assistant professor and Director of Historic Preservation at the University of Maryland's School of Architecture, Planning and Preservation. In 2004, Dr. Mason joins the University of Pennsylvania as Associate Professor of Architecture in the Graduate Program in Historic Preservation. In addition, Mason is a partner in the nonprofit conservation group Minerva Partners. From 1998 to 2000 he was Senior Project Specialist at the Getty Conservation Institute, researching economic and social issues relating to the conservation of cultural heritage.

CONTRIBUTORS

Daniel Bluestone is a specialist in nineteenth-century American architecture and urbanism. His book *Constructing Chicago* (1991) was awarded the American Institute of Architects International Book Award and the National Historic Preservation book prize. He is currently a member of the Board of Directors of the Society of Architectural Historians. In 1998 he was invited to participate in the Getty Conservation Institute's Agora project, a small international panel charged with formulating new approaches to cultural heritage preservation, education, and economics to complement international programs in material conservation. Bluestone is working on a book that surveys the history and politics of historic preservation in the United States.

Briann Greenfield is an assistant professor of history at Central Connecticut State University where she also serves as coordinator of the Public History M.A. Program. She received her Ph.D. in American Civilization from Brown University and a M.A. in Museum Studies, also from Brown. She has worked for several museums and historical societies, including Slater Mill Historic Site and the Society for the Preservation of New England Antiquities. Currently, she is writing a book on public memory in New England.

Michael Holleran is an Associate Professor of Planning and Design, and coordinates the Graduate Program in Historic Preservation at the University of Colorado, Denver. His *Boston's Changeful Times: Origins of Preservation and Planning in America* won awards from the Society of Architectural Historians, the Society for City and Regional Planning History, and the Society for the Preservation of New England Antiquities. He has served as chair of the Boulder Landmarks Board, and is a current board member of the Recent Past Preservation Network. His next book is on preservation of irrigation landscapes in the American west.

Ned Kaufman is a consultant in historic preservation and heritage conservation, living and working in Yonkers, New York. He is also co-coordinator of the graduate program in historic preservation at Pratt Institute in New York City. Previously he served as director of historic preservation at the Municipal Art Society of New York and was founder and co-director of Place Matters. He has also been a professor at the University of Chicago and at Columbia University's School of Architecture, and guest curator of the Canadian Centre for Architecture's inaugural exhibition.

Rudy J. Koshar received his Ph.D. from the University of Michigan in 1979. He taught at the University of Southern California from 1980 to 1991, then moved to the University of Wisconsin–Madison. Recent publications include *German Travel Cultures* (Berg, 2000); *From Monuments to*

Traces: Artifacts of German Memory, 1870–1990 (California, 2000); *Germany's Transient Pasts: Preservation and National Memory in Twentieth Century Germany* (North Carolina, 1998); (with Alon Confino) "Regimes of Consumer Culture," theme volume for *German History* (May 2001); and an edited volume, *Histories of Leisure* (Berg, 2002). He has held Guggenheim, ACLS, German Marshall Fund, DAAD, Jean Monet, and other fellowships. He is series editor for Leisure, Consumption, and Culture with Berg Publishers. His current research is a study of automotive driving practices in Europe and North America from ca. 1900 to the 1960s.

James M. Lindgren has explored the cultural roots of American historic preservation for a quarter century. He earned his Ph.D. in history at the College of William and Mary in 1984, and is currently professor and chair of the history department at the State University of New York in Plattsburgh, where he teaches a variety of courses in public history. He is the author of *Preserving the Old Dominion: Historic Preservation and Virginia Traditionalism* (University Press of Virginia, 1993), *Preserving Historic New England: Preservation, Progressivism and the Remaking of Memory* (Oxford University Press, 1995), and a book nearing completion, *Preserving Maritime America: Marine Museums and Cultural Politics in the United States.*

David Lowenthal, emeritus professor of geography and honorary research fellow at University College London, is a gold medalist of the Royal and the American Geographical Societies and a Senior Fellow of the British Academy. He has taught at a score of universities on both sides of the Atlantic, and has been a Fulbright, a Guggenheim, a Leverhulme, and a Landes Fellow. Among his books are *Geographies of the Mind* (with M. J. Bowden, 1975), *The Past Is a Foreign Country* (1985), *The Politics of the Past* (with P. Gathercole, 1989), *The Heritage Crusade and the Spoils of History* (1996), and *George Perkins Marsh, Prophet of Conservation* (2000).

Judy Mattivi Morley received her Ph.D. from the University of New Mexico in 2002. Her dissertation, "Making History: Historic Preservation and the Creation of Western Civic Identity," examined the connection between historic preservation, city planning, tourism, and identity in post–World War II western cities and is under contract with the University Press of Kansas. Dr. Morley is also the author of "Albuquerque, New Mexico, or Anywhere, USA?: Historic Preservation and the Construction of Western Civic Identity," published in the *New Mexico Historical Review,* April 1999. Dr. Morley currently teaches at Metropolitan State College of Denver and the University of Colorado at Denver.

Robert R. Weyeneth is professor of history and co-director of the Public History Program at the University of South Carolina, where he teaches historic preservation, social history, and environmental history. He is the author of *Historic Preservation for a Living City: Historic Charleston Foundation, 1947–1997* (2000) and *Kapi'olani Park: A History* (2002), a landscape history of Honolulu's "Central Park." Much of his writing has focused on the challenges of remembering the problematical past, often through the enterprise of historic preservation. His research has explored efforts to commemorate sites associated with the modern civil rights movement, the current vogue for the present to apologize for past injustices, and public memory of the Centralia Massacre, a controversial chapter of community history in Washington State. He is currently at work on a study of the architecture of racial segregation.

Chris Wilson is J. B. Jackson Professor of Cultural Landscape Studies at the University of New Mexico School of Architecture and Planning in Albuquerque. He is the author of *The Myth of Santa Fe: Creating a Modern Regional Tradition* (1997) and *Facing Southwest: The Life and Houses of John Gaw Meem* (2001), and co-editor of *Everyday America: Cultural Landscape Studies after J. B. Jackson* (2003). He directs the Graduate Certificate in Historic Preservation and Regionalism program at UNM, heads an interdisciplinary study of the historic squares and plazas in New Mexico, their potential for community revitalization, and for the adaptation of these urban forms to new town design.

INDEX